"I dreamed last night we were together...
I dream about you often...
But worst of all I dreamed you died."

Mary McAdam

SUICIDE:
SURVIVORS
WHAT PROFESSIONALS SAY:

"I thought I would just peruse the manuscript of
SUICIDE: SURVIVORS, but I couldn't put it down. It's
written with extraordinary sensitivity and insight; the reader
will find a wealth of practical wisdom in this poignant and
indispensable book." Dr. Earl Grollman, Rabbi, Belmont,
MA — Speaker and author.

"SUICIDE: SURVIVORS is filled with a great deal of
experientially based wisdom. Wisdom, for me, is much more
than knowledge...Your sharing of your own pain and empathetic
understanding of the needs of other suicide survivors is
extremely helpful because you go beyond knowledge to
wisdom." Paul E. Irion, Millersville, PA — Religious consultant
to the National Funeral Director's Ass'n.

"SUICIDE: SURVIVORS is clearly written, sensitive
and an extremely helpful volume... written by someone who has
experienced the pain herself...The humanity and warmth that
characterized Ms. Wrobleski's earlier work is seen again...It is a
book that provides hope and and reassurance." Andrew Slaby,
M.D., Ph.D, M.P.H., Summit, NJ — past president of the
American Ass'n of Suicidology.

"SUICIDE: SURVIVORS is a long over-due book. It
offers explanations, education, comfort and hope...It goes into
concerns not addressed in other books...The book contains
insights into why or what may have contributed to the death. A
terrific book that will be more helpful to suicide survivors than
any book I have read." Helen Fitzgerald, Springfield, VA,
Coordinator, Grief Program, Mt Vernon Center.

SUICIDE: SURVIVORS

A GUIDE FOR THOSE LEFT BEHIND

SUICIDE: SURVIVORS

A GUIDE FOR THOSE LEFT BEHIND

Adina Wrobleski
2615 Park Avenue, Suite 506
Minneapolis, Minnesota 55407
(612) 871-0068

Copyright © 1994 by Adina Wrobleski
Published by: Afterwords

Adina Wrobleski
2615 Park Avenue, Suite 506, Minneapolis, MN 55407-1046
(612) 871-0068

Printed in the United States of America
Second Edition 1994
  Second Printing 1995

PUBLISHERS CATALOGING IN PUBLICATION DATA

Wrobleski, Adina Suicide: Survivors — A Guide for Those Left Behind
  1. Suicide — North America 2. Mental Illness. 3. Psychiatry.
  4. Psychology. I. Title.

Library of Congress Catalog Card Number: 93-090615

ISBN 0-935585-06-0

FOR ALL MY FRIENDS

Faye Bland, Karen Deviny, Mary and Al Kluesner,
Reuel Nygaard, Bonnie Scherer, Dean and Mary Swanson,
Ben Van Sant, and Ron and Marian Weiss.

TABLE OF CONTENTS

About the Author

Adina Wrobleski is an internationally recognized authority on suicide and grief after suicide. She helps people understand that suicide is not a bewildering mystery that cannot be understood. There is a worldwide body of science about suicide, and her specialty is taking complicated psychiatric and psychological evidence, and explaining it in clear and interesting language through writing and speaking.

This is the second book Adina Wrobleski has written. Her first book **SUICIDE: WHY? — 85 Questions and Answers About Suicide** (1994) was the culmination of her quest for information about suicide that was lacking in 1979 when her twenty-one-year-old daughter, Lynn, killed herself.

SUICIDE: SURVIVORS — A Guide for Those Left Behind reflects Wrobleski's personal experience of suicide grief and recovery. She extends her hand to new suicide survivors, and gives them guideposts, reassurance, information, comfort, and hope.

ACKNOWLEDGMENTS

I am very grateful to the following people who read and critiqued this book in manuscript. Their help, encouragement and kind words improved this book, and meant more to me than I can say. They are: Lee Beecher, MD; Catherine Carson; Wilma Carry; Helen Fitzgerald; Rabbi Earl Grollman; Ron Hunter; Paul Irion; Bonnie Scherer; Andrew Slaby, MD, PhD, MPH; Mary L. Sulesky (Hermitage, PA); Mary L. Sulesky (Arlington, VA); Mary Swanson; Joseph H. Talley, MD; and Al and Linda Vigil. I especially want to thank my friend and editor, Ravina Gelfand.

PREFACE

A suicide survivor is any person grieving a suicide death. (Suicide attempters are people who have attempted, but not completed suicide.) **SUICIDE: SURVIVORS** is a personal message from Adina Wrobleski to survivors. **SUICIDE: SURVIVORS** gives friends and professionals a look at the world of pain survivors inhabit.

There are some fine books written for suicide survivors, but **SUICIDE: SURVIVORS** is unique in its detailing of what survivors can expect on their road through grief and recovery. They will be reassured by the fact that someone they have never met can describe what they are experiencing.

SUICIDE: SURVIVORS is practical. It speaks to common problems of survivors, offers advice, gives solutions that have worked for others, and above all it offers encouragement and hope.

Minneapolis, Minnesota September 1994

PROLOGUE

About 6:30 on the evening of August 16, 1979, my husband Hank and I were feeling particularly happy. It had been a nice day, and we had just finished dinner dishes when the doorbell rang. Since my husband had been a police officer for thirty years, we smiled when we saw a uniformed policeman at our door — he was a friend.

We knew him well and were glad to see him, so it took a bit of time for him to get our attention. And then he told us — just the bare facts the Lakeville police had given him "I have bad news; your daughter Lynn is dead. She shot herself." Her husband had found her body around 4:00 P.M.

Physical shock is an interesting phenomenon. It is the mind's way of anesthetizing us from pain, and it lets in reality in small doses, enabling us to do what has to be done. (It causes people to say of us, "My, how well they are doing.")

Hank's first impulse was to go to the town where she lived with her husband. But first we had to call Lynn's brother Joe and her sister Dawn, as well as my sisters and brother. It was a terrible night. We couldn't reach Dawn because she travels, and we had to ask our local police department to request the Bangor, Maine police to find and tell Joe. He called three times that night to convince himself it was true.

The next morning, through her work in Washington, D.C., we found out where Dawn was. She had a double shock because the message I left at her work to "call her father" got changed to "call home," and she thought that Hank had died. As her relief flooded in about Hank, she had to absorb the blow that Lynn had died.

We did drive the twenty miles to Lynn's home that night, and then back to our home to make the calls to our relatives and friends. We told them what we knew: Lynn was dead; she had shot herself.

THE FUNERAL

The rest of the funeral experiences were the same, probably, as all bereaved people suffer. We were lucky because Joe and Dawn were able to stay for two weeks. But then they were gone, and we were on our own.

In the next months we discovered what a blessing shock really is. The heavy numbing, zombie-like shock of the first few days gradually lifts. But it stays a long time, enabling one — most of the time — to go through the motions of returning to ordinary life.

WHAT HAPPENED?

So what happened to Lynn? It was so clear afterwards. I divide the last eight years of her life into the bad five years, and the good three years. Lynn was a "terrible kid," and we had a lot of what we thought were behavior problems with her. That's what the counselors and therapists told us. And I was a "terrible mother" too. I was punitive and angry, and she and I had a lot of power fights. Often Hank was in the middle. There were a lot of good times, but her junior and senior high school years were marked by anxiety, frustration and anger for all of us.

Lynn refused to go to school much of the time, and often would sleep until five o'clock in the afternoon. We now know that this excessive sleeping was one symptom of her deep depression. So were most of the other things she did. She was sick, and we didn't know it!

She was defiant, rebellious and disobedient. It was about her junior year in high school — after trying punishment, bribery, incentives, and periodic counseling — that we gave up and just let her run. She was doing poorly in school, doing everything she could to push our buttons, and was completely out of our control. She got jobs and quit or was fired. We were fortunate that she was never promiscuous, on drugs, or in trouble with the law.

In the middle of her senior year, she moved out, and truthfully, we were relieved. She had met her future husband. They soon bought a house, and somewhere along the way she and I forgave each other. Through the bad five years (when she lived at home), our love for each other stayed alive, and in the good three years (after she moved), we often talked about the "bad" years. She used to laugh and say, "The way for kids to learn to get along with their mother is to move out." It's not good advice, but it worked for us. She and I began to develop a true mother-daughter relationship.

THE NEW BEGINNING

I remember when it started. She had just been gone a couple of days when the phone rang. I answered and it was Lynn. She wanted to know, "How do you make pot roast?" She always adored her father, but now our love began to grow deeper — phone calls — meeting her for lunch — she dropped by our house. Occasionally, the four of us got together. Lynn seemed happy and busy all the time.

Only after she died did we remember the annoyance we felt when she called us and there were long silences on her part. She said something, we replied, and then silence. She was reaching out to us; she wanted something, but she couldn't tell us what it was, nor do I think she knew. We forgot these awkward conversations after we hung up.

Also, twice in the months before her death, she came over wanting reassurance. Once she was frightened about predictions by evangelists that the world was coming to an end. The other time, she was worried whether we would go to war with Russia. (This kind of 'eschatological' thinking is frequently found in mental illness.)

THE WEDDING

It was 1977, and Lynn was nineteen, and suddenly (it seemed), we were planning her wedding — that whole bit that mothers and daughters do. And it was a lovely wedding. We did something fun. We left all the presents unopened, and the day after the wedding they came over, along with her mother-in-law, and Dawn and Joe, and we had a big party opening the presents. The last two gifts were from us — completing her china and tableware to eight settings. The day after they got back from their honeymoon, they came over with a gift to thank us for the wedding.

Lynn's depression had lifted, and she seemed happy for the first time in years. Her father said afterwards, "I had always worried about her — both consciously and unconsciously — until she got married. Then I thought she turned the corner." (I think she lived three years longer than she would have if she hadn't met her husband.)

Our relationship grew. She was a great one for sending cards — whether there was an occasion or not. For an event, she usually sent two cards. I'll never forget the first time she sent me flowers on Mother's Day. A couple of days after she died, I came home and saw all the flowers our friends had sent, and in my fog, thought: "That's funny. The only one who ever sends me flowers is Lynn." Then reality crashed around me again.

Lynn occasionally bought me small presents, but most importantly, we continued talking, doing things and growing together. Where had this beautiful, thoughtful young woman come from? I never clearly felt — except for those last three years — the joy and pride of mothers as they see bits and pieces of themselves reflected in their daughters. I recalled all those years she fought me, and I fought her — trying to instill my standards, tastes, ideas and practices. She had heard me. In those three years I saw things in Lynn that she could only have learned from me.

And they were achieving so much! Lynn was a driver — we thought then; now we think she was driven. They bought a lovely home, but almost as soon as they had it, Lynn wanted to build their dream house. She was only twenty years old, and her husband a year older. Maybe she knew her time was short. They bought and sold nine acres for a homesite that didn't work out. We hoped she would stop her search for awhile, but back out she went looking for the perfect site. And she found it; twenty acres in the country.

A FRENZIED TIME

Looking back, it was a frenzied time. She did all the running to courthouses, lawyers, contractors and banks. She was working too. We shopped for carpet and curtains and tile. Their new house was a month away from completion when she killed herself. She was twenty-one-years-old, and she had everything going for her. But she also had a brain disease called major depression, and the way one dies from depression is by suicide.

Figuratively, I think that Lynn kept all her pain and anger behind a locked door which she kept closed through sheer strength all her life. I think that about three months before she died, that door started opening. She forced it shut again, and went about picking out the furnishings for her new home. But it kept opening, and she had to use more and more of her diminishing strength to keep that door to death closed.

THE NEW HOUSE

About three weeks before Lynn's death there came a key danger sign which no one understood. I saw it two days before she died, and didn't understand it. The big, unrecognized signal she gave was a complete reversal in her feelings about something she cared for. She suddenly hated, feared and felt hopeless about their new house. This was the house she was a month away from moving into — her dream house.

Her husband saw another abrupt change. She had loved horses since her childhood, and as soon as they bought their first house, Lynn finally got her own horse. About three months before she died, she suddenly and abruptly lost all interest in Roxanne. She took care of her, but she didn't ride or enjoy Roxanne any more.

People have asked me, "Didn't her husband see any signs?" And I reply, "Of course he did," as do all survivors after a suicide. At the time we didn't know what we were seeing, and were too afraid to look. One gets awfully smart about suicide after it happens, and a lot of things are clear then. But to a young man working eighteen hours a day, and trying to figure out what has made such changes in his wife, it is not clear. As bad as it was for us, I felt horror at her husband being a twenty-two-year-old widower!

I didn't see any really visible tearfulness and dejection in Lynn until two days before her death. She called me in the morning of August 14, and I met her for lunch. We talked for four hours. Instead of taking her to a hospital emergency room, because she was near death, I reasoned with her.

I knew and recognized then that she was depressed, and even talked to her about it. I knew in the back of my mind that there is something called major depression — a serious brain disease — but in my great wisdom, I thought she had the "ordinary" kind of bad mood most of us experience — the kind one "gets over" or "comes out of."

Mostly we talked about the house that day — of how to cope with living there when she didn't want to — because she had to live in the house at least until they could sell it. I told her she had no other alternative, but Lynn knew that she did.

She had cheered up when she left, and I did too, assuming the crisis had passed. When we were waiting at the cash register, she put her arms around me and said, "Thanks for caring." I told her I loved her, and she told me she loved me too. Her husband later said she came home feeling optimistic, and had discussed with him what she and I had talked about. But she couldn't hold on to it. She called me three times the next day wanting to hear again some point we had talked about. She was having a very hard time concentrating.

THE END

The day after that she got up, but didn't go to work. I called and talked briefly with her about 8:30 A.M. She was depressed. Then she mowed the lawn, and after that she had a bowl of soup. And after that she went down the hall to her bedroom, locked the door, lay down on the floor, and shot herself in the heart.

INTRODUCTION

What is a suicide survivor? Usually the term "survivors" refers to the relatives listed in obituaries who are left behind after a death, but here suicide survivor means any person who is grieving a suicide death. One can grieve just as deeply for a friend as for a relative. This book is intended to be a guide and support to those of you just starting the awful journey after someone you love has died by suicide.

This book is based on years of study and my own personal experience when my daughter, Lynn, died in 1979. I have also met and known hundreds of other survivors since then. In the word "survivor" there is a challenge to be met: to survive after the most crushing loss that can happen, and to go on. First, however, you need some basic information. (I have written in detail about suicide in my book, *SUICIDE: WHY? — 85 Questions and Answers About Suicide.* AW)

WHAT DOES NOT CAUSE SUICIDE?

Quite a bit of what is "known" about suicide is not so. Suicide is not caused by losing jobs, having fights with people, or having ambitious parents who move a lot.

We can blame anything or anyone for a suicide, but neither will be the *cause* of a suicide. The social conditions we live in affect us and our lives, but neither poverty nor enormous wealth account for suicide. Living in anxious times does not cause suicide; stress and pressure do not cause suicide.

Bad parenting does not cause suicide, and good parenting does not prevent suicide. If it were, then all the children of "bad" parents would kill themselves, but they don't. It also does not account for why children of "good" parents kill themselves. Divorce and broken homes do not cause suicide. Fifty percent of marriages end in divorce these days anyway.

Suicide represents about 1.5 percent of all deaths. There are millions upon millions of people in the population, but only that small fraction kill themselves each year. There has to be something extra that accounts for these deaths.

MYTHS AND FACTS

About forty years ago, someone made a list they called "Myths and Facts About Suicide." Over the years, it has been copied over and over stating several "facts" about suicide that are not so.

Among the so-called "myths" and "facts" are:

• Are people who kill themselves "crazy?" No.
• Are people who kill themselves mentally ill? No.
• Is suicide inherited? No.

These "facts" deny a connection between mental illness and suicide, because both mental illness and suicide are so stigmatized that people dealing with mental illness don't want the additional stigma of being associated with suicide, and people who have suicides in their families don't want the added burden of mental illness.

The people who wrote these "facts" also contend that depression is not an illness; they say that depression is normal and that everyone gets depressed. That is not true. Everyone gets unhappy, sad, blue, regretful, miserable, and all the other shades and varieties of normal human sadness.

Another of these "facts" denies any connection with a genetic inheritance. The fact that these diseases have genetic components is wonderful news. It alerts us that people in our families may be predisposed to these diseases just as others have vulnerabilities to heart disease, alcoholism or diabetes in their families.

The question about "crazy" should ask, "Are people who kill themselves psychotic (out of touch with reality)?" The correct answer is that a few are, but the great majority of people who kill themselves have unrecognized and untreated major depression often concealed by illegal drugs or alcohol. Major depression used to be, and still is by some, called clinical depression.

THE OLD MESSAGE

Most of what is "known" about suicide carries the old message that if suicidal persons are loved and understood well enough, and listened to carefully enough by caring people, and allowed to talk out their problems, they will not kill themselves. This thinking resulted primarily from the belief that suicide stems from unresolved conflicts and psychic injuries that have to be "talked out."

Some people still believe that "depression is anger turned inward," which was an old way of looking at the anger seen in people who have major depression. Now we know that this anger results from the fact that one of the chief symptoms of major depression is irritability. People who live with someone who has major depression often say that they had to "walk on eggshells" to keep from "setting them off."

THE SUICIDE PREVENTION MOVEMENT

About the time the myths and facts were written there also came the "suicide prevention movement." Starting with the fact that often suicidal people are very upset and in crisis, and that they can be "talked down" from their emotional storm, the idea arose of creating a suicide prevention phone line that would be manned by volunteer lay people trained in intervention techniques. The concept took hold, and suicide prevention lines were started all over the country. Why not? They hardly cost anything. The only problem was that they did not prevent suicide.

More properly it should have been called the "suicide *intervention* movement." It became clear that only a very small percentage of calls to these phones involved a suicidal person. Eventually they were called "crisis" or "hotlines" handling a wide variety of problems. They are very effective and helpful in doing this, but after a suicide in a community, there is still a knee jerk reaction to put in a hotline.

SUICIDE IS A BEHAVIOR

Suicide is a behavior. One has actually to commit some action to hurt or kill oneself, and there are degrees of suicidal behavior. Suicidal behavior is on a scale, or continuum, from zero to a hundred with only one hundred as death. Every behavior below one hundred is a frantic, and finally despairing attempt, to find solutions other than death.

These include obvious behavior such as threatening or attempting suicide, reckless driving, or abusing illegal drugs. These are often attempts to find solutions other than death for overwhelming emotional pain.

Most people who write or speak about suicide start with the danger signs, but that is almost too late. The danger signs are about ninety-five on that behavioral scale. To reduce suicide, it is necessary to go back to twenty or twenty-five on the scale when the symptoms of mental illness first show themselves.

CAUSES OF SUICIDE

The causes of suicide actually are multiple, and don't involve dramatic scenes of tragedy or failure in love. The causes have to do with 1) the biology of a person's brain, 2) their genetic inheritance, 3) the psychology of their mind or personality, 4) events in their lives and 5) the society that surrounds them. There are no villains here to blame; a suicidal person has a combination of these factors that put him or her in danger of death.

One researcher calls it "The overlap model for understanding suicidal behavior."[1] This says that suicide results from a *combination* of the biology of the brain, family history and genetics, personality traits, life events or chronic physical illness.

What have been called "mental illnesses" are actually brain diseases, and the brain is just another organ of our body like heart or lungs. The brain has chemicals in it that regulate how we think, how we feel and how we behave. Brain diseases and mental illness will be used interchangeably in this book. Basically, when these chemicals get out of balance in various ways, a person will have 1) major depression, 2) manic-depression, 3) anxiety diseases, or 4) schizophrenia. These are the primary brain diseases from which suicide results.[2–6]

People who have manic-depression and schizophrenia usually have such extreme symptoms that people recognize they are ill. They have psychotic symptoms such as hallucinations and delusions, plus an inability to think and speak normally. Psychotic means being out of touch with reality. Hallucinations cause a person to see and hear things that are not there, and a delusion is a fixed false belief in which, for example, a person believes he is destitute when he, in fact, has $200,000 in a box under his bed.

Schizophrenia affects the ability of people to think and perceive reality. Major depression, manic-depression and anxiety disease primarily affect a person's mood and emotions. They all result from a chemical imbalance in the brain.

The majority of people who kill themselves have major depression. The balance of suicide deaths result from the other three brain diseases. Sometimes they are in combination; anxiety disease is often seen with major depression as is substance abuse. One percent of people who attempt suicide will kill themselves within a year, and 10 to 20 percent of people who attempt suicide will ultimately die by suicide. [8]

Evidence reveals that people who kill themselves had a "psychiatric disorder" (brain disease), and that the majority of these suicides resulted from major depression. [9–13] It also reveals "that most people who commit suicide were suffering from a major psychiatric illness at the time of their death, although only a small percentage were being treated." [14–16]

MAJOR DEPRESSION

Major depression is the brain disease from which the majority of suicides result. At any given time, there are about twelve to fifteen million people who have major depression. Eighty percent of them can be successfully treated with medicine, psychotherapy, or in combination of the two, but only 20 percent of people who have depression get any treatment.

The majority of people who have killed themselves had unrecognized, undiagnosed and untreated major depression. Various symptoms of major depression (such as irritability, loss of concentration, poor sleep and an inability to feel pleasure) lead to disruptions in relationships in marriage, work and school.

To the untrained eye these symptoms often look like deliberate and willful angry words and actions — things the depressed person could change or stop if he or she wanted to. Untreated, these symptoms can eventually disrupt and destroy marriages, friendships, school achievements and careers. These end results are the consequences of the depression not the cause of the suicide.

There are some people who receive good medical and psychological treatment who still kill themselves, just as the sickest people with heart disease will also die, even with the best treatment available. The tragedy is that 15 percent of the people who have untreated major depression will ultimately kill themselves. This is the pool from which most suicides result. Most often their families and friends did not know they were sick until they died.

If you are a suicide survivor, you have a long and terrible road ahead of you. I do not want you to have to walk it alone.

ADINA WROBLESKI

September 1994

CHAPTER 1

THE WORST HAS HAPPENED

There is a story about the mother of a family talking to John; she is telling him he must go to school. "But I don't want to," he says. "You must," she replies. He complains, "I don't want to; all the kids pick on me." She says, "Never mind, you have to go to school." He says, "I don't want to; all the teachers pick on me too." "Never mind," she says, "John, you are the principal and you *have* to go to school!"

BECAUSE WE HAVE TO

When devastating grief hits us, we feel much the same way about life. We don't want to go on; we just want to stop. Our emotional pain feels so crippling that we think we can never go on again. We can think neither forward nor backward without pain. The reason we do go on, however, is because *we are the principal in our lives, and we have to go on.* We go on to plant a stake in the future when we feel least able to do it. We go on for our own sake, for our family's, for our friends and for the memory of someone we loved who died.

Suicide! That awful word — that word that has always been whispered when it happened in someone else's family. Suicide! The word that used to make us wonder about "that family" where a suicide occurred.

SUICIDE SURVIVORS

Survivors are the names of the people listed in the obituary — the deceased's living close family or friends. Now, *you* are the survivor of the tragedy — the awful tragedy of suicide death. But you are not alone; you are joined to several million people who are also suicide survivors.

You will meet some of them; some of your friends will suddenly confide that they too had a suicide in their family. But why *confide?* Why not tell? Why didn't you know before? Why should suicide be any worse than cancer or a heart attack?

TABOO AND STIGMA

Almost since the beginning of time, people have tried to "outlaw" suicide by placing a taboo on the subject, and a stigma on the people who killed themselves and on their families. A tabooed subject is something society decides is so terrible that no one may be allowed to do it, talk or learn about it. A stigma is the mark of shame and ridicule placed on those people who do kill themselves, and on their families. The stigma is the punishment for breaking the taboo. There are still some people who shun families who have experienced a suicide.

As badly as you may be feeling as you read this, take some comfort that things are much better now. Society used to do terrible things in the aftermath of suicide. They used to mutilate the bodies of suicides, hang their bodies in town squares, bury their bodies without religious rites and outside the cemetery. They would bury them at a crossroad with a stake driven through their heart. They would confiscate the money of persons who killed themselves, and would drive their families from their homes.

Some of these things still exist. There are still insurance policies that deny life insurance and even hospitalization payments for those who die by suicide.

THE NEW PUNISHMENTS

The families of teenage suicides are punished in new ways. Students at their schools are not permitted to attend their funerals. Schools refuse to allow memorial tree plantings in memory of a student suicide. One family offered a school their memorial moneys for a scholarship in their son's name. The school was willing to accept the scholarship, but refused to put his name on it.

These things are done under the guise of not wanting to make suicide "attractive," " romantic," or "glamorous" to young people. Behind this is the ridiculous belief that suicide is contagious in teenagers. A study published in a prestigious journal, and which received widespread publicity in 1986, claimed that reporting teen suicides or seeing programs about suicides will cause other teens to kill themselves.[1] Four studies, the final one by the Center for Disease Control (CDC), were unable to achieve the same results. [2–4]

The CDC study reported that "We did not demonstrate increased exposure to media presentations of suicide among those who killed themselves. In fact, these teenagers were reported to be less likely to have seen television shows about suicide." [5] The effects of this belief that suicide is contagious is causing horrific punishment on grieving survivors.

The memories of those teens who die by suicide are not allowed to be commemorated. "Experts" — many with impressive degrees, have told the schools that going to the funeral of a suicide should not be allowed. They say it will suggest to his friends that "all the attention paid" to a suicide victim will cause them to say to themselves, "Hey, look at all the attention John is getting at his funeral! Golly, I think I'll go kill myself too." It is as if a teenager would say, "Wow! David hanged himself! Hanging is so glamourous, I think I'll do it too." It is as if another will say, "Gee, all that blood is so romantic! I think I'll shoot myself too."

What is happening is that just when the centuries-old religious taboo has been easing up, we now find some people attempting to re-impose an elitist taboo. Those people say it is all right (safe) for them to talk about suicide, but dangerous for anyone else. And, above all, we must not talk, write, or learn about suicide.

There are still a few churches that deny religious burial to suicides. There are still some denominations that think suicide is a sin. How did a cause of death become a sin? Well, a lot of harm in the world is done by well-meaning people, and around 400 years after the birth of Jesus, well-meaning people thought they could prevent suicide by passing a religious law against it — by making it a sin.

People, then as now, did so because they really thought that suicide was a *choice* that suicidal people voluntarily took. In those days, they knew nothing about the chemicals in a person's brain that affect how they think, feel and behave — the chemicals that can get so out of balance that people kill themselves. They naively thought that if a person saw how much suffering it would cause their family, they would not kill themselves. They were proved tragically wrong.

Suicide continued down through the centuries, as it does today. The difference is that there is unparalleled promise of recovery from a suicidal depression today. The similarity with the past is that too few people today know that depression is a brain disease that can be treated with medicines and psychotherapy, and a disease from which most people could recover. The medicine is needed to correct the chemical imbalance in the brain, and psychotherapy to sort out the problems that result from the depression. Without this knowledge, ancient superstition and modern ignorance combine to keep suicide rates high.

TOO MANY SUICIDES ARE NOT ENOUGH

In addition to the chilling effect the taboo has on research into suicide, the reason there is so little interest in suicide is that *not very many people kill themselves*. Even with suicide being the eighth leading cause of death in the population, and the second leading cause of death among young people, there are not enough suicides to get more than momentary attention from people who don't want to see it at all.

For example, in the United States, every year 5,000 young people (ages fifteen through twenty-four) kill themselves, but the population of young people is 20 million. That isn't enough to make people care. Out of a population of 240 million people, 30,000 kill themselves every year. Apparently 30,000 suicides aren't enough to make people really care.

In the mid-1980s, the public heard many voices saying that teenage suicide had reached "epidemic" proportions. Parents were scared and concerned for their children. But fear lasts only so long. Since millions and millions of parents' children didn't kill themselves, their heightened fear subsided. The public felt deceived by people who tried to whip up concern about teenage suicide when they looked around and saw that their children weren't killing themselves.

It also sent a message to the public that only teenage suicides mattered, and this was tragically unfair. No one had told them the truth: that teenage suicide is rare. Few young people die of anything. Sociologist, Ronald Maris, had the courage to say that "one question no one...has asked about young people is why so *few* of them suicide." [6] Teenagers represent about 7 percent of all suicides. If the hue and cry had been about *all* suicides, enough people might have been mobilized to demand more attention be paid to suicide. It wasn't that people said to themselves, "I'm not going to care about teenage suicide," but that they didn't like being scared and fooled.

SUICIDE IN YOUR FAMILY

But when suicide occurs in *your* family or to your friend, it is not rare; it is a gigantic fact of life. When it is *your* husband, wife, child, brother, sister, mother, father or friend, it is *your* whole world that is torn apart.

There are so many survivors. For every suicide, there are at least ten people closely affected by the death. That means that for the 33,500 suicides each year, (30,000 in the United States and 3,500 in Canada) there are at least 335,000 people who become new suicide survivors. In just ten years, that means another three million new suicide survivors.

The general public has been so bombarded by confusing and misleading messages, it has not realized it needs to energize itself with righteous indignation. The public needs to tell the experts that if they don't have answers, they had better learn them. The public needs to demand this, and suicide survivors need to lead the way. If suicide survivors ever become organized, they can demand that priority be given to preventing suicide. They have the numbers to get things done.

It is a tragic fact that we have the tools right now to prevent thousands of suicides every year, and they are not being widely used. With the present arsenal of medicines and psychotherapies now available to treat depression, we could substantially reduce the number of suicides every year. It will be the same as was the case with diabetes deaths when insulin was discovered. There must be a commitment to see that these tools are used on the part of the government, medical, psychological and sociological communities, as well as business, the media and the public. Until there is such commitment we are saying by our inaction, "We really don't care."

SOMEONE YOU LOVE HAS DIED

But who cares? Right now you are dealing with the fact of suicide, not its history or social implications. Someone *you* loved has died. This makes everything different. It is often imagined that the death of a child is the worst thing that can happen to a person, and when it is the suicide death of *your* child, it is the "worst" — whether he or she was fifteen or fifty years old. Almost all the publicity about suicide concerns young people who die, however, and this minimizes and ignores the grief of many thousands of people every year.

It is a tragic fact that about that 5,000 elderly people kill themselves each year. But we don't value our wonderful old people as we should. One cynic said, "An old lady takes an overdose of her medicine. She's old and she's dead; who cares how she died?" (There are even people who say we should "help" old people kill themselves — the so-called "rational suicide" advocates.) These older people who kill themselves have spouses and children and grandchildren and friends who grieve. They matter too — those who die, and those who survive them.

Then there are all the people who kill themselves who are not very old or very young. They are the men and women in their late twenties to early sixties. All these people too, have parents, spouses, children, brothers and sisters, other relatives and friends. These people matter too — those who die, and those who survive them.

Parents, spouses, children, brothers and sisters — these are the primary people that matter — those most affected by all suicide deaths. But suicide causes pain to other relatives and friends. It causes pain and shock among acquaintances. So when is suicide the worst? It is the worst when someone *you* love has died.

THE WORST HAS HAPPENED

Suicide! It has happened in your family or to your friend. You feel stunned; you feel the worst shock you have ever received. It seems like the suicide death came suddenly and from nowhere. You have a funeral to plan, or to go to. Your feeling of shock is real; it is your body's protective response to terrible pain.

Grief is like a raging river, and shock is like ice on that river that enables one to walk on it — to do the things we have to do. But the ice is thin in places and we fall through, and have to climb out again, and go on. Eventually, through the many months ahead, that river of grief will gradually change to a brook and finally to a small stream.

But that is months and months away. Shock continues to be your friend. It helps you get through the funeral, going back to work and your daily routine, and finally leaves when you are once again strong enough to walk alone. Why say months and months instead of years and years? Because there are too many dire and pessimistic forecasts about suicide grief. You will hear people say:

- that your guilt will be massive and overwhelming;
- that you were somehow in complicity in the death;
- that you will not be able to "admit" it was a suicide;
- that your marriage will probably breakup;
- that if only you had loved and understood well enough or listened well enough, the suicide would have been prevented;
- that you and your family are now at high risk for suicide;
- that you will be "arrested in your grief" and need intensive therapy; and
- that you will never "get over" a suicide death — that you will (should) suffer from it all your life.

You may hear some or all of these things, and you may think or fear some or all of them will be true. It may *seem* they are all true, but given your experience, these are normal thoughts and fears. In the pain of grief, however, you may be particularly vulnerable to self-fulfilling prophecies. You will have a terrible scar, and it will pain you from time to time for the rest of your life.

It is never going to get worse than it is now. Hang on to that thought. There are many dark days and months of grief ahead, but remember that you got through the worst; you will get through the rest. You will go back and forth — believing and not believing that someone you loved has died. You will suffer, and suffering is painful! But on your dark days *remember that the worst that can happen already has.*

Suicide survivors have a right to recovery from their grief as other people do. You will survive — because people have always survived — because they had to. It is what makes us human — that we go on and become stronger and better because of the pain in our lives. You are the principal in your school of life and you *have* to go on.

LIVING WHILE GRIEVING

But first you must grieve while going on. No one has ever been immune to suffering. The pain of your grief may hit you right away, or shock may stay a month or so, and then plunge you into that raging river of grief. Whether the pain hits you early or is delayed, it will feel like you are drowning in it, and you will feel convinced it will never go away. *Feel that. Give into the pain when you can.* Cry, if that is the way you grieve. Beat your fists on the wall, go to the grave and scream at him or her, or just sit tight and endure if that is the way you grieve. Don't let any one tell you *how* to grieve.

We have a feminine, middle class standard of what proper grief is. Traditionally, men have not grieved by crying, or crying a lot, as women do. It has been fashionable to fault men for this, and it is good that young men are increasingly learning that they can be vulnerable and cry. But the only way a lot of men in our society *can grieve* is by "toughing it out" — by "holding it all in." We must recognize the difference in the way men and women grieve in our society, and not blame men for being what they are.

There was a tradition in our now changing society that told men they *had to* "pull themselves together." The presumption was that women, being more sensitive, needed more time to grieve. The presumption was that women grieved *more* than men.

But people flow into vacuums. In the past, if men were told they must return to work immediately, they did it because they had to. If women were permitted more time, it is human that they took it, and it is human that they flowed into the roles that society cast for them. With more equality between the sexes, we are seeing changes — women are treated as men in the work force, and they are behaving as men have: "toughing things out" at work and "pulling themselves together" at home for the family's sake *because they have to.*

Our country was founded by men and women at a time when it was the norm to lose two or three children to death; and our pioneer women may not have worked outside the home, but they worked side by side with men "toughing things out" and making things work. People grieve as they always have; we grieve at the same time as we continue living and moving toward the future.

It will not be easy, but whoever said, or expected, suffering to be easy? What kind of a person would you be if you could quickly "get over" the death of someone you loved so deeply? You have a long period of grief ahead of you; you will be changed by it; your life will be forever changed by it.

There is a saying that when you lose a parent, you lose your past; that when you lose your child you lose the future. That is not true. You cannot lose your past; your past cannot be changed. You cannot lose your future; your future is continuously being changed into the present. It is up to you how you live in the future, and it is up to you how you react to events in the present. It will be hard to go back to life, but you will.

WHAT WILL HAPPEN?

It is never too late to grieve. The suicide death you are grieving may have happened a week, several months or years ago. The reason it is necessary to grieve — to feel all the pain and all the emotions associated with grief — is to help us rebuild our lives without the person we loved so much.

Whether it was your child, spouse, parent, grandparent, sibling, or friend who died, there is now a huge, gaping hole in your life where all your memories of the past and dreams for the future combined to make your life meaningful with someone you loved who died.

What's ahead? Lots of pain, anxiety and heartbreak. Each day may seem like it is worse than the other, but each day you endure your grief will be a building block of your future. It is hard to realize this day by day, so it is best if you do just that: go from day to day.

An important part of grieving is to check on yourself. At first it is just enough to get through one day. Many grieving people are surprised when they look back after two months, for example, to find they *are* a bit better. Not much, but a bit better. The period of time is past when they thought they couldn't make it through, and they're still holding on and going forward.

People are very impatient in grief — they want it to "be over," and quickly. We are not as realistic about emotional pain as we are about physical pain. If we break a bone, we *expect* it to be painful, maybe agonizingly painful, but we remind ourselves that it will get better.

Our experience with pain tells us this, but we seem to forget it when our pain is emotional. If your spouse, or parent,or brother, or sister, or child, or friend has died, you cannot "get over it" quickly. If you could, it would mean there was not very much love there in the first place.

It is helpful to look back and compare, and to measure your progression through grief. You will discover that grief is one of the most chaotic experiences you will ever have. Some people also think that your *first grief* may be the worst, because you do not have the experience to call on as we do in physical pain. We grieve differently for different people, and in accordance to our relationship with them.

BACK TO A NEW NORMAL

Things will never be back to the *"old normal;"* grief means building a *"new normal."* People tend to take things for granted, but death is no respecter of times or occasions. Our grief after a loved one's death interrupts our lives; it seems to cut us off at the knees. It feels as if the bottom has dropped out of our world.

Who will be your guide? You need to call on all the resources in your life for support: your spirituality, your family, your organizations, your work, your entertainment and your friends. Learning to grieve may be learning to share your grief. This is important for families. If everyone goes around "holding themselves together" it may look as if no one cares.

You can become a better person, more sensitive to hurt, and stronger than you were before. You will find a "new normal" because you *have* to go on living just like the principal who has to go to school.

CHAPTER 2

DEALING WITH OTHER PEOPLE

After the death of someone you love, every day may seem an ordeal, and everything you do may seem extremely difficult. One of those difficulties is that there is so little understanding about suicide death that people often do not know what to say or do in its aftermath. Most people are well-intentioned, but even the best of people may feel inadequate in the face of your pain. They don't know what to say, and sometimes they say things that hurt.

It is not uncommon for people to feel so uncomfortable about suicide that they say nothing for fear of saying the wrong thing, or worse, for them, is that you will cry (so what if you do?). This causes some people to act as if nothing has happened, which is pretty extraordinary in the face of a suicide death. Some people may fail to talk about the person who died; they may act as if he or she never died. It's hard to keep perspective, but most people intend well; they just may not always know how to act that way. You do not have to go out of your way to help them help you, however.

Another thing to remember is that this is a time of super- sensitivity on your part; six weeks or six months after your tragedy, acquaintances may well forget, or not realize that you are still deeply in pain. It may seem as if your world has stopped, and everyone else is speeding by you.

Remember the wisdom of the musical title: "Stop the World, I Want To Get Off." Your world has stopped, and it will be a while before you get back up and on with

your life again. At first, you will just take short trips out
into the world again, but eventually your life will get back
on the road of your future.

TRYING TO UNDERSTAND

Some people say you will *never* know *why* someone
you loved killed him or herself. Well, that is true and
untrue. This whole book is about trying to help you
understand why the suicide happened from a medical and
psychological point of view — to give you factual
information about suicide and why people die by it.

The *why* you will never know is that haunting
question: What was in their mind at the moment they
decided the time is "Now?" What were they thinking of?
Were they thinking of us? Why didn't they give us another
chance? Why didn't they let us know how bad things were?
Even those few who were left notes didn't get adequate
reasons for their suicide.

More time has been spent blaming people for
suicide than finding explanations for suicide. Numerous
studies have been made counting the divorces, moves to
new communities, ambitious or absent fathers, and
smothering mothers in the families of suicides. The
assumption is that a lack of love and understanding of the
suicidal person was at fault in our relationships — that we
didn't love them well enough, pay enough attention to
them, and were so preoccupied with our own lives, we
ignored their cries for help.

LOVE — UNDERSTANDING — LISTENING

There is a widespread belief that if one just loves and understands people well enough, they will not kill themselves. It is also widely believed that all a suicidal person needs is to be listened to. North Americans have such a touching belief in *talking things out.* Consequently, when people — especially teenagers — do kill themselves, the assumption is that had they been listened to well enough, and loved and understood well enough, by good people, their suicides could, or should, have been prevented.

Conjectures are also made about the sibling rank order in families; overbearing and aggressive mothers and weak fathers are blamed; and speculations are made about childhood losses. Extremely pessimistic predictions are made of the ability to continue without immediate and extensive "counseling" — often involving the whole "sick" family. The fact is, in most suicides someone in the family *was very sick, and they died;* the rest are well.

Think about this. If your parenting was so terrible, why haven't all your children killed themselves? If you were such a terrible wife and person, why was it just your husband who killed himself? If you were such a bad child, why did only one of your parents kill themself? The answer is because someone in your family was very sick, and they died.

Trying to make sense of so shocking and tragic a death as suicide, in the face of your own and society's blame, is more than one person should have to bear. You feel you can't carry on, but you do. You think it is more than you can bear, but it isn't. You feel it is tragically unfair, and it is. You feel you will never get over this, but

you will. Why? *Because you have to* — just as all those
millions of suicide survivors since the beginning of people
on earth did before you — in the face of even worse
censure and punishment than we have now.

Will you always have a scar? Of course. Will it hurt
from time to time in the future? Of course. Will you feel
better and eventually get back on the road of life? Yes.
Ultimately, it is not *how* they died, but *that* they died that is
so terrible.

HOW MUCH, AND HOW LONG WILL IT HURT?

The pain and shock of grief soon after a death hurts
so much that many people want to know how long it will be
before they are "over it." You think it is too much to bear.
Too many people say a suicide death is something you will
never get over, and there is an the implication that you
shouldn't get over it. Some slightly more cheerful people
will tell you that — *if* you do get over it — it will take
years. Sometimes that is true of a few people, but most
people survive, endure, return to the future, and are happy
again. That doesn't mean it will be easy. No one ever
promised a rose garden in life, and no one ever said
suffering is easy, but throughout history people have
suffered, been changed, and become better and happy
again.

The work of grief is to linger and say good-bye to
the one you loved, and eventually take those intense
feelings and once again apply them to the present and
future. You do not ever want to forget someone you loved
who died, but it is in the nature of humans to forget pain.
It's hard to believe at first, but it will happen — the pain

gets less and goes away. You will remember it from time to time, and feel pain, but that is not the same as "never getting over it." To make the suicide death of someone you loved the focal point of your life is not fair to yourself, your family, or friends.

For centuries society has recognized the collective experience of humans that grief takes a year or two to resolve. Going through grief, however, is like climbing up a mountain that has a lot of peaks and valleys; there are ups and downs, but movement is upwards. Grief is a huge emotional wound, and it takes time to heal. But time, by itself, will not help you get "over it." If you just stay still, holding all your pain inside, it will lie waiting for you. The more you stamp down your pain, the more it will hurt. Time needs some help from you. You need to grieve in your own way, and you need to go on. While all the turmoil and pain is happening to you, you *have* to do your work, you *have* to care for and about the rest of your family (if you are alone, your responsibility and care are for yourself) and you *have* to be with, and care about other people outside your family.

Is there any agenda for grief? Yes and no. People vary. Usually, however, the first two months are the worst; they are when you feel most hopeless. Some people feel relatively numb the first month, and then the pain hits; other people feel absolute despair right away, hardly thinking they can pull themselves together. After a couple of months, there is enough time to look back — often in amazement — and realize you did get through "all that." And it is good to compare; remember how you felt at the funeral, for example, and gauge what you have accomplished since then. Aren't you just a little bit better? It may only be that you got from there to here, but that's progress. About three months after the suicide, you start to concentrate better, and it's a little easier to fall asleep. You may still cry a lot, but not as much as you did before. It still seems a pretty bumpy road you are trudging along.

Through all this misery, suddenly it's six months since someone you loved died. You wonder how you ever made it this far. But what a terrible thing it seems that the world is impersonal and goes on heedless of your pain. You can "get off the world" for awhile during grief, but the world still goes round and round, so you can get back on again. You are the principal in your life, and you have to go back to living. It is this process of *having to go on* — at the same time as you are grieving — that makes grief normal, and you stronger.

THE HURT AND PAIN OF RECOVERY

Feeling guilty for feeling happy is called *recovery guilt*. Perhaps you saw a movie or had lunch with a friend — and you enjoyed it! You suddenly realize you have gone two whole hours without thinking of someone you loved who died. You *knew* you would never forget; you *vowed* you would never forget. And here you did; you had a good time, and you feel guilty about it. It may not seem like it, but this is progress — this is good news for you. Recovery guilt can happen anytime. It did, perhaps, after the funeral when everyone got together, and there were old friends and distant relatives, and you laughed and talked with them. Many people wonder how they could forget at a time like that. They "forget" because that's our mind's way of giving us a little break, and giving us the first indication that we are going to be all right — the fact that we can still laugh is our first hopeful indication.

It is not uncommon, about six to eight months after the death, to have a big setback. Maybe it's prompted by recovery guilt; maybe it's a reluctance to begin to let the past start to slip away. Whatever its cause, to you it feels as if you are right back at the beginning. It feels as if all the progress you thought you'd made is gone, and you were wrong to think you would ever be better. But it *is* a setback. Maybe it is a stop to rest before you set off to climb the rest of the way back onto the world and into the future.

Somewhere around the midpoint in your grief, the pain begins to feel less sharp — to feel as if it's a dull ache that you will live with forever. You won't. Most people who talk about grief forget to remind you that *people forget pain.* You have to call on your experience to remember this — to believe that even the horror of a suicide death will diminish. But first you need to give yourself a chance. If one drew a line to represent the months after grief, it would be very jagged, but the overall course would be steadily upward. What happens is that as you get further from the death, the times you are down begin to get less deep, and the times between your low points begin to be further apart. As you approach the one-year anniversary, you feel pretty good most of the time, and the sharp pain and dull ache changes to a heavy sadness.

You need to be aware that grieving people may also have major depression. Over a period of months, if the intensity of your pain is not relieved, if you lose weight, sleep poorly, and feel desperate and hopeless, you should see your doctor. Since 4 out of 100 people get depression, and since it is already in your family, it is wise to watch for it in yourself and others in your family.

GETTING "OVER IT"

You will think, and hear "experts" tell you that you will *never* get over a suicide death — especially if it is one of your children. If getting "over it" means being happy and productive again, yes you will. If getting "over it" means forgetting the death and all that has happened, you won't. The holidays or their birthday may always bring back painful memories, but it will change to having a good cry two or three years afterwards, and a short period of sadness many years after the death.

One of the difficult things for you at first will be going to other funerals. You may always cry a little in remembrance, but what makes you human is that you care. Other things that are difficult are seeing other couples together if it was your spouse who died, or seeing mothers or fathers and their children together if your child died, or just seeing other people having a good time. You may get angry at them for appearing so happy, and for appearing to take each other for granted. You vow this will never happen to you again, and keeping that vow is one of the good things that can come out of grief.

WOMEN, GUILT AND GRIEF

Clear genetic, biological, psychological and sociological links are present in brain diseases and suicide. Despite all these factors governing each human, mothers and women generally have been held responsible for the psychological health of the entire family. Folk wisdom says, "The hand that rocks the cradle, rules the world," and "Behind every good man there is a good woman." The actual power of women has always been a good deal less;

the placing of responsibility, blame and guilt has always been a great deal more.

Two researchers studied major psychiatric and psychological clinical journals for the incidence of mother-blaming. They wanted to know if the women's movement during the 1970s had affected the amount of mother-blaming involved in the psychological health of families. It hadn't. "Professional ideology...crystallized by the 1950s, in which the causation of all psychopathology, from simple behavior problems to juvenile delinquency to schizophrenia itself, was laid at the doorstep of the mother. The guilt and anxiety created in mothers whose children had even minor behavior deviations were enormous."

In the same study researchers repeated the traditional notion that "women's physiology and hormones — but not men's — naturally suit them for child rearing. What has not been pointed out is that, if women come by child-rearing skills naturally, it is curious that they (are blamed for) emotional disturbances in so many of their children." They also said, "mothers were by far the most likely to be discussed" and the "authors of the 125 articles read for this study attributed to mothers a total of 72 different kinds of psychopathology" in their children. "In no article was the mother's relationship with the child described as simply healthy, nor was she ever described only in positive terms." [1]

What does this have to do with suicide and grief? Well, if women are considered to be more responsible for how their children turn out, they are then more likely to feel guilty and are thought to grieve more. Historically, as today, women are thought to grieve more deeply than men. They are *expected* to grieve more, and they often are

treated differently from men after a suicide. People expect
men to tough things out and be strong for the sake of the
women and children, and women are expected to *feel* more
deeply. Women often are given more time off after a
suicide death — especially the death of a child. It is
assumed they *need* more time to "pull themselves together"
than men. Men had no choice; their role was to be the
strong supporter.

Now that women are seeking and approaching
equality, these assumptions of weakness and the need for
more time to recover are still being held by society, but
many more women now are in the same position as men.
Most working women have no more choice now than men
do as employees; they are given three days off for the
funeral and expected back at work. Many women now say
that they wanted to go right back to work because it helped
them keep their mind off their pain. But the point of this
discussion is not to say that old or new assumptions are
good or bad, but to point out that when the same
expectations are made for women as for men, they perform
the same — *because they have to.*

ROCK MUSIC AND SATANISM

Other kinds of blaming are certainly alive. Some of
the new targets are the ever unpopular rock music and
Satanism. There have been a few lawsuits and many claims
that certain rock bands cause some teenage suicides. In one
famous case, two teenage suicides were blamed on the
English rock group Judas Priest. The parents sued the
group, but the judge ruled that claimed subliminal
messages urging teens to "do it" were chance sounds in no
way related to the deaths. In an article blaming the parents

of the boys, a writer claimed the lawsuit was a "sad attempt by grieving grown-ups to find blame for their own failures." [2]

As for Satanism, adults have made this another hot button for some teens to push. Even though a few teens who kill themselves may have dabbled in Satanism, a far larger group of teenagers who killed themselves went to church, but we do not blame religion for their suicides. A small number of teens who played Dungeons and Dragons killed themselves, but a far larger number played Nintendo games. Society always has an eye out for unpopular causes for which to blame suicide. When these are absent society can go back to the old faithful mother-blaming.

RELIGION AND GRIEF

The fact that *you have to go on* is the hope of the future. The worst of all things about grief is the temporary loss of hope. It is rebuilding hope that is the work of grief. You may think you can't do this now, and perhaps, right now, you can't. But know that you will.

Most people today have grown up with a legacy of fear and shame about suicide. Before there was scientific understanding of suicide, it seemed to people that suicide was something people did deliberately — sometimes to hurt other people. Hundreds of years ago in our culture, people thought that they could prevent suicide by making it a sin. It was a vain attempt, and it caused centuries of pain for suicide survivors. There are still some churches that preach that the soul of a suicide will suffer eternal damnation, but they are very few. Some people are surprised to find that it has been many years since the Catholic Church had harsh and punitive attitudes toward suicide. Today the religious community is in the forefront of concern for genuine suicide prevention, and for the care of survivors when prevention fails.

The death of someone we love shakes our faith in ourselves. The work of grief is also rebuilding our faith — in ourselves, and daring to place it again in others. Hope and faith are two of the most important religious principles there are, and that is why so many people find that their religion plays so large a part in being a fortress against despair.

You may feel supported by your religion, or temporarily betrayed. Many people feel that doubt is an important part of religion. Your religion may be of any faith — Protestant, Catholic, Jewish, Muslim, Humanist or any of the number of other ways people relate to their spirituality. Spirituality is the part of us that helps us transcend or rise above ourselves — the part that makes us better and stronger. Most people will find their churches and synagogues very supportive, and their pastors, priests and rabbis willing and able to help.

CHAPTER 3

WHY IS THIS GRIEF SO DIFFERENT?

Research on suicide grief has found that suicide survivors have extra problems due to the taboo and stigma, but despite this, recover as other people do. [1–6] A case could be made that suicide survivors are sturdier than other grieving people because they recover despite all the extra problems they have.

BEWILDERMENT

"We did not know, and the professionals we dealt with did not know she was sick until she died!" "We never knew anything was wrong until he died." Only in suicide death are survivors put in this ludicrous position. The taboo and stigma have prevented public education about suicide. There has been virtually no public education about depression, and what little education there has been about depression and suicide sometimes has been confusing and many times, outright wrong. They say, "We did not know he had "problems" (a disease) until he died." It is little wonder that you may be feeling that your loved one was a perfectly healthy person one minute, and the next minute dead by his or her own hand? It is no wonder you are left feeling there were no clues, and that the death mysteriously came "out of the blue?"

It is popular to say that "Why?" is the one question that will never be answered about suicide death. It's interesting that people don't use the words "never", "ever", and "forever" about other causes of death. We are much more realistic and optimistic about other deaths. It is almost

as if the taboo and stigma say we *should* never be allowed
the gradual recovery that occurs in other deaths — that we
should be left in the dark about our loved one's death.

There are two aspects of the question "Why?" The
first we can know; that is, "Why did they die?" The simple,
but truthful, answer is that the person we loved so much got
so sick (usually with depression) that they died, and the
way someone dies from depression is by suicide. The
chemicals in their brains that affected how they thought,
felt and behaved were out of balance, causing them to view
the future and their world as places they could no longer
live — places where it was too painful to live.

The "why?" that we won't know is why they
decided that, after all the pain they'd been through — after
all the things they had tried to make their pain go away —
after all that others had tried to do for them — *"now"* was
the time for them to die. On the day that my daughter killed
herself, what made her decision after lunch that *"now"* was
the time when absolutely all hope was gone? That is the
"why?" I will never know.

DENIAL OF THE CAUSE OF DEATH

It used to be more common to "cover up" a suicide
death than it is today, but it still occurs. The oppressive
stigma makes some people feel they will help themselves,
and protect the good name of the person who died by
saying it was an accident or a heart attack — anything but a
suicide.

Nonetheless, it is still fairly common to lie in some
circumstances and to some people about the cause of death;
for example, a family may tell the truth to everyone but

eighty-year-old Grandma who lives a thousand miles away. They think it is "nicer" for her not to know. They may tell a casual acquaintance the death was a heart attack; it seems simpler to do than dealing with that person's shocked reaction.

Another reason for lying about the cause of death is to avoid the cruel penalties imposed by some insurance policies. Most whole life policies contain "suicide clauses." It is understandable that insurance companies want to protect themselves from the person who kills him or herself and wants the survivors protected by insurance. The irony is that this post-death wish for survivor benefits is granted for people who kill themselves two years *after* the issuance of the policy, but not before. However, few people who kill themselves are thinking of their insurance coverage. If they had been thinking this well, and had logically seen the consequences, they might not have had to kill themselves.

Even worse are some hospitalization policies that will not pay the hospital bills for persons who die by suicide. Not all persons who die by suicide die quickly. Sometimes they are hospitalized from a few to several days. For families to suddenly discover that their hospitalization policies have suicide clauses is devastating. While they are still trying to absorb the fact of the death, they have the additional shock of incurring a huge financial obligation as well.

It is not that insurance companies are unable to foresee and regulate premiums accordingly. Many group life policies do not have suicide clauses, but most individual policies do. If insurance actuaries can compute premiums for all other deaths, they can surely do so for suicide death. Because they don't, some people *have* to lie about the death — just to survive financially. Just the fact that some insurance policies pay off and others don't is a grave injustice. Suicide survivors have not been strong enough so far to band together to demand that they be treated fairly.

In the past, professional people such as doctors, police officers, medical examiners, funeral directors and others often counseled people to cover up the suicide, and "helped" by putting another cause of death on reports. This is not done very often today, because professionals know that it is harmful for families to live the lie of a secret suicide in the family. Caregivers would have never had to "help" people lie if there hadn't been such severe social and financial consequences following from suicide.

Realistically, suicide survivors have to make decisions about what and how much to tell people. A rule of thumb is that it's on a "need to know" basis. If, for example, your child died, and you visit with someone at a coffee counter you will likely never see again, and they ask how many children you have, tell the actual number without elaboration. However, if that person becomes your friend later, he or she needs to know about this major and tragic part of your life.

It is absolutely the best policy, however, to tell the truth about the suicide. It is best for you; it is too difficult to keep juggling lies, and to remember who knows the truth and who doesn't. If other people can't handle the truth, that is their problem. Also if you lie, it suggests that you really are a "bad" person, and have something terrible to hide. You need to marshal all your resources to remember that you and your family are good people who have had a terrible tragedy happen.

THE METHOD OF DEATH

Today most people die away from their homes —
usually in hospitals, and most people die nonviolent deaths.
But this usually is not true of people who kill themselves.
Because people who kill themselves are otherwise
physically healthy, they have to resort to shocking and
often violent methods of death. And they most often die at
home.

A suicide survivor may have the burden of
discovering the body, and seeing the death scene of
someone who died from gunshot, hanging, carbon
monoxide poisoning, or worse. Many survivors have to
clean up the death scene of a loved one. Few can afford the
luxury of moving, so they must become desensitized to the
room where the death occurred. A person whose relative or
friend jumped in a river faces the probability of a disfigured
body, or the possibility that the body will not be found at
all.

Most people who kill themselves do so with
methods that are *available* to them, and consequently, most
Americans kill themselves with guns. In Canada, where
handguns are much less accessible, most people who kill
themselves use poisons and hanging. Suicide methods are
also culturally determined. In a study of three generations
of Chinese male suicides in the United States, a researcher
found that the grandfather generation, who had come from
China where hanging was the preferred method, continued
that method after they came to the United States. Their
grandchildren who killed themselves were products of the
American culture, however, and used guns.

The more bizarre the suicide method is, the more
difficult it is for us to understand. Shocking as suicide

death is, it is even more so when people burn themselves to death or barricade themselves with hostages and eventually shoot themselves. It is even harder still to understand homicide-suicide. It is not known why, but there is a chemical in the brain called serotonin, and when one of its component parts is low, it is associated with more violent and aggressive methods.

Some of these people are psychotic (not in touch with reality). A mother who jumps to her death with her child may actually believe she is protecting her baby. But most people who kill themselves are too much in touch with reality — the reality of their desperate, never-ending emotional pain. Their thinking is distorted by the pain.

Some people consciously wish to disguise their suicides, and die in "accidents" of their own making. It also has been widely reported that many single driver car accidents are really suicides. In two studies of single car-single person accidents, it was found that between 2 percent and 5 percent were actually suicides. (There were no attempts to swerve or take protective action before the crash.) Whatever the cause, from the survivor's point of view, dealing with the method of suicide is a problem no other survivors have to contend with.

SEPARATION IN AND OUT OF THE FAMILY

Only in suicide is the first question, "What will we tell people?" Sometimes not every one in the family will be told the truth. This is usually done to "spare them." Only in suicide are there divisions among family and friends that stem from the taboo and stigma.

One of the "comforts" of grief is to blame someone for the death, and nowhere is this easier to do than in suicide. We have been taught to blame. Historically, the stigma placed on the "bad" family suggests blame *should* be placed. While there is not always a scapegoat, spouses, for example, are frequently blamed by in-laws.

Americans have eagerly adopted Freud's belief that all psychological problems originate in childhood, and that to relieve them one has to "talk them out" and "deal with them" or dire consequences will occur. With these ideas came the indictment of suicide survivors that assumed that *if the victims had been loved well enough*, and *listened to well enough* by *good* people, they would not have killed themselves. To this day, these are themes of movies and plays where characters die by suicide. Parents and spouses are usually the people who are blamed; it is assumed that if they had been caring enough, they could have prevented the suicide.

This assumption, along with real grievances within families and among friends, leads to disagreement and separation. As a rule, only in suicide do people find they can talk about the death with some, but not other family members. Only in suicide, do people decide who outside the family they will talk to about the death. The question always is, "Who shall we tell (the truth to)?" Society has taught even the kindliest people to recoil when they hear the word suicide.

RECONSTRUCTION

When people talk about grief they often mention "acceptance." Acceptance is that sought-after goal when we are "over" the pain. In suicide death, acceptance is more difficult because of the bewilderment felt about the cause of death. Sometimes early, sometimes later, we almost always remember things that scared or troubled us when our loved ones were alive — that now seem to make so much sense. They had, for example, talked about suicide, and we pooh-poohed it, or thought they weren't serious. We remember all the many things we could or should have done. We remember all the times when we could have acted better or done more than we did.

Among all the blaming it is perhaps most potent when we blame ourselves, especially if the suicide occurred after harsh words or a parent's punishment of a teen. It also is very common after the breakup of a relationship. Survivors need to remember all the times harsh words were exchanged when the person did not kill him or herself, or how many times a teen had been grounded after which he or she did not kill themself. If breakups of relationships were a cause of suicide, there might be no one left on earth.

It's painful to look back. We see clues that seem so obvious now, but which frightened us at the time — frightened us so much that we "forgot" we heard and saw what now seems so clear. Possibly we remember how difficult it was to live with the one who died. Because he or she wrestled death from nature's hands, and left us no defenses, we alternate our wonder with anger and bitterness. "Why didn't our loved one give us a second chance?" we ask over and over. At a certain point, we have to remember things as they were, rather than the way we bitterly wish they were.

We are so forcefully faced with the way things *are now* that we must begin to remember things *as they were*. Very few people who die are saints, and our people who died often were more difficult to live with than some others. Sometimes suicidal people are angry people, who are difficult to please. Sometimes just seeing their desperate suffering was the worst part of living with them. Sometimes they were so quiet and well-behaved, their death was the loudest thing they ever said.

Whatever your past with someone you loved, you must now build the future without that person. It seems impossible to pull yourself from the past, which is the only place your loved one still lives. But part of suicide grief is to reconstruct the past, without assigning yourself the role of villain. The hard task of grief is to begin to pull yourself back to the present from the past where everything seems so clear now. Reconstruction and acceptance mean we put the past in better perspective. We have to remember the past accurately — that many times we walked the extra mile — that *we did the best we could with what we knew at the time*.

CHAPTER 4

THE MANY PAINS
OF GRIEF

Right now there is the pain! At first it seems it is all one huge pain, but we quickly discover this huge pain is made up of many different kinds. The pains of suicide grief include all the extra problems you have because of the taboo and stigma. On top of that, many common grief reactions have unique characteristics when it is suicide grief.

FEARS

Fear is generally viewed as weakness in our society, so most people suffer with their fears silently. But fear and all the other emotions are what make us human. It is normal and human at this terrible time to have thoughts about our own deaths — even our own suicide deaths. Here you are devastated that someone you love has killed themselves; how can you have these awful *thoughts of suicide* popping into your head? You can because it is normal.

Experience has shown that in the aftermath of suicide death, it is not unusual for survivors to have thoughts of suicide. It may sound unusual, but having any kind of awful and terrible thoughts is a symptom of anxiety. If you have occasional sudden, awful, and frightening thoughts of suicide, they are probably symptoms of your anxiety and are normal. If they persist over a long period, and involve specific plans for death, you need to run, not walk to your doctor.

Speaking of your doctor, it is a good idea after the death to have a physical exam. Grief has many physical manifestations — headaches, stomachaches, sleeplessness and poor concentration — and it is reassuring to know that you are healthy, or at least no worse than you were before. Some conditions, such as high blood pressure, may be aggravated by the death, and your doctor may want to give you medication, or watch you more closely for a while.

Because a vulnerability to major depression runs in families, some people get depression while they grieve. Antidepressant medicines are necessary to take away the severe symptoms they may think are reactions to grief. The difference between depression and grief is in the intensity of feelings or reactions. You have reason to suspect depression if there is weight loss over a few months, sleeping is particularly disordered, and the emotional pain is excessively sensitive. Almost all grieving people can give themselves some relief from grief; they can laugh at a joke or be diverted by a movie. People who have depression cannot do this. Check your reactions against the list of symptoms of depression in the back of this book. If four or more symptoms last more than two weeks, see your doctor. It may be that depression is making your grief worse.

Do not fall into the foolishness of thinking medicine is something to be avoided. Some people take pride in "handling things" by themselves without the "crutch" of medication. Medicines are a blessing we are lucky to have; there is no nobility in needless suffering. (What is absolute foolishness is any attempt to "treat" your pain with alcohol or illegal drugs. It may seem to dull your pain, but it does so at great potential harm to you.)

Another very common fear is that *someone else you love will die*. When a spouse dies, the remaining spouse may be more worried about a child or children. Children may be afraid that if one parent died, so could the other. Who you worry about depends on your relationships. But be assured is it normal to have this panicky fear that someone else will die, and what will you do then? With time it will gradually go away with your other fears.

It is also normal in the aftermath of suicide to *worry about mental illness* — even in people who deny a connection between the two. You may wonder who will be struck next. It might be sensible to do so, because illnesses run in families. This may be your first indication that your family has a vulnerability to depression. You need to realize, however, that your family is in no way "foredoomed" because there has been a suicide.

Our health is determined, like our eye color, by the combination of genes we inherit from our parents. Unless we are identical twins, we all inherit different combinations. Even identical twins are not identical in their illnesses or deaths. This is because our destinies are strongly, but only partially determined by our inheritance; it has long been known that our environment is a large determining factor in our lives. Both have a powerful influence.

Another thing that is fairly common in the aftermath of suicide is a *panic attack*. With a panic attack, the individual is suddenly, usually without provocation, filled with waves of fear that last for a minute or two — but seem like hours. Panic attacks are spontaneous; they can occur anywhere or time — away from home or possibly just as you are trying to go to sleep. The panic feeling itself is frightening — and the fear of the panic returning causes great anxiety.

WHAT IS FEAR?

Some information about what actually is happening when you are afraid is helpful. The feeling of fear is awful, but all the other things that happen when we are afraid are *physiological effects of adrenaline in our bloodstream.* It is so frightening to be afraid that we don't notice the purely physical things that accompany fear. None of them are harmful:

- your heart beats faster, sometimes skipping beats, and booming in your chest
- you break out in a sweat on your forehead and hands
- your skin may feel tingly
- you may feel as if a tight band is around your head
- your muscles knot up
- your stomach muscles contract
- your eyes see bright sparks
- you feel dizzy
- everything may go dark, and you fear passing out
- you feel nauseated

When you consider having all these physical reactions at once, you can see why the fear often increases. The best thing you can do is *talk to yourself — reassure yourself.* Tell yourself, "It's just adrenaline. It always goes away." Take deep breaths, and move your body to dissipate the adrenaline. It is a fact that adrenaline can only do so much physiologically to our bodies; there is a maximum amount of effect adrenaline can have. Consequently, the panic attack you have already experienced is probably the worst it will ever get.

Your anxiety and fear about the panic returning, however, are very uncomfortable. Fear is fed on anticipation so the best prescription for fear and panic is to *stay in the present*. People who are phobic get into a frightening circle described as "fear of the fear." The time when you are not panicking is spent worrying and fearing the panic will come back. So there is always fear. Don't ask yourself "what if" questions. Staying in the present is good grief advice as well. Ask yourself "Am I all right now?" Too often we catastrophize when we are grieving. We worry about the future, and feel we can't stand it. In fact, you are grieving because *the worst that could happen already has: some you love has died.*

SHOCK AND DENIAL

Denial is a *psychological* protective mechanism, just as shock is a *physiological* protective mechanism. Shock and denial will be your friends in the early months of grief. In suicide death there are two kinds of denial: denial before and denial after the suicide. Suicide survivors are victims in more than one sense. They are victims of the tragedy of death, but also victims of a society which left them unprepared for the events leading up to the death.

DENIAL BEFORE DEATH

Suicide has been so wrapped in secrecy, fear and superstition that even "well-known" facts about suicide are not known by the unsuspecting public. People instinctively know when things are not right, and most of you saw things you knew weren't right. The taboo has deprived us of information about mental illness; even the professionals who are meant to help us may not know more than we do.

In fact, most of us were raised with the "information" that "depression is normal" and that "everyone gets depressed." The word depression is misused. Everyone sometimes is unhappy, sad, forlorn, blue, miserable, or dismayed by the normal ups and downs of life. Depression is a brain disease involving an imbalance of the chemicals that regulate how we think, feel and behave. Most of us did not know that depression could kill until it happened in our families. In retrospect, most of us realized the one we loved was depressed. We often say things like, "I knew he was depressed, but I didn't know he was that depressed!"

Consequently, before the suicide, we were frightened when we heard statements about hopelessness and suicide. We were frightened into doing nothing. Because we didn't know what to do, we convinced ourselves that we hadn't heard or seen what we did and we "forgot" it — to protect ourselves from what was too awful to contemplate. This is the denial mechanism. We "forgot" and hoped for the best. *After* the suicide, all the things we "forgot" come tumbling out of our memory as things we *should* have known and *should* have done something about.

CHAPTER 4. THE MANY PAINS OF GRIEF 91

DENIAL AFTER DEATH

The worst has happened, and our first response is likely to be one of protest. "I don't believe it," or "It can't be true," may be our first reaction. This is denial after a suicide combined with shock. Shock is that physical reaction that makes us feel as if we are wrapped in cotton, that we are sleepwalking, and that makes our pain feel far away. Denial helps us tell our family and friends what happened, make arrangements for everyone to get home, plan a funeral, and meet and greet all the people who come.

It's the time when people sometimes say of us, "My, she's taking it so well." It seems if we manage to stand up and behave ourselves appropriately in public, some people want to think we are doing "so well." Shock and denial are protective; they help us get through these end-of-life rituals. More and more, since churches and synagogues support instead of punish, it *is* easier on us, and easier for our friends and relatives to rush to our side.

Many of you will have had this experience of support, but almost all of us have had at least a few bad experiences as well. Over and over we hear that gasp of shock from people when they hear it was suicide. Almost all of us have run into some awful boor who makes a really thoughtless or insensitive comment. We are suddenly sensitive to anything about suicide, and we become so sensitized that we suddenly realize how many television shows, movies and books utilize suicide as entertainment. A suicide is added to give a little "edge" or shock value to a story. We now realize that suicide isn't "entertaining" anymore.

There are stories run in the newspapers all over the country telling of ordinary and unknown people who kill themselves in grotesque ways. Maybe it was someone you loved who was written up this way, and your tragedy was spread all over the continent for the titillation of others. Suicides of unknown people are not usually news. Unless the suicide is by a well-known person, who has killed him or herself in a very spectacular and public manner, it is not news.

What helps you through all this horror is denial after the suicide death. Denial which helps us forget — while we are going on with our lives — because *we have to*. Most people feel as if they will completely fall apart, but almost none of us does, nor do we have the luxury to do so. We have jobs, children, spouses, parents, siblings and friends, and we have responsibilities to all of them. As hard as it is, most people find the routine of living helps them get through those first days that seem agonizingly long.

Most people don't realize that their "friends" — shock and denial — are helping them go on, and that these friends stay with them for many months. Shock and denial leave slowly and gradually. They often dump us unceremoniously into that raging river of grief, but they also help us get back out a tiny bit stronger for the effort. Each time it seems to take all our strength, but suddenly — it seems — we begin to see little signs of hope.

We look back and say, "It's been a month since it happened, and I can't believe I got through it!" It comes as a relief, and a little bit of pride of survivorship. It helps us up when we fall again and again into tears of despair. After our tears have helped relieve some of our emotions, we remember, "Well, I went on before." We compare and realize, "Well, if I did it then, I can do it again."

RELIEF

Who could be relieved when someone dies by suicide? You, for one. Because many of us lived under extreme tension with someone we loved who died, and since most of us did see signs of suicide or things that might have been signs of suicide, his or her death can be like the other shoe dropping. The anxiety is over. The worst thing we feared has finally happened, and we can be allowed a breath of relief.

It is not true that all people are ignorant of what is going on. There are those survivors who have dealt with the chronic mental illness of a loved one in the form of manic-depression and schizophrenia. These are terrible crippling diseases that can torment people for years. A small number of people with these illnesses kill themselves, and when they do, it is normal and natural for the survivors to feel relieved. They are relieved that a great and long ordeal has finally ended.

Some suffered so long watching someone they loved who was so ill, there is hardly any emotion left for grief. Most of the survivors have watched the illness turn someone they love into a stranger for whom they are responsible. There are physical illnesses, such as cancer, that cause people to say after the death comes, "It was a blessing." This is often true of the terrible "mental cancers" called manic-depression and schizophrenia.

This relief comes because your own stress is gone, but many people feel equally relieved that the suffering of someone they love has ended. Often we didn't realize how badly they were suffering, and only in retrospect do we know how they hurt. Many people feel guilt when they

experience these normal feelings of relief. Relief is one of
the only things in grief that feels good, so don't waste time
and energy feeling guilty about a normal human reaction.
Be as realistic as you can. As awful as it sounds to say it,
for some survivors there are positive benefit — such as
financial or emotional — when a long illness results in
death. In other situations where alcohol or illegal drugs
made the relationship a nightmare, the death may be a net
benefit to family peace. There is nothing terrible about
acknowledging it. This doesn't mean you are glad they are
dead.

Again remember there are so many terrible things in
the basketful of grief we carry that we would be foolish not
to let ourselves feel the benefits of one of the few good
things. In some relationships, so much attention had to be
devoted to caring for someone with a chronic illness that all
the others, including yourself, have been deprived. Of
course it was done gladly, but don't ignore the bit of
happiness that seeps through when you realize the potential
for a new freedom.

DELAYED GRIEF

Some people were never allowed to grieve, or
didn't allow themselves to grieve, and they carry their
burdens as best they can. Sometimes when there is a
suicide death in the family, small children are "protected"
by lying to them, or forbidding them to talk about the
person who died and/or their death. There is also a
tendency for some people to put their grief "in the past"
and not think about it. Some adults who grieve a suicide
death try to shut things out in the past, and do their best to
"carry on." Some other people seem to devote their lives to

the past, and carry their pain with them all their lives. Delayed grief usually occurs when people try to stamp their pain down, but every time they stamp, it hurts more. Taking time to grieve may also be a luxury of the middle and wealthy classes. Everyone has to go on, but people in grinding poverty must go on for their very existence, or to sustain the existence of others.

After a suicide, some survivors act as if they can change the past. This results in the normal "what-iffing" and "if-onlys" people do so frequently after a suicide death. It is a necessary look at the past, but when it becomes exaggerated and excessive, grief may be delayed. Sometimes people hang onto their grief, feeling they deserve punishment for having failed the one who died. Some people, such as young children, who hadn't been allowed to grieve, carry their pain like a permanent ache. Delayed grief can be like carrying a rock everywhere one goes. Sometimes belated grief and tears can dissolve the "rock." (*Kristen and the Rock*, Karen Dahl, privately printed, 1984.) It hurts to carry these "rocks" from the past. A few people are permanently damaged by their delayed grief.

Other people store their grief away in a sealed compartment. There is a common belief that this sealing away of grief will greatly damage, if not destroy people. This isn't necessarily true. The brain has ways of protecting us, and this is one of them. If one thinks of the brain partly as a storehouse, it may be desirable to close off one "room." It doesn't necessarily prevent people from living productive and full lives; in fact, it may help them. It may be their only way of defending themselves. This is normal grief for many people.

Some people who use this way of sealing off their pain are afraid of what might happen if they "let go." Most of them have a vague dread of being overwhelmed — of being incapacitated by their grief if they "let it out." If this is your situation, ask yourself, "What is the worst that could happen?" You might completely go to pieces. What does that mean? Well, you might break down crying and sobbing, and find it hard to regain control. Has total loss of control ever happened to you before? No? Well then, it won't now. But what if you break down emotionally in front of someone else? What if you did? It would likely be a kind person who cares about you, and wouldn't think badly of you if you did. The fact is that the worst that could happen to you is that you would temporarily lose emotional control. That's not so terrible; if you have held all your grief in for months or years, you have a lot to cry about. You deserve to feel sorry for yourself.

You might begin by pouring out your grief and pain to your pastor or rabbi, a relative or friend. If you feel you can't do that, pour it all out on paper. Tell the person, or tell the piece of paper, the whole terrible story. Pour out all the things too terrible to talk about. Lose control, break down and cry. Maybe you are angry; you probably should be. Perhaps someone made you hide it all away when you were too little or weak to fight back. You have a right to be angry. Perhaps there are things you feel guilty about — perhaps you feel responsible in some way. Tell it all, or write it all. The worst that can happen is you will lose emotional control for awhile. That's not so awful; it probably has happened before in your life. It's only temporary; you always regain control. Almost everyone has experienced feeling better after a good cry, and you will too. If you are too fearful, or just can't do it, you may want

to see a professional if your delayed grief is getting in the
way of things you want to do in the present. It is never too
late to grieve.

SLEEP, DREAMS AND VISIONS

It is not unusual to have difficulty sleeping for a few
months after the suicide. Common problems are difficulty
falling asleep, or falling asleep but waking early and being
unable to go back to sleep. Some people see the death scene
or other terrible things in their minds, which keep them
from falling asleep. You may feel more tired than usual
during the day, or have problems concentrating. Generally,
these problems are worst in the first few months, and begin
to go away six or seven months after the death. Not
everyone has any or all of these problems, but they are
normal and should not alarm you if they happen.
(Remember that if any of these are extreme, long lasting,
and you are unable to function, it can be major depression
on top of your grief. See your doctor if this is the case.)

A majority of people dream about the person who
died. The most common dream is that they didn't die. Very
often the person who died will "come back" in the dream to
reassure or to explain — sometimes that the death was all a
mistake. People sometimes have dreams about the
childhood of their loved one, and these dreams generally
have the theme that the one you loved is still alive. There
are also "second chance" dreams in which people dream
they are rescuing their loved one in some way. Dreaming
gradually recedes, and suicide survivors often report that
their dreams change to "searching" themes. One may
dream of a house, in which in every room they search, the
loved one has just left — just when they are so close, they

are lost again. Dreams rarely occur often, and dream activity recedes with time.

It is also fairly common, especially shortly after the death, to "forget they died." If the phone rings, you may think for a second that your loved one is calling you; you may find yourself setting a place at the table for them. You may "see" or "hear" them. Your memory may be so vivid that you see their face in someone who resembles them, or you may imagine you hear some distinctive sound they made coming in the house, or "hear" their voice. These "visions" rarely last more than a second or two, but it's enough to make you feel acute disappointment when reality makes you remember they are dead.

ANNIVERSARIES AND HOLIDAYS

If you read other books on grief, you will find there is a lot of talk about how badly you are going to feel on anniversaries and holidays. There is often a suggestion that supportive friends and relatives call you on anniversaries of the death, and other special times. Some people do cope by "storing up" their grief until the day, and letting it all out on the anniversary day. Many suicide survivors, however, have much more trouble with the *anticipation of the special day* than the day itself.

Survivors may start to fear and anticipate the anniversary date — even a month ahead of time, and it seems to get worse the nearer the day comes. But by the time it does come, many people have spent so much time anticipating and fearing the day that the anniversary itself is anti-climactic. With the passage of years, many survivors report a brief anticipation prior to the anniversary, but some feel guilty because they did not have this anxious anticipation, and even forgot the day. In fact, this is a sign of returning to normal, of not letting the terrible thing that happened in the past control the rest of your life.

Of course, holidays, birthdays and anniversaries will be very sad — especially for the first year as each milestone marking their lives passes without them. But these special days can begin to gather even more importance if, with the sadness and loss, you determine that the surviving members of your family must enjoy each other all the more because you now realize how important you are to each other.

When you find yourself dreading some holiday, remind yourself that *the worst that can happen already has happened.* The worst that can happen now is that you will have a very unhappy day — you may collapse in sobbing and feel you will never get over it. But this has happened to you before, and you did get through it — and you will again. You might try something called challenging: try to imagine what the day will be like — try to make yourself feel the worst you can. Usually when you try to make yourself feel a particular way, you can't. Usually if you tell yourself to "Do your worst, I don't care," it has the effect of strengthening you, because you are accepting the fact that you *can* take what comes.

As painful as it may seem, anniversaries and holidays are good occasions for remembering the person you loved who died. It might seem too painful, but many families have discovered that a time set aside for everyone's memories will bring back some of the happiness of the past through the pain of the present. A lot of people like to have pictures around, and "talk to them." Other people put their pictures away for awhile; the reminder is just too painful. A lot of people wear an old shirt or sweater that belonged to their loved one who died.

You might make their favorite dinner on their birthday, or make a donation in their memory. Of course you may shed a tear or many. These are examples of the only way you can still "do" something for someone you love who died — and you will discover it also is doing something for yourself. You need memories — good and bad — because they are a living monument you will always have. You can gather memories from other people in the family, from the loved one's friends, and add these to yours. As long as you live, someone you loved will still be alive in your memory.

CHAPTER 5

ANGER, BLAME AND GUILT

We often don't stop to realize it, but another thing that feels good, in moderation, is anger. To feel anger, to scream and accuse, helps us "get it out of our system." For a long time, people have realized that bottling up anger only hurts us, but to sit quietly and hold our anger inside a little helps us in the same way. Nursing our anger — if we don't do it too much — is sensing the injustice done to us "after all we did" for someone who has left us so brutally.

ANGER

Many of us cry in anguish, "How could he do this to me?" We are not ready yet to realize that he was probably in such emotional pain that he *couldn't* think of you, or if he did, he thought you would be better off! Anger is energy. Angry people often have a tremendous amount of strength. To a certain extent, we can let anger's energy work for us. To tackle cleaning out the garage in a fury of energy helps us "get *it* out of our systems," and has the positive benefit of "finally getting that job done."

BLAME

Anger becomes dangerous when we use its energy to hurt other people. One of our defenses against painful angry feelings is to blame other people for the suicide. Seldom is there a clear-cut villain we can blame for "causing" the suicide, but any person, group or even a corporation is a candidate for blame. It is most often anyone near us, and we usually want it to appear that it is "they" who are the bad people and "we" the good people. It is so easy to blame, because all of us are so fallible. It is easy to blame because all of us are imperfect and guilty of many things. We often are angry and placing blame to put distance between us and that desolate feeling of isolation and aloneness —where each of us has to face the reality that someone we loved has died, and there is *never* anything *any* of us can *ever* do about it. Only with death are the words "forever," "ever" and "never" true. This is the desolation of grief. There are no second chances. In this life, they are beyond us *forever*, and the terrible reality of grief is our knowledge that we will *never* see them again on this earth. *No wonder we are angry!*

The person we are most likely to be angry with is the person who died, and we innately realize how silly this is. They *are* gone, and we can't *ever* reach them here again. Mercifully, they can't hear us; their pain is gone. But *their pain has been transferred to us*, and one way of dealing with this pain is through anger.

As healthy as it is to feel and release anger, we might think about what anger really is: one writer said at the most basic level, we become angry because *we did not get our way*. Things did not turn out the way we wanted them to, and now there is *never* any hope they will. Not only has someone we loved died, but so have all our dreams for them — and us. This is a lot to be angry about. We need to try to remember to let the steam off our anger harmlessly, and not vent it on other people who may be feeling just as bad as we are. It hurts us just as much being angry at really "bad" people, because we, not they, feel the brunt of our anger.

Anger and other emotions are neither good nor bad; they just are. We may not be able to control how we *feel*, but we can control what we *do*. We might feel like driving the car at eighty miles an hour, but we keep ourselves from doing it by remembering our responsibilities. We might want to scream and break things, but we control ourselves. We may want to accuse and blame others for the death and our pain, but we have to control our tongues and remember the parable that reminds us that "he who is without blame may throw the first stone." Anger is normal. Feel it, feel its cleansing fire, and control yourself until it burns itself out and you feel better.

UNPOPULAR AND GUILTY VICTIMS

The public stigma on suicide creates a perception that we and our loved ones are "unpopular" and "guilty" victims. This has prevented suicide survivors from banding together in strength to throw off the stigma. Since 1978 about 200 support groups for suicide survivors have sprung up in the United States and Canada. All of them are individual efforts with no united national group to give advice, guidance and support. No national celebrity suicide survivor has put more than token effort into suicide reduction. There are no telethons raising millions of dollars every year.

By contrast, a group that has "popular" and "innocent" victims is Mothers Against Drunk Driving (MADD). They richly deserve their success, but suicide survivors can only envy them their strong national headquarters, and chapters in each of the United States and Canadian provinces during the same period our individual and isolated efforts have struggled to bring suicide survivors together. MADD has permanently changed the way people feel about drunk driving. That needs doing about suicide as well.

SOCIETY BRANDS SURVIVORS GUILTY

After a suicide, virtually the first message that gets through is how guilty we *must* feel. Combined with this, is the message of how ashamed we *must* feel. People say, "Oh, that poor family; they *must* feel terribly guilty." Others say, "Oh, it *must* be awful for them, dealing with *all that guilt.*" What do they mean? Why *must* we feel guilty and have "all that guilt?" How do they know how guilty you feel? Would they assume you *must* feel guilty if someone you loved had died from cancer? No. And it is not that they are bad or unkind people; they have inherited the centuries-old condemnation of suicide that says only "bad" people kill themselves, and, consequently, they *must* come from "bad" (dysfunctional) families who have "all that guilt."

This is the public assumption that suicide survivors are guilty in a way that other people are not. This assumption, from the Dark Ages, that we should have some brand to show people our guilt and shame for having a suicide in the family lives on. Unfortunately, the stigma has affected us so much that we often accept this brand, or place it there ourselves. But this is not fair. You are a good person who did your best, loved your most, and had a terrible tragedy happen.

REAL GUILT

This is not to say that you don't feel guilty; you wouldn't be human if you didn't feel guilty after the death of someone you loved. This is *real* guilt. In this life, there is no second chance for us to do things we should or could have done differently, nor can we call back unkind or angry words, nor change decisions. Resolving real guilt is one of the important jobs of grief. Our family and friends may try to comfort us by saying, "Don't feel guilty." This is well-intended, but, painful as it is, real guilt has to be looked at, admitted and grieved over. The fact that you do feel guilty proves you are a good person; the fact that you have not always been able to do the right things, say the best things, and make the correct decisions proves you are human.

Your intentions were always good, but you weren't always good. Part of the work of grief is to be able to look at the things you were guilty of, cry over them, and gain strength to be better after you have healed. And you will heal; *you have to*. There are some people who say you will be consumed with guilt and shame the rest of your life. That's nonsense! You need to gradually switch emphasis from your real guilt, and remember how many times you were forgiven, and how much you were loved by someone you loved who died. If there is one incident that seems too terrible to think about, force yourself to think of similar situations in which you *did* do what you now think was right. Think of all the times you said, thought, and decided things that *didn't* result in suicide.

Suicide is not a rational or clearly thought-out action. If suicide is any kind of a "choice," it is a coerced choice, in which someone you loved was unable to see alternatives and consequences. Having said that, it is nonetheless true that it is the person who died who decided *when* all else had failed, *when* everything he or she tried hadn't worked, and *when* the pain was too much to bear anymore.

WHAT-IFFING GUILT

Because someone you loved didn't *have* to die as a result of a terminal physical cause, we are prone to attribute omnipotence to ourselves. We should have known; we should have done things differently, if we had only done one thing extra, we think *"then* they would still be alive." Whatever you did or didn't do just before their death, you had done or hadn't done many times before. If you were mad at them, you had been mad at them many times before when they hadn't killed themselves. If you were gone from home when they killed themselves, you had been gone from home endless times when they didn't kill themselves. If you failed to say,"I love you," before they died, you need to remember we don't go around expressing our love every minute of the day to those we love, and take for granted they will be there.

A certain amount of "what-iffing" and "if-only" thinking is a good process to help you come to grips with the fact that you probably did do all you reasonably could. We tend to idealize the dead, but we must remember that depressed people can be very unreasonable, and oftentimes downright difficult to live with. Depressed people tend to have two sides to their personalities: 1) depressed and dependent, unhappy and clinging, and/or 2) irritable, angry and so touchy one can hardly talk to them. One has the feeling it is necessary to walk on eggshells to keep from "setting them off." People who have manic-depression or schizophrenia can be very difficult to live with, which is an understatement given the severity of the symptoms of these brain diseases. They do and say bizarre things, are abnormally suspicious, and although they do not do it on purpose, can destroy relationships, jobs, school or lead to bankruptcy.

At a certain point, you need to look back realistically at the person who died, and remember how he or she actually was before death. The loved one certainly hadn't the saintly image you may be trying so hard to impose on yourself. You likely are remembering happier times before they were so sick and upset. You need to remember all the things you tried, all the times you were loving and patient, all the times you wracked your brain for one more thing that might help, all the times you gave things up for someone you loved, and nothing worked. That's right — nothing worked — and your loved one died.

It's *normal* to feel you will never be happy again, but you will. It's *normal* to wish you could just crawl in a hole, and give up, but you won't. It's *normal* to doubt your ability to relate to the rest of your family and friends, but you will. It's *normal* to think if you had only done or said things differently, then that loved one would still be alive, but he or she wouldn't. It's *normal* to hurt so much you think you won't ever recover, but you will. You will *because you have to;* you will because down the road, the future will beckon you to come back.

GRIEF AND POWER

Things did not turn out the way we wanted, and we are angry and desperately hurt by it. One person [1] has pointed out an important distinction about our personal power. He says that in any situation in life there are some things that a person can do, and some things that are up to others, or to outside factors, or to chance. We can set goals and do our best, but we cannot, by our own power, make things turn out the way we want.

To imagine that the entire outcome is up to us, *that we have the power* to determine what will happen or, in retrospect *that we did have the power* to determine what happened in the past, is illusory or imaginary power. One can set goals and do one's best, but one cannot by one's own power ensure success. When you go over and over pre-death circumstances and events, searching for acts of omission or commission that you believe caused the suicide, you are attempting to maintain an imaginary power.

We do not have a power that somehow says the past will be magically changed if we only do enough penance, or refuse to believe the present. You may say that you don't really believe your loved one can be brought back by your efforts, but the danger is that if you remain at the "what-iffing" and "if-only" stage, you will *act* as if you have this power, and you will waste your energies in a vain attempt at having a second chance.

Some people take the energy which had been expended in real relationships (real power) and shift it toward maintaining a relationship with the deceased (illusory power). The fear is that without the illusory power, there will be no power at all.(1) The fear may be that living in the past is the only way to stay with someone who died. While we cannot bring the person back, and while there are no second chances with the person who died, there are many second chances with the living — with others who need and want us here and now. This is where your real power lies. It's hard to come back to the present, and to face the future, but that too, is the work of grief. You will come back to the present and the future, not only because you have to, but because you will want to.

CHAPTER 6

WHO DO YOU TELL? WHAT DO YOU SAY?

Because there have been hundreds of years of stigma and taboo on suicide, the simple matter of notifying people of the death poses the question of what do you tell them? It isn't just at the time of the death, but in the future. Who needs to know? What should we tell people? Which of the relatives should we tell? What about children? In all cases *tell the truth*. Often you have no alternative, but where you do have a choice, you will do harm to yourself and other members of your family if you try to "hush it up." There is nothing so awful that mankind hasn't seen before. The suicide will be a terrible shock to your friends and family, but get the information out fast so you won't have to go on and on telling people who haven't heard.

If you are worried about gossip and rumors, realize that the truth is the best way to squelch rumors. If you try to make up some "cover story" it will be more difficult. Your self- consciousness will probably show and only make people suspicious or pity you if they know the truth. Let other people help you. Their shock and surprise is their problem; you don't have to worry about shielding them. Many suicide survivors report that their friends and family rushed to help them, but people can't do this for you if they sense they are being held at a distance by a lie.

LET YOUR CLERGY HELP YOU

It may not seem so at the time, but if your pastor or rabbi discusses the suicide at the funeral service, they are doing you a favor. He or she is telling a large group of

people the awful fact that is so hard for you to repeat over
and over. Clergy who deal compassionately with the
suicide in the funeral service are also setting a wonderful
example of support for you. Your friends and
acquaintances can learn from them how to help you.

If your clergy *isn't* helpful, or condemns your loved
one, look around and realize that the majority of religious
people today are not like that. Obviously, this is easier said
than done. But remember that people change churches and
religions all the time. You don't have to associate with
people who say awful things about you and about someone
you loved who died. It hurts terribly if your clergy
condemns your loved one, you and your family. Good and
kindly religious people don't do this.

TELLING CHILDREN

It is plain to see that your friends and people at
work need to know about the suicide in your family, but
little children? Yes, they need to know the truth as well.
Being the only one who doesn't know, places your child in
a terrible position. Young children are smarter than we
sometimes think; they certainly are sensitive and tuned to
the currents and undercurrents in their homes. They know
when something is wrong; they often have seen things —
sometimes they have seen the body. You can't turn around
and tell them it was an accident. This could cause a terrible
rupture in your relationship. If you lie to them about
something as important as a death in the family, it can hurt
them in the short and long run. All the children in your
neighborhood know, and if you don't tell your child they
will. Children need to be told by people who love them.

After a suicide in your family, you need to call the principal, the counselor, or your child's teacher, and tell them of this terrible thing that has happened. The school needs to be aware that your children are grieving, and it needs to hear the facts from you. Children often think that if they just go back to school and say nothing, somehow things will be okay. They are always self-conscious, and may be doubly so when there is a death in the family. As bad as it is, it certainly is better if you tell the school than if it hears it through rumor and speculation. Your children may not like your doing this, but you must. If the school people know the facts from you, they can help the rest of the students.

Your child's friends need accurate information so they can befriend as best they can. They also need to understand about grief and be prepared for some of the perfectly normal, but scary things that happen to their grieving friend. There just isn't any way you can take the pain of grief away from children, but you can make it worse by closing them out.

When a student kills him or herself, it is a good idea to have some kind of intervention by counselors and mental health people in handling shock and grief. Sometimes, however, when a student kills him or herself people from outside come into a school and act as if the whole student body is somehow is at risk for suicide. Schools have been advised by "experts" that it is dangerous to talk to young people about suicide.

But imagine the fear, worry and hurt of a young person who knows what happened but is swept adrift in a ocean of silence. Young people see the fear in the adults around them, and they hear the whispers used to talk about suicide. The majority of students in a large school won't know the person who died, and they will be surprised, fearful and shocked. They need information, reassurance and an explanation of how suicide happens. They don't need to hear hysterical predictions that they can somehow be lured or enticed into killing themselves.

IF YOU HAVE ALREADY LIED

If you have already lied to your child or children, you should make it right — now. You need to get him, her or them with you, and say you thought you were doing the right thing when you told them the death was an accident, but you realize now they need to know the truth. Apologize to them for lying, and explain how you thought it was for the best at the time. Tell them simply what the cause of death was, and then answer their questions. Be prepared for them to be angry with you for lying. It can be a valuable lesson for them to see that adults sometimes do lie, and that this is the way people correct lies. You and they will probably be relieved to get it out in the open.

But surely one shouldn't tell really young children. Perhaps not. Babies and two-year-olds need to understand that the person who died is gone permanently. Three and four-year-olds need to hear the truth simply, because if you don't tell them, they will find out, and it may be in an awful way. Obviously, little children don't need every single detail, but they need to know that the person did it to him or herself, and how, with a simple explanation of why. They need to know that some people feel so badly inside themselves that sometimes they kill themselves, because they can't think of any other way of taking the hurt away. They need to know that people can be sick in their emotions as well as in their bodies.

But how can you explain the method of death that was chosen? There are so many guns on television that it is not difficult for young children to understand a gun death. They probably have seen suicide deaths on television. It is harder to explain when the method of death was hanging, poison or one of the bizarre methods some people use to kill themselves. Be truthful. Tell them you don't know why he or she picked that method. Children can get funny and unrealistic ideas, and need to be assured that they can ask questions and have honest answers. As they grow older, they will want to understand the death in more detail. Answer questions simply, accurately and as they come up. *There is nothing too awful to talk about; everything in the world has happened before.*

Honesty about emotions is just as important. If you are angry, it's all right to let them know that. They probably are too. Don't "spare your children." You need to cry, they need to cry, and they need to see you cry. They despair and you despair sometimes. They need help from you to understand that these emotions are temporary. They may come and go, but they are a normal part of grieving. They need to know they won't always feel this way; *you* need to know you won't always feel this pain.

TELLING EVERYONE

At first it seems you have told everyone, and that everybody knows. Even in small towns this isn't necessarily true — that "everyone knows." There are some people who should know who may not. That friend who hasn't called you probably doesn't know yet. We all have acquaintances and friends who we don't see very often, and they have other sets of acquaintances and friends. We assume the news of the suicide is going to "spread like wild fire," but that often isn't the case. People are gone when things happen, they have their own problems that distract them; they just simply may not have heard about it. Whatever the reason, you will run into people who don't know. It happens less and less as time goes on, but you probably will run into people six months or a year afterwards who don't know that someone you loved has died.

It is a good idea to decide on a short explanation of what happened, and memorize it, if necessary. Some examples: "It was a terrible shock to us, but he killed himself." — "She died; she took her own life in January." — "We didn't realize how depressed he was, and he killed himself." Make it short and fast, and be prepared for the other person's shock. It's not fair, but suicide is a shocking death, and one of the extra burdens suicide survivors have is dealing with other people's gasps of shock or disapproval when they hear the news.

Another matter is whether to tell the method of death in the explanation. An example, "It was a terrible shock; he shot himself." People are curious about methods of suicide, and some boors come right out and ask what method the victim chose. To prevent speculation, it probably is better to tell the method. If it was a very public suicide, they will already know. Some people may blurt out, "Was she on drugs?" or make some other tactless comment. It is easier said than done, but try not to get upset by all this. Some of these people mean well, and the others are not worth getting upset about. Still other people will be genuinely concerned for you, and you will need to say something soothing to them. Can you believe this? You are the one who has had the tragedy, and you have the extra burden of telling people, "That's all right; I know it's a shock." *We have to take care of them before they can turn around to console us!*

TELLING PEOPLE IN THE FUTURE

Who should we tell and who needs to know? Your family and people who marry into your family need to know about the suicide. They need to know that there is depression, manic-depression or schizophrenia in the family, the same way they need to know if there is diabetes or heart disease. It is part of our health history. We need to know about the illnesses in our families so we can spot them in time in the future. Couples need to know the family medical history when planning children. There is nothing that foredooms you or your family because there has been a suicide, or more than one.

If you meet someone at a coffee counter, and visit over lunch, that person doesn't need to know your whole history. If you're a widow, you can just say you're single. If one of your children died, and you're asked how many children you have, just say the remaining or original number. People you meet casually don't need to know about this particular tragedy in your life. If that person subsequently becomes your friend, however, you will need to tell your new friend and explain the circumstances. People who care about you need to know. The suicide of someone you loved is just too big an event in your life for your friends not to know.

One final warning! You will run into any number of people who will boorishly foist on you their *half-baked* opinions about suicide. There are professional people who have *half-baked* ideas about suicide, and who may press their pet views on you, often insisting you and your whole family need counseling. You just don't need, and you don't have to tolerate, unsolicited opinions and advice about this tragedy in your life.

CHAPTER 7

RELATIONSHIPS

One of the biggest lessons death teaches us is to value our friends and family. They are always our best support. Everything is so difficult, but one of the worst things you can do for each other is to try to maintain a "stiff upper lip" for the sake of others. Parents must see their children cry; how else can you know when to give them comfort? Children need to see their parents' grief; how else will they know how deeply you care?

Brothers and sisters need the example of their parents' grief to learn how to manage theirs. Husbands and wives often try to "hold themselves together" for the other's sake. Your relatives — your aunts and uncles and grown sisters and brothers need to know how and when to help you. Some relatives and friends who didn't know your loved one well will grieve more for you and your pain. Our friends want to help us, and the very difficult thing is that we have to let them. We are so used to being self-sufficient — so reluctant to "impose on anyone" that sometimes we don't give our relatives and friends the opportunity of helping us.

Another thing you need to remember is that there are never ideal circumstances in families. In some families there are real breaks between people. Sometimes people will be brought together by tragedy, but more often the problems in relationships that were there before the death are still there, and perhaps they become worse. In the real world, death puts a great strain on relationships, and the strengths and weaknesses that were there before will still be there. Many people become better and stronger because of tragedy. But if you were on the verge of divorce before the suicide, you still are. If your marriage was so-so, you will still have a lot of ups and downs with your partner. If your marriage and other relationships were good and strong, you will reap those rewards in comfort and love.

CONTEST FOR WORST PLACE

You will hear many people say that the worst thing that can happen is the death of a child. Not always. Couples who have good marriages often find great comfort in having each other. Facing death forces many people to revise their priorities. Death forces a change in basic values. The basic value is being alive! It can cause some things thought so important to be revised. We can start to ask this question: "Tomorrow, will this seem worth making an issue of now?" A lot of things we get upset about seem unimportant when put to this test.

Is the death of a child worse? Think of the widow or widower left alone, or left alone with young children. Think of the seventy-year-old mother whose forty-five-year-old son kills himself. What about his children and wife? What about his brothers and sisters scattered across the country? Think of the twenty-year-old widower. How can his parents comfort him; how does he feel about his in-laws? How do they feel about him? Think of the divorced couple whose child kills himself? Think of the thirty-year-old man whose father or mother dies by suicide? Think of every imaginable relationship in suicide death, and you have the real world of suicide grief. When it is someone *you* love, it is the worst!

It may not seem so now, but when you realize you can still think and care about other suffering people, when you learn that you can still reach out, that you can still sympathize with someone else, when you can still see people worse off than you are, then acceptance and return to life after suicide begins. Beginnings and endings are the circle of life. The beginning, however, is only the first step of our return to our new lives. Your life will never be entirely the same again because someone you loved has died — has died in a ghastly way, and there is just no quick route back to life without your loved one. The hole left in our lives after the death of someone we loved seems so huge that all we can do at first is step around it. This is why the relationships we have in our lives are so important.

This is why the demands on us to go on are so important. And we go on because we *have to*. Use your families and friends for help. Depend on them, rely on them; ask them for what you need. Then let them depend on you, rely on you; give *them* what they need. When you learn that even in this terrible grief you can still give and that you get help while you give it, you will have learned what is best about people and how they survive. *We get help and we give it — and we get help by giving it.*

RELATIONSHIPS HAVE UNIQUE PROBLEMS

Whether you grieve deeply or not at all depends on the relationship you had with the person who killed him or herself. It is always assumed that the closer in blood relationship one is to the person who died, the more deeply one will grieve, and the further away from blood relationship, the less one will grieve. This is generally true, but there are many exceptions. For example, it is wrong to assume that a person is grieving less because he or she was "only" a friend, or "only" an aunt or uncle. It is wrong to

assume that siblings or spouses or anyone else will
automatically grieve deeply.

A long-time friend of someone who killed himself
may be closer to the person than a sister who is fifteen
years older and lives across the country. That sister cares,
but may never have had the time it takes to maintain a close
and intimate relationship because of distance and time. A
wife may not always grieve a husband's death. He may
have been an abusive alcoholic for years, and she,
understandably, may feel only relief after his suicide. These
examples serve to show only that one should not assume
the degree of grief is the same for everyone — even in the
same family or in close relationships. The point is, don't
feel guilty for what you are or what you feel. There are no
right or wrong feelings, just right or wrong actions. If you
are grieving a little less than someone else in your family,
let them know they can lean on you a little bit more.

PARENT SURVIVORS OF A YOUNG CHILD

Popular and professional literature often assumes
that the death of a child is the worst grief that can occur,
and that the probability of recovery from this grief is
dubious at best. This assumption further implies that this
desperate grief occurs only with the death of a *young* child.
This assumption that parents of a child grieve more
minimizes the grief of other people grieving the suicide
death of their sibling, parent or grandparent. It minimizes
the grief of spouses, fiancees, or people living together.
Other neglected grievers are grandparents, friends, and
other relatives. Suicide grief is worst when it happens to
you when someone you love has died.

Having said this, parents probably are unique in feeling more responsible for a child who dies than when someone else dies. Parents have the whole life history of their child to review for things that might have, or should have been done differently. Like every other griever, they have to face the irrevocability of the loss. They have the added burden of bearing the blame of people who say they are a sick and "dysfunctional" family that somehow contributed to the suicide. Blame is especially placed on busy, ambitious, career-oriented parents who move a lot. They are regarded as parents who care more for their careers and possessions than for their children. These individuals are not granted the assumption that someone in their family was very sick and died, and that the rest of the family is well — the assumption they would be granted if it had been a cancer death.

Parents who face the suicide of their child hear dire predictions for their marriage. They hear that the divorce rate after the death of a child is anywhere from 60 to 90 percent. The 90 percent figure is questionable if for no other reason than not that many people can *afford* a divorce. The 60 percent figure is not particularly surprising as about 50 percent of all married people divorce anyway. On the other hand, if you are a single divorced parent, the likely assumption is that your child killed him or herself because of a broken family. The deck is stacked so you can't win either way. The fact is, the kind of marriage you have going into the suicide death grieving period predicts the way you and your spouse will grieve together.

If your marriage was on the brink of divorce before the death, the extra pressure of grief may well cause you to separate. If you have a close, helpful and loving relationship, you will probably pull together and deepen your relationship. When people say the death of a child is worse, they don't take into account the fact that couples have each other, whereas, for example, a spouse is left alone or with small children. But there is no better or worse in grief, it is all bad. When it happens to *you*, it is the worst.

PARENT SURVIVORS OF A GROWN CHILD

Elderly parents of grown children who kill themselves have different problems from parents of young children who die by suicide. The parents of a young suicide most often have other young children, and they must cope with their grief at the same time they have to guide their other children in their grief. Parents, being human, often want time out from parenting their other children, and it is not unusual for a family to drift in their own ways for awhile. People are resilient, and this muddling through things often works out well. The ideal parent, of course, would grieve deeply, and at the same time be the fully nurturing mom or dad they've always been expected to be. Unfortunately, there are no ideal parents.

Families, like marriages, will tend to be the same after a suicide as they were before. If they were close and talked a lot with each other, or if there were substantial problems in the family leading to a lack of communication, those same frameworks will still be there. Most families pull together in one way or another. After a suicide is not the time for telling parents and families how much better other families are.

An older or elderly parent who has a child who kills him or herself, has different problems and sets of relationships. The parent is more likely to be single or widowed and living alone. Consequently, the feelings of desolation and loneliness may be greater because of physical isolation. These parents may have longer memories to cherish of their children, but they have a shorter time to recover and appreciate them than young parents do. These parents who are closer to their own deaths, often feel it is unfair for their children to die first. In these days of long and healthy lives, children are expected to grieve for their parents, not the other way around.

GRANDPARENTS AND IN-LAWS

Grandparents have special problems surrounding the suicide of a grandchild. They often have a double grief; they grieve not only for their grandchild, but for the grief of their child. Many times they are a stabilizing influence for their children, because they have had more experience of great loss. They will put aside their own grief, and rush to help their children with theirs. They do it lovingly and willingly, but their sacrifice should be noted and appreciated.

Older or elderly parents whose grown child dies by suicide may have problems with the remaining in-law spouse and vice versa. Sometimes there has been friction with the in-laws before the death, and it is increased afterwards. There may be mutual accusations between them and the spouse. Even where there aren't bad feelings, a spouse may move to another city or state after the death. Or, after some time, the spouse may remarry. In any or all of these situations there may be problems for the grandparents in seeing their grandchildren, and this is felt as a deep loss by them.

The worst situation occurs when there is hostility between the remaining spouse and the in-laws. The spouse may refuse to let the grandparents see the children, and there may not be much they can do about it. One avenue they can try is to find an intermediary such as a mutual friend, relative or a pastor or rabbi who can try to find some guidelines and rules for visitation. Going through the courts to resolve this problem is not uncommon any more. When the remaining spouse moves to a different city or state, the grandparents will have to reconcile themselves to the fact that they will see their grandchildren only on short visits. Often grandparents cannot afford to travel and the relationship has to be maintained by phone and letters. When widowed spouses remarry, it might not be unusual for grandparents to feel resentful. Nothing can replace children, but people do find new spouses. If you do find yourself resentful, try to realize where your resentment is coming from, and do your best to like the new partner. It may be your only alternative for a harmonious relationship with your grandchildren.

SPOUSES

When a spouse kills him or herself, a great deal depends on the age of the remaining spouse and the relationship they had with each other. Wives and husbands, as well as people who were living together, have a wide variety of relationships with each other. Most spouses left behind will be widows, because more men kill themselves than women do. Consequently, a great deal of emphasis is placed on the problems of widows, and widowers find less support for themselves. This is because there are fewer suicide survivor widowers than widowers from other deaths. The problems of spouses, however, are generally the same, and be assured that what follows applies to men as well as women.

Generally, younger spouses recover and remarry rather quickly — probably because they are more resilient, forward-looking and stronger. Initially, however, because of their youth, they may be more shocked and overwhelmed by the thought of the future, and have less financial resources. The twenty-six-year-old widow of a bus driver left with four children is in a different situation than that of a forty-year-old electrical engineer who is left with a house and four children after his wife's suicide. Remarriage at older ages is never simple due to difficulties of blending families, and simply because there aren't very many marriageable people available.

Widows and widowers, even in marriages which they thought were equal, discover after a suicide how many important things the other spouse had taken care of, and a host of little things which had been completely taken for granted. Financial resources always make a tremendous difference regardless of age. A young widower may have parents he can turn to for financial aid; a middle-aged widow may have to turn to welfare. With so many mixed marriages, a widow may not be able to get social security for her children because they were not legally adopted by her husband. In one very narrow situation, a widow can be denied social security for her children unless she can prove the suicide was an accident!

The relationship of the couple before the death determines how or whether the remaining partner will grieve. If there was a very loving relationship, though it may also have had lots of stress in the relationship, there will be genuine feelings of loss and grief for the surviving spouse. There may be very little or no grief if the couple had been just barely getting along, or even hostile. In these unhappy marriages, survivors may feel a good deal of relief. They may also, however, grieve for the lost dream and hope of a happy marriage. In some situations, where, for example, the person who died had depression and alcoholism for a long time, the death — although not longed for — may produce a positive benefit for the remaining family. There had been someone who was very sick in their family who died, and after the death they were able to start fresh to build on their strengths.

SEPARATED COUPLES

Sometimes suicides occur after a couple has separated or divorced. In some cases, the remaining spouse often grieves for that part of the marriage that was good — that person he or she originally loved. It is not uncommon for separated people to feel that if they had only stayed and tried harder, the suicide would have been prevented. Some relationships had so little left in them at the end, the spouse mourns more the loss of the dream — the dream that things would turn out all right — or return to the way they used to be. Sometimes when the divorce is long past when the suicide occurs, the remaining partner will have no grief at all, but will be concerned for their children's grief. These parents conscientiously respect the relationship their children had, and will try to help their children mourn.

The problems in-laws have go both ways after a suicide. There may be friction between spouses and in-law parents. In life, there are some people who are just plain hard to get along with, and sometimes they are in-laws. Some grandparents, or some spouses, were cranky, selfish and disagreeable people before the suicide, and remain so after it. The remaining in-laws may have tried everything to get along with them to no avail. The temptation will be great to sever the relationship. Where there are grandchildren, the temptation should be resisted because children often see a different side of people than adults.

A different situation prevails when there are no children to tie in-laws together. There often has been a loving relationship between in-laws which may be continued and strengthened even if there is a remarriage. Where the relationship has been strained and still is, the time is ideal to go separate ways. Even where there was a loving and supportive relationship between them and their in-laws, in the case of very young widows or widowers, they often drift away to begin new lives unencumbered by the past in-laws they didn't know well. A nineteen-year-old widow or a twenty-one-year-old widower deserves the chance to recover and begin anew with the blessings of in-laws. This is not to say that relationships should be severed, but only that, realistically in these cases, it is not unusual that in-law relationships fade away after a death when there are no children.

UNMARRIED COUPLES

Unmarried partners will have the same problems as spouses, and more. After the suicide of one of a couple living together, the remaining partner may be in a difficult legal position. Without a will, he or she is not the legal heir or partner of the person who died, and if the in-laws decide to exclude them, there is not much that can be done. It is easier if there was a good relationship, and the family includes the friend or fiancee left behind. More and more frequently, one does see a friend or fiancee listed in the obituary as a survivor. It is a dubious position to be in, however, and roommates, close friends, partners and

fiancees are often the neglected grievers. This may be
especially so when the couple was gay or lesbian.

YOUNG, TEENAGE AND OLDER CHILDREN

Young children, teenage children, and older
children have different needs and capabilities. Young
children tend to be neglected in the urgency of the
aftermath of suicide, but they must be remembered quickly.
They do not have the life experience to understand what
has happened, and need information and reassurance.
Everyone needs practical help after a death, but children
especially need to understand what has happened, and need
help in dealing with their friends and school. Children's
friends do not call on them or send flowers when someone
dies. Very young children may not really grasp the
magnitude of what has happened, and may appear to chatter
quite indifferently about the suicide. It is not unusual to
hear a child say, "My daddy killed himself," as if it were
ordinary conversation. Children may go around saying it
freely to their friends. Their natural inclination to be open
could be copied by grown-ups. Young children need
simple, accurate information, with more details provided as
they grow older and want more information.

Teenage suicide survivors are familiar with the
family situation, and have a more complete grasp of the
implications of the death. Many parents report their
teenagers just don't want to, or won't talk about the suicide.
Teenagers experience a great deal of self-consciousness,
and they are often very, very embarrassed by the suicide.
They need to receive concerned care, and to hear that they
can talk about it when they want to. They also need a good
role model in their family who talks in a normal way about

the person who died and how much they are missed. When a person dies, it is *not* normal to have absolute silence about the fact. Suicide is too big an event to be undigested and ignored. If the school does not know about the suicide, a caring adult ought to inform it so allowances can be made for a temporary loss of concentration, a drop in grades, or a change in behavior. The teenager who is informed about the suicide, and about his or her part in the reorganization of the family — the teenager who is involved in plans for the future and has open communication, will get along very well.

Older children, in their twenties on up, tend to pull together for the sake of their parents when one of their siblings dies. Older children's needs often are neglected during the funeral period, and they may not be able to realize their own grief until they are back in their own homes. It is a great shock when one of your brothers or sisters kills themself. It is a terrible shock. Siblings expect their parents to die eventually, but not one of themselves! Often the sibling who kills him or herself lives far away, and there may be a great deal of unreality about the death. They are used to not seeing that member of the family and it is easy to "forget" they have died. If people are separated by great distances, they know there is the *possibility* of seeing each other, even if it is remote. But when one of them dies, they are removed from the earth! The possibility is gone. Older children grieve according to the closeness of the sibling who died. There are exceedingly close families, and those that tend to spin off and go their own ways. Older children have a lifetime of memories with their brothers and sisters, and their grief should not be minimized.

CHAPTER 8

RECOVERING AND GOING ON

The biggest need people have in grief is to be reassured. Reassurance is a guide that helps us gauge ourselves; to compare ourselves with a norm or standard. Being with other suicide survivors helps break down the isolation and fear we have when we are alone. Your difficulty in going through your grief, and getting back to your "new normal," may depend on the kind of messages you hear. If someone tells you immediately after the suicide that, "This is something so terrible you will never get over it," it can become a terrible self-fulfilling prophecy. On the other hand, your outcome may be very different if the message you hear is, "Yes, this is terrible, and you probably feel you won't ever get over it, but you will. It's hard for you to believe right now, but many people have done it, and so can you."

SUPPORT GROUPS FOR SUICIDE SURVIVORS

One of the most helpful things you can do for yourself is to attend a grief group for suicide survivors — if you are lucky enough to have one in your city. In a group you can talk to other survivors and compare your situation with theirs. We need to have our pain acknowledged, and to be supported by others. At the same time we are receiving support, we discover we can also give help to others. Support groups are based on this principle — that one gets help by giving it.

Self-help groups are divided two ways. First, they are divided as to whether the group is for a temporary problem, like grief, or for chronic problems, such as having a retarded child. Secondly, grief groups fall into closed or open groups. Closed groups work well in small communities where there aren't very many suicides. These meet weekly for six to eight weeks, and follow a structured agenda. They cover stages of grief, and seek to complete the cycle of grief. Open groups do not have programmed agendas, and meet regularly on fixed dates each month. At these groups, survivors deal with the problems they are experiencing at the time, and they have a mix of people close and faraway from the suicide. Group leaders are also survivors. They are very altruistic people who are through their grief and have a strong impulse to help others.

Dependency is a tendency to become unnaturally attached to a group, and some people worry this will happen with suicide survivors. Some open-ended groups are formed like clubs which one joins, as opposed to groups where people come together temporarily because of a common problem. There is nothing wrong with forming new friendships in a grief group, but it seems unwise to urge suicide survivors to join, and stay in a group for months and months — or years. To make a suicide death in your family the central focus of the rest of your life will take away necessary energy and attention that needs to be on you and your surviving family and friends.

Attend a group meeting as soon after the suicide as you can. The longer you flounder around trying to figure out what happened and what hit you, the more confused, helpless and hurt you will be. You may feel you just can't talk to a bunch of strangers, but take a deep breath and go.

You will meet role models. You will meet survivors who are further away from their loved one's suicide. You will see, for example, that they have gotten through the first six or nine months. You will also see and hear other recently bereaved survivors who are still reeling from shock and bewilderment as you are.

You may be shocked to discover that you are laughing in commiseration over some gross thing that happened. Early on in the grief group experience, you may need more from others than you can give. As you go on, you will find that you reach out to other people, because you have been there too. In rural areas or small towns, where there are no groups, suicide survivors can get together informally with newly bereaved suicide survivors. Ask your funeral director or pastor or rabbi if they know other suicide survivors who would get together with you. Other survivors can provide you with a measurement stick, a source of encouragement, and a haven for times of discouragement.

A suicide survivor's grief group is a supplement to one's natural support system; it is a temporary haven where a person can go to be with people who understand how they feel. You may feel freer to "let down" with other survivors than people close to you. The group is a place where you realize you are getting your own strength and confidence back to go on by yourself. Some survivors, after they are ready to leave the group, stay awhile longer to help newer people. A suicide survivor's grief group is one no one ever joins voluntarily, but it can be a lifeline to a future without someone you loved who died.

To say that grief is chaotic is to understate the problem. If only grief were a steady, upward progress from the death of your loved one to remembrance and renewal, it might not seem so bad. But grief is a period of falling down, picking yourself up, falling down, picking yourself up again — and again. As time passes, you won't fall down so far, and the times between falls begin to lengthen. But even still, it will not steady. Many people, around six or eight months after the suicide, have a setback. It *feels* like you are right back at the beginning, and that you've lost all the progress you thought you'd made. You haven't. You're human; you are healing. The other despairing times have passed, you have gone on, and you will again.

DO YOU NEED A PROFESSIONAL?

Most grieving people don't need professional help. They need support not therapy. If you do need therapy, there are many professionals available. You should see someone who practices psychotherapy or counseling, and many professionals do: psychologists, psychiatric nurses, social workers, and pastors are the most common. There are also grief counselors. Before going to any professional, check them out. This is not as difficult as it sounds. Ask someone you trust if they know of a good psychotherapist; more and more people are going to therapists for help with problems in their lives. There is very little stigma attached any more.

If there is a mental health clinic in your area, call it; it will have someone on its staff who can help you. (It also will have a psychiatrist in case you have depression.) Funeral homes sometimes have bereavement counselors. There are many resources. Whomever you go to, you should talk to personally first — either in person or over the phone. State simply what your situation is, and ask if they have had experience in helping grieving people. Good therapists will answer honestly, and if they don't have this kind of experience, they probably know someone they can refer you to.

You should know, however, that you will still have to do the work of grief. Psychotherapists are people who can help you with your problem; they do not solve it for you. Psychotherapy is talk-therapy, and you do most of it. Psychotherapy is rather like sitting and talking in front of someone while you talk and figure out solutions to your problem. The psychotherapist may guide you by asking questions or making occasional comments, but you do the work. What is the work of psychotherapy? It is to help you learn to think differently about your problems, and to look at new ways of solving them.

SOME HELPFUL CLICHES

A cliche is a truth that is so obvious, it sounds corny and old fashioned. Cliches are old truths — and they represent our legacy from all the collective wisdom of the past — put in a short phrase. One old cliche says: *Things turn out for the best.* That is not true in itself, but you can *make* things turn out for the best. Even though there are many things beyond our control in life, we are responsible for what is inside of us, and we have much more power to call on than we realize.

The great psychiatrist Victor Frankel says that the one thing no one can ever take from us is our *attitude* toward life. *We* are the ones who will decide how we look at the tragedy of the suicide in our lives; we *can* let it ruin the rest of our lives. We also can decide, as humans always have, that *we're not going to let this defeat us. Where*

there's life, there's hope. One of the reason cliches like this
are hackneyed sayings is because people have found them
to be so true over the ages.

One of the tasks of grief is to regain your strength.
Not only can you regain the strength you had before, but
grief survived increases your inner strength. It may make
you *sadder, but wiser;* enduring catastrophe taps that bit of
extra strength you didn't know you had. Grief isn't solely
related to death; it relates to all the losses we have in life.
Each loss builds on the other, but the grief of death is the
worst loss.

And the *first grief* for a person is worse than
subsequent ones will be, because you have to go through it
alone and discover your own guideposts. If your first real
grief is a suicide, it may seem that you will never get over
it. When you do, you may look back, with a justifiable
pride, and wonder, "How did I ever get through it?"

One of the benefits of surviving an ordeal is that
your added strength gives you more confidence. *If I
survived this, I can survive anything!* you can say proudly.
Suicide survivors not only get "through it," but can feel an
extra pride of survivorship, because they not only survived
the death, they did so even with all the extra problems
created by the taboo and stigma on suicide. You can even
feel a little bit superior about it. You've been *tested by fire.*

Another good that can come out of grief is your
realization of how precious time is. *There's no time to
waste,* our ancestors taught us. Now we know what they
mean. Grief can teach us to *take time to smell the roses* and
to value how important *now* is.

Cliches teach us that *there's no time like the present.* If we can learn to say those kind or loving words now — while we have the chance — we can avoid the kind of regrets we had for the things done and undone in the past. We can't do any more for someone we loved who died, but we can *make up for it* with the living. We may also need to learn that *all work, and no play, makes Jack a dull boy.* People in the past learned that workaholics lose out in life, or maybe we have not worked hard enough in the past, and need to *pull ourselves together* — we need to get organized.

There are any number of ways we may learn the wisdom of these ancient truths that are now cliches. Grief can teach us to *appreciate what we have* more, and to value what we have. Instead of yearning for what we can't have, we need to *take stock in ourselves.* We can look closely at our lives, and what is important and what we may have overlooked.

After a loss like a suicide death, you will find that just being alive is the basic value in life. There are all sorts of ways you can make changes in the quality of your life. But being alive is the *bottom line.* Grief teaches us that death is the one thing on earth that is irrevocable. One definition of spirituality is transcendence — to go beyond ourselves — beyond what we thought we were. This is one reason people sometimes become more deeply religious after a death; without realizing they could, they transcended themselves.

When will you "get over it?" When will you *be back on an even keel?* — back to your "new normal" again? Generally speaking, it takes time for a huge emotional wound to heal, and you need help. You may need to learn to ask for the help you need from the people around you. *I'll believe it when I see it,* you may be thinking, but you can and will.

We have the benefit of the ancient wisdom that tells us that *nothing new has happened under the sun. There are no new things; just the same old things happening to new people.* There have been suicides since men and women have been on earth. People survived then, and you will too. The future beckons to us, and we have a healthy impulse to return because of that "persistent breeze that blows towards us from the future." (Albert Camus.)

WORKING AT HAPPINESS

It sounds strange to say you must work at happiness, but what it means is that you should be good to yourselves and each other. Just because such a devastating thing as a suicide happened doesn't mean you shouldn't participate in enjoyable activities and can't have a small period of enjoyment.

There is no reason in the world that you cannot have the diversion of a movie, picnic, trip to the zoo, dinner out, or any other thing you normally enjoy. Yes, it will be bittersweet, and you may cry. So what? Getting back into life after suicide means getting back into your routine, which involves work, obligations, and things you enjoy.

Food won't taste good, your loss of concentration means you will miss half the movie, the sky will not be as blue, nor will the sun shine as warmly. But it will come. If anyone deserves the consolation of a bit of enjoyment, you do. The fact that you can laugh — even for a moment, or that you can divert yourself with a book for half an hour means you are going to be all right. It will take a long time and be hard, but you will be happy again. You have a right to recover from grief just as other people do.

THE FUTURE

Despite the low priority given to the problems surrounding suicide death, the future is bright. The progress made in the last half of the twentieth century in understanding the brain —how it works, how it gets sick, and how it gets well — cannot be turned back. The director of the National Institute of Mental Health said in 1990, that "90 percent of what we know about the brain was learned in the last ten years." There is a field called neuroscience that has made remarkable discoveries.

President Bush signed a proclamation making 1990 to 2000 "The Decade of the Brain." Congress has even increased appropriations for research. There is a strong commitment to research on major depression, manic-depression, schizophrenia and the anxiety diseases. We will also benefit from research that explores the organic things that go wrong in the brain, such as brain tumors and Alzheimer's disease. Scientists and pharmaceutical companies will continue developing medicines that are more effective, and have fewer side effects, for the treatment of mental illness. Families of individuals who have mental illness will begin to demand better educated psychiatrists, psychotherapists and other caregivers. Mental illness will be seen as the physical illness of the brain it really is. When people discover that antidepressants can take away the terrible emotional pain in two or three weeks, they will refuse to suffer a year and a half or more while their depression runs its course.

People won't stand for their loved ones suffering from untreated mental illness. They won't be silenced by the people who say it is all right to take medicine for physical illnesses, but people who have mental illnesses must suffer untreated, and pull themselves together by their own will. Suicide survivors banding together will be the new people who won't stand for being treated as outcasts because someone they loved died by suicide. Their friends and caregivers will become increasingly supportive. It's not fair, but only the families and loved ones of someone who died by suicide can banish the stigma; only those who wear the heavy cloak of stigma can throw it off. No more will suicide survivors be in the ridiculous position of not knowing someone they loved was sick until they died — by suicide. We must honor their memory.

The big "hot" topic of teenage suicide which surfaced will give way to a real concern and understanding of why *anyone* kills him or herself. And it won't just be teenagers that people care about — it will be all of the suicides. Suicide survivors aren't different from other people; they aren't saints, nor are they terrible sinners — just good people who have suffered a terrible tragedy: someone they loved has died. Only suicide survivors can say, "There was someone in our family who was very sick, and they died, and don't you dare try to place shame on their memory, or place blame on the family for their death." While grieving the past, a suicide survivor's task is to return to the future. All of history tells us that suicide survivors did because *they had to.*

Remember John? The man who had to to go school because he was the principal? You have to go on because you are the principal in your life. The work of your life is to rebuild after suicide. You always have two choices in life: you can quit or keep going. You know what will happen if you quit, but there is always promise and hope in the future. Things won't always go your way; you can't change the past, but you can take charge of your own life and make things "turn out for the best." You *have to* — because *you* are the principal of your life.

WHAT IS MAJOR DEPRESSION?

Depression is a brain disease in which the chemicals that affect how we think, feel and behave get out of balance. It is a state of constant, unrelieved misery. People who have depression often are angry and irritable. They often are dependent to a point of clinging to, and dragging down people near them. Sleep, appetite and sex are affected. They are unable to feel pleasure about anything. Unless the depression is recognized, it is very easy to dislike people who have depression, and blame them for things they can't control.

Major depression is a disease that goes away by itself in most people, but usually lasts for a year to a year-and-a-half, during which time there is immense suffering. Antidepressant medicines take away the painful symptoms in two to four weeks. The treatment for depression is medicine, psychotherapy or a combination of the two.

SYMPTOMS OF MAJOR DEPRESSION

The following is a list of symptoms of major depression seen in the at-large population and in young people. Some young people who have depression do not appear unhappy and sometimes look and are treated as if they simply have behavior problems.

SYMPTOMS OF MAJOR DEPRESSION	SYMPTOMS OF MAJOR DEPRESSION OFTEN SEEN IN YOUNG PEOPLE	
Obvious unhappiness	No apparent unhappiness	
	Defiance	
	Rebelliousness	Various
Inability to feel pleasure	Disobedience	Acting out
Preoccupation with sad thoughts	Running away	Behaviors
Crying and tearfulness	Drinking or on drugs	Commonly
	Refusing to go to school	Seen
	Failing in school	
Irritability and touchiness	Irritability and touchiness	
Feelings of helplessness worthlessness and hopelessness	Feelings of helplessness worthlessness and hopelessness	
Periods of withdrawal and isolation	Periods of withdrawal and isolation	
Loss of energy	Loss of energy	
Signs of self-neglect	Signs of self-neglect	
Loss of concentration	Loss of concentration	
Loss of interest in surroundings	Loss of interest in surroundings	
Loss of interest in favorite things	Loss of interest in favorite things	
Physical complaints (headaches, etc.)	Physical complaints (headaches, etc.)	
Sleep difficulties: insomnia or excessive sleeping	Sleep difficulties: insomnia or excessive sleeping	
Appetite difficulties: losing weight or overeating	Appetite difficulties: losing weight or overeating	
Loss of interest in sex	Loss of interest in sex	
Thoughts of suicide	Thoughts of suicide	

Not all people who have depression will have all of these symptoms, or to the same degree. If a person has four or more of these symptoms, if nothing can make them go away, and they last more than two weeks, he or she should see a psychiatrist, doctor or mental health professional.

CHAPTER REFERENCES

INTRODUCTION

1. Blumenthal SJ, Kupfer DK, NY Acad Sci 487:327-340, 1986.
2. Winokur, G, Clayton, P, *Medical Basis of Psychiatry,* 1986.
3. Andreasen, NC, *The Broken Brain,* 1986.
4. Roy, A. (Ed.) *Suicide* Asberg, M. et al, 1986.
5. Papolos, F. & J. *Overcoming Depression,* 1987.
6. Gold, M. *Good News about Panic, Anxiety & Phobias,* 1989.
7. Weissman M et al, New Eng J Medicine V321, N 18, 1989.
8. Blumenthal SJ, Medical Clinics of N America, V 72, N 4, July, 1988.
9. Robins E, Murphy GE, Am J Public Health 49:888-898, 1959.
10. Dorpat T, Ripley H: Comp Psychiatry 1:349-359, 1960.
11. Barraclough B, et al, Br J Psychiatry, 125:355-373, 1974.
12. Hagnell O, Rorsman B, Neuropsychobiology 6:319-332, 1980.
13. Blumenthal SJ, presented at the annual meeting of the American Psychiatric Association, Los Angeles, May 1984. 14. Robins E, *The Final Months,* New York, Oxford University Press, 1981.
14. Shaffer D, Gould M, Trautman P, Presented at the NY Acad Sci - NIMH Conference of the Psychobiology of Suicidal Behavior, New York, 9/85.
15. Shafii M, Carrigen S, Whittinghill JR, et al, Am J Psychiatry 142:1061-1064, 1989).

CHAPTER 1

1. New England J Medicine, 9/11/86.
2. New England J Medicine, 9/24/87.
3. Suicide & Life-Threatening Behavior, V 18(1), Spring, 1988.
4. American Journal of Psychiatry, 145:11, November, 1988.
5. The Journal of the American Medical Ass'n, V 262, No. 19,11/17/89.
6. Suicide and Life-Threatening Behavior, V 15, No. 2, Summer 1985.

CHAPTER 2

1. Caplan, PJ, Hall-McCorquodale, I. Am J of Orthopsychiatry 55(3), July 1985.
2. Anne Quindlen, Minneapolis Star Tribune, September 23, 1990.

CHAPTER 3

1. McIntosh, Death Studies, 12:21-39, 1988.
2. Wrobleski, Omega, V 15(2), 1984-85.
3. Wrobleski, Israel J of Psychiatry, V 24 N. 1-2, 1987.
4. vander Wal, Omega, V 20(2), 1989-90.
5. Barrett, T, Scott T, Suicide and Life-Threatening Behavior, 19(2), 1989.
6. Death Studies, V14, N5, 1990.

CHAPTER 5

1. Mark Solomon, excerpts from paper presented at the annual meeting of the American Association of Suicidology, April, 1985, Toronto.

NOTES

DATE DUE

DEC 4 2001			
JAN -7 2005			
FEB 27 2007			
NOV -7 2003			
JAN 0 3 2013			
			Printed in USA

HIGHSMITH #45230

The Overnight Socialite

"If Edith Wharton reincarnated in a Marc Jacobs
dress with the humor of a Park Avenue Nancy Mitford,
that would be Bridie Clark. Hats off to *The
Overnight Socialite*, a distinguished froth of rich
social satire and romance."

ong the

ct

A delicious, escapist treat." —Vogue

the
Overnight
Socialite

the
Overnight
Socialite

WEINSTEIN BOOKS

ISBN: 978-1-60286-128-2

First Paperback Edition
10   9   8   7   6   5   4   3   2   1

Dedicated to John

the
Overnight
Socialite

1

Mallory Keeler, Editor in Chief
Invites you to celebrate the launch of
Townhouse
The Magazine
December 2nd
7 PM
Doubles
783 Fifth Avenue
Dress to be photographed

W yatt, sweetie, please! I can't breathe if you're mad at me!"
Wyatt Hayes IV lit his Dunhill, struggling to keep the expression
on his face placid. The girl in front of him—stunning, lithe as an
island cat, eight years his junior—looked to be in almost as much
discomfort as she deserved. And true enough, as the party music
throbbed and the extravagant crowd milled around them, she did
appear to be moments away from hyperventilation.

Her name was Cornelia Rockman. Dark blonde hair, green eyes
fringed with dark lashes, the most adorable nose money could buy.
Maybe you've heard of her. If you'd been dragged to the launch party
for *Townhouse*, as Wyatt had, you couldn't miss her photograph. She
beamed smugly from the new magazine's inaugural cover, which
was on display around the posh private club—and the city, for that

matter—in poster-size blow-ups, like a portrait of a Renaissance pa-
tron saint. Which goes to show how deceptive looks can be.

"I'm sorry, Wy! I said I was sorry." Cornelia dropped her voice to
a low whisper. "I barely even know Theo. Daphne—my publicist—
just told me to stand next to him for a few photos. I've got to boost
my image a little if I want that Badgley Mischka campaign. It's not
enough to show up to parties wearing pretty dresses!"

*Boost her image? Her goddamn image was already plastered all over
Manhattan, the anorexic little . . .*

Wyatt took his time exhaling. He pulled down on the lapel of his
festive velvet blazer. With every passing second of silence, Cornelia's
chiseled face grew more contorted with anxiety. Wyatt studied the
burning tip of his cigarette. (Only he could get away with indoor
smoking, which is why he maintained the habit.)

"Please say something!" she pleaded.

What was there to say? He could no longer look the other way
as his girlfriend devolved into a lowbrow celebutante. If Cornelia
wanted to degrade herself for publicity, popping up next to other
men on the red carpet like a human whack-the-weasel game, he certainly wouldn't be waiting on the sidelines.

"No big deal, Corn," Wyatt finally answered, using a nickname
she loathed. He was sick of watching Cornelia's eyes flit around the
room; she was so worried that other people were noticing the tension between them. Her need for approval exhausted him. "I've got
an early start tomorrow. I'm going to call it a night."

"Call it a night? But you just got back from Zimbabwe, I haven't
gotten to see you yet—"

"Tanzania," he corrected.

"Tanzania! I *meant* Tanzania! What about tomorrow?" She lowered her chin to give him her most kittenish look. "I could come
over—"

"I don't think so," he said. He kissed her dewy cheek in the most
perfunctory way, and walked away, ignoring the throng of super-
charged socialites and social wannabes who nodded or waved for his
attention as he slipped by.

If the economy was tanking, if the nation was at war, if the world was teetering on the brink of devastation, you'd never know it from the women at Doubles, Wyatt thought. The club was a teeming garden of cocktail dresses that night: red Valentinos, green Pradas, pink and gold Oscar de la Rentas, and on the more exotic flowers, a smattering of Cavallis in swirling blue and purple. Bright Young Things waiting to be plucked, so to speak, by a man like Wyatt Hayes IV. They'd arrived decked out in their great-grandmother's jewelry, hoping their presence at the right party would be documented on Parkavenueroyalty.com the next day—or even better, in the pages of *Townhouse*, the much hyped new magazine. These were beautiful girls. Not just stylish—sexy, too. But tonight, Wyatt just shrugged past them.

Striding into the gilded foyer, past the incongruous five-foot jar of jelly beans, Wyatt could still see the shocked, nearly tearful expression he'd left on Cornelia's face. Good. At least there was that.

Upstairs and outside, the air was thick with imminent rain. Standing under the gold awning, hunched in his raincoat against the cold, Wyatt could hear his pulse in his ears. If he were a different kind of man, a barroom brawl would be just the thing right now. He felt like shoving someone. He felt like throwing all his weight behind a punch.

Cornelia had been contrite, but that was only because he'd gotten angry. Her remorse didn't erase the fact that she'd slipped away from Wyatt a moment before being photographed by Patrick McMullan and the pack, only to pop up next to Theo Galt, the hotshot son of private equity billionaire Howard Galt. Not that Wyatt wanted to mug for the camera himself—he avoided it whenever possible. He just didn't appreciate his girlfriend seizing a photo op with another man.

Striding past the typically esoteric Christmas display in the Barneys storefront, Wyatt tried chalking up the slight to Cornelia's addiction to attention, to be expected in a woman desperate to be the reigning hen in the chicken coop that was the Upper East Side. He had no real attachment to Cornelia, he reminded himself, even though he had been seeing her regularly for many months. True, she'd won the approval of Wyatt's mother, the queen of hauteur, and that was not a hurdle many of his ex-girlfriends had cleared. (Not that Mrs. Hayes had particularly warm feelings for Cornelia. She simply knew her parents from Palm Beach and felt comfortable that a Rockman heiress wouldn't be after her son's fortune.)

True, Cornelia was a knockout—the tawny hair, the flawless skin, the pouty lips, the size-two body. In appearance and carriage, she was a thoroughbred, and Wyatt relished how good they looked together. They were the alpha couple in any room. At least, that's how he'd always seen it. Obviously she felt otherwise.

He'd even made a stop at Harry Winston that afternoon to pick out an early Christmas present: a classic diamond tennis bracelet, set in platinum. It would go back tomorrow.

Wyatt Hayes IV wasn't feeling heartbroken. What he felt was worse than heartbreak. Though he'd never stoop to admit it, even to himself in the darkest hours of the night, Wyatt felt *humiliated*.

In all his thirty-seven years, he'd always been the bigger, better deal, the sleekest lion in the pride, the kind of man that any woman—whether she was a socialite, heiress, It girl, model, actress, or some hyphenate hybrid—would ditch her date for. Indeed, it had happened countless times, some young woman locking in on him across a crowded room despite the man at her elbow. Women, for as long as he could remember, had been primed to look him in the eye, listen to him, and take him seriously.

And why wouldn't they? He was tall, aristocratically handsome, tops at tennis and squash, a member of the best clubs, the proud descendant of *Mayflower* bluebloods, cutthroat robber barons, and more than one dead president. He was also—as someone outside his own social set might put it—massively loaded.

But most important, he was a respected scholar, a Harvard man . . . a thinker! Maybe his career had more or less stalled for the past five years, but he'd always have those three prestigious letters— Ph.D.—anchoring his good name. Hadn't *Quest* referred to Wyatt as "the world-renowned biological anthropologist and New York's most eligible bachelor"? They most certainly had—he had the clipping to prove it.

So what if he was going a little gray at the temples? He was Wyatt Hayes; aging shouldn't matter.

But now he couldn't help but worry. Since when did his girlfriend trade up for photo ops? Cornelia hadn't even attempted to coax him into a shot. She'd been too eager to share the frame with twenty–something Theo, with his slicked-back hair and gleaming, bonded smile. It was a terrifying shift in the natural order. Wyatt knew a lot about the natural order; he'd spent his adult life studying it. The young lioness knew when to move over from the aging head of the pack to the up-and-coming male. Had Cornelia just done the same?

The game was changing; he couldn't deny it. Take Southampton, studded with McMansions, brand-new Bentleys, and various arrivistes waving their wealth like nautical flags—the place felt utterly transformed since his youth. Uproars in the economy had separated the bulls from the steers, and the bulls that survived were hardier, fiercer, tougher to ignore. The socialites were far worse. Unlike their predecessors—well-bred, civic-minded young ladies—the current "socials" were self-serving, calculating, press-hungry parasites. Their sense of responsibility had disappeared along with the Botoxed wrinkles on their foreheads—replaced with a hunger for fame. Vanished was any notion of contributing to the public good, of using one's position of privilege for something loftier than buying shoes or selling handbags. The new socialite grabbed as much spotlight as she could. She took, and took, and took. And now, with her picture plastered on *Townhouse*, Cornelia was the poster girl for a world gone wrong.

Wyatt stared through the window of the Hermès store, bitterness etched across his face. He wished life could be as it once was.

Maybe his friend Trip was around. Wyatt needed a drink, or several.

Leaving Cornelia whimpering at Doubles had left him feeling empty and alone. Something deep inside Wyatt—as well as something shallow—demanded that he make his world right again.

2

*A*t exactly seven o'clock, Lucy Jo Ellis emerged slightly breathless from the East Sixty-Eighth Street subway stop. It would have been better to arrive fashionably late, but she couldn't bear to sit home a minute longer. Not when the biggest night of her life lay ahead of her, wrapped up in shiny paper like the most fabulous gift ever.

Her big break had come that afternoon, when one of Nola's assistants—Clarissa, the red-haired one never seen without a Starbucks double espresso clutched in her white-knuckled fist—had come sprinting into the workroom, waving the extra invitation. Lucy Jo dove on it before anyone else could. "Take it easy," Clarissa had muttered. "Just get there on time, okay?"

Nola Sinclair—technically her boss, although Lucy Jo was such a peon that the designer never bothered to offer eye contact—had decided to create a show around the collection she'd unveiled to buyers and press the previous spring, adding a few new pieces, in order to take advantage of the way the city was done up for the holidays and to drive some more press. The collection was just arriving at the hippest, hautest boutiques, and the designer wanted to give it some extra buzz. No expense had been spared in transforming the inside of the Park Avenue Armory into the world's largest igloo, with a clear plastic runway customized to look like ice. Nola had wanted the real thing, and pouted for weeks when her father—the sole investor in her company since its inception—deemed it too dangerous for the models. Silvery cocktail tables had been set out for the glitterati, with a mink muff (theirs to keep, of course) waiting on each tufted white leather seat.

All this Lucy Jo had garnered from trade rags, gossip columns, and at the watercooler. Now she'd be seeing the spectacle in person.

Too bad she hadn't gotten the nod just a day earlier—then she could've whipped up a one-of-a-kind creation that really showed her design chops. As it was, she'd barely had time to slice-and-dice a flamingo pink chiffon gown (Loehmann's, $19.99) into a kicky little minidress, using some of the extra fabric to add a flounce at the hem. The color was a little brighter than she remembered from the store—but the whole point was to make an impression, not to blend into the sea of little black dresses.

She squared her shoulders and marched toward the huge brick Armory on Sixty-Seventh. Tall, with a tendency to stoop, Lucy Jo had often been called big-boned. She'd never once been called beautiful, which had more to do with the people she knew than her looks.

You can do this, she coached herself. She took a breath so deep she could feel the chiffon strain against her rib cage.

How could she not feel nervous? Madonna was being flown in for the night. Margaux Irving, the fiercely chic editrix famous for her withering stare and influence throughout fashion's highest echelons, had RSVP'd yes and was bringing along Roger Federer. The glossy posse, comprised of the chicest girls from the chicest magazines, would be present and accounted for, along with everyone from Uma to the Olsens. And now Lucy Jo Ellis—the twenty-seven-year-old

daughter of a manicurist from Dayville, Minnesota; assistant pat-
ternmaker in a packed Garment District workshop that always
reeked of BO and Funyuns; and aspiring designer—would be there,
too. Fêteing with the best of 'em. And with any luck, landing that
coveted job doing creative design work . . . the job that narrow-
minded Nola Sinclair refused to consider her for.

How did it happen, Ms. Ellis? Lucy Jo could imagine some deferential fashion reporter asking her years from now. *How did you go
from being an anonymous worker bee to one of the most influential designers in the history of the industry?*

And Lucy Jo would sit back in her chair, tickled by the memory
of her humble start. She would recall her early days spent huddled
over a crowded worktable, barely looking up until she sensed that
her fellow workers had gone home. Only then could she pull out her
design portfolio, diving into the sketches that would one day thrust
her to the center runway of American fashion. She would tell the
reporter how some nights she could feel the folds of lustrous silk
run through her fingers, so real was the illustration she'd painstak-
ingly created.

Then, of course, she would fondly recount the night she was
about to experience, the turning point in her career. "I always knew,"
she'd tell the admiring reporter, "that it was just a matter of time before my life caught up with my dreams."

And she had, truly, always known. Growing up in a small town two
hours outside Minneapolis, Lucy Jo Ellis had harbored a secret belief that life would deliver on its big promises. Fashion had been her
passion ever since she could remember; at age four, she'd pointed
her little index finger at a gown in one of her mother's celebrity magazines and declared, "Too much ruffle." She'd started making her
own clothes when she was only twelve, mimicking the trends she
could never afford to buy. As a teenager, she'd memorized tattered
copies of *Vogue*, absorbing how iconic '90s designers such as Gianni
Versace and Azzedine Alaïa glorified the female form, delighting in
the gritty glamour of Herb Ritts's photography. On the walls around
her bed, she pinned fashion ads from the old *W*, and they hovered
like sophisticated, angular angels over her sleep.

After high school, with no cash for college, she'd tried working for Annie Druitt, the local seamstress. Annie was a sweet woman and enjoyed having company in her shop—but hemming pants and taking in hand-me-down prom dresses barely paid one salary, let alone two, and Lucy Jo's big things remained at large.

So on the day she turned twenty-six, with a hard-earned two thou in savings, she packed a bag, ignored her mother's watery discouragement, said a few goodbyes, traveled across the country on a Greyhound, found via Craigslist a Murray Hill studio with a floor so sloping she constantly tripped over her feet, and lucked into an entry-level job at Nola Sinclair. The job was only marginally more inspiring than working for Annie Druitt—but at least she was in New York, epicenter of all things fashion, and working for an industry darling no less.

A year later, however, she hadn't made any progress. A year wasn't long, in the grand scheme of things, but it was too long for Lucy Jo. Her learning curve had grown flatter than Kate Moss, and Nola refused to consider anyone for a design position who wasn't vetted by the hallowed halls of FIT or Parsons.

It didn't matter. Nola was the gateway, and tonight was Lucy Jo's opportunity to meet her real mentor—someone who would recognize that her talent and drive went far beyond assembly-line work.

Things are finally clicking into place, Lucy Jo thought. She unzipped her enormous blue parka as she hurried down Lexington Avenue with her design portfolio clutched in one arm, wishing again that she owned a nicer coat to go with her dress. Once she got her next job, she'd buy herself a cashmere overcoat suitable for evening events. And she'd walk right into Saks Fifth Avenue and buy a pair of strappy gold Louboutins, no matter how much they cost. She hoped that tonight nobody would notice the scuff marks on her Aldo heels.

Shoes and coat aside, Lucy Jo was ready. She'd read *The Secret*. Her handshake was strong. She'd practiced maintaining eye contact. And she knew exactly what she wanted—an opportunity with a designer who wouldn't consign her to stitching zippers. Though she was slightly terrified to show her design portfolio to the design stars who'd be in attendance—not to mention the business cards she'd had printed up at Kinko's and planned to distribute like party favors—she knew she had to get the word out that Lucy Jo Ellis would make Thakoon, or Brian Reyes, or Rachel Roy a fabulous assistant designer. (Only Nola would have the cojones to stock the crowd with competitors, and only Nola could inspire them to say yes— presumably because they knew how much press she'd draw.) Lucy had even jotted down some conversation starters on index cards, stashing them in her bag just in case. If she happened to find herself standing next to Margaux Irving, there'd be zero chance of dead air.

She'd put equal effort into her appearance. She'd bought her first-ever pair of Spanx, holding her breath hoping that the $40 charge would go through on her credit card. She'd fake-tanned, smearing toxic-smelling cream all over her body and face. Now it looked as if she'd spent Thanksgiving in St. Barts, not on her futon nursing pad thai every night. She'd curled her hair. Wonderbra-ed. Applied three coats of mascara to make her eyes really pop. Painted her nails and toes bright pink to match her dress. And then there was the dress itself—a walking advertisement, she hoped, for what she could do with a needle, thread, and twenty bucks.

You can do this, she repeated to herself, climbing the stairs toward the velvet rope at the Armory. The other arrivals swirled around her, the women's bare legs goose-pimpling beneath the flourishes of designer frocks, the men looking sexy and severe in black jackets and skinny ties. Lucy Jo stopped briefly to reapply her lipstick, give her hair a quick flip-and-brush, and spritz herself with a Chanel perfume sample she'd been saving for a special occasion. Then she marched herself up to the velvet rope.

"Name?" said the PR flack with a clipboard, eyeing her.

"Lucy Jo Ellis," she replied, flashing her brightest smile.

The girl scanned her list, then looked up. "Ellis, you said?"

"E-L-L-I-S. Yup, that's right."

"Sorry, I don't have you on here."

Lucy Jo's first instinct was to scream. She fought it down. The PR girl's empty eyes moved to the next person in line.

"Hang on!" Lucy Jo said loudly, diving into her tote bag and pulling out the now-creased invitation. "I have the invitation right here! Nola's assistant Clarissa gave it to me. I work at the company—there's just been some mistake!"

"What can I tell you? You're not on my list. The only Ellis we have is Bret Easton Ellis. Why don't you call Clarissa?"

"I—I would, but I left my cell phone at home. Please." Lucy Jo cursed herself for buying groceries instead of paying the phone bill. The service had been cut off last week.

"Sorry, but I can't let you in if you're not on—"

"Your list. I know. Could *you* call Clarissa, by any chance?" she pleaded, but the girl just shook her head.

Before Lucy Jo was reduced to plopping her knees down on the cold steps to beg, the front doors parted and a flash of red hair caught her eye.

"*Clarissa!*" she screamed at the top of her lungs, wild in her desperation. The red hair turned around—and sure enough, it was Nola's assistant, looking as though the strands of black pearls around her neck were choking her. Relief surged through Lucy Jo's body. "Thank God! For some reason my name's not—"

"You're the girl from the workshop, right? You're totally late!" Clarissa hissed. She motioned for Lucy Jo to hustle through the doors and then grabbed her wrist. "Didn't I tell you to get here at six?"

"What? No, I'm sure it said eight on the invitation—"

They were interrupted by the woman of the hour, Nola Sinclair, cutting through the crowd with her usual look of hell-bent determination. Lucy Jo shivered.

"Clarissa!" Nola called, jerking her head toward a vacant room off the main hallway. Clarissa, still gripping Lucy Jo's arm, followed her boss with terror in her eyes. Lucy Jo could understand why. At five-two, with a thick shock of prematurely white hair, Nola commanded a presence far bigger than her actual size. Though her look hadn't deviated in ten years—spiky hair, bleached skin, kohl-rimmed eyes, black long-sleeved shift, and dominatrix platforms—there was something about her that never failed to startle. Nola was a mercurial personality who loved to take risks with her collections, and move in unexpected directions, and her unpredictability was sometimes hailed more than her actual talent. Lucy Jo, though she didn't always "get" Nola's style, knew she had something to learn from her moxie.

"The seating is a fucking train wreck," Nola hissed once they were sequestered from overhearing ears. "You have Margaux Irving four seats away from Menon Whittemore! Fashion One-Oh-One: they loathe each other! I distinctly told you that they should be seated on opposite sides of the runway." She noticed Lucy Jo and pulled a face. "Who is this?"

Clarissa's face blanched. "One of the girls from the workshop— she came to help out—"

"She's wearing *color*," Nola said, revolted. Then she cast her eyes over Lucy Jo's face, neck, and décolletage. "And why does she look like a human carrot?"

"I, um—" Lucy Jo felt her cheeks turn crimson.

"Whatever. One disaster at a time. You need to fix the seating immediately." With that, she stormed off. Clarissa rushed after her, and Lucy Jo scurried after Clarissa, into the central hall that seemed to be filling up by the minute. She was winded from Nola's harsh appraisal, and her face burned with embarrassment. Maybe the self-tanner wasn't so St. Barts after all; maybe her dress wasn't quite ready for its close-up in *Vogue*. Fortunately, the crowded hall was illuminated by long tallow candles that cast dramatic but shadowy light, so nobody could see her blush.

Beneath magnificent vaulted ceilings and stained-glass windows designed by Louis Comfort Tiffany, the who's who of the fashion scene sipped cocktails and air-kissed each other hello. Lucy Jo watched Carla Bruni and Naomi Campbell gossip in one corner, Naomi stubbing out her cigarette in one of the abstract ice sculptures. There was Patrick Demarchelier, just five steps away; Graydon Carter kissing Natalie Portman hello; Jennifer Lopez showing off pictures of her twins to Kelly Ripa; Caroline Kennedy waiting for a martini behind Ian Schrager. It was like visiting some kind of fabulous zoo, where the exotic animals were very expensively dressed.

"Stop staring," Clarissa whispered after Lucy Jo had whipped her head around to get a closer look at Sting, who was chatting with Julianne Moore at the martini bar. "And hurry up. You heard Nola—I have way too much to do right now."

Why was Clarissa cattle-prodding her through the hall? The question flew out of Lucy Jo's head when they stepped into the enormous Drill Room, the main chamber of the old Armory. It was like stepping inside a dazzling glacier that had cracked to form a hidden cave of ice. Cocktail tables, covered in virgin linens and crystal votives, dotted each side of the sleek runway. Enormous white imported peonies that looked like giant snowballs were piled up haphazardly around the runway, and art deco chandeliers hung low, casting a glittery cabaret light. All that was missing were the models, the clothes, the audience—and Lucy Jo striding down the runway, the designer modestly accepting her end-of-show accolades.

"This is amazing!" Lucy Jo was struck still with awe.

Clarissa glanced up at their surroundings. "Yeah, well, it better be. There's a lot at stake. Nola's super stressed." She grabbed Lucy Jo's down-coated elbow and hurried her along. They passed through the backstage area, where a dozen cadaverous models were wriggling into their clothes, and then through the swinging double doors of a . . .

Catering kitchen?

"Extra uniforms are back there, I think. Get ready *fast*, okay? Marco—over there—will give you your marching orders."

"Marching orders? I don't understand—"

"What's to understand?" Clarissa's eyes widened with annoyance. "You carry a tray with caviar blinis and champagne. Offer it to the guests. You're not removing a brain tumor."

Huh? The kitchen suddenly felt as small as a coffin. Lucy Jo just blinked. "I'm here to work?"

"Of course! I told you, half the catering staff came down with some nasty virus, and they're super short-staffed. We got a few people from accounting to fill in, some interns, and you. Why are you looking at me like that?"

Lucy Jo was too stunned to speak, too embarrassed to protest. She was afraid if she tried to force words, a sob might come out instead.

Clarissa's face suddenly opened up, as she realized the extent of Lucy Jo's delusion. Then her face snapped shut again, as firmly as a Judith Leiber clutch. "Okay, well . . . see you later." Clarissa spun on a five-inch heel and shoved through the doors into the party.

"This might be a little small." Marco, the goateed head cater-waiter, eyed Lucy Jo up and down before tossing her a skimpy black patent-leather dress that she'd be lucky to squeeze over one thigh. It had an extra bunch of fabric on one shoulder, like an abscess— a sure sign that Nola had a hand in its design. "What size shoe do you wear? Hope it's seven, cuz that's all I got left." He tossed her two dominatrix boots. They looked dangerous.

Reality hit her with a sickening thud. How ridiculous she'd been to assume that she'd been invited to rub elbows! She was the hired help, nothing more. Lucy Jo put down her portfolio, and held the size-two dress against her size-ten hips. "Do you have anything bigger?" she gulped.

There was a loud crash from the back of the kitchen. "Nah, but don't sweat it," Marco called over his shoulder as he headed to do damage control. "Nobody's gonna be looking at you tonight."

3

Yesterday's sale of Important Watches at Sotheby's in Geneva did not disappoint the packed room in attendance, most notably when a Patek Philippe chronograph wristwatch, selling for the first time in fifty years, was purchased for a historic $1.2 million dollars by an unknown U.S. collector.

—Hans Depardieu, www.antiquewatchwatch.com

*M*y usual," Wyatt told the bartender, an older man whose first name he should have mastered years ago. He had felt more at peace upon entering his favorite darkly lit watering hole, one of the last bastions of smoker tolerance in the city. When a cool tumbler of single-malt scotch materialized in front of him on the mahogany bar, Wyatt exhaled for the first time since leaving Cornelia.

"What happened to you, man? You look like hell!" Trip Peters clamped a hand down on Wyatt's shoulder, and Wyatt turned around to greet his friend. Trip was short, balding, thirty pounds overweight, and seemingly unaware of any of these shortcomings. "Double martini, Saul."

"Yeah, I know I do," Wyatt lamented. Actually, he looked like a mildly disheveled aristocrat getting liquored up as quickly as possible, but hell is relative.

Drinks in hand, the two men snagged a table toward the back. "I like the watch," Wyatt said, noticing the Count Trossi Patek on his friend's wrist.

"I couldn't resist," said Trip, glancing at the timepiece, his infatuation obvious. "One of the first single button chronograph wristwatches the company made. One of the earliest with horizontal registers, too. Paid seven figures for it at the Sotheby's auction." Trip was a watch guy. Also a car guy, a plane guy, and a wine guy.

It's a law of New York City: no matter how much money you're making, you're surrounded by people making more. Trip, however, was a bit of an exception. Even when the seas of the international economy grew so rough that many financiers were puking over the railing, the SS *Trip Peters* had proved to be an ocean liner bigger, sturdier, and more secure than just about any other vessel it encountered. After using some of his considerable but not gargantuan inheritance to launch his own hedge fund at age thirty, Trip had made fuck-you money starting year one. Wyatt had to admire his friend's indefinable knack for mining gold where others dug up lead. Nobody posted higher returns, and nobody played the game better. "I didn't know he had it in him," old friends of Trip confided to each other. Trip was smart enough, they said, but c'mon—his parents had donated a baseball diamond to get him into Pepperdine.

He and Wyatt had known each other since they were kids. They'd been a grade apart (Wyatt was older) at St. Bernard's, and both families wintered in Palm Beach. From a very young age, their mothers had insisted that the boys were best friends. Three decades later, they'd shared so much history that it had become more or less true.

"So what happened to you?" Trip asked. "Where are you coming from?"

"A launch party at Doubles for a waste of paper called *Townhouse*. I left early. After breaking up with Cornelia, as a matter of fact."

"Seriously?" Trip looked surprised.

"Long overdue, I know."

"Actually, Eloise and I thought you guys were good together. You seemed—I don't know, well matched. Why'd you end it?"

"Are you serious, man?" Wyatt didn't feel like talking about the snub, even to his closest friend. "This whole socialite thing's gone to Cornelia's head. The girl preens in front of anything with a flash-bulb. She actually thinks she's got a *career* to manage. Apparently nobody's told her that landing on party pages isn't a career."

"So she's a little caught up in the scene," Trip said. "That seems pretty harmless."

"Harmless? Gertrude Vanderbilt founded the Whitney. Jackie Onassis made Grand Central shine." The muscles in Wyatt's neck had grown taut. "Cornelia's primary goal in life is to climb to the top of Parkavenueroyalty.com."

"What's Parkavenueroyalty.com?" Trip asked. He popped some peanuts into his mouth and then, checking the time, gazed at his watch with the kind of elation that would have done a new father proud. "Eloise is probably expecting me home soon."

"It's a completely inane website that *ranks* all the socialites and reports on their every move." Wyatt took a gulp of his scotch. "They rank men, too. They've got you down as the number six most eligi-ble bachelor in Manhattan. I'm number three myself. I was num-ber two last week, until this kid Theo—"

"Sounds like Cornelia isn't the only one obsessed with this thing," Trip remarked. "Not that the kettle is black, or anything."

Wyatt glared at his friend. "She checks it constantly. I look once in a while to satisfy a morbid curiosity."

"Whatever you say."

"All those girls are just the same. I'm telling you, Peters, of all the wildlife I've observed—and my fieldwork has taken me to every con-tinent—the most bizarre creatures on the planet are socialites on the Upper East Side."

Outside, winter lightning split the sky.

4

"Many critics say my work—and particularly this collection—pushes the collective discourse about fashion in a revolutionary new direction. They say I don't play by the rules. That I don't aim for mere beauty—that I aim at something far less pedestrian. Perhaps this is so."
—*Nola Sinclair as quoted by* The Daily Fashion

C hampagne?" Lucy Jo asked a Posh Spice doppelgänger in current-season couture. The woman accepted the flute and continued her conversation without pausing for a comma, never mind a thank-you.

At first Lucy Jo had been shocked by how invisible she felt. Considering that she looked like an overweight Jetson in her ridiculous outfit, she felt it was bizarre to walk around the crowded room and have guests notice only the marinated sea scallops or risotto balls on her tray. It wasn't the triumphant night she had dreamed about, that was for sure. Hustling back and forth to the kitchen whenever her tray felt light, bussing empty glasses and used napkins from guests—working instead of networking. But she was somehow managing to smile despite the raw ache of her disappointment. When she had changed into her catering costume, she'd even tucked a few business cards in her Wonderbra, refusing to give up hope. And at least she could soak up the scene.

And what a scene it was. The models—all looking recently exhumed from their crypts, clad in Nola's inky palette and sporting androgynous buzz cuts—charged down the runway to the primal beat of a bass drum. Edge before beauty—that was Nola's style. Her dresses looked like geometric configurations created by Mondrian on acid. One model looked as if she had a badly deformed left hip, but it was just the strange lines of her suit. It was the type of fashion that critics ate up and real women hated, thought Lucy Jo, and she agreed with the real women (or the unenlightened masses, if you were on the critics' side).

The audience watched with rapt attention. Lucy Jo could feel the undeniable electricity in the air. Some jotted notes; some just followed the models with their eyes as though they were watching a slow match at Wimbledon. The phalanx of photographers at the end of the runway flashed so many shots that the room seemed to dance in a Studio 54–esque strobe light.

Lucy Jo rebalanced her tray and pushed a damp lock of hair off her forehead. *One day I'll be in Nola's shoes*, she thought. Figuratively speaking—those S&M-inspired platforms looked as crippling as the boots into which Lucy had been forced to wedge her feet.

A model in a long charcoal-gray dress paused for effect at the end of the runway, its glassy surface reflecting her image. Lucy Jo's breath caught in her throat. That dress had been her baby at the workshop—the only remotely "pretty" piece in the collection, it had struck her as both a fluke and a gift. Tonight Nola had strung full rounds of bullets around the ferocious-looking model's neck, but the dress was still pretty. Lucy Jo had made the pattern with painstaking precision, staying late for days to get it just right. And now the brightest stars of the fashion universe were admiring it.

"Are you doing your job or watching the show?" Clarissa was suddenly at Lucy Jo's elbow. Before Lucy Jo could defend herself, the room exploded into thunderous applause and the two girls looked up to see the last model exit the runway. A beat later, a single spotlight illuminated a beaming Nola Sinclair.

"Oh God," she heard Clarissa pant next to her. "*Champagne*. She asked me to get it for her, but she asked me to do ten other things at the same time—"

Nola held up both hands to stop the applause. It wasn't exactly typical for a designer to make a postshow speech—but Nola, thought Lucy Jo, liked to grab as much attention as she could. "Thank you. Thank you all for coming tonight to toast the season and my collection." Nola took a step or two out on the runway, smiling into the darkness around her.

"She's going to kill me," Clarissa hissed.

And so began the worst two minutes of Lucy Jo's life. It started with a shove from Clarissa, along with an order: "Champagne. Nola. *Now!*"

It was hard to see her way in the dark toward the spotlight, let alone to balance a tray, but Lucy Jo hurried to the edge of the runway—Nola was squinting impatiently in her direction—and then some demonic person pointed Lucy Jo toward an empty chair to climb onto, and then—

She was standing at the end of the runway, blinded by the blaring spotlight, which seemed to be shining directly into her eyes, walking the few feet toward Nola as fast as she could to deliver the champagne—all too aware of her tiny skirt, her sweaty face—

Lucy Jo felt the sole of her left boot slide too quickly on the shiny, slippery plastic—

And then she was tray over heels over head, all limbs flailing—

Falling is one thing. Models slip all the time, and they rebound to their feet before anyone has time to gasp. But when Lucy Jo's ample butt hit the runway full force, she felt the plastic split beneath her with a shriek, like thin ice giving way—an earsplitting sound that echoed throughout the cavernous room. The last thing she saw before she plunged through the runway were Nola's platform shoes, and then came the crash of a dozen champagne flutes shattering around her ears.

Not the big break she'd been praying for.

She looked up and saw her legs sticking out of the hole, silhouetted in the spotlight. She couldn't move.

"She's stuck!" a familiar Australian accent gasped from a few feet away.

Nicole Kidman. Lucy Jo hoped for a fast death.

It was too terrible. Not only had she broken through the runway, but she'd somehow wedged herself in, her body folded up like a clam, and she couldn't seem to wiggle out no matter how feverishly she tried. Her hair was sticky with champagne. She could hear the crowd tittering, and in the glare she could glimpse photographers leaning in, snapping pictures. Lucy Jo covered her face with her arms, perp-walk style.

"Grab my hand!" commanded one of the beefier backstage workers, crouching above her. After much heaving and grunting, he managed to yank her out and heft her onto terra firma. The audience applauded—even louder than they had for Nola. As he stopped to catch his breath, Lucy Jo, still covering her face with both hands, vaulted off the runway and raced toward the kitchen.

"What happened?" she heard Nola ask, trying to sound concerned and not livid.

"Runway's not built to support that much impact," the guy muttered. Nola's microphone somehow picked up his reply and amplified it across the whole room.

Lucy Jo pushed her way through the kitchen door, past the other waiters looking on in sympathetic horror. Her backside throbbed, but in that moment the pain didn't even register. Ducking behind some cabinets, she squeezed out of her uniform and back into the pink dress that now struck her as the most hideously bright monstrosity she'd ever seen. Then she threw up in a nearby trash can.

She was just wiping her face with the back of her hand when Nola rounded the corner, her face blood-blister maroon. Clarissa was on her heels, looking petrified.

"*How could you?*" Nola bellowed.

"It was an accident!" Lucy Jo felt hot tears spring to her eyes. *No!* No crying. She had already just humiliated herself enough for three lifetimes. "You think I meant to—"

"Don't you *dare* cry! Do you realize that you single-handedly destroyed my entire show? Do you know how much effort went into this night? How much money? And time? And now all anybody will be talking about is how some fat-assed cater-waiter broke the fuck-ing *runway* and flashed her Spanx to the entire crowd!"

Oh God. Lucy Jo was going to be sick again.

"Don't even *think* about coming into work tomorrow, or ever again," Nola raged on. "You're fired! You're over!"

Lucy Jo grabbed her parka, and her bag, heavy with portfolio and business cards, and dashed for the exit.

5

My dear, descended from apes! Let us hope it is not true. But if it is, let us pray that it will not become generally known.

—Attributed to the wife of the Bishop of Worcester, upon hearing Darwin's theory of evolution

Cornelia, devastated though she was by Wyatt's abrupt departure, was not about to let his blowup ruin a perfectly good party—especially one that starred her as its prime attraction. She'd spent three hours getting her hair and makeup done, and her outfit—a one-shouldered green mini by Zac Posen, not available to the public for months—demanded an audience. And so did she. She swallowed her hurt at how Wyatt had treated her. He just didn't understand the immense effort it took to be a prominent social, and she had to forgive him for that. Wyatt was old school; if he had his way, they'd hang out with the same dozen couples all year long, living exactly the way their parents all lived. He'd come around, once she opened his eyes to how much fun the spotlight could be.

"Ta, Cornelia!" Binkie Howe, one of the old crusties (her parents' friends), blew a kiss in her direction. "Divine cover photo of you."

Cornelia smiled. Now that she had made the rounds with the Manhattan media types, and done kiss-kiss with her friends and frenemies, she needed to find Theo Galt.

Theo, only son of a private-equity king, had his own record label in L.A. She'd met him several times, but they'd never exchanged more than a few words—perhaps because of the supporting role Cornelia had played in his father's last divorce, four years ago. During cocktails at their Park Avenue triplex before the season's opening night at the Met, Wife Number Three had caught Cornelia, then twenty-three, and Howard Galt, then fifty-two, in the master bathroom, engaged in the kind of clinch that was undeniably what it looked like. Theirs wasn't much as far as affairs went—they'd never gotten past the initial grope—but it was enough. At first Number Three had been surprisingly cool—stepping around them to freshen up her lipstick, then sharing the same box at the opera without any visible sign of distress. She'd even kissed Cornelia goodnight. But the next day she hired a team of bulldog lawyers to take Howard for close to half his net worth. Cornelia's mother had made a few calls to keep the Rockman name out of the gossip columns, but Theo knew the truth—and whether it was because of his fondness for that particular stepmother or, as sole heir, for the lost half of his father's megafortune, he'd seemed a bit aloof afterward.

Before she set her sights on making an album, Cornelia had never given Theo Galt or his cold shoulder much thought. But in the past year, Cornelia had realized that she deserved a fate greater than marriage, children, and the Junior League. Watching her peers settle into that life made her itch. Who said adulthood had to be so boring? Why shouldn't it resemble one long debutante ball, only with just one debutante and much more interesting dresses? She could have it all, just like that old lady who used to run *Cosmo* had said. She could be a brand, pulling the Rockman legacy into the twenty-first century. She could be big in Japan.

A music career was a key part of Cornelia's five-year plan to build a major multimedia empire: hit albums, book deals, a television series, maybe one day her own magazine. When the Stevens—

Spielberg and Soderbergh—came calling, she wouldn't say no. She didn't believe celebrities who said they felt hunted by the paparazzi; she herself would feel duly appreciated by constant coverage. Frankly, she had the cheekbones for it. At Brearley and Groton she'd always been Most Popular, and now achieving fame beyond her own ZIP code seemed like manifest destiny.

Not that Wyatt approved. Of course he wouldn't; not yet. When Cornelia divulged her ambitions to him in Monaco last summer, he'd just scowled and said, "Why add another layer of detritus to the cultural trash heap?" But she knew he would come around. If her mother had taught her one thing—which seemed about the accurate number, given her absentee approach to parenting—it was how to manipulate a man into believing that he wanted whatever *she* wanted. She'd marry Wyatt, and have her cake, too.

When Daphne tipped her off that Theo Galt was flying in to support Mallory Keeler, his old friend and the brains behind *Townhouse*, Cornelia knew she had to seize the opportunity. (Daphne, Cornelia's forty-something publicist, had studied semiotics at Brown and now spent her days hawking $500 facial moisturizer, $300 tracksuits, rapper-size bling, and the clients who licensed it all.)

Maybe it's better that Wyatt stormed off, Cornelia thought, watching Theo make his way over to the bar. She followed him. *Easier to corner a man when you don't have another one looking over your shoulder.* Wyatt's reaction to one stupid photo had certainly proved that.

"Just in town for the night, Theo?" She tapped her glass with a slender finger, sliding it over the counter to the bartender for a refill.

Theo looked mildly surprised to see her next to him. "Not even. I'm flying back right after the party. I have a few meetings in L.A. tomorrow morning that I couldn't miss, but I wanted to be here for Mal."

"That is so sweet. I'm sure she appreciates it." Cornelia wondered why he'd *really* made the effort. He seemed too much like his father—street-smart, driven, self-serving—to waste his NetJets miles on the frumpy editor-in-chief. "You're sure you didn't decide to come when you saw I was on the cover?" she asked playfully.

"Dad wanted me to meet the latest wife," he said, ignoring her question. "I couldn't make it to his annual wedding." Theo smirked, and then revealed two rows of ultra-white teeth. "Plus Mallory promised a room full of hot women."

Cornelia felt a prick of annoyance; she disliked when other women were praised in her presence. Not that she cared about Theo's opinion. He was good-looking enough in his perma-tan, black-button-down shirt kind of way, but her grandmother had warned her, "Never trust a man who spends too much time on his hair," and Theo's artfully tousled highlights and boy bangs gave him a syndicated-television look. Still, she lowered her eyelashes. Her opinion of Theo was irrelevant; she needed to win him over. "I'm sure you don't have to leave Los Angeles for that."

"New York girls are worth the trip." Theo wasn't tall, barely reaching her eye level, but his direct stare was oddly imposing. "So you're Mallory's first cover."

"I was flattered that she asked me." Actually, Daphne had hounded Mallory for weeks to win Cornelia the spot—but Theo didn't need to know that. "And I'm so glad you're here. I've been meaning to call you. I'd love to have your professional advice."

"Let me guess, you want to record an album." He snorted lightly. "A woman of many talents."

"Yes," said Cornelia. Theo was clearly enjoying his position of power. Men always did. "So would you recommend I start by making a demo? Maybe I could sing something for you, a private performance, and you could tell me what you think."

Theo tipped back the remaining sip of his martini. "You're something else. Didn't your great-great-grandfather get in on the ground floor of that whole 'railroad' idea?"

"You know your history," Cornelia said, secretly delighted. "Why?"

"A music career can be grueling. Besides requiring *talent*, it can exhaust even the hungriest girls. You know, girls whose plan B involves a hairnet or a stripper pole. Where'd you go to college?"

She didn't like the direction he was heading. "Yale."

"Yale. Rich girls who go to Yale don't become pop stars. Buy a house with twenty showers to sing in. That's my professional advice, sweetheart."

Theo made as though to leave, but Cornelia grabbed his arm. Enough was enough. "Sweetheart, your father's company went public for *five billion dollars*." She kept her voice calm, so as not to make a scene, but she was pissed. Nobody spoke so condescendingly to Cornelia, especially not some Armani-clad runt who'd once dated Jennifer Love Hewitt. "You of all people understand that ambition has nothing to do with what you have in the bank. I'm going to have a music career. I was asking for help, not permission."

Theo didn't say anything for a moment. Then he reached into his jacket pocket and produced a shiny black business card. "I can see why Dad was into you. You're cut from the same cloth."

"I'll call you," said Cornelia triumphantly as she slipped his card into her tiny beaded purse.

Mission accomplished, she thought, bestowing a few quick but effusive goodbyes to Mallory and other key people, and making her way upstairs to Fifth Avenue. She had two more events to hit: a book party uptown, zzzzz, and Parker Lewis's holiday bash in Tribeca, which wouldn't be much better. After the cocktail-hour high of being the center of attention, everything else tonight would be a letdown—but at least most people she saw would know she was the toast of *Townhouse*. That gave the other parties more promise.

As she strode out onto the street, Cornelia felt two things: rain, steady and cold, and a spasm of wistfulness. It was too bad Wyatt wasn't with her to enjoy her success. That would make it perfect.

But hell, it was still success. She'd call him first thing in the morning.

She scanned the street for her jet-black Town Car. Not seeing it, she phoned the driver. "Where are you?" she demanded when he picked up.

"Just ten blocks, but there's traffic," the driver answered.

Cornelia hung up immediately, fuming mad. She'd fire him tomorrow. It was her strict policy never to blow up at her staff in public; that just looked bad. Cornelia stepped out onto the street, raising her hand to snag a cab. She was nothing if not resourceful in the face of adversity.

Lucy Jo wouldn't allow herself to cry until she got home. That was the deal. She ran toward 68th Street, chomping on her cheek to distract herself from the real pain. Her humiliation at Nola's show was terrible enough—she didn't need to follow it up by sobbing on the subway.

When she reached the station, Lucy Jo was thwarted by a heavy current of people exiting onto the street. "Flooded," an old man in a Mets cap told her. "Trains aren't running. Don't bother."

Lucy Jo had barely noticed the pelting rain, since it seemed like such a natural extension of her mental anguish. *Humiliated, unemployed, and now forced to fight for a cab.* She'd never mastered the bus routes, and during a torrential downpour on the worst night of her life didn't seem like the time to try. The street was crowded with cab competition, so Lucy Jo decided she'd have better luck heading north and over to Fifth Avenue, a straight shot home to Murray Hill. She flipped up the hood of her parka.

By the time she reached Fifth and then made her way down to 60th, she looked like she'd jumped into a swimming pool fully dressed, and she'd still had no luck. She'd almost given up hope when she saw a dim light in the distance moving down Fifth toward her. The number on the taxi's roof glowed like a beacon signaling *Home.* Like an island castaway spotting a plane in the sky, Lucy Jo darted into the street, frantically waving both arms to get the cabbie's attention. He pulled over just steps away.

But before she reached the back door, another girl dashed past her—unseen behind her umbrella—grabbed the door handle and slid into the backseat.

"Excuse me?" Lucy Jo was shocked by the stranger's audacity. "This is my cab! I've been looking for a really long—"

"So you're already wet." The umbrella quickly collapsed to reveal its owner, a glamorous blonde with catlike green eyes. She looked expensive and vaguely familiar, and she laughed a little as she slammed the door in Lucy Jo's face. Then she rubbed a circle on the fogged window so that Lucy Jo could see her victorious little smile as the cab pulled away.

Lucy Jo watched the taxi disappear into the rain. *Maybe I'll catch a fatal case of pneumonia*, she thought, struggling to see the bright side. She glanced at the bus stop, only to see her cab thief's smugly beautiful face on a huge poster for *Townhouse* magazine.

"IT" GIRL CORNELIA ROCKMAN TAKES MANHATTAN, read the headline.

Lucy Jo ducked under a nearby awning. Who was she kidding? MANHATTAN CHEWS LUCY JO ELLIS UP AND SPITS HER OUT, that's what her headline would read—right next to a photo of a drowned rodent in fluorescent ruffles and an old ski parka.

6

To: trip@alliancecapital.com
Sent: December 2, 9:22 PM
From: elcarlton@mycingular.blackberry.net
Subject: heading to your place in 20. xox

Trip's BlackBerry vibrated in his pocket, and he held out the blue screen in front of him. "Eloise. I should get home."

Wyatt rolled his eyes. "For the record, I don't see what you're holding out for. You're more or less married already. Just give the girl a ring."

"You're either married or you're not." Trip's speech might have been a little slurred from drinking, but his defensive edge was sharp.

"Touchy!" Wyatt laughed. But he couldn't help feeling a little impressed. Who would've guessed that roly-poly Trip Peters, of all their friends, would be the one most unwilling to commit to marriage? Then again, who'd have guessed he'd be the one to bank $500 mil by his thirty-fifth birthday?

"Eloise is the best. I love her to death. All I'm saying is, marriage isn't for everyone. It's not for us."

"Hear, hear," toasted Wyatt, enjoying the last of his scotch. He waved for the check. It was reassuring to have one wingman he could still count on. Most of their buddies had been swept into the vortex of domesticity, guarded by wardens who used to dance on tables at Bungalow 8 or Moomba. Many had moved off-island to Greenwich or Locust Valley, their lives surrendering any real spontaneity. Wyatt didn't envy them a bit. Neither, apparently, did Trip.

They stumbled out of the bar and into the downpour. "Where's Raoul?" Wyatt asked. He glanced down the block, expecting to see the midnight blue Mercedes that trailed Trip wherever he went.

"Gave him the night off, his daughter had a ballet recital. Shit timing. We'll never get a cab." Trip pulled his Barbour over his head.

"We'll walk. You've got four blocks; I've got six," Wyatt said. Trip's pursuit of convenience had become almost comical, he thought. His household manager now packed and shipped his luggage before every trip to spare him the chore of wheeling a roller bag onto his private plane.

They set off, weaving through the already deep puddles. "Any interest in Turks and Caicos for a few days?" Trip asked, tripping over a fire hydrant that shot out in front of him. "Wheels up tomorrow at eleven, weather permitting. We've got room."

"Yeah?" Wyatt considered it for a moment, but he felt too glum to motivate himself. "Maybe next time. Now that I'm a free man, I might head to London for a visit. I keep promising friends I'll make it there, but work's been keeping me busy."

He knew he was playing fast and loose with the definition of busy. The truth—that his career as a biological anthropologist had become as strenuous as his "gentleman's workouts" (five-minute swim, followed by a fifteen-minute steam) at the Racquet Club—made him uncomfortable. Although from time to time he'd publish a small piece (on such arcane topics as male mating effort among the bonobos, or the effect of predation pressure on social systems), Wyatt hadn't broken an intellectual sweat in a long time. Still, he kept up a good act, claiming that all the far-flung safaris he took each year were in the name of "research."

It was a shame, really. Back in his Ph.D. days at Harvard, Wyatt had been lauded as a star on the rise. His professors and mentors expected an august career to follow his dissertation (subordinate behavior in chimpanzees, in keeping with his childhood crush on Jane Goodall). But it hadn't.

What happened instead: after working himself into the ground to finish his doctorate, Wyatt figured he deserved some time off. He felt blissfully liberated from academia, freed from the dusty stacks of Widener Library, where he'd spent countless sun-deprived hours. To make up for lost time, he spent that first winter stationed in St. John, importing friends and models to keep him company, windsurfing off Cinnamon Bay Beach and napping in catamarans off Trunk Bay. Then he took up residence in his mother's guest cottage in Southampton, where he could count on three lavish meals prepared daily by her Cordon Bleu–trained chef and served by her staff of twelve, along with more invitations than one man could possibly accept. But accept Wyatt did. It was a charmed existence, dotted with boondoggles and jet-setting long weekends that stretched into weeks if such was his pleasure. Wyatt hit the international social circuit with a vengeance, flitting about the glittering *über*world of the rich and beautiful. The months stretched on, quickly becoming a year and then two.

Not having to earn a living can be an insurmountable challenge to a person's career. The path to tenure at Harvard was too steep; it required years of unappealingly hard labor. Nor did Wyatt dream of teaching at Podunk University (which was every school but Harvard, as far as he was concerned), living in a town where you couldn't find a decent scotch and where sushi was considered as exotic as space travel. Besides, it wasn't like he needed the spending money a teaching job could provide.

So he'd more or less given up—a fact that he refused to fully admit, even to himself.

"Busy, huh? Working on anything interesting these days?" Trip asked.

"I'm thinking about writing a book." It was a bluff with a tiny seed of truth: Dr. Alfred Kipling, the publisher of Harvard University Press, had been after Wyatt to write a book for years. Kipling—a stubborn old gentleman whom Wyatt had met through his Ph.D. adviser—refused to give up hope that the younger scholar could produce something original, provocative, and valuable (or at least worth more than Lehman stock). Wyatt had written a scholarly dissertation, Kipling reasoned—why not a book? So far, Wyatt had only proved these hopes to be misplaced.

"A book about what?" Trip asked. Then something caught his eye, and he paused for a split second in front of a bus stop. Wyatt stopped alongside him, forgetting the rain. There was Cornelia, staring out from an oversize advertisement for *Townhouse*, larger than life. Flawlessly beautiful in a mint-colored cocktail dress, Cornelia modeled a plunging neckline accentuated by a rope of diamonds. Her character flaws aside, Wyatt had to admit that she was a 12 out of 10. He couldn't avoid reading the enormous headline: "IT" GIRL CORNELIA ROCKMAN TAKES MANHATTAN.

It could just make you sick.

"Hey," Trip said, giving Wyatt a light punch on the arm. "It's a good photo, and she's a hot girl, but you made the right call. She drove you insane, right?"

"Right," Wyatt repeated, still staring. She looked so smug. So sure of herself. So obnoxiously . . . *superior.* Why hadn't he noticed how much he hated her while they were dating? "I need a smoke," he said, gesturing toward a deep storefront awning.

"C'mon, man, we've barely made it a block," protested Trip. But he too jumped under the awning. "Are you okay?"

Wyatt's head was spinning. It wasn't just the amount of alcohol he'd consumed. And it wasn't just Cornelia, either—it was everything she represented. Then, in cinematic style, a thought struck him just as a vein of lightning crashed above their heads. "I have an idea," he said slowly. The four little words felt dangerous and exciting as they left his mouth.

"Yeah?" Trip pushed his hands deep into his coat pockets and shifted from side to side. He didn't seem to grasp the magnitude of the moment. "What's that?"

"An idea that I could develop into a book!" Wyatt could feel his passion escalate. It was the first time in a long time that anything

connected to his career had done *that*. "And if it worked—if I could
pull it off—it would knock Cornelia down a few notches. It would
reveal the farce of society as it now stands!"

That got Trip's attention. He looked at his friend, illuminated in
the yellow glow of the streetlamp. "Okay, let me hear it."

"It might sound a little strange—"

"That's a given."

Wyatt ignored him. "Socialites in Manhattan have wealth, privilege, beauty, and youth working for them. Designers curry their favor and send them free clothes; magazines run fluff pieces about
their so-called 'businesses'; every PR flack in town begs them to
make an appearance at parties. Like it or not, they're alphas—the
top of the pecking order."

"Okay," Trip said. "So what's your idea?"

"I'd conduct a social experiment answering the question: Could
anyone become an alpha socialite if she wanted to? Or is there something inherent in these girls' backgrounds, personalities, or genetics
that predetermines their social status? My theory is that there isn't."

"Uncharacteristically democratic of you," Trip remarked.

"And to test this theory," Wyatt continued, "I'd take a random girl
off the street and turn her into the most sought-after socialite in
New York City. Convince everyone that she was the real deal—the
number one It girl, the cover of *Townhouse*—in just a few months.
I'd turn her into the next Cornelia Rockman, so to speak, only better. Show how hollow the system has become, and what a joke today's 'socials' are. Show that any girl—no matter who her people are,
no matter where she comes from, no matter how little she has in
her trust fund—can be passed off as the reigning socialite."

"Are you serious? I can't tell if you're kidding, man."

"Completely serious! I'm a keen observer of human nature, Peters,
and I've been playing the game in New York for twenty years. Then
there's my academic expertise. The animal kingdom is full of tricks to
gain social dominance. All I'd need to do is apply a few of those to
the socialite game. Kipling keeps telling me to work with what I
know. It's the perfect merger of two worlds I know well." Wyatt
sensed an inner stirring that he hadn't felt in years. He could write

this book—and without doing time in the stacks of a university library or in the bush of the Serengeti. "And just *think* of Cornelia's reaction—"

It took the two men this long to realize they weren't alone under the awning. If the poor girl hadn't issued a rather wet sneeze from her corner, they might not have noticed her at all. She was drenched to the bone, teeth chattering. She tried pulling herself together when Trip looked over, but it was no use.

"Bless you," Trip said. He offered his handkerchief.

"Thanks," she said, accepting it. "That's real nice of you."

Wyatt lowered his voice. "If I could teach a common, average wallflower . . . a girl you'd never look twice at if you passed her on the street—" The girl sneezed more loudly, and Wyatt instinctively stepped away from her. She sneezed again. And again. On the sixth sneeze, he finally looked back at her.

Her dark hair hung lifelessly on either side of an open, friendly face. *From the Midwest,* he judged, *and she hasn't lived here longer than a year.* She was tall, maybe five-nine, and not thin. Even though she was buried under a Michelin-man-size winter parka, Wyatt could tell there was meat on her bones. But her features—particularly her dark, expansive eyes—weren't bad. All in all, she struck him as a fixer-upper; a block of clay ready for Pygmalion's chisel. "What's your name?" he asked.

"My name?"

"That's right, your name." Wyatt handed her his business card, hand-engraved on card stock that was thick enough to cut butter.

"It's . . . um, Lucy Jo Ellis," she said reluctantly, taking the proffered card.

Wyatt scratched his chin. "Not much of a name, but we could work on that."

"Excuse me?"

He studied her carefully. She was the walking definition of average. Except for her outfit, a soggy rag of a neon pink cocktail dress, there wasn't anything memorable about her appearance.

"Wyatt! You're scaring the poor girl." Trip admonished under his breath.

"That's ridiculous." He guessed she lived in Murray Hill, or maybe in the nineties near the FDR, possibly with a roommate. No wedding ring—he guessed she was single. There was just something about her that said *alone in the world*. "Please, Peters, I'm offering to expand the girl's entire social status, her entire life."

"Improve my *social status*?" Lucy Jo repeated, her voice rising about an octave.

"Give me a few months," Wyatt continued deafly, still addressing Trip, "and I could turn her into a social luminary. She'd make the rest of the pack look like dim little tea lights."

"Are you insane?" the woman spat at him. "You don't even know me!"

"I'm really sorry," Trip said. "My friend's been drinking." She just shook her head. Her lips were pursed into a tight line, and a blotchy red circle had formed on each of her full cheeks. "Please just ignore him. Wyatt, let's go."

But Wyatt felt more certain than ever. Meeting this girl tonight— it felt like fate. And her selection would be *truly* random, making a perfect start to his book. "I could turn her into the toast of Manhattan. She'd make those silver-spooned heiresses green with envy. I'd put her up in a nice apartment. With the right clothes, education, social grooming—"

Whaaaaaaaaap! The girl's right hand laid twenty pounds of slap against his cold cheek. "What the hell was that for?" Wyatt bellowed, rubbing his face to erase the pink impression of Lucy Jo's palm. "You idiotic—"

"Do I look like the Happy Hooker? Or a charity case? I don't know what your issue is, buddy, but I'm not that kind of girl!" Lucy Jo yelled. She stepped indignantly out into the rain, which beat down so hard on her that she could barely open her eyes.

"Calm down." Wyatt grabbed her arm to pull her out of the waterfall. In one motion she wrenched it free, and he quickly stepped back, surprised by her strength. "You think I'm trying to pick you up or something? You're missing the entire point!"

"Well, you're—you're missing some marbles!" Lucy Jo shouted

over a peal of thunder. But she stepped back under the awning. There were no taxis in sight.

Wyatt, still pressing his injured cheek, felt his temper rise. "Imagine flying off the handle because someone offered you the opportunity of a lifetime!"

"Imagine having your head so far up your ass that you feel entitled to insult a perfect stranger!" Lucy Jo snapped back.

The two of them stood silently under the awning, huffy as an old married couple having the same fight for the umpteenth time. Then, as though remembering she was free to go, she stepped back toward the street. "Your handkerchief—" Lucy Jo glanced down at the wet linen square that Trip had given her.

"All yours. And here, please take my umbrella."

"Nah, that's okay—"

"It's the least I can do," Trip insisted. "I'm sorry that he upset you like that. He's a moron—"

"Hey!" Wyatt shouted. "I'm standing right here."

"But I promise he wasn't trying to suggest anything sketchy."

"You got the moron part right," said Lucy Jo, but her expression softened. She accepted Trip's umbrella with a thankful nod, and hurried off down the block.

7

his is precisely why we need a driver," Fernanda Fairchild, thirty-one and counting, whined to her mother. The two stared glumly out the front door of Nello. Nightmare! The rain had started during the endive salad. Now it was coming down in sheets.

"Always the nights I wear velvet," clucked Martha Fairchild, running a protective hand down the sleeve of her Chanel jacket. Maximilian, Fernanda's older brother, had gone out to hail a cab. He'd been at it without success for the better part of five minutes, and the ladies were beginning to panic.

"I knew it'd be a disaster tonight!" Fernanda exclaimed. She'd honed a special gift for predicting disasters. "Is Max, like, getting out there? You've got to be aggressive to get a taxi on a night like this. You've got to throw yourself in front and dare the cabbie not to run you over!"

"You know your brother," Mrs. Fairchild said pessimistically.

For those who don't: Max Fairchild was thirty-four, gorgeous, out-doorsy, athletic, blond, and gentle natured. The only thing he was missing was a backbone, which his many female admirers gener-ously forgave. He wasn't what you'd call brainy, either, but he did just fine at his uncle's firm.

Fernanda, who took after their pale, beaky late father, pulled the ends of her jet-black hair in agony. "I knew we shouldn't have tried to squeeze in dinner after the *Townhouse* party. I'll be drenched and curly by the time I get to Parker's!" Fernanda's hair was her one van-ity. Lovely and thick, it took a full hour to blow-dry during twice-weekly appointments at Garren. And that very afternoon—after a month on the waiting list, not to mention her entire week's salary at Christie's—she'd finally gotten her first cut-color-blowout ap-pointment with the Lower East Side shut-in that Cornelia and all the girls raved about. The guy's musty apartment made Fern's skin crawl, but Cornelia insisted he was the best. She was totally right, of course. Cornelia was just lucky that her astronomical bills were handled—and never questioned—by one of her family's account-ants. Anyway, it was too infuriating; now all Fernanda's effort would be for naught.

A very wet Max suddenly emerged from the street, his cherubic blond curls matted dark against his brow, his ravaged black umbrella looking like an origami swan. "It's awful out—"

"Did you get one?" Fernanda demanded, peering out through the cloudy glass.

"I tried," Max said. "I walked over to Park, too, and then up a few blocks—nothing!"

"So what do you suggest we do, Maximilian? Take the bus?" Mrs. Fairchild was only being sarcastic, of course, and was not pleased when Max fished out a yellow MetroCard from the pocket of his trench. "Stop being ridiculous! Go get us a taxi *tout de suite!*"

"Hey, there's one!" Fernanda shouted, pushing her drenched brother back out the door and toward a barely visible on-duty light making its way up Madison.

"Someone's got it already—" Max called over his shoulder, pointing toward a young woman who'd been desperately trying to hail a cab since he went outside. "That girl's been waiting—"

"*That girl* is not wearing Carolina Herrera and python Manolos!" Fernanda shrieked. Nor, presumably, was that girl heading to the home of a man she'd been doggedly hunting for months. Fernanda couldn't be late for Parker Lewis's party. He was ideal husband material: forty-five, recently divorced, distinguished, social, wealthy. Not much to look at, but who cared? If Fernanda showed up late—well, she just knew that the circling hyenas would beat her to the kill. This was a pivotal night. She'd invested four grand in her outfit alone, and she needed to see a return.

"Just get it already, Max," Mrs. Fairchild commanded, in a quieter but equally emphatic tone.

Max charged out the door and raced toward the taxi. The girl was closing in on it, too, and as she saw Max coming, a wave of disbelief—then disgust—transformed her face.

He gulped; this was not a proud moment. But what was the fleeting wrath of a stranger compared to the hours of verbal thrashing he'd get from his mother and sister? Max lunged, beating the girl to the door by less than a step. All those squash matches at the Racquet Club were good for something.

"What is *wrong* with you?" the girl yelled as Max threw open the door and dove into the backseat. She struggled to maneuver around him, but he played great defense.

"I'm really sorry," he muttered. God, she was soaked. She clutched an umbrella, but it still looked like she'd been out in the rain for days. Max slammed the door as kindly as he could, under the circumstances, and the girl smacked her open palm against the window in protest.

"My sister and mother are right . . . up . . . there, under that awning," Max told the driver, ashamed of what the man must think of him.

The girl—much to Max's chagrin—followed the car right down the block, refusing to accept defeat.

"H-he just stole this taxi from me!" Max heard her appeal to Martha and Fernanda as they scurried out from the restaurant under borrowed umbrellas, opened the door, and dove in. "It was mine—"

"Sorry, dear," the elder lady called out, shutting the door.

Once safely inside, Martha turned sharply to her pouting daughter. "Do you think I don't *know* we need a driver, Fernanda? You think I *choose* to live like this?"

Fernanda let out a deep sigh. Max shifted uncomfortably in his seat, pretending to stare out the fogged-up window.

The Fairchilds possessed one of those painful family secrets that everybody knew. Henry Fairchild—Max and Fern's father—had been a fourth-generation wastrel who'd squandered a shocking amount of his family's once robust steel fortune. Unlike his savvy forefathers, Henry had a nose that pointed him toward get-poor-quick schemes and dot-com fiascoes. Then he'd had the gall to keel over at age fifty-three, leaving his family stranded in a classic eight on 82nd and Park.

They weren't penniless. In truth, the Fairchilds spent more money in a year than most people could hope to see in a lifetime. None of them had ever scrubbed a toilet, hemmed a pair of pants, or walked their own dachshunds at an inconvenient time. They still had some of the influence and power conferred by their last name. So all had not been lost.

But the rich have their own sliding scale for what it means to be truly comfortable. And thanks to Henry's ineptitude, the Fairchilds had slid. Max couldn't be counted on to restore the family fortune to its onetime glory. Fernanda still lived at home, which galled her. Just the other day, she'd had to ask her boss for a raise. Because *she'd needed one*. That had not been an easy moment to bear. Being past thirty and single made it all the worse.

"Laight Street, between Hudson and Varick," Max said to the taxi driver. His sister and mother sat in grim silence.

The long and short of it: Fernanda needed a husband immediately, if not sooner, but she'd already struck out with a stable of eligible men. Thank God for divorce, as mother and daughter agreed. The mere rumor of a marriage on the brink could buoy both their spirits. Thus they'd been downright thrilled to hear that Parker's wife had left him for her Vedic astrologer and a "simple life" in Arizona. *Bon riddance*, Fernanda thought, with the thirst of a vulture stumbling across juicy roadkill.

Now she just had to get there first.

Watching the second stolen taxi of the evening speed off, Lucy Jo could no longer hold back her tears. She was exhausted from trolling the lower 60s in the rain, the skin on her bare legs now rubbery-wet, her lips purple. Another cab pulled over to pick her up just minutes later, but the psychic damage had been done. As the red and yellow lights of the city melted down Lucy Jo's rain-streaked window, she slumped in the backseat, the night's events flashing through her mind like a torturous slide show. Her entire world had collapsed along with that runway. She'd been humiliated in front of a room full of her idols. She had been fired from a job she'd pretty much hated, but would now beg to have back. Then that rich bitch Cornelia What's-her-face had shamelessly stolen her cab. She'd been insulted and propositioned by a stranger, before losing another cab to another heartless preppy.

She leaned her head against the gray pleather seat. It was slimy from a previous passenger, but she didn't care. A dull backache had set in, along with a deep chill. And Lucy Jo felt a little dizzy, too—the way she had when she first moved to New York and the city made no sense at all.

"Nine dollars," said the cabdriver when they'd reached the white stucco walk-up building she called home. She handed him eleven, cringing to see how few dollars she had left in her wallet.

As she reached into her pocket for her keys, Lucy's hand grazed the business card Wyatt Hayes had given her. *I'd have to be out of my mind*, she thought, opening the door.

8

Marriage means commitment. Then again, so does insanity.

—*Unknown*

"Turks and Caicos? Well, doesn't *that* sound awfully romantic!"

"It's supposed to be beautiful," said Eloise Carlton into the telephone, not sure how else to respond to her mother's enthusiasm. She peered into her overstuffed closet, rising up on tiptoes to pull a suitcase off the top shelf. "Trip says we're right on the beach—"

"So? Do you think this could be *it*?" Ruth Carlton, incurably hopeful, squealed into her daughter's ear.

Eloise held the phone away. You'd think by now her mother would have clued in that sometimes a fabulous island getaway was just a fabulous island getaway, no rings attached.

"Mom," she said in a warning tone, tossing a violet and indigo Allegra Hicks caftan into her suitcase.

Eloise Carlton had been dating Trip Peters for eight years, since she was twenty-eight, which was two years before he'd shown any hint of hedge-fund prowess. Back then he'd lived in his mother's pied-à-terre, conveniently located close to Dorrian's and Mimma's Pizza. Now Trip owned a six-bedroom townhouse inches from Madison Avenue, complete with wine cellar and indoor movie theater. "Well, you said he planned the whole thing as a surprise. As 'part' of your Christmas present. So your father and I thought, maybe—"

"Now Daddy's speculating on my love life, too?" Eloise blew her bangs, currently Titian red, off her forehead (she dyed her hair a new color every few weeks, during her rare nights at home). *Focus.* Trip had just sprung their pre-Christmas trip on her that afternoon, right in the middle of a chaotic and ill-conceived fashion shoot ("farmyard chic," which essentially meant models dressed in designer overalls and Galliano plaid, riding tractors and wrestling pigs). Now she had less than an hour to pack before heading over to his place and collapsing in an exhausted heap onto his bed. After dozens upon dozens of spontaneous Trip-engineered getaways, Eloise was starting to loathe the sight of her Goyard overnight bag. Sometimes all she wanted was to stay put, to sink into the couch and not move for a week. She loved her cute two-bedroom apartment on tree-lined 73rd Street, the best investment of her life, but she got to enjoy it so little.

"Your father and I just want you to be happy," said Ruth.

Pack, Eloise told herself. The trick to discussing her relationship with Trip with her mother—which lately was the only thing her mother wanted to discuss—was to multitask. SPF 30. Malo cashmere traveling mask and slippers. The turquoise Eres string bikini that Trip had drooled over during their last trip to Mykonos. Her favorite floppy straw hat. Vivier sunglasses.

"All your sisters are married," her mother reminded her.

"Lucky them!" chirped Eloise. Passport. Oversize makeup case, even though she rarely wore more than a hint of mascara and lip gloss. More than that weighed down her porcelain complexion. Her Jennifer Aniston look for travel: Miu Miu gold leather sandals, comfy but well-fitted Superfine jeans, and two white tops with barely-there straps. An H&M dress that she could throw on for lunch. Two slubbed-silk sarongs, light as air. Her white Genetic jeans, plus a slinky bronze-colored top she'd scored at a thrift shop and strappy Choos. Next month's *Harper's Bazaar*, not available to the public for another two weeks. These were the perks of being a stylist: free magazines, unbeatable swag.

"And your friends, sweetie. How many times have you been a bridesmaid?"

"Um . . . fourteen, I think?" Eloise refused to sound anything but delighted by this fact.

"You've hosted four baby showers in the past year alone," Ruth continued. "I hate to say it, sweetie, but it can be a bit harder to get pregnant at thirty-six—"

Eloise's neck tightened. She rubbed it with one hand, tossing a bottle of Bulgari perfume into her suitcase with the other. Not that she felt any need to correct her mother, but she'd actually thrown six baby showers that year. Eloise could fill an Olympic pool with all the pink and blue buttercream icing she'd ordered from Magnolia. She loved doing it, was always quick to offer—but sometimes those little baby things made her heart ache.

"And don't tell me you don't care about getting married, I will not buy it." Ruth Carlton could no longer keep the frustration out of her voice.

"I certainly don't care as much as you do," Eloise said quietly. "Trip and I aren't like you and Daddy."

Not being like her parents had been a selling point when she was thirty. She and Trip had lived for their benders at Marquee, their impulsive trips to Morocco or Ibiza or Tokyo or wherever Trip decided they had to fly next. They were constantly surrounded by friends—crowded into overflowing banquette tables, ordering one more bottle of Cristal just to keep the night going. Their nights ended at 4 AM and their mornings began with greasy egg-and-cheese sandwiches from the corner deli. They loved their life together. They always seemed to be on the same wavelength, best friends who happened to have great chemistry and identical taste in Turkish takeout. What could be better?

"Believe me, I *know* you're not like us," Ruth clucked. "I would've kicked Daddy out on his—"

"Mom, stop!" Eloise interrupted. "All I'm saying is that just because Trip planned a vacation doesn't mean he's going to propose."

"You never know," her mother insisted.

Jewelry! From her case Eloise pulled out a delicate gold necklace from Cartier and the pair of freshwater pearl earrings Trip had given her for her birthday last year.

"Can't you just ask him what he's thinking?" Ruth asked for the millionth time. "Just ask him when he sees himself getting married. Not an ultimatum, just a question."

"I've been busy, Mom," Eloise answered, evading the question. "Work's been nonstop. Last week I had a shoot in Palm Springs and Telluride. I had a shoot today. The week after next I'm in Rome for Italian *Vogue*. I'm not sitting around obsessing about this."

"I'm not *suggesting* that you *obsess* about it. All I'm saying is that it shouldn't be this difficult. If he cared about your feelings, he wouldn't drag things out like this."

Eloise and Trip had met on a humid July evening in the backyard of a Bridgehampton house some mutual friends were renting. Trip was working the barbecue, but he dropped his tongs and zeroed in on Eloise the moment she arrived. Later, when one of their pals griped about his charred burger, Trip grinned sheepishly. "Blame whoever brought *her*," he'd said, pointing his chin at Eloise. He wasn't the best-looking guy in the world, or even in that Bridgehampton backyard. He was four inches shorter than she was when she wasn't wearing heels; Eloise always had a pretty good view of the balding crown of his head. But there was just something about him. Or something about them that she couldn't imagine finding with anyone else. They'd gone home together that summer night and hadn't been apart since.

"I've got to hang up, Mom," Eloise said briskly, glancing at her watch.

"So is Wyatt still dating your girlfriend?" Ruth asked. She prided herself on staying current on the latest couplings, and thanks to a new rash of socialite-focused blogs, she could track everything from Duxbury.

"I wouldn't call Cornelia a friend. She's just a girl I know socially," said Eloise. "I've gotta go—"

"Well, I hope it works out. My friend Donna thought that if Trip ran out of single friends, settling down might strike him as the natural next step—"

"Mother!" Eloise had reached her limit. "Enough, okay? I'm going to be late."

"Fine, sweetie. Have a wonderful time on your trip. Call us if anything interesting happens," Ruth said in a singsongy voice.

"Thanks. But don't wait by the phone," Eloise answered, trying to sound lighthearted. After she hung up, she flopped backward onto her bed. She'd barely had time to breathe all week. A few days at the beach with her honey was just what she needed. Why was she being such a stick in the mud? It really was so thoughtful of Trip to plan it, to surprise her—

Why not? Eloise thought suddenly, springing up and heading toward the closet with purpose. She pulled out the wispy Alberta Ferretti dress she'd been saving for a special occasion, along with her fabulous white lizard Choos.

After all, a girl shouldn't be caught unprepared for a wedding proposal she's totally not expecting.

9

Oh, honey, *no*. When we first heard about the now infamous cater-waiter incident at Nola Sinclair's show, we cursed the fact that we weren't fab enough to see it in person. But then one reader took pity, and oh-so-generously sent us this photo. Not enough to make a positive ID, but hey, we'll take it.

www.fash-addict.com

11:56 PM

The Cherry NyQuil wasn't working.

Lucy Jo pointed her flashlight at an Idaho-shaped stain on her bedroom ceiling. Even that cheapo wine in a box her mother guzzled, which smelled like it could fuel a car, was out of her budget at the moment. When she'd found an old bottle of cold medicine at the back of her bathroom cabinet, it'd struck her as the luckiest thing to have happened in the two weeks since Nola's show. But it wasn't working. Despite having slugged down the better part of a bottle, she still could operate heavy machinery without exercising extra caution.

The 11:56 dragged its feet clicking to 11:57 on her '70s-era alarm clock. All the thoughts that had been bruising and bullying her all day refused to fade to black. Normally Lucy Jo loved to be alone—it gave her time to sketch—but tonight she just felt stuck with herself.

Thanks to an overdue electricity bill, she didn't have basic cable as a distraction—or light, for that matter, besides the jumbo flashlight she'd borrowed from the overgrown frat boys across the hall. Even before her public debacle at Nola's show, Lucy Jo had been living on the financial edge, waiting for her big, salary-raising break, juggling bills so she could pay the rent on her overpriced and pitiful studio, which she'd chosen because she wanted to live in the center of things.

Her cell phone rang—it was the one bill she'd paid since Nola's—and she lunged across the futon for it, idiotically hoping it was a potential employer. Calling at midnight.

"Will you accept a collect call from Rita Ellis?" asked the operator.

Lucy Jo inwardly groaned. Her mother. "Of course," she said. "Hi, Rita. How are you?"

There was a pause at the other end of the line. "I won't lie to you," said her mother, her voice gruff. "Been better. I had to take Faye Dunaway in for surgery the other day." *Here comes the windup,* thought Lucy Jo. Faye was one of Rita's six beloved cats, all of whom had been named after her mother's obsession: movie stars. "I knew something was wrong when she wouldn't touch her Iams," Rita went on. "That's not like Faye."

One time, just one time, she could call to see how I'm doing, or to wish me a happy birthday.

"Just be glad you're living the good life in New York City, Lucy Jo, and not trying to earn an honest living in Dayville."

"Trust me, Rita," Lucy Jo said, holding the NyQuil bottle upside down for the last drops. She'd never been able to convince Rita that her income didn't go far in New York. "I'm not living the good life."

"Well, it beats inhaling nail glue, day in and day out."

Lucy Jo felt an involuntary pang of guilt. Each month, she sent her mother as much money as she could—and each month, she wished it could be more. Although Rita's employment as a manicurist had always been sporadic at best, she'd managed to keep a roof over their heads during Lucy Jo's childhood. So what if she'd already used the excuse of Faye's surgery twice before. Maybe the cat really *had* been under the knife more times than its namesake.

"And then this surgery comes up, out of the blue—well, I had to use all the money I'd saved for my prototype."

"Your prototype?"

"I told you about my celeb-inspired acrylic nails! My nail art, baby! I've got a set with Brangelina and their kids, one with the cast of *Dallas*. I'll send you a handful"—she giggled at her bad pun—"as soon as they're ready. Then we'll be in business."

"We?" The prospect of eating out of restaurant Dumpsters was more appealing than going into business with her mother. "How much do you need?" She wanted to help, of course, but felt a bit queasy at the prospect of emptying out her meager savings account.

"Two hundred ought to do it, hon."

That would leave Lucy Jo with $100 to her name. She'd need some money to print out more résumés, to keep her cell phone turned on . . . God willing, she'd be able to line up something before rent was due.

"Would a hundred and fifty be okay?" Lucy Jo asked, biting her lip. She thought briefly about telling her mother she'd been sacked, but then Rita would try to persuade her to come home to Dayville. She couldn't handle that.

"I won't lie," Rita said. "Two hundred would be a much bigger help."

Lucy Jo sighed. "I'll send it in the morning."

"You're a good girl. Overnight the check, if you don't mind."

11:59 . . . midnight.

Staring at the ceiling stain, Lucy Jo decided to take an inventory of things that could be worse. The fallout from her public debacle at Nola's show hadn't been nearly as bad as she'd expected. A few photos—none of which showed her entire face, miraculously—had popped up on blogs, but she'd managed to remain anonymous. Even the aftermath at Nola Sinclair had seemed strangely devoid of drama—the next morning, a messenger had returned the few personal belongings she'd kept at work. A few of her former co-workers had called to check in; her friend Doreen, a single mother and expert seamstress, had even offered up some contacts. But by day two of her sudden unemployment, the phone had stopped ringing.

In the past two weeks, she had spent her days hustling back and forth between the FedEx office, the post office, and the local library with free Internet—a gray triangle of fluorescent lights and disgruntled workers—trying to rummage up a job lead. So far, nothing. Worst time of year to look for a job, she was incessantly reminded. A teetering economy didn't help, since most companies had imposed a hiring freeze or were shedding staff. She hadn't gotten any severance from Nola, needless to say, and although she'd signed up for unemployment, the first check—which wouldn't even cover her rent—had yet to arrive.

The clock released another minute it'd been holding hostage. *Maybe I'm ridiculous for thinking I could make something of myself.* She couldn't afford denial much longer. *Maybe I should just move back home, get it over with.* The thought hit Lucy Jo like a gut punch.

There was one other option, one that had been creeping its way to the front of her mind more and more often with each passing day. *Wyatt Hayes IV.*

Snow was expected; the air was crisp and begging for mink. Just the sort of day Lillian Edgell would have requested for her funeral, remarked Dorothea Hayes to her son Wyatt when they entered St. James Church. Dottie, as she was known, had flown in from Palm Beach to pay her respects and demanded that a recalcitrant Wyatt escort her.

Lillian Edgell, a grand dame who'd stayed on top of her game until her death at age ninety-three, had planned her own funeral years earlier—from the elaborate floral arrangements (white lilacs, ranunculus, snowball viburnum, lady's slipper orchids, sweet peas, and Dutch fringed tulips) to the guest list (two hundred hand-selected friends, not a nose more). In her final years, it had pained her to imagine a funereal sendout planned by one of her bumbling sons or, worse, her overeager daughters-in-law, so she'd taken matters into her own hands.

It was December 16, and although many of Lillian's friends had already departed for sun or ski, the church was still packed with those who'd stayed in New York for the glittery merry-go-round of holiday parties. After so much champagne and revelry, it was almost refreshing to attend a somber event.

"There's Courtney Lennert," Dottie Hayes said to Wyatt. They were seated in the sixth pew, as usual. "She ought to wear a name tag. All that work has made her virtually unrecognizable."

"Mmm," answered her son.

"You're not listening to me."

"No," Wyatt agreed. He was thinking about Lillian Edgell, which he suspected put him in the minority. She had lived the kind of life that ended with a full-page obit in the *New York Times*, and she was a throwback to a time that seemed to be slipping out of grasp, when the so-called Four Hundred reigned over New York society and contributed generously to the public good. After her husband's early death, Lillian had never remarried, choosing to focus on philanthropy. She'd donated a wing to the Met and championed several other organizations vital to the city's culture. A life well spent, Wyatt had always thought. He too was a philanthropist, doing his share of good—each year he wrote as large a check to the Vanderbilt and the Museum of American Heritage as his accountants would allow—yet something was still missing. Something he couldn't quite articulate. Maybe it was a unique feeling of purpose. Anyone could write a million dollar check—well, almost anyone—but sometimes Wyatt craved the feeling that he had accomplished something only *he* could.

"What is it with you?" his mother whispered. "You've been so gloomy all day. It's Cornelia, isn't it?"

"It's a funeral, Mother."

There was nothing in his life to be unhappy about, but in the two weeks since he'd been blown off by Cornelia, he'd been feeling less and less inclined to drag himself out of bed every morning. One of the liabilities of being a deep thinker, Wyatt mused, was that it left him vulnerable to existential crises.

"You should come back to Florida with me, darling," Dottie suggested. She brushed imaginary lint off her flawlessly tailored black Bill Blass suit. "Some sun would do you good. I don't see why you'd choose to stay here in freezing Manhattan."

Like many of her wealth and pedigree, Wyatt's mother was a conformist, frequenting only the art dealers, interior decorators, restaurants, salons, clubs, manicurists, and clothing designers preferred by her circle of friends. Winter invariably meant three months in Palm Beach and a week skiing in Switzerland. Spring and fall were spent in Manhattan, punctuated by weeklong jaunts to London (fall) and Paris (spring). On Memorial Day, she and her pack traveled two hours east to their eight-bedroom cottages on the beach in Southampton, where they met daily for tennis at the Meadow Club. In Dottie's life, only the chintz ever changed. It was a lifestyle that had been passed down and perfected over generations.

"I'll be down next week for Christmas." Wyatt raked a hand impatiently through his hair. He knew his mother had ulterior motives.

She didn't waste time in revealing them. "I heard Cornelia was at the Beach & Tennis yesterday for lunch, looking radiant. Have you considered giving her a second chance, dear? I really don't understand why you're being so stubborn."

"Please, Mother, we've been through this. She's an insufferable—"

"Fine, fine." Dottie waved her hand. "No need to get worked up."

"No need to get worked up? Did you read Page Six?" He'd gotten at least twenty e-mails teasing him about the not-so-blind item: *"WE HEAR . . . a certain wealthy anthropologist got a red carpet heave-ho from his young socialite girlfriend, a ravishing blonde whose star seems very much on the rise. . . ."*

"Oh, that's silly. You can't blame Cornelia for that—"

"Her publicist probably didn't fight it much, since it was flattering to Cornelia. 'Star on the rise' my ass."

"Wyatt, language." Then Dottie registered what her son had said. "Her *what*?"

"You heard me. Her publicist."

Dottie, looking stricken, turned in the pew to face him. It was as though Wyatt had announced that his ex had a dope dealer on Ninth Avenue. "Why would Cornelia Rockman have a . . . a *publicist*?" she asked.

"How quaint of you." Wyatt sat back, relishing the moment. "Cornelia's got a publicist, a stylist, and an image consultant. She's a career socialite."

Shocked, Dottie Hayes turned to face the altar. "What is our world coming to?" she murmured. "A *publicist*! In my time, a re-spectable young lady's name appeared in the papers—"

"At birth, marriage, and death." Wyatt smiled. It was one of his mother's favorite adages. "Times have changed. Today's socialites hope to see their names three times a week. That's why Cornelia will show up to the opening of an envelope, as long as there'll be some press there."

"What do her parents say?"

"Who knows." Wyatt decided to nail down the coffin, so to speak. "I've heard Cornelia's in talks to star in her own reality TV show. She wants to conquer the music industry, the media, Hollywood—"

"You were right to part ways," Dottie said firmly. She shook her head. "I had no idea. *Not* the girl for you, Wyatt."

"That's what I've been telling you." There were times when Wy-att appreciated the predictability of his mother's disapproval, and that she was as horrified as he was by the ways the world around them was changing. They sat in silence for a moment, eyes trained on the closed casket.

"Courtney Lennert's daughter is quite the beauty. Takes after her father's side."

Wyatt rolled his eyes. "She's a snore; all she talks about is horses."

"Serena Simmons?"

"Half the members of the Racquet Club recommend her."

"Fernanda Fairchild?"

"Gold-digger. Not cute. And best friends with Cornelia, to boot."

"Aren't there any nice girls in New York?" asked Dottie incredu-lously. "No one like Trip's lovely Eloise?"

"Not as far as I can tell."

"You're too picky, that's the problem. No girl will ever measure up to your impossible standards."

Wyatt looked at her. As annoying as her meddling and matchmak-ing could be, he could see that his mother was genuinely worried about his happiness. Marriage had brought her enormous content-ment, and she hoped that the same would be true for her son. He reached over and patted her arm. "Maybe so. But Dad was picky, too, and it served him well."

"Sometimes you surprise me." Dottie smiled. She folded her hands gracefully in her lap and looked toward the altar, where the rector had just appeared. "I just wish you'd surprise me by finding a nice girl and settling down."

10

What is life but a series of inspired follies?
—*George Bernard Shaw, Pygmalion*

*L*ucy Jo squinted through the elaborate wrought-iron leaves covering the front door of Wyatt Hayes's Fifth Avenue building. She didn't know which was more intimidating—the gargoyles snarling down from the gray-stone façade, or the white-gloved doormen guarding the soft-lit marble lobby. With thudding heart and desperate resolve, she pressed the doorbell.

"I'm here to see Wyatt Hayes, please," she told the doorman. She hoped he couldn't smell her fear. *Breathe*, she reminded herself. *What's the worst that can happen?*

And then her mind, without her consent, answered the question: *He's as arrogant as he seemed and you're humiliated and forced to move back to live with your mother and her six cats. You spend the rest of your life gluing on tips and double "dating" passing vacuum salesmen with Rita. Or Wyatt turns out to be some perverted wackadoo who*

drugs you and sells you into human bondage, like on that Dateline
special—

Lucy Jo struggled to regain her composure. *Okay, just breathe.
Forget thinking. Thinking makes breathing a lot harder.*

"Is he expecting you?" the doorman asked.

"No, not exactly," she said. "But he gave me his card." Lucy Jo
flashed it as if it were a security badge. The paper was soft from being overhandled.

*Breathe, Lucy Jo. It's easy. You've been doing brave things your whole
life.*

Moving to New York had taken guts, no doubt about it. But taking the subway thirty blocks uptown and walking to the address listed
on Wyatt's card had required deep drilling into reserves of courage she
never knew she had.

"I'll call upstairs. Your name, please?"

"Lucy Jo Ellis. Thank you."

"Wyatt?" Margaret, the broad Irish woman who'd cared for Wyatt
since he was in diapers, popped her head into the dining room
where he and Trip had just finished dinner. "There's a girl downstairs
in the lobby to see you."

Wyatt groaned, mainly for Trip's benefit. "Cornelia! She's relent-
less. Phone calls, e-mails—and now she's taken to just 'dropping by'
the building."

"So? Are you thinking about taking her back?" Trip asked.

"Why should I? Nothing's changed."

"It isn't Cornelia," Margaret interrupted. "It's a young woman
named Lucy Jo Ellis."

Wyatt frowned, trying to place the name. Trip found it faster.
"Hey, isn't that the girl we met during that downpour? The one who
walloped you? You don't think she's here to take you up on that crazy
proposition—"

"That horrible girl?" Wyatt shot up from his chair. "So she shows
up here with her tail between her legs! Well, maybe she's smarter
than she seemed."

"She slapped you?" Margaret didn't ask why. "And what proposition did you make, Wyatt? Are you sure you want her—"

"Yes! By all means, have Harold send her up," Wyatt said. For the first time in longer than he could remember, he felt genuinely curious about what would happen next.

Wyatt watched intently as Margaret ushered the nervous, flush-faced girl into the dining room and then reluctantly excused herself. The only eye contact this Lucy Jo Ellis person could make was with the Alex Katz portrait hanging in the corner. Wyatt stepped closer. Even in the generous cast of the chandelier, she was more of a fixer-upper than he'd initially realized. Maybe he'd been overconfident. At the bar that night he had been overserved, and the two were famously correlated.

"So what brings you here?" he asked, after Trip had risen from his seat to shake the girl's hand.

The simple question seemed to heighten her terror. Lucy Jo stood tensed in the doorway, as if bracing for an earthquake. He could see beads of sweat crystallize above her upper lip. "You said you could transform my life," she managed to say. "I—I'm just here to find out more."

Wyatt couldn't help feeling flattered by both her interest and her nervousness. It almost made him forgive her initial rudeness on that rainy night two weeks earlier, but not quite. If she was here to appeal for the same opportunity she'd previously found insulting, he saw no reason to make it any easier. "Sit down," he told her, gesturing toward an empty chair.

Lucy Jo did as he instructed, hurdling her way across the long dining room. She moved with a complete absence of grace, Wyatt noticed, her hips swiveling and arms pumping more vigorously than was necessary. *Fixable.* He'd dated enough models to know that walking gracefully was more of learned skill than one might think. When she did plop down in the chair, the girl still looked ill at ease. A three-tiered silver tray of chocolates and Ladurée macaroons rested in front of her on the table, classical music tinkled softly in the background—but judging by the expression on her face, you would've guessed she was facing an interrogation lamp and a hostile cop.

"So you want to be a socialite?" Wyatt began, breaking the silence.

"Well . . . not exactly."

Wyatt stopping pacing. "I don't understand, then. Why'd you come?"

"I want to work in fashion. That's why I moved to New York in the first place—"

"Fashion?" Wyatt looked at her incredulously. Half the girls he knew worked in fashion, and he couldn't imagine any of them being caught dead in Lucy Jo's outfit. Her pearls were the size of golf balls and looked less valuable. Her dress wasn't awful—a basic shirtdress in oxford stripes, cinched with a thick leather belt—but she wore penny loafers, a Shetland sweater around her shoulders, and screaming pink polish on her nubby fingernails. It looked like she'd gotten her hands on *The Official Preppy Handbook*, circa 1980, and imitated the look as inexpensively as possible. "I wouldn't have guessed that."

"Dude, cut it out!" Trip shot Wyatt a warning look.

Lucy frowned but moved on. "It's hard to get a job on the creative side. You need more than talent. You need to know the right people."

"Ah," Wyatt said. This young woman had her own agenda. "So you think you have the talent? And you think we know the right people."

"Yeah, well, I googled you—"

"She googled me, Trip. And?" But he knew exactly what she'd turned up. Photos from parties. Mentions from his graduate years at Harvard. Ancestral records dating back to the Battle of Hastings. Wyatt googled himself biweekly.

Lucy Jo looked newly flustered. "And, well, clearly you're a well-connected guy. I want a career. And to get that career, I need connections. Visibility."

"You know, she even sounds like a socialite. Opportunistic! Ambitious! Very promising." *Maybe there really is a Cornelia Rockman trapped beneath that frumpy exterior*, he thought, frowning at her, trying to assess her bone structure. Could it be he'd stumbled onto the perfect case study on that rainy night, and that this really was the book he was meant to write? He thought about his last conversation with Kipling, in which they'd discussed how the publisher wanted to publish more books with not only academic, but commercial, appeal. If Wyatt could document Lucy's rise from obscurity to alpha status, it might be right up Kipling's alley.

"If you could turn me into a socialite," she said, "then all's I have to do is—"

"*'All I'd* have to do,'" he corrected. See? It wasn't so hard.

"It'd be much easier to get the job I want. I mean, look at all the socialites who've become major players in fashion. I'm not saying I could be the next Tory Burch—but I thought maybe I could find a job working for a great designer, you know, if I was on the inside of the social world."

Wyatt clapped his hands together and then began to pace the dining room once more. "So you'd be willing to do as I say for the next few months? Live by my rules?" He saw Lucy Jo visibly squirm. "Trust me, nothing untoward will be asked of you. Just a lot of hard work."

"I'm not afraid of hard work—"

"What *are* you talking about?" Margaret poked her head back in from the kitchen, apparently not getting quite the information she needed by listening through the door.

"Wyatt's got some crazy idea in his head, Margaret," Trip answered. "He wants to take this nice girl and turn her into a socialite. Talk some sense into him, will you?"

Wyatt was glad his friend hadn't mentioned the prospective book in front of Lucy Jo. Knowing she was being studied for that purpose might make her self-conscious—besides, she'd likely be less eager to pass herself off as an heiress if she knew his plans to publish an exposé of her ordinary beginnings. Wyatt felt a stab of conscience, which he quickly dismissed. The girl wanted to work for a designer. He could make that happen today, if he wanted to, just by picking up the phone—but she didn't need to know that. The point was, at the end of their time together, she would be better off than she was at the moment. And so would he.

"You can't just take over a stranger's life, Wyatt," Margaret was saying.

"If she's game, why can't I? Lucy Jo, I want to turn you into *the* most glamorous socialite New York has ever seen." He stopped, experiencing yet another flash of genius. "All in time for the Fashion Forum Ball this March! That's the perfect finish line—it's the biggest event of the year. Only leaves us three months, but we can do it."

"Did you just say the *Fashion Forum Ball?*" He could see Lucy start to salivate, her eyes big as plates.

"Back up," said Margaret, setting a hand on each of her significant hips. "Did you just say 'we'?"

Wyatt resumed his pacing. "I'll need your help, Margaret. And the help of the best trainer, nutritionist, makeup artist, and so on. We already have the best stylist in the business, if Eloise will take the job—"

"Wait!" Lucy Jo interjected, looking more nervous than ever. "Um, time out. Maybe we should talk about the cost of all this—"

"I'll cover all your expenses. You have nothing to worry about."

"Mr. Hayes." Lucy Jo straightened in her chair. "I've taken care of myself my whole life, and I'm not looking for a handout. I was thinking, if I gave you a percentage of my future earnings—a stake in Lucy Jo Ellis Designs—you'd be making an *investment.*"

"An investment!" Wyatt gave Trip an amused look across the table, but he didn't get one in return. Actually, his friend appeared to be glowering at him. "I think that's a great idea. I'll take a small stake in your future empire. Now, as for a place to live—you could live here, I suppose—" Both Lucy Jo and Margaret showed their clear dislike of that idea. "What about Eloise's place on Seventy-Third? She'd jump at the chance to move in with you, Trip, even if it's only temporary."

"Eloise is your girlfriend?" Lucy Jo, horrified, glanced at Trip. "I can't take over her apartment!"

"A word in the kitchen, Wyatt?" Trip asked, standing up and walking briskly out of the room. Wyatt, with a shrug, followed behind him, leaving Margaret and Lucy Jo alone in silence. Once he got to the kitchen, he found Trip rummaging through the pantry for sweets. "What the hell are you thinking?" Trip asked, ripping off the wrapper of a Toblerone. He'd always been a comfort eater. "First of all, this poor girl thinks you can magically deliver the life she's always dreamed of . . . what's going to happen if you can't?"

In truth, the thought hadn't crossed Wyatt's mind. "It's her choice. She came here today because she wanted something more for herself. I'm going to do my best to help her."

"And you honestly believe she could be the next Cornelia? She's a real person with feelings. You can't get her hopes up like this. I mean, let's face it, looks play a big part in this whole socialite business—"

"Her looks are just fine." Trip's doubt had strengthened Wyatt's conviction. "Trust me, I know what I'm doing and have every confidence in our success."

"You're a crazy man. You truly are." Trip exhaled deeply, popping another triangle of Toblerone into his mouth. He frowned up into Wyatt's face. "If you're expecting this girl to hand over her life to you, maybe you should have skin in the game, too."

"You're proposing a bet?"

"Why not? If you fail, your watch—the 1927 platinum minute repeater that Henry Graves Jr. commissioned from Patek Philippe, your grandfather bought at auction, and you inherited, you lucky s.o.b.—is mine."

"How the hell do you know *that* much about *my* wristwatch?"

"I've been eyeing it for years. If you win, I'll pick up the tab for the whole thing."

"*And?*" Wyatt had a vague understanding of how much his timepiece was worth.

"Your choice of five bottles from my wine cellar."

"Deal," Wyatt grinned, shaking Trip's hand. The two of them headed back to the dining room, where Margaret and Lucy Jo were waiting. "Now, Lucy Jo, if we're to undertake this, you'll need to approach our work with a great deal of seriousness. You'll need to be tough, work hard. The schedule will be grueling."

She nodded. "I always work hard."

"Good," said Wyatt, clearing his throat. "We have to remake you from the ground up, giving you an entirely fresh identity. Jane Gatsby, if you will. You'll be at several parties a night—twenty, thirty a week. Lunches, too. We'll get you invited to the best shows during fashion week. And launch you onto some important committees. We'll start first thing tomorrow. The Fashion Forum Ball will be at our throats before we know it. There's not a minute to lose."

A little laugh escaped from Lucy Jo's pursed lips. "All that partying sure sounds grueling."

"Laugh now," he said. "You underestimate just how much work is involved in being social."

11

The foremost requirement to be possessed by a young lady preparing to enter society is a wise and judicious mother, herself schooled in the mores and morals of civilization, who can shepherd her innocent child through its perilous wilderness. Failing the presence of such a maternal figure, it is to be hoped that the novice will find some other firm hand on her shoulder to steer her, and resolute voice to guide her.

—*Sarah Birmingham Astor,* The Navigation of Society: A Guide for Young Ladies and Others Who Wish to Establish Themselves in Good Company, *1889.*

Day One, 7:12 AM

As dawn's first light began to stream through the large window in his study, Wyatt consulted the long to-do list he'd compiled. To his enormous satisfaction, he'd managed to immediately check off the first item yesterday: pitching his book concept to Kipling, who'd responded with even greater enthusiasm than Wyatt had hoped, calling back just an hour later to offer a (needless to say, minimal) advance. Wyatt had immediately accepted. Harvard University Press was the right home for his first book. Kipling said he'd send contracts right away.

Now the only thing separating him from successful publication and Trip's finest vintages was . . . the girl stifling a yawn and resting her uncombed head against the armrest of his couch. It was no small thing, he realized, looking at her. "We've got a lot of ground to cover," he said, feeling energized if a little daunted.

"I should warn you, I'm not much of a morning person," Lucy Jo mumbled.

He ignored her. "First, there's the matter of your name."

"What's the matter with my name?" she asked, speaking the last three words through a wide-mouthed yawn.

"Lucy Jo?" Wyatt grimaced. "Screams Middle America. You might as well get a tattoo of a Disney character, or an anklet."

"Are you usually this rude?" She pulled down the hem of her dress, which only drew his eye to notice the tiny Tweety Bird on her thigh. "And what's wrong with Middle America? I'll have you know—"

"We can go one of three ways," he interrupted. "Initials, like C. Z. Guest—"

"L.J.? I don't know . . ."

"Or we could invent a nickname. Like Happy, or Fizzy—"

"Fizzy?" She snorted. "Seriously, you think *Fizzy* is an improvement on *Lucy Jo*?"

"For our purposes, yes. Or we could simply drop the Jo. Your full name will be Lucia. That's pretty. Now we just need a middle name, to round it out a bit. What's your mother's maiden name?"

"Ellis."

"What's your father's last name, then—maybe we can use that."

"No clue," she said flatly. "And don't ask me his first name, because I don't know that either."

Wyatt frowned, and then picked up the black Social Register. "Let's see." He flipped it open at random. "Would you prefer to be Lucia Montgomery Ellis? Lucia Haverford Ellis? Lucia Bancroft Ellis?"

"Lucia, um, Haverford has a nice ring to it, I guess," Lucy said.

"Settled. And everyone simply calls you Lucy."

And just like that, a new identity was born. Well, more or less.

Day Two, 2:54 PM

"Help!" Lucy yelled when she saw Wyatt walk past the doorway to his home gym, where she was currently imprisoned with Derrick, her ex–Navy SEAL trainer. Wyatt poked his head in. She'd never sweat so profusely in her life. It felt more like melting. As if the predawn run in Central Park with Derrick wasn't a big enough insult to the system, now the guy was whipping her through a weight-lifting circuit. "How long is this torture going to last?" Lucy panted, expending what little oxygen she had left.

"Just until you're a sample size," Wyatt answered. He had his finger in a book—*Social Dominance in Primates*, she read on the spine. Nerd.

Derrick pushed a three-foot box toward her. "Jump-ups," he said with a twisted smile. "Go!"

"Isn't it enough that I froze my ass off doing wind sprints this morning?" Lucy jumped, narrowly clearing the box's edge, arms flapping to help her keep her balance.

Wyatt, crossing the room, made a big show of checking out her backside. "No, it's definitely still there." He and Derrick laughed.

"That's not funny!" she shouted indignantly, almost falling off the box for a second time. "And you want to teach me manners?"

Wyatt scowled. "Maybe I picked the wrong girl," he said brusquely. "You can quit today, no hard feelings."

Lucy Jo jumped back to earth. "I never said I wanted to quit. I just don't want to be exercised to death."

"Don't be so melodramatic. I'm telling you, if I hear one more complaint—one more 'do I have to?'—you're out for good, and there *will* be hard feelings. Got that?"

She caught her breath, reminding herself that her dream was on the line. Wyatt was just her means to an end. If she could put up with him for just a few months, he'd help her find a job with a designer, and her career could accelerate toward producing a line of her own someday. "Fine," she said, feeling a fresh determination.

"Jump!" Derrick barked.

When Wyatt headed for the door, Lucy couldn't resist sticking her tongue out at him—which she promptly bit, so hard she could taste blood. "Ow!" she hollered, blaming him for the pain.

"Serves you right," Wyatt said, his back still toward her.

Day Three, 12:24 PM

"I'm sorry," Margaret said, setting a murky green shake in front of Lucy Jo. It looked like pond scum. "How do you expect the poor girl to drink this stuff, Wyatt? Honestly, it's cruel."

"It's just a seven-day juice cleanse, Margaret," said Wyatt impatiently, pulling his napkin onto his lap and digging into his steak frites. He tossed the brochure with a skinny yogi on the cover across the table at them. "All the models swear by it."

"Today's lunch is a rejuvenating combination of kale, broccoli, and seaweed—with a few shots of wheatgrass," read Lucy Jo in a dismayed voice. "Sounds like code for *swamp*, if you ask me." From across the table, Wyatt could hear her stomach growl in protest. But she picked up the shake, pinched her nose, and swallowed.

"Not so bad, right?" he said lightly, choosing to ignore the seconds-from-puking expression on Lucy's face. He dipped a fry in béarnaise sauce and popped it into his mouth. "Now, we've got ground to cover. There's the matter of your education. I don't dare try to pull off Brearley or Exeter. We'd be exposed in a minute. We'll say you went to Miss Dillard's School in New Hampshire. All the women in my family went there."

"Couldn't someone just dig a little? Find out we're lying?"

"I've made arrangements. It'll check out." Wyatt had called in a favor with the headmaster, who happened to be an old Hasty Pudding buddy and was willing to pretend that Lucy Jo was an alumna.

"Arrangements?" Lucy looked thoroughly baffled.

Sometimes her naïveté is astounding, Wyatt thought, making a mental note for the book. How did she think things got done?

"Once we get our stories straight," he continued, "I thought it'd be a good idea to get Rex Newhouse to write a short profile on his blog. Just a little something introducing you. Once the 'facts' have been written a few times, nobody will bother to check them."

"So I'm a graduate of Miss Dillard's High School—"

"Miss Dillard's School. All girls. Even when you were accepted to Andover, Mother wouldn't hear of it. That reminds me—leave off the pronoun when you're speaking about members of your family. It's Mother, Dad, Grandmère, and so on."

"Grandmère?" Lucy giggled. "Sounds like a horse."

"No college, you said?" Wyatt asked, consulting his notebook.

"I had to work," Lucy said, chin tipped.

Wyatt thought for a moment. "Well, college is less important.

We'll say you went to the New School, here in New York, but never graduated because you wanted to travel."

"This is totally amazing." Lucy wiped a few drops of foul juice that had escaped down her chin.

I've seen chimps with better table manners. "What's that?"

"In just three days, I've become Lucia Haverford Ellis, a blue-blooded, prep-school educated daughter of fortune."

Wyatt, looking up from his list, peered at her across the dining room table. "It's not quite as simple as saying the right things, or wearing the right clothes. It's your carriage, your delivery, your manners, your . . . aura. We're just sketching out some outlines that you'll have to fill in, and that's no small task. Everything about you will need to change for this to work."

"Awesome pep talk," Lucy muttered. "Hey, what do I say if someone asks about us?"

"Us?" Wyatt repeated. Margaret looked at him with curiosity.

"Yeah, *us.* I mean, I assume we'll be going out together a lot. What's our relationship?"

A good question. Wyatt couldn't decide what was riskier to his rep—claiming Lucy as a relative, or as a girlfriend. "We'll tell people we're old family friends. Known each other since birth. Practically cousins."

Lucy gave him a sideways look. "Got it, coz."

"Yeah, don't call me that. I'm just your wiser, older friend, showing you around the city as you take your place in society."

"Wiser, huh?" She took another swig of her juice, forgetting to pinch her nose. The shake left a disgusting algae-green residue over her top lip.

What have I gotten myself into? Wyatt blanched as she wiped her lip with the back of her hand.

Day Four, 4:52 PM

"Allow me to get the door for you, Miss Ellis," insisted the driver, rushing around to the side of the car before Harold, the doorman, could scramble out from Wyatt's building. Wyatt came out the front door just steps behind him.

"Thank you, Mark," Lucy said, feeling like royalty. She was sheathed in a mod navy minidress that made her legs look surprisingly long and attractive. Sliding out of the backseat, she caught her own reflection in the shiny window of the Town Car and tried not to gape. But *wow*. Pair Eloise's black book of beauty gurus with Wyatt's black Amex, and the results were pretty astounding.

That morning, Lucy's hair had been layered into a soft bob that reached almost down to her shoulders. Very Katie Holmes, claimed the hairstylist, after declaring Lucy's previous $9.99 Supercuts chop a crime against humanity. Her brows had been perfectly, painfully, painstakingly shaped by a so-called eyebrow doctor. Her smile had been brightened. Her skin, lavished with attention during an oxygen-infused facial, had never looked more radiant. Her feet and hands had luxuriated in warm almond-honey butter. She'd been waxed, buffed, shined like a BMW after a long winter.

"Ta da!" She curtsied before Harold and Wyatt.

"Not so fast." Wyatt looked stern. "Back in the car."

"Do I have another beauty appointment?" Every square inch of Lucy's body had been polished to a sheen. What more could be done?

"You're not Britney Spears. You need to learn how to get out of a car without flashing an entire city block. Try it again."

Lucy flushed. Not that she'd been expecting a compliment or anything crazy like that—but she couldn't help feeling a bit deflated. It was so like Wyatt to find something to criticize. "I'm *wearing* underwear."

"I know. Purple."

"And I know how to get out of a car!"

"Apparently not."

She got back in the car, cursing him silently. Then she slid out— *again*—this time scooching across the backseat in little jerky motions.

"Again," he ordered.

"Okay, I know I didn't flash anything that time. Harold, did you see anything?"

Harold shook his head. He seemed disappointed.

"You looked ridiculous," Wyatt said, sounding exasperated. "This time keep your knees firmly pressed together, and don't wiggle so much. It should be a smooth, graceful movement."

She tried it again.

"No," he said.

Again and again, she piled in and out of the car door. Several taxis beeped at the parked car, but Wyatt waved them off. "I'm getting butt burn!" Lucy complained on the fifth take.

"Not perfect, but better," Wyatt finally declared when she'd managed to keep her ankles together. "Come inside. Now we're behind schedule."

Could he be any more condescending? "Thanks for the lift, Mark," Lucy called to the driver, who'd returned to the front seat.

"Anytime. You look great, Lucy, like a real movie star."

"Aren't you nice?" She gave Wyatt a pointed look as they headed inside, but he didn't seem to notice.

Day Five, 10:43 AM

"Right hip forward, left leg back." Angelique, the German model Wyatt had recruited to teach Lucy proper carriage, demonstrated the pose in front of the floor-to-ceiling mirror that took up one entire wall of Wyatt's private dressing room. She gestured for Lucy to do the same.

"It looks like you're about to steal second base," Wyatt chimed in from his armchair in the corner.

"I'm trying!" she yelled back. Lucy adjusted her back leg but she still looked awkward. There was just nothing natural about standing like this, even if it did "shave inches off her hips," according to Angelique. Lucy wondered briefly whether Wyatt and Angelique had a romantic history. Judging by the flirty little smiles the model kept sending his way, she guessed they did—or soon would.

"Why don't we try walking instead?" Angelique was losing patience.

"Don't let her off the hook that easily, Ange. Lucy can't walk before she's mastered at least one camera-friendly pose."

"But that could take hours." Angelique's full lips popped into a pout.

Lucy felt her temper flare. A towering six-foot beauty with long blonde locks and cheekbones that could cut stone, Angelique probably couldn't relate to anyone who didn't roll out of bed ready for a close-up. Annoyed, Lucy jutted out her hip again, throwing back her chin slightly.

"Yes!" Wyatt exclaimed. "Much better."

"*Finally,*" Angelique said. "Now try this one." She pivoted her willowy frame so that the imaginary camera in front of her caught one side of her body and a bit of her back. Then she coquettishly turned her head, chin nearly at her shoulder, and smiled.

Lucy imitated, casting an insouciant grin at Wyatt in the mirror.

He squinted back, examining her clinically, and then nodded. "Not bad," he declared. "Great job."

"Hey, thanks!" Lucy spun around to face him, shocked to hear praise escape his lips.

"Great job, *Angelique*. Now, Lucy, you may try walking."

Day Six, 3:12 PM

"Fill in the blank," Wyatt said. When Lucy emerged from the dressing room at Bergdorf in a black satin Dolce & Gabbana, he immediately shook his head. The dress was too overtly sexy for their purposes. He sent her back behind the black velvet curtain to try on the next outfit. "The gay male walker is a *blank* part of the socialite's arsenal."

"I don't know." Her voice was muffled by whatever she was pulling over her head. "Outdated?"

"*Essential*. Charming, stylish, erudite men never go out of style. I've booked you several lunch dates at La Goulue with the best in the business, so to speak. I won't be able to go with you to every event, you know. I've got my own work to do."

Lucy pushed back the curtain, flush-faced from the exertion of trying on three racks of clothes in record time. Now she modeled a sophisticated Rodarte cocktail dress in muted pink chiffon. It showed off her figure, which had already been significantly whittled thanks to Derrick. Wyatt gave a thumbs up.

"Give me three *As Mother always says*," he said.

Back in the dressing room, Lucy was working her way into a cashmere sweater-coat and black cigarette pants. "*As Mother always says,* better to be overdressed than underdressed. *As Mother always says, you can tell a great deal by the way a man eats his soup.*" She threw back the curtain for Wyatt's input on her latest ensemble.

He nodded appreciatively. "Perfect for weekends, you know, around the house."

"Around the house?" Checking the price tag, she pulled a face. "You seriously think an eight hundred dollar sweater is appropriate loungewear for a Sunday at home?"

"Of course. You have to be camera-ready at all times. What else does Mother always say?"

Lucy sighed. "One can't put a price on quality."

Wyatt smiled. She was learning. And he was getting everything he needed for his book, working feverishly at night after fourteen-hour days with Lucy. *The Overnight Socialite*, he and Kipling were thinking about calling it. This experiment would be a landmark in anthropology—and it could jump-start his stalled career.

Day Seven, 1:54 AM

"How many times do I need to tell you? The G in Gstaad is silent!" Wyatt circled the couch where Lucy was now slumped like a wilted tulip. Though they'd been working tirelessly on her elocution, Lucy's *a*'s remained as wide as the Great Plains, and her frequent "you knows" and tendency to rush-right-through-a-sentence-without-pausing-for-air were putting up a tenacious fight.

"The snow in Aspen puts Gstaad's to shame," Lucy repeated life-lessly.

"Get the marbles out! You're still mumbling." Growing impatient, Wyatt tapped his notebook with his pencil. "From the top."

Lucy held up an index finger instead, taking several thirsty gulps from her water glass. *Another ugly habit.* Would he have to reteach the girl everything?

"Can we finish this tomorrow?" she whined. "I'm seriously about to pass out. And it's Christmas Eve."

"We'll be finished when you've got it right!" Wyatt barked. Did she think he was enjoying hour six of listening to her butcher the English language? That he wouldn't rather be drinking southsides on his mother's terrace, the white lights of her twelve-foot Christmas tree twinkling behind him? "From the top, Lucy. And for God's sake, sit up straight."

She cleared her throat and collected herself into an erect posture on the front of the couch. "Didn't we meet in Capri last July?" she continued, saying each word cautiously.

"Yes!" Wyatt stopped in his tracks. "Yes!" It was the first time she hadn't pronounced the name of the island like those unflattering three-quarter-length pants. "Go on, go on!"

"I don't want to be known merely as the *Ellis heiress*," Lucy continued, looking surprised herself. "I prefer to be judged on my own merit."

"Yes! That was actually good!"

"I was raised in Chicago, and my family summers in Nantucket." Lucy looked equally shocked by the patrician accent leaving her lips. "You remind me of my roommate from boarding school." They stared at each other in disbelief as she continued. "Who sets foot in Manhattan after Memorial Day?"

"That's it!" Wyatt could barely restrain himself from jumping up and down. He closed his eyes. "Again!"

"The snow in Aspen puts Gstaad's to shame!" Lucy shouted.

"I think you've got it!" Wyatt exclaimed. For six entire sentences she had sounded like a born-and-bred socialite, blue blood coursing through her veins. He grabbed her by the hands and pulled her up off the couch.

"One week in Ibiza and I don't need to go clubbing for the rest of the year!" she said, pronouncing the z as "th."

"By George!" Wyatt, unable to contain his excitement, scooped Lucy around the waist—smaller, now, he noticed—and began to dance with her around the room.

"Didn't we meet in Capri last July?" She beamed up at him.

"You've got it!" he exclaimed, twirling the girl in his arms.

12

Wyatt's Book Notes:

Dominance among male cichlid fish is correlated to bright coloration. When researchers experimentally manipulated subordinate male cichlids into developing this bright coloration, they found that the fish began to exhibit dominant behavior within minutes. Similarly, the effect of a simple makeover and improved wardrobe on L.'s psyche was an astonishing phenomenon to behold. Though our work is just beginning, there's no doubt that designer clothes—and never the same outfit twice—do indeed make the socialite.

"How do you properly thank someone for hooking you up with a personal chef who usually keeps a six-month waiting list?"

"Handwritten thank-you note, delivered by messenger the next day?" Lucy tried to hide her breathlessness as Wyatt took the front steps at the Heritage Museum two at a time. With their experiment now almost two weeks under way, Wyatt had gotten into the habit of drilling her constantly. Ever since she'd had her breakthrough, she'd stopped hating it so much. When she answered correctly, it could actually be fun—and that was happening more and more often.

Wyatt made a buzzer sound. "Wrong!"

"An elegant arrangement from Plaza Flowers?" she panted. After double sessions each day with Derrick the ex-SEAL, she should have been able to scale the side of the museum without breaking a sweat. But she was huffing for air keeping up with Wyatt's long stride. They were going to see the new Pierre Bonnard exhibition, and Lucy had been up late the night before learning about the Nabis, the group of Post-Impressionist avant-garde artists of which he'd been a member. Required reading, but it was actually pretty interesting, and Bonnard's use of intense, high-keyed color spoke to her as a designer.

"Try again," he said.

"An invitation to join my table at an upcoming benefit?"

Wyatt rolled his eyes. "Not even close."

"I know! A dozen pairs of Christian Louboutin shoes." Wasn't that what Jessica Seinfeld gave Oprah? Lucy felt sure she'd gotten it right this time. Wyatt had spent yesterday afternoon explaining to her the rules of reciprocity in establishing "tribal ties." He called it tit-for-tat behavior, explaining how chimps—and humans—used mutual back scratching to build alliances. Reciprocity was the glue that held social groups together. And what woman wouldn't appreciate Louboutins as barter?

"Unless the chef is Thomas Keller, you massively overshot. The correct answer is: invite her to your weekend home in Millbrook."

"Wyatt, I don't have a weekend home in Millbrook!"

He halted at the front entrance of the museum, considering this fact. "Fine, then, the flowers."

Flashing his "Friend" card at the ticket counter, he waltzed by with Lucy in tow. Then he typed something quickly into his Black-Berry and hit send before tossing it back into the pocket of his cashmere overcoat.

Cornelia—got your messages. Thanks for the wine. In midst of new project and very busy. Be well, W.

Be well? *Be well?* fumed Cornelia, examining her poinsettia-red thumbnail. She was lounging by the pool in Palm Beach. *He might as well have written "eat shit and die."* And who sends a half-assed text message in response to a bottle of '82 Château Mouton Rothschild? How rude. She laid her right hand on her taut stomach, toasty from the morning sun, and thrust her unpainted left hand toward the manicurist.

Although she'd spent the past week at her parents' home (they were in London, making it an ideal time to visit Palm Beach), Cornelia had continued her now monthlong campaign of contrition for posing next to Theo Galt. Days after the *Townhouse* party, when Wyatt hadn't returned her phone calls, she'd e-mailed him a Patrick McMullan snap of the two of them, a reminder of how good they looked together. No response. Then, before leaving for Florida, she'd pounced on Margaret as she left his building, pressing into her hand a small package for Wyatt containing the handkerchief he'd forgotten at her place the first night they'd kissed at Socialista. She hoped it would spark memories of their private after-party. Apparently, it had not. Finally, after too many unreturned calls and e-mails, she'd been reduced to raiding her father's wine cellar. And still all she'd gotten in response was his stupid text!

"Still bumpy," she whined, holding the nail two inches away from the manicurist's face. The young Hispanic woman had been sent by an agency that delivered manicurists, masseuses, acupuncturists, and yoga instructors to Cornelia's door, which kept her from having to mingle with the hoi polloi.

"I don't see any bumps, Miss Rockman," the woman answered. "I've redone the nail three times. I think it looks perfect."

"Excuse me?" Cornelia's nostrils flared slightly. She jumped up from the chaise longue and stretched her legs, casting a shadow over the shallow end of the pool. "I'm not paying for a mani-pedi that looks like it was done by a blind chimp." Mentioning the chimp reminded her of her anthropologist ex-boyfriend, of course, which made her even more irritated.

"Okay, I can redo—"

"Nor do I have time to sit here watching you botch it up again!"

The manicurist sighed. "That's fine, Miss Rockman. See you again the same time next week?"

"I suppose. But tell Esmerelda no tip. I check the petty cash, you know." The woman began to shuffle toward the house with her heavy kit. "Just because I'm a Rockman doesn't mean I'm an ATM!" Cornelia yelled after her. Her mother, Verena, had always warned her about people—from men to manicurists—looking to "get theirs." Gold diggers. Parasites. Verena knew something about the profile:

she'd married Cornelia's father when she was a twenty-three-year-old Scandinavian swimsuit model and he was a sixty-two-year-old senator with a heart condition. Against all odds, Cornelia's father was now past ninety, and Verena was a smokin' fifty-two-year-old rumored to have men in many ports.

Shameless, Verena would say if she knew about Cornelia's current situation. It was not the woman's role to woo, she would scold. Men—even rich, powerful, intelligent men—were easy to manipulate, if you knew how. Knowing how was the art of being a woman, and Cornelia's efforts had been kindergarten-level finger painting.

But then she'd never expected Wyatt to put up such a fight! Most men would have overlooked Cornelia's minor lapse in judgment at that stupid party, and *every* man she knew (except Wyatt, apparently, the one she now wanted more than ever) would've taken her back at the first whiff of an apology.

Cornelia arranged herself in the lounge chair again, adjusting the top of her minuscule white bikini. The view of the water, contrasted with the cool pink façade of her parents' home and the gently swaying palm trees dotting their property, evoked such an air of prosperity and peace that there were days when Cornelia didn't reach for her antianxiety medication more than twice. Today, unfortunately, was not one of those days.

Her marriage to Wyatt Hayes was inevitable, thought Cornelia, reaching over to take a sip of her mint-laced iced tea. That was the conclusion she'd reached last winter, resting on this same slate blue chaise, the morning after she and Wyatt were reintroduced at a cocktail party on the Morgans' docked yacht. He'd stood at the bow, the lights of the Okeechobee Bridge dotted in the distance behind him. Cornelia was immediately riveted. Everything about Wyatt screamed aristocracy, though he wore just jeans and a white button-down rolled up to his forearms, and her immediate thought had been: "We'd look perfect together." She'd spent the night charming his best friend, Trip Peters, and feeling Wyatt's eyes on her. A month later (it would have happened sooner, but for all his safaris), he'd asked her to dinner at Per Se, which turned into drinks at Socialista. They'd been dating ever since.

The morning of the *Townhouse* party, her source at Harry Winston called to inform her that Wyatt had stopped in to do some Christmas shopping, and that before he was guided toward the tennis bracelet she'd set aside he'd cast an eye over the engagement rings. Cornelia had been pleased, but hardly surprised. It was all part of her plan. Wyatt would propose by the following spring, giving her a full year to plan a June wedding at her family's estate in Northeast Harbor. The rehearsal dinner could be at *his* family's estate in Northeast Harbor. The Hayes-Rockman wedding would net a four-page spread in *Vogue*, maybe more.

Their tiff was a glitch in that scheme, but one she could recover from. If Cornelia had learned one profound life lesson in her twenty-seven years, it was that she could always get what she wanted. She'd relished the high of scoring her croc Birkin, snagging her front-row seat at Marc Jacobs, and capturing not one but three tickets to the *Vanity Fair* Oscar party—and to win Wyatt back would be her most satisfying triumph yet.

"Isn't it enough I'm letting the girl live in my apartment?" Eloise laid a finger on the top of Trip's *Wall Street Journal* and pulled it down so that he had to look at her. They were twenty thousand feet and climbing en route back from Aspen, where they'd spent the holidays. "Now you're asking me to spend my entire Friday with her, hunkered down at some spa?"

"You make it sound so torturous," Trip said, folding up the newspaper and storing it neatly in his briefcase. He smiled. "Besides, don't pretend you weren't thrilled to move in with me."

Eloise swatted him lightly. "I'd be even more thrilled to have my own closet."

"You have too many clothes. Anyone ever tell you that?"

"I'm a stylist, sweetie. It comes with the territory." She snuggled under the thick cashmere blanket, folding her legs underneath her. "Why can't Wyatt spend the day with her? I don't need a forced friendship. She's his project, not mine."

"I told you, he's got to be in Boston on business."

"Oh, please. When's Wyatt going to stop *pretending* he works?" Eloise didn't know why she was being so difficult. She suspected it had less to do with Wyatt and this Lucy person, and more to do with

Trip's last-minute insistence that they spend the holidays skiing instead of driving to Duxbury to be with her family. She'd spent the first twenty-four hours of their trip doing damage control with her mother. Worse, she couldn't seem to make Trip understand why it was a big deal. "It's like he's trying to engineer his perfect woman. He called me yesterday asking for my opinion on highlights versus lowlights!"

Trip just laughed. "Trust me, Lucy is as far from Wyatt Hayes's perfect woman as the Cubs are from winning a World Series."

Eloise wasn't entirely convinced. She hadn't actually met Lucy yet—the girl was never at the apartment when Eloise went over to retrieve her mail or get more clothes. Apparently she was spending night and day at Wyatt's, in socialite boot camp. Wyatt had been in isolation mode, too, even bailing on his mother for the holidays so they could keep up their so-called training. "I swear, this is his strangest diversion yet."

Trip pulled a lock of her hair—now a strawberry blonde—off her face. "All I know is, he keeps hounding me to ask you to spend time with her. Just be nice to the girl. You get a massage, get your nails done, talk a little. How painful could it be?"

Eloise slumped in her seat, knowing she was acting like a petulant seven-year-old. Ever since their trip to Turks and Caicos earlier that month—which was just as beautiful as Trip had promised—she'd been in an inexplicably sour mood. "If it means that much to you, I'll spend the day with her. But that's it, okay?"

The opening notes of "Rich Girl" bleated from Cornelia's BlackBerry, interrupting her stroll down Worth Avenue. *Daphne Convers: Office.*

"Are you sitting down?" Daphne burbled. "Because big news! Dafinco just called, and guess whom they want to develop a fragrance with?"

"Who's Dafinco?" asked Cornelia, peering into the display window of Cartier. She needed more gold jewelry. A few bangles, or something. She pushed through the heavy red door, and the woman behind the counter immediately perked up. Cornelia loved being recognized.

"Only the biggest makeup and perfume distributor in the entire country, doll!" Daphne was saying. "And they want you to launch their next perfume, Cornelia. You! We're talking major seven figures—"

Cornelia stopped in her tracks. That *was* big news. "So, like, would my name and face be on all the ads?" Cornelia held up a finger at the frothing saleslady.

"Everything and anything, doll. We'll walk through the whole thing. Can you be in New York next week for meetings?"

"I'm in St. Barts through Tuesday. Any day after that is fine."

"We'll make it work! You're the star. This is the beginning of big things for you, sweetie," Daphne said. "They're already putting together a couple of prototypes for you to smell. They think 'Socialite' should combine lilies of the valley, jasmine, and citrus with under notes of cedarwood. Classic, timeless, clean—"

"I don't know," Cornelia said. She motioned to see an eighteen-karat Love bracelet embedded with diamonds, and the woman whipped it out of the display case with remarkable alacrity. "I'd prefer something with a bit more mystery. More sex appeal. Lots of ooomph."

As Daphne sycophantically agreed, Cornelia could feel her back muscles begin to unclench. Pushing her oversize sunglasses to the top of her head, she handed the saleslady her credit card and felt content for the first time since the *Townhouse* party.

She had a perfume deal. And if she sent Wyatt one of her garters scented with "Cornelia," he would be man-putty in her hands.

13

Wyatt's Book Notes:

Betta fish flare out their gill covers—opercula, the scientific term—in order to appear more imposing to their peers and impressive to potential female mates. Park Avenue princesses act curiously like male Betta fish; they spend hours and hundreds each week having their hair voluminously blown out. They wedge their feet into four-inch stilettos. All this, it would seem, is intended make them imposing to their peers and impressive to potential mates. I encouraged L. to wear her hair as full as possible and to avoid flats, so that she would flaunt an intimidating presence to her fellow socialites. I intended that she perceive these women not as friends but as rivals.

*P*erfume?" asked Dottie Hayes, one eyebrow raised.

"She's quite the go-getter," said Binkie Howe.

While the parties continued to churn fifteen hundred miles north, many of Manhattan's social set had migrated down for the high-profile charity benefits of Palm Beach's season. Binkie's veranda, shaded against the midday sun by a grand banyan tree, was crowded with the Flagler Museum's planning committee, an assortment of women ages twenty-five through seventy-five who, regardless of age, dressed remarkably the same.

Cornelia Rockman was the sole deviant from the unspoken dress code, wearing a body-hugging dress whose square inches were overwhelmed by the length of her coltlike thighs. She held court among the junior committee members.

"Go-getter," Dottie repeated, eyeing her warily. "That's one word for it, I suppose."

Binkie leaned closer. "You know I think it's fabulous that so many women today have careers. I myself worked tirelessly for the Junior League when I was a young bride. But to market some product with your name on it just seems so—"

"Say no more," Dottie said, pressing her hand into the air. Where was the girl's mother, one had to wonder? Verena Rockman was a bit flashy, but Dottie still would've expected some maternal intervention. Her daughter was splayed across the cover of this month's *Palm Beach Scene*, for pity's sake! Then again, Verena had been a swimsuit model herself. Maybe in birthing Cornelia she had added too much chlorine to the Rockman blood.

"So don't kill me, Dot." Binkie cringed. "Cornelia asked to be seated next to you today. She was so forward about it; I was caught off guard—"

"Of course," Dottie said, immediately dreading the luncheon she'd been looking forward to all week. It irked her that Cornelia had infiltrated the board of a cause so near and dear to her heart. Dottie had served on the board of the Flagler Museum for two decades, as her mother had before her. Since her teenage years, the museum had offered a cultural escape during the social season in Palm Beach. Designed by Carrère and Hastings—the famed architects who'd also designed the New York Public Library—the Flagler made Dottie feel like she was stepping back into the Gilded Age, when her family, her in-laws, and most of their crowd had accumulated great wealth.

"Lunch is served," announced a maid in a crisply starched uniform, and the ladies began to drift across the stone veranda to their seats.

"Sorry," Binkie whispered, squeezing Dottie's arm before heading off.

Dottie found her table right away, admiring the daffodil-yellow edge of the salad plates while the other ladies made their way to the table. As long as it didn't involve saying *no* to forceful young women, Binkie knew how to do things correctly. She kept six china services in Palm Beach, so her weekend guests wouldn't see the same pattern twice. The elegant calligraphy on the name cards had been penned by Binkie's longtime assistant, Mary Sue, a wiry woman who accompanied her employer wherever she went and, if you believed the rumors, which Dottie emphatically did not, occasionally shared Binkie's bedroom. Binkie, like many of their friends, had lived down the hall from her husband for at least twenty years. Why crowd into one bedroom when there were so many from which to choose?

"Are we seated next to each other?" Cornelia asked, giving Dottie a boisterous double kiss. "What a treat!"

"Isn't it?" Dottie replied.

Lunch passed quickly in group conversation, as the ladies poked at field greens and Chilean sea bass and discussed the museum's latest fund-raising efforts before diving into gossip about mutual friends. Cornelia, to Dottie's dismay, was endlessly persistent in tying every thread of conversation back to Wyatt. When Susannah Gray, whose family had recently purchased the Morgans' family yacht, deliberated over which interior designer they should hire to give it a fresh look, Cornelia gushed over Tikki Morris, who'd done a stellar job on Wyatt's apartment. When Jacqueline Griffin brought up the recent election, Cornelia enlightened the table with Wyatt's insights on the candidates. Dessert would be lemon meringue pie? Wyatt's favorite, Cornelia noted, fascinating nobody.

Dottie successfully ignored the efforts to start a conversation about her son until the dessert plates were cleared, and Cornelia's feline eyes bore down on her.

"You've probably heard that Wyatt and I are no longer," the young woman said rather too dramatically.

"Such a shame," Dottie replied. "Though I'm sure a beautiful girl like you must have no shortage of interested suitors."

"I'm not interested in other men," Cornelia said, her intensity startling Dottie. "I know that Wyatt and I are meant to be together. We want the same things out of life. We're both so committed to our work—Wyatt with his study of primates and people and I with my philanthropy and my . . . business efforts. We share the same *values.*"

Dottie, trying not to show just how insulted she was by that suggestion, was reduced to fiddling with her napkin. Imagine, she'd once urged her son to give this girl a second chance!

"Maybe if you were to talk to him, he'd reconsider. He holds you in such high esteem, Dottie—I'm sure he'd listen to you."

"Wyatt can be very stubborn," Dottie said. Selling her son short was the only diplomatic way she could think of to handle the situation. "And difficult. He always needs to get his own way. He's incorrigibly rude. Nothing like his father, I have to say, when it comes to temperament. His father was a true gentleman, through and through."

"Wyatt's a gentleman, too," Cornelia insisted. "His manners are flawless—he just chooses not to use them."

"And then there's his constant travel," Dottie continued. "I never know where in the world my son is. How that works in a serious relationship, I couldn't begin to imagine."

A chilling look passed over Cornelia's face when she grasped that Dottie would not be getting in her corner. Dottie, unnerved, changed the subject. "I think it's wonderful that you've decided to get involved with the museum, dear. We need more young people to take on civic responsibilities."

"Oh, I'm very civic-minded." Cornelia sat back in her wrought-iron chair, arms now folded across her chest. "I'm on thirty-seven committees."

Dottie was flabbergasted. "Thirty-seven, did you say? But how could you possibly find time for all of them?"

"Mostly they want my name for the invitation. You know, so people will show up for the events. I'm just glad to do my part."

"I see," Dottie said. The girl's arrogance was downright frightening. *This* was the future of the Flagler's board? "Well, it's certainly a different world than when I was your age. You girls have much more . . . energy." She glanced at her watch. "I should be going. Tennis at three. Good to see you, Cornelia. Please give my best to your parents."

"I will," Cornelia said, no longer bothering to hide her annoyance. "Will Wyatt be in town anytime soon?"

"Sadly, it doesn't look likely. Work is keeping him in New York."
Dottie watched Cornelia digest the information. The two women,
standing, parted ways with a hostile kiss.

Lucy dropped her Birkin—on loan from Bag Borrow or Steal—on
the floor and locked the door of Eloise's apartment behind her.
Funny how the place already felt like home. It was the kind of home
she'd always hoped to have someday, with its softly feminine colors
and warm, eclectic furniture.

She fished out her ringing BlackBerry—an upgrade provided by
Wyatt—and flopped onto the couch. Every muscle in her body
ached, thanks to Derrick, especially her throbbing brain, thanks to
Wyatt. *Caller Unknown.* "Hello?" she said, picking up.

"You were going to tell your mother you moved, right?"

Damn. Rita. Lucy could hear the too-familiar din of O'Shaugh-
nessy's in the background.

"I've left you five voice mails this week," Rita continued. "My
nails got returned! Your landlord tacked on a note saying that you
hadn't picked up packages in weeks, and he didn't know where to
find you. Nice guy. Single?"

"Married," muttered Lucy. She'd been avoiding giving her mother
the update on her life, because she wasn't sure just how to describe
her new circumstances. Nor did she need Rita, sniffing money, paw-
ing at her door. "I'm house-sitting for a friend. Just a temporary
thing." *Not a complete lie, relatively speaking.*

"Well, you better give me that address, then. I'll remail the nails.
They came out super, by the way. You'll love the one of Oprah Win-
frey at her various weights. And your boss will flip for them."

"Uh-huh." Lucy gave Rita the address at Eloise's.

"So you'll pitch them to Nola Sinclair? They're a gold mine, I'm
telling you—"

"To Nola? I don't think that's the best idea." *A blushing understatement, considering she despises me and canned me a month ago.*
Why did her mother have to be so pushy? "Nola's a nail biter."

Rita gasped. Nail biting, to her, was an offense on par with book
burning. Worse, actually. But she quickly recovered. "Well, the city

must be full of potential investors. Maybe I should come stay with you and we can pound the pavement together. I'll cut you in for fifteen percent. Or maybe ten. What do you say, kid? Ten percent of a million dollar business is still . . . um, a lot of money."

Lucy bit her cheek. Just what she'd been afraid of—Rita barreling in and taking over the best opportunity she'd ever had. If she knew about Wyatt, she'd maul him. "I'll talk to some people," she said. That wasn't a lie. She just wouldn't talk about Rita's nails. "See what I can put together. Stay put for now." Much to her relief, her mother seemed to accept that. Now she just had to stay Rita-free for the next two and a half months until the Forum Ball. After that, she'd get her break working for a fabulous designer, start paying her own way again, and be able to give Rita more of a boost. It was just a matter of time.

Fernanda Fairchild's ankles began to wobble in her ugly brown rental skates the moment she shoved off from the wall. (She'd begged for some white ones to better match her ruched-sleeve parka and cashmere chapeau, but was told that brown was *it*.) "*Parker!*" she yelped, forgetting to act cool as her arms shot out and she struggled to catch her balance. Parker, sporty in a down puffer vest and earmuffs, flew to her rescue. "Hey, thanks," she said, once her equilibrium was restored. "You're pretty good on those things." As surprised as she'd been when Parker had suggested the Wollman skating rink, tourist trap, as the site of their third date, Fernanda was downright shocked to find that she was enjoying herself. Parker had packed a huge thermos of hot cocoa with plenty of marshmallows, and he was getting a kick out of seeing Fernanda out of her element.

"Do you think I would've asked you to go skating with me if I didn't have skills? Played hockey in high school," Parker said, not letting go of her arm. They moved smoothly around a corner, avoiding a close call with the eight-year-old show-off who cut in front of them. "Granted, that was three decades ago." When he laughed, his eyes crinkled at each corner. Fernanda would have been terrified to see such deep crow's-feet on her own face, but she found Parker's to be strangely endearing.

"The last time I went skating was when I was five years old," she found herself reminiscing. "Our old country house in Bedford had a pond in the backyard, and Dad let Max and me skate on it one weekend when Mom wasn't around. I loved it, actually. I didn't want to stop. My feet got so cold he had to carry me back up to the house."

"You had your very own rink?"

"Yeah, well, a lot of fun we had with it. Mom was very overprotective."

"Can't blame her," Parker said, giving her a squeeze as they rounded another corner. "But now you can make up for lost time. Live on the edge!" Parker released Fernanda's arm and skated around her in a little circle.

Then the same eight-year-old speed demon veered right into her path, sending her into another violent wobble. "Hey!" she shouted. Parker grabbed her arm again.

Fernanda had come to think of dates as work, the way an actress would think of auditions. But the afternoon with Parker hadn't felt like work. "Have dinner plans tonight?" he asked as they cruised the rink.

"With Mom"—normally she would have fabricated something more glamorous, but Parker made her feel honest—"but I can reschedule."

"Or the three of us could have dinner?"

Fernanda fought the urge to pinch herself. "Really? I'm sure she'd love that!"

"Great," Parker said, clapping his gloved hands together once in what seemed to be genuine enthusiasm. "How about my place? I'll cook."

"You cook, too?"

He smiled. "I studied at La Varenne for the year after college, before the high-stakes world of international finance lured me with its siren call."

She stopped skating. "Okay, Parker, what's the catch?"

"What do you mean?"

"No man is this perfect. Do you go to Hannah Montana concerts? Make sculptures with your toenail clippings?"

"The catch?" Parker stroked his chin as though deep in thought. "I don't know. Well, there *is* Mr. Fursnickety—"

Oh God.

"Sounds worse than it is. He's a ferret."

It's worse than it sounds, she thought. Fernanda disliked furry creatures. Unless they'd already been made into yummy fur coats, they weren't of much interest to her. She was only mildly fond of her own dachshunds, George and Barbara.

"Mr. Fursnickety belonged to my ex-wife, originally—she's responsible for the terrible name. But she left him behind. So I adopted him. He's actually a cute little guy, once you get used to him."

Fernanda nodded politely, but in her mind she'd already packed her step-ferret off to boarding school. No skinny rodent could mar her happiness. Parker was everything she'd been looking for. She could envision their lives together—two adorable children, an ample spread on Park Avenue, and a home in Hobe Sound so she no longer had to stay with her mother. She'd quit her job to focus full-time on perfecting her body, decorating their homes, getting the kiddies into the right schools. She was enjoying these reveries when the front edge of her skate caught on a thick groove; Fernanda's body pitched forward and then, overcompensating to find balance, wobbled backward. Mere nanoseconds before she connected with the ice, Parker caught her with both arms. If you were watching from the sidelines, it appeared that Fernanda Fairchild had swooned.

Eloise had no idea what to make of the attractive young woman sitting next to her in the backseat of the Mercedes. Trip had badgered her into spending "girl time" with Lucy Ellis, so now Raoul was driving the two of them to a rose-scented Fifth Avenue spa. Not that she would expect sympathy, but it wasn't the way Eloise would have chosen to spend her afternoon.

"You probably have a strange impression of me," Lucy said, breaking the silence. She played with the cuff of her buttery cashmere sweater and then smoothed her trousers, a dove gray. She seemed stiff and uncomfortable in her clothes, like a little girl in a starchy Christmas dress.

"What? Of course not! You seem, um, very nice." Eloise glanced out the window as Bergdorf Goodman flew past, not knowing what else to say. How could she not have doubts about the kind of girl who would submit to Wyatt's weird social experiment? Or skepticism about someone who would strive to be a socialite, lamest of all ambitions? Fashion styling wasn't exactly Doctors Without Borders, but Eloise took pride in her independence.

"Thank you again for letting me stay at your place," Lucy said as they said goodbye to Raoul and headed toward the spa's golden doors. "I still feel bad, kicking you out of your own—"

"Don't! Seriously, it was about time that Trip and I moved in together. It's been great." She smiled, hiding her irritation at Lucy's need for reassurance. Truthfully, she didn't love having a total stranger set up camp in her guest bedroom and bathe in her antique claw-foot tub. But since Lucy's arrival had finally pushed Trip into co-habitation, Eloise wasn't complaining. And Lucy would be there for only three months, anyway. After that, according to Trip, she'd be rereleased into the wild—and Eloise would probably put her apartment on the market.

"Well, thanks." Lucy seemed to sense that the subject should be dropped. "So Wyatt said you're a stylist?"

Eloise nodded. "Yup, I've been doing it since college. The travel can get exhausting, but I really love the work." They approached the stern-looking receptionist. "I think the reservation is under Peters. Facials and massages."

"Did Wyatt mention that I want to be a designer?" Lucy asked as the woman led them back into the luxe changing room, where two adjacent lockers bore their names.

Eloise couldn't help crooking an eyebrow. If there was one thing that irked her more than vapid socialites, it was vapid socialites who thought they could just throw out a shingle and be the next Diane von Furstenberg. Like it was a snap, or something. They didn't realize it took talent, vision, the capacity for endless hard work. "Good for you!"

she said with false enthusiasm, hoping she wouldn't be asked to open up her Rolodex. Ugh.

"Well, we'll see. It's my crazy dream. I've been making clothes since I could walk, practically, and I've got a portfolio full of my more ambitious sketches—the couture stuff I've never been able to afford to make. I know I'm just a random girl from Minnesota and the odds of my 'making it' are next to nil, but I can't seem to give it up."

Eloise slipped into the fluffy white robe that had been hanging on the hook in her locker. She decided to speak her mind. "So Wyatt is supposed to be your golden ticket? It takes more than social status to make it in the fashion business."

Lucy blushed, but nodded vigorously. "You're right. But I couldn't seem to get beyond factory work with Nola Sinclair on my own."

"You worked for Nola?"

Lucy hesitated. "Yeah, actually . . . do you remember the cater-waiter who crashed through her runway last month?"

"Who could forget?"

"That was, um . . ." Lucy finished her sentence by pointing at herself.

Eloise's heart flew out to the girl. "That was *you*? You poor thing! I felt so bad after that happened—it looked like it really hurt. And I'm sure Nola wasn't easy on you—"

"She fired me. I felt stuck before it happened, and after, of course, I felt even more stuck. So I started to consider Wyatt's idea about becoming a socialite. When the experiment's over, I'm hoping I can get a job working for an emerging designer, you know, like Thakoon or Isabel Toledo—someone I can really learn from. It just seems like those jobs come more easily when you have social connections. My ultimate goal is to become a designer myself—someday."

Not totally illogical, Eloise had to admit. "If you want to be a designer, you need to know your stuff. You need the talent, the skill, the vision."

"I know," Lucy said. "It's overwhelming, but I want it so badly."

They were ushered into the facial salon, where the air was laced with eucalyptus and a waterfall trickled down a pebbled wall. Eloise found herself liking Lucy more than she'd expected to. They reclined on terry-cloth chaises for the facials. "Wanna play a game? Match the following fashion adage to the icon who first said it. 'I always wear my sweater back-to-front. It is much more flattering.'"

"Diana Vreeland. Next!" Lucy grinned.

"'A woman who doesn't wear perfume has no future.'"

"Coco Chanel."

"'In difficult times, fashion is always outrageous.'"

Lucy looked momentarily stumped. "Okay, I'm going to need a hint on this one."

"Italian, collaborated with Dalí, mother of Marisa Berenson—"

"Elsa Schiaparelli, of course. I knew that—"

"Who's credited with inventing the miniskirt?"

"Um, Mary Quant? At least, she brought it mainstream from the streets of London."

Eloise was impressed. "So what's your style? As a designer, I mean?"

Lucy sighed as the facialist smeared her face with thick cream. "I guess it depends. I'm inspired to work in a new direction all the time. One day I'm trying a new take on the Hervé Léger bandage dress, the next day I'm reenvisioning a Chanel vintage flapper dress. You know, unpredictable."

First wrong answer she's given me, Eloise thought, *and the most important one by a long shot.* She'd never known a successful designer who flitted between styles. There could be shifts, sometimes dramatic ones, but not a whole new set of rules. No, that wouldn't work. Lucy Ellis would either figure that out, or she'd fail. But Eloise held her tongue. She'd just met the girl, and she'd already given her a lot.

"He wasn't at the Townsends', either?" asked Cornelia, swerving her silver Jaguar to narrowly avoid hitting a woman crossing Worth Avenue with a Bugaboo stroller. She tucked her phone under her chin and leaned on her horn.

"No show," Fernanda reported. "Nobody's seen him for two weeks. It is the most bizarre thing. You're sure his mother said he was in New York?"

"Positive. She was practically crying about how he'd 'abandoned her for Christmas.' Not that anybody could blame him for not wanting to spend time with that old bag of bones."

Fernanda lowered her voice. She shared her office at Christie's with two assistants and couldn't talk loudly, which always annoyed Cornelia. "But Channing told me that her maid is friendly with some Sant Ambroeus busboy who has been delivering a lot of food to Wyatt's. Apparently he's been holed up a lot with Trip."

"Just the two of them?" Cornelia asked, bracing for the name of her temporary replacement. Not that it mattered, but she wanted all the facts.

"That's what I hear. Honestly, I don't know how Eloise deals. It's bad enough that Trip won't commit—"

"Poor thing," Cornelia said. But she had no real sympathy. Eloise and Fernanda were two peas in the same hand-wringing pod—they let men call the shots and then moped when they didn't like the shots called. Cornelia whipped around the corner and pulled into the Rockmans' driveway, jamming the stick shift into park. She, on the other hand, was a woman of action.

"At least she and Trip finally moved in together," Fernanda said. "She's spending all her time at his place now. Finally brought her whole winter wardrobe."

"Listen, sweetie, I should jump. I just pulled in—"

"Hang on!" Fernanda said frantically. "I've been dying to share something fun. You remember Parker?"

"Of course I remember Parker." Cornelia rolled her eyes as she slammed the car door and strode toward the house. Fernanda had only been sweating the guy for months. "Almost fifty, big schnoz, divorced. What about him?"

"Actually, he's forty-five," Fernanda corrected. There was an unmistakable note of pride in her voice. "We're going out tonight for dinner. Our fifth date already! Last night he took me to the opera—"

"The opera? God, he *is* old."

"No, it was fabulous. *Candide*. And Park has the best seats—"

"Did he bring his ferret?" Cornelia squealed. "Tamsin told me about that thing. I'm sorry, but that's gotta be the creepiest pet ever."

"You're telling me, but—"

"Did he keep the ferret under his seat? In a little cage?"

"Cornelia, please. He's a lovely man. He cooked dinner for Mom and me, how cute is that? She adores him, of course. I know it's early, but it's really working."

"That's great. No, seriously, that's great. You sound excited, which is what matters." Cornelia held the phone away from her mouth. "Hey, Pablo! I'll be with you in one minute—Fern, sorry, that's my new Pilates instructor. He's waiting for me—"

"Go, go! Just had to share. See you this weekend. I'll call you when Mom and I land."

But Cornelia had already hung up. As she entered her parents' house, the frigid air-conditioned air sent goose bumps straight up both arms. She grabbed the mail that had been set aside for her on a sterling silver tray, kicked off her shoes, and headed for the media room.

She pulled the latest installment of *Townhouse* from the stack of mail and felt a splash of disappointment that she was no longer gracing the cover. The weekly's current cover boy was a grinning Theo Galt, resting one buttock on the edge of his Dordoni desk, under the headline GALT GETS GOTHAM. Behind him in the photo, Cornelia could discern a large framed photo of Theo sandwiched between Jay-Z and Beyoncé. She would have to call to congratulate him. And, of course, remind him that she was the next big thing to hit the music scene.

Flopping down in an armchair, she hungrily leafed through the glossy pages. There she was at the Philharmonic in that sexy Derek Lam dress that accentuated her skinny arm–to–C-cup ratio. And there was Wyatt next to her, at the *Townhouse* launch party—his tall-dark-and-handsome the perfect complement to her petite-blonde-and-beautiful. He had a bitter-lemon expression on his face and he wasn't looking at the camera, but one of his hands rested on her back. Staring at the candid photograph made her feel calmer. It reminded her of how perfect her life seemed to everyone who read the magazine—to the entire outside world.

And it made her more determined than ever to win Wyatt back. Then Fernanda could run off into the sunset with her divorced and decrepit troll-man, for all Cornelia cared. She wouldn't be alone.

14

Dorothea Hayes invites you to
dinner at home
800 Park Avenue, PH A
Wednesday, January 13th
Cocktails starting at 7 PM

Dottie Hayes, wearing a crimson dress and diamond studs the size of grapes, had been enjoying the serenity of the six o'clock hour with a stiff vodka gimlet when she heard her son come crashing through her front door.

"Mother! *Moooooother!*"

She cringed but remained silent. Did he expect her to holler back, as if they were playing a game of Marco Polo? Dottie shut her eyes and took a medicinal sip of her drink.

"I believe she's in the library, sir," Dottie heard Graciela confess.

"There you are!" Wyatt yelled, rushing in and immediately sucking all the tranquillity out. "This place always had too many goddamn rooms." His cheeks were flushed from the wintry evening, and as often, Dottie was taken aback by how much he looked like her late husband. They had the same thick shock of dark hair, the same tall, athletic build, and the same penetrating blue-gray eyes. But appearance was where the similarity ended. For as much as she loved her son, Dottie hadn't been lying to Cornelia about her assessment of Wyatt's shortcomings. Her son had been lost for years now, squandering his considerable talents by chasing the next good time, running through girlfriends. If she thought about it too much, it gave Dottie a deep ache. And so she forced herself not to think about it. She made herself accept that her son—her bright, handsome, brimming-with-potential only son—was more or less a flash in the pan. Maybe she'd failed Wyatt as a mother. In any case, it was too late. He was now close to forty and set in his ways.

"You've found me," Dottie sighed. "You're early. Scotch?"

"I'll help myself in a minute. I want to talk to you."

"That's nice," Dottie said. "Your absence at Christmas might have suggested otherwise." She'd been hurt that he hadn't made it down to Florida, even when she offered to fly him down private. Wyatt was all the family she had, if you didn't count her needle-nosed sister Lydia, a joyless woman who'd devoted her life to raising English springer spaniels and who refused to travel. "Well, it's good that you're here. Maybe I can convince you to behave yourself this evening. I'm not in the mood to be embarrassed."

"What makes you think I'll embarrass you?"

"Thirty-seven years of experience. You know your manners are atrocious, and it's a reflection on the woman who raised you."

"It can't be Margaret's fault entirely."

Dottie just rolled her eyes.

He sat down on the couch and rested his hand-sewn John Lobb shoes on the coffee table. "So I've got news. Big news. Harvard University Press is going to publish my first book. Alfred Kipling's going to edit it himself. I just signed the contracts."

Dottie gasped. "Wyatt, dear, that's wonderful!" Could it be true? Dottie hoped he was serious this time, that he'd found some purpose. It made her Christmas dinner for one seem like a worthwhile sacrifice. "Well, tell me, what's the topic?"

"It's an anthropological experiment, one that studies the influence of nature and nurture on social status. I'm chronicling the de-

velopment of a new alpha female. It's been occupying my every waking thought. And if my experiment works, it should make for a
groundbreaking book."

"Are you studying chimps again? Apes?"

"Humans. You know I've long been intrigued by how closely our
behavior mirrors that of our closest primate relatives. Anyway, you'll
get to meet her in a few minutes," Wyatt answered. "She's coming
with Trip and Eloise."

"*Her*?" Now Dottie's interest turned to concern. "And she's coming to my dinner party? I'll have to tell Graciela right away."

"I'll tell her. I think you'll like Lucy. She's wasn't born with a silver spoon in her mouth, but she's learned pretty fast which silver
fork to use. She has a certain . . . spirit."

Spirit, coming from her son, could mean a wide range of dinner
party–disruptive things. "This is so typical of you, Wyatt. Please tell
me she wasn't raised by wolves."

"No, no. By a single mother, blue collar, in Minnesota. You have
nothing to worry about. I've been grooming the girl for weeks, and it
seems to be sticking. Of course, we can't know for sure whether she's
adapted to her new role until she's thrown into a social gathering."

Dottie felt one of her headaches coming on. "I have no idea what
you're talking about, but I do know that you've picked the worst
night possible. An anthropological experiment at my dinner party—
honestly, Wyatt! For starters, where will I put her?"

"Next to me," Wyatt suggested. "That way I can keep an eye on
her. Make sure she doesn't drink from the finger bowl or try to clear
her own plate."

Dottie ran through the new arrangement quickly in her head. She
had a gift for seating tables that bordered on mathematical genius.
"Fine, then. What's her name?" she asked.

"Lucy Ellis. It won't be bad, I promise. I've taught her the social
graces—"

"How can a man without social graces possibly teach them? You,
who recently told my friend Millicent she resembled her French
pug?"

Wyatt just laughed. "I'll admit that wasn't my finest moment, but there've been studies showing that after a period of sustained proximity, humans and their pets—"

A maid in a blue uniform appeared in the doorway. "Guests, Mrs. Hayes."

"Thank you, Graciela. Will you ask Pammy to write out a place card for Lucy Ellis? She's to sit on Wyatt's right. Move Mimi Rutherford-Shaw between Bancroft Stevens and Roger Rosenthal. Thank God we happened to have a spare man at the table."

Wyatt rose with his mother. "Lucy doesn't know about the book, yet. And it's essential that nobody know the truth about her. My career hangs in the balance."

"Of course I won't say anything about your strange experiment. The poor girl. You think I need to be told not to embarrass one of my guests?"

"I appreciate your support, Mother."

"I'm not sure you have it, darling." Dottie let out a loud sigh. She had never been able to say no to her son, which explained a great deal.

"Martha, hello!" Wyatt said, leaning in to her cloud of Amarige to give the dour dowager a kiss. Martha Fairchild looked momentarily surprised to see him—he rarely made appearances at his mother's dinners—but quickly reset her expression to its customary jaded disinterest. Behind her stood Max and Fernanda, who struck Wyatt as being more overgrown children than adults. Max was exhibit A for the argument that generations of blue-blood inbreeding deoxygenated the bloodstream. And seeing the dark and shifty-eyed Fernanda, Wyatt was instantly on his guard. Fernanda, he knew, was enthralled by Cornelia, who had the cash and pizzazz that Fernanda furiously longed for. If he wasn't careful, she would report back to Cornelia every detail of the evening, including news of the tall, striking, and unfamiliar woman sitting at Wyatt's side. Wyatt wanted no publicity from tonight. It was best to keep Lucy's debut low-key, the way you took a new sailboat around the harbor before you raced her.

"So you're back from . . . where were you, again?" Fernanda asked.

"I was here." He knew she was fishing for information, so gave little.

"Well, we missed you at the Red Cross Ball. It was epic this year."

"I'm sure," Wyatt said. He glanced over Fernanda's bony shoulder to see if Trip, Eloise, and Lucy had arrived yet. Now that the high priests and priestesses of the social set had filled his mother's drawing room, Wyatt couldn't help but feel a little nervous about whether his protégée would sink or swim in these perilous waters. She was still so damned unpredictable.

With most of New York society away for the holidays, he'd risked taking her out to restaurants, where they'd dined unseen. Two nights ago they'd gone to Amaranth with Trip and Eloise. Wyatt had looked across the table at the refined, lovely young woman opposite him, holding her own in a conversation about an exhibition of Rembrandt drawings at the Metropolitan Museum of Art, which they had toured earlier in the day. Hours of walking with a Social Register on top of her head had cured Lucy of her heavy stride; she now moved as if she weren't ashamed of her height, and she didn't bend into an osteoporotic crouch to converse with Trip, who came up to her chin. The endless, grating phonetics lessons had rid her speech of thoughtless um's and that wide *a* that had made Wyatt resolve never to set foot on the Minnesota tundra.

Thanks to her daily double workouts, she'd slimmed down almost immediately, revealing a firm but womanly body. She would never be the willowy waif, but now she was slender and athletic, looking as though she'd spent Saturdays playing field hockey at Wellesley. She had a waist now, and when Wyatt recently had popped his head in on one of her workout sessions, he had no choice but to admire the long, lean line of her thighs. Thanks to her healthy eating, her exercise regimen, and weekly facials, her skin had a new glow. She knew what to talk about at a dinner party, which was essentially nothing, and she knew *how* to talk about it, which was with a demure disinterest. Equally important, she knew where she was supposed to come from: they'd rehearsed the details of her background so thoroughly that she'd started to take a certain pride in her family's imaginary timber fortune.

Still, the girl was a wild card. Just when he'd start to relax—
poof!—ol' Lucy Jo would be back, butchering one of the French
phrases he'd taught her to pepper into conversation, blowing her
nose at the table, bringing up how much things cost. She still smiled
too much and too indiscriminately for his liking, wore yoga pants
and sneakers when she had no intention of working out, and used
words like "classy" and "fancy." That same night at Amaranth, when
he'd caught her checking her teeth in the reflection of a butter knife,
Wyatt had seen the prospect of book publication go egg-shaped before his eyes. Without a triumphant ending, Wyatt knew the book
would fall flat. Not to mention, he'd lose his bet with Trip—his
watch and his pride. Tonight, he knew, could be the first victory in
his Lucy experiment, or it could be a decisive failure.

"Wyatt?" Fernanda asked, looking a little peeved. "I asked if you
were going to Tamsin and Henry's wedding?"

"Sorry," he said. "I'm a little distracted."

Fernanda laid a sympathetic hand on his arm. "No, I completely
understand. You're nervous about seeing Cornelia for the first time
since—"

The loud hum of chitchat all around them seemed to fall silent.
"What are you talking about?" Wyatt sputtered, causing Fernanda
to fall back on her heels. "Cornelia's not coming tonight!"

"What, didn't your mother tell you?"

"Will you excuse me for a moment?" Wyatt fixed his mother with
a death glare. She well knew the two of them had split; she'd even
approved of the breakup. What could she possibly have been thinking? Cornelia's presence tonight was more than a nuisance; it was
a potential disaster. Lucy wasn't ready for sniper fire yet. Wyatt
stepped back from Fernanda so fast he ground his heel into Max's
loafer, and then charged across the drawing room, pulling his
mother out of a conversation with the Dutch ceramics collector Lars
van Sever and his wife.

"How could you invite Cornelia into your home without telling
me?" he hissed. "I thought we were on the same page about her."

"We were. We are. The girl is a social juggernaut. Martha Fairchild
called to see if she could come, and wouldn't give up even when I told

her the table was already too full. Martha even offered to stay home herself so Cornelia could be here! Last time I invite the Fairchilds— live and learn. But I couldn't think of a graceful way to say no."

"Next time, how about *no*?"

Dottie laid her hand on Wyatt's arm and looked at her son with maternal concern. "I've never seen you this nervous. Do you care for this Lucy girl?"

Wyatt looked up to see Trip and Eloise in the doorway, with Lucy behind them, her dark hair gleaming against the oak woodwork. "She just walked in!" he exclaimed, feeling a fresh surge of panic. "Too late. I'll just have to keep them separated as much as I can." He took an urgent sip of his scotch. "And to answer your question, I care for my *book*. A premature encounter with Cornelia could jeopardize everything Lucy and I are working toward."

Dottie Hayes followed her son's gaze. Two steps behind Trip and Eloise, a statuesque young woman scanned the room with large, dark eyes. She wore a deep aubergine dress, belted at the waist to create a feminine silhouette. Her dark brown hair was smooth as a sheet of silk, and a saltwater pearl dropped off each earlobe. Complemented by a fabulous pair of Roger Vivier shoes, her legs looked about a mile long.

She was one of the most beautiful young women Dottie Hayes had ever seen.

"The book, of course," she said to her son.

The stern-faced ancestral portraits in Dottie's gargantuan drawing room glared at Lucy, reminding her how many fathoms she was out of her depth. If this classy crew knew who she really was, she'd be relegated to passing out champagne glasses. It had happened before.

She shivered and looked doubtfully at the other guests. It wasn't just that the crowd was impeccably dressed, although that they were. The men looked straight off Savile Row, their suits precisely tailored around the shoulders but not cinched and show-offy around the body, their silk neckties subdued but gleaming. But the women were the main attraction, turned out in gorgeous cocktail frocks and one-of-a-kind bejeweled shoes. Given the heady aura of opulence, the five-carat diamonds flashing from most earlobes managed to seem understated. Lucy's eyes fell on one older woman whose silvery hair and three strands of good pearls offset her dark velvet jacket as she stood next to a younger brunette with Maria Shriver cheekbones. The two of them looked vaguely familiar, but then the rich and powerful were New York's particular genre of celebrity.

These people have nothing to prove, Lucy thought. It struck her at that moment, after weeks of training, that she had finally grasped the essential difference between old and new money.

Like a toddler clutching her mother's skirt, Lucy stayed a cautious step behind Eloise as they hello-ed their way into Dottie's drawing room. Thank God for Eloise—since their day at the spa, her no-nonsense sweetness had been a refuge for Lucy against the tempests and squalls of Wyatt's demands. The two women had bonded quickly. Eloise had savvy and style, but was also more openhearted than Lucy had expected. Lucy had shared the true story of her life, from the discomforts of growing up the daughter of Rita the celebrity-addicted nail artist to her struggles to make it in Manhattan, and Eloise in turn had confided her frustrations with Trip, whom she adored but who seemed less likely to propose to her than was His Eminence the Cardinal of New York. If Eloise weren't here tonight, Lucy knew she would collapse into a little pile of purple silk—especially now that she glimpsed Wyatt's mother, so regal that she made Queen Elizabeth look like Sharon Osbourne. Lucy recognized her from the family photos Wyatt had on the walls of his study.

"Try to relax," Eloise whispered, giving Lucy a warm smile. "Everyone will love you, I promise. You have nothing to worry about."

Wyatt's mother came right up to greet them. "Eloise, your dress is marvelous." She drew out her *r*'s. "You know exactly what works."

Eloise smiled at her. "Thanks, Dottie. This is our friend Lucy Ellis."

"A pleasure to meet you," said Dottie, extending her hand. Her spun-white hair was cut into an elegant, understated bob, reminding Lucy of a meringue. "I'm Wyatt's mother."

"Thank you very much for including me, Mrs. Hayes," Lucy said, shaking her hand stiffly. She desperately wished she could be as laid-back as Eloise; instead she sounded as if she were reading from a teleprompter. "Your home is, um, magnificent." There was that *um* again. She was glad Wyatt wasn't within earshot.

"Call me Dottie, please. That's very kind of you. It's in the process of being redecorated, so, you know, it's a bit of a mess at the moment."

Lucy scanned the room. Not so much as an Hermès ashtray out of place. "If this qualifies as a mess, I'd hate for you to see my closet!"

Dottie laughed politely. "What will you have to drink, dear?"

"Oh, whatever's easy."

"Anything's easy," Dottie answered.

Judging by the flanks of waitstaff poised to serve, Lucy guessed that was true. "Well, um, perhaps a Singapore sling?" She'd blurted out the first fancy, umbrella-adorned drink that came into her head, but judging by her hostess's uncomfortable reaction, she'd blurted wrong.

"A Singapore sling?" Dottie frowned. "I'm sorry, I'm not sure—"

"Or maybe some champagne?" Eloise suggested.

"Oh, yes, that would be perfect," Lucy said, relieved. "I'd love some champagne, if you have it." She was so nervous she was making basic blunders. *Champagne* was the official drink of socialites, duh! Had Nola's party taught her nothing? But Wyatt hadn't told her what to order during the cocktail portion of the evening. What else had he neglected to mention?

"Of course. The server will be right back with it. Excuse me a moment—I see the mayor and his fiancée." Dottie swept away.

"I don't belong here." Lucy suddenly felt overwhelmed. "Everyone keeps looking at me. They all look so perfect. So expensive. So—"

"And you don't?" Eloise subtly directed her attention to the large antique mirror on the wall next to them. "People are looking at you because you're beautiful. But listen, I do know how you feel. As a crowd, they can be a bit imposing. There are good people mixed in. Oh, like Mimi Rutherford-Shaw. You'll like her, I promise." She waved at a mammiferous blonde in pink Pucci. Everyone seemed to adore Mimi, Lucy immediately noticed, and not just because her proximity made them seem thinner. Even in this stuffy environment, she appeared to be having the time of her life.

"El!" Mimi came barreling over.

"Mimi, you've got to meet my friend Lucy."

"Aren't you the most gorgeous thing?" said Mimi, kissing Lucy hello. Wyatt had given Lucy the rundown on Mimi, as he had on many of the usual suspects. She was a proud southern belle whose down-home drawl had grown more pronounced the longer she lived in New York City. By now most people could hardly make out what she was saying. "Pleased to make your acquaintance. Where're you from, doll?"

"Chicago," said Lucy, cringing. She hated lying, especially to someone who seemed so friendly, but she had to stick to the script. It was part of the deal. "And I'm guessing you're from the South?"

"Atlanta, born and bred. But I married a Yankee, and he gets the bends if we go below Virginia."

"Lucky for us," Eloise said. "Lucy, Mimi founded an amazing nonprofit called Baby Love. Maybe you'd be interested in getting involved—"

Before Lucy could form a response, Wyatt descended upon her. He was dressed in an oxford gray suit she'd never seen him wear, and it fit perfectly. "I've been trying to get your attention!" he said.

"Wyatt, hi. You know Mimi?" Lucy asked politely.

Wyatt glanced over. "Hey, Mims. Is Jack here?"

"No, he's got another work dinner. Second one this week! Honestly, I *hope* that man is having an affair. Otherwise, he works too damn much." Mimi paused, as though feeling a sudden shift in the room's energy. Lucy felt it too, and turned around.

Cornelia Rockman, never one to downplay an entrance, had swept into the drawing room. Finding an opening in the crowd, she paused, smiling lightly as though her photograph might be taken at any moment. Which, given her ubiquity on the party pages that Wyatt had assigned Lucy to read daily, seemed entirely possible.

"Cornelia Rockman, right?" she whispered to Eloise. She recognized the girl from her rainy Nola Sinclair night, when she'd so brazenly swiped Lucy's cab. And of course, Wyatt had given her a full debriefing on the reigning Queen Bee.

"Yeah. Wyatt broke up with her last month. I'm surprised Dottie invited her tonight."

Wyatt's ex? Wyatt had left out that little detail! Lucy looked at Cornelia with a mixture of curiosity, envy, and professional interest. She was stunning, of course. She was channeling a 1950s housewife—a very expensive 1950s housewife—in a cocktail dress that seemed to hug every curve of her body. It was as if Christian Dior had arisen from the grave long enough to dress her, just to remind the world what feminine beauty really was. As a designer, Lucy had to admire how well Cornelia wore her clothes, and how she clearly knew what cuts flattered her slim but ample body. She made no eye contact with the other guests, even though half the eyes in the room were now on her. Judging by Cornelia's carriage, you'd have guessed the dinner was being held in her honor.

Meanwhile, Wyatt's face had taken on a pink tinge. Lucy could feel him tense as Cornelia, after deigning to greet a few of the other guests, approached their little group. "Wyatt!" she said, pressing both his cheeks gently with her own. Lucy watched the reunion with unblinking attention. She'd never seen a more gorgeous pair of people. Wyatt had actually dumped this woman? She wasn't the sweetest soul in the world—but then, was he? Cornelia seemed to possess all the physical perfection and poise that he was trying to drum into Lucy. "I'm glad to see you," she said.

"Why did you insist on coming tonight?" Wyatt demanded, jaw tightly clenched.

"Your mother included me, of course," Cornelia answered smoothly. She twisted a mammoth emerald that she wore on a long gold chain. "But if it makes you too uncomfortable, I can leave."

"Don't flatter yourself. I'm perfectly fine." He seemed to collect himself. "Lucy, this is Cornelia Rockman. Cornelia, Lucy Ellis."

"Pleasure," Cornelia said, sizing up Lucy the way a cheetah sizes up a gazelle. If she recognized Lucy from that night in the rain, she didn't show it.

"So good to meet you!" Lucy said, sticking out her hand. "I love your dress."

Cornelia looked down at Lucy's hand as if she were offering her a dead pigeon. Then she leaned over and kissed Lucy twice, off the coast of each cheek.

"Shall we see what my mother wants?" Wyatt asked, seizing Lucy by the elbow and propelling her across the room.

15

Wyatt's Book Notes:

In the early twentieth century, the Norwegian zoologist Thorleif Schjelderup-Ebbe described a system of social dominance among flocks of poultry, known as the "pecking order." He observed that subordinate birds refused to feed until the more dominant birds had finished. Similarly, in our modern society, good manners dictate that guests wait until their host takes the first bite before starting to eat. Unfortunately, I had neglected to tell L. that bit of information.

*C*ornelia had to agree that Dottie's dining room had never looked more elegant, the table gently illuminated by towering silver candelabras and draped in vermilion linens. The visual feast was topped off by an heirloom china collection that was making Martin Matheson of Christie's—Fernanda's boss—drool. All in all, it was the perfect backdrop for her overdue reunion with Wyatt.

"Your mother must be up to something," Cornelia said flirtatiously as she and Wyatt found their seats next to each other. Of course, she'd switched the seat cards herself just moments before, stealing into the dining room before anybody else came in. Now that Lucy person was next to the duke of dull, Max Fairchild, and Cornelia could have Wyatt all to herself. No random interloper was going to thwart her efforts to win him back.

"You switched the cards," Wyatt said. He didn't look amused.

"What if I did?" Cornelia cooed, a bit unnerved by how easily he saw through her. "We need to talk. This is ridiculous, don't you think? People don't break up over one minor misunderstanding."

"This isn't the time or place," Wyatt said. He turned toward Esther Michaels on his right, an old family friend who'd been among those responsible for the restoration of Central Park in the 1970s. That left Cornelia with nobody to talk to but the drearily intellectual Morgan Ware, who was an ex-vice chairman of the Federal Reserve. As Morgan droned on with his doom-and-gloom economic forecast—apparently nobody had clarified that this was a dinner *party*—Cornelia felt the warmth of Wyatt's body next to hers. A thrill ran all the way down to her pewter-colored stilettos. She couldn't deny it—he was hot when he played hard to get. She crossed her leg and moved her foot so it would gently—seemingly accidentally—brush his leg. More electric current. He moved his leg away.

So he wants me to work for it, Cornelia thought with a sly smile. She turned back to Morgan, pretending to listen.

Stranded on the table's opposite bank, Lucy looked helplessly across at Wyatt, wishing he were beside her, guiding the conversation, giving her the little verbal and facial cues they had rehearsed in preparation for this night. She felt as if she had been abandoned in a foreign country where everyone but her spoke Lockjaw.

"You look so familiar to me!" Martha Fairchild, seated on the other side of her son, declared. She tilted her head, then pushed Max back in his chair so she could have an unobstructed view of the new girl. "I feel sure we've met before, but I can't think where."

"You look familiar to me. And Max—you do, too." She'd seen him before, she was sure of it. Maybe on the party pages. That was probably it.

Max fixed his sky-blue eyes on her. "Really? I feel sure that I would remember meeting you before."

Is this hottie actually flirting *with me?* She'd noticed Max glance her way several times during cocktail hour, and he seemed delighted to be seated next to her for dinner. Lucy didn't know which was scarier: that Max might be on to her, or that he might be into her. Wyatt had warned her about talking too much to any unattached men she might meet tonight. "They'll pretend to be interested in your life," he'd cautioned, "and before you know it you'll be giving them directions to downtown Dayville. Less is more."

"Ellis is your family name?" Martha asked, leaning past her son again. "Who are your parents, dear?"

"My family's from Chicago. You might know my father, Raymond Ellis." Lucy repeated verbatim what Wyatt had told her to say. He knew nobody would recognize the name, but he also knew nobody would admit that. It was enough, Wyatt suggested, that Lucy convey the distinct impression that Raymond Ellis was a person that every person *should* know.

"Of course," Martha said. "How is he?"

"Oh, same as ever," Lucy said with feigned affection. Maybe Wyatt was on to something. "And where are you guys from?" Oops. *You guys* was Lucy-Jo–speak. But the Fairchilds didn't seem to notice.

"On the Fairchild side, New York. But my mother was an Edgell." Lucy detected the pride in Martha's voice. It must mean something to be an Edgell. Maybe some of these superrich folks had something to prove after all. "Most of my family is still in Boston, although there's a subset living in Paris."

"Paris, how wonderful!" Lucy had long dreamed of visiting the fashion mecca. "Have you ever been over to visit them?"

"Of course. Many times."

"Is the city as beautiful as it looks in movies? I'm dying to go."

"Paris?" Martha asked, seemingly confused by the question. "You've never been?"

Stupid. Lucy felt her stomach drop. "Um, of course I've been to Paris. But not since I was a little girl, I'm afraid, and I barely remember it." Martha seemed to accept the answer, and she drifted into conversation with Lars van Sever as their first course was placed in front of them.

"Is that, um, raw fish?" Lucy whispered to Max, staring grimly at her plate. It looked as if it had been cut from the belly of some unidentifiable creature and rushed directly to the dining room without benefit of a saucepan. It glistened in the candlelight.

"Yeah. Tuna tartare." He smiled. "Not your thing?"

"I've never had it," Lucy admitted. "I don't do raw. Not after my friend Doreen got such violent food poisoning from the sushi place on her corner that she lost thirty pounds."

"Thirty pounds?" Max repeated incredulously.

"More, actually. That was just the first time."

"She got food poisoning more than once? Same place? Why'd she keep going back?"

"Oh, Doreen. She wanted to lose ninety pounds in time for her sister's wedding."

"You're joking." Max ventured a smile. "I mean, she didn't really do that."

"She did!"

He seemed at a loss for words, but then he nodded. "I can see why you'd hesitate." As for Martha, she'd tuned in late and was gazing down at her plate with what looked like a brand-new, Lucy-supplied perspective on raw fish. "Here's some bread," said Max to Lucy. "I think you're safe with that."

"I should at least try a bite, don't you think? I don't want to insult our host." Lucy bravely stuck her fork into the quivering tower of pink flesh. She brought it to her lips, held her breath, and slid a few of the slimy chunks to the back of her mouth.

The fish seemed to return to life in her mouth. She struggled to swallow, but her throat wouldn't allow it. It fought the fish with loud, guttural sounds.

"Are you choking?" Max jumped up from his seat and pulled Lucy out of hers, quickly locking his arms around her rib cage for the Heimlich. "Stay calm!" he shouted. But now Lucy *was* actually choking a bit, thanks to his rescue efforts, and after two hoists from Max, two fish chunks came flying out of her mouth, across the beautifully set table, before landing squarely on the décolletage of Cornelia Rockman.

Lucy wished there was a runway she could fall into. The room was silent as a mortuary as all eyes turned from Lucy to Cornelia.

"You're okay now," said Max, proud of himself.

"Am I?" She glanced at Wyatt, who seemed to be avoiding her eyes, disclaiming ownership, and then looked apologetically toward the head of the table. Dottie was doing a poor job at hiding her horror. "I am so, so sorry, Dottie—Mrs. Hayes. Dottie. And Cornelia! Here, let me get that off you—" She rushed around the table, napkin outstretched, but Cornelia held up both hands to ward her off.

"That couldn't have been more disgusting," Cornelia hissed, and Lucy, not sure what else to do, slunk back to her seat.

When she sat down, Max laid a hand on her shoulder. "You tried. I'm witness to the fact that you really tried to eat that fish."

She glanced across the table fearfully, but Wyatt kept his eyes on his tartare. Only Trip and Eloise flashed her their sympathetic smiles.

"Binkie," Dottie asked, when the two women retreated for a moment to her bedroom to smooth their hair and share a secret cigarette, just before the main course was to be served. "What on earth is a Singapore sling?"

As the roast pheasant plates were cleared away, Wyatt monitored Lucy as she talked with Morgan Ware and nodded in profound interest as he held forth on why young ladies as lovely as herself should consider inflation-indexed or municipal bonds for their portfolio. Seeing as she couldn't get in much trouble with Ware, who never let anyone get a word in edgewise, Wyatt slipped down the long hallway that led to his old bedroom. Going into the room still decorated with his adolescent collection of poisonous stuffed frogs, a taxidermied rhesus monkey with glowing red eyes, and a genuine Native American talking stick that his father had brought back from Alaska after buying oil leases from the Eskimos, Wyatt sat down on the king-size bed where he had slept his first eighteen years and lit a cigarette—the first of the evening. He might smoke illegally in public places, but he dare not light up in front of his mother.

He exhaled and sighed. This Lucy-training was hard work. And, on a night like this, nerve-racking. Not only had he introduced his protégée to the crème de la crème of society, but he'd inadvertently inflicted Cornelia upon her, which was like introducing a bunny rabbit to a fox. They'd been lucky to escape with only the regurgitated tuna.

Overall, Lucy had acquitted herself well. Even his mother had been impressed, Wyatt suspected. That clod Max Fairchild had mooned over her; Morgan Ware had practically offered her a government-guaranteed loan.

Of course, Wyatt still had work to do. When Lucy got nervous she moved too fast, used her hands to talk, and ate actual food off her plate. And she laughed too easily. Max Fairchild had never said anything remotely clever or funny in his life, as far as Wyatt knew, and yet Lucy had been in stitches for the better part of dinner. He would have to remind her to curb her friendliness in social situations.

Still, he thought, as he blew smoke toward the moose head above his bed, she had what it took. Which meant he'd have what he needed for his book. He extinguished his cigarette on an old Snapple cap he'd kept in the top drawer since boarding school, then pulled out the ziplock bag he'd remembered to bring and dumped in the butt and the ashes. *His book.* Contrary to what his mother might think, that was what he cared about.

"Remember Camp Wokonoba?"

"Of course." Fernanda grinned. As a girl she'd lived for camp. She and Cornelia had first bonded there, despite their age difference. "We snuck out of our cabin every single night—"

"Do you remember the little trick we played on that heifer Penelope?"

Fernanda tapped a finger to her lips, trying to pull up the memory. They'd terrorized a lot of girls that summer. "We gave her a mullet while she was sleeping?"

"No, no, no. Remember you stuck your apple pie à la mode under Penelope before she plopped down in the mess hall?"

"Ah, right." Fernanda grinned. "A classic."

Cornelia squeezed her arm. "Look—Dottie's serving crème brûlée for dessert."

"Delicious." Fernanda glanced across the dining room. Lucy must have gone to the powder room, leaving her chair open for attack. Fernanda hustled wordlessly toward her brother and took a seat, first swiping a large blob of brûlée off the plate. "Having fun, Max? You seem rather taken with your dinner partner." Carefully, silently, she deposited the eggy custard on the chair behind her. Fernanda felt the familiar rush she got whenever Cornelia pushed her into mischief.

"Oh, hi there!" Lucy had returned, smiling widely. "You're Max's sister, right?"

Fernanda stood. "Sorry, sorry, I stole your seat!" she said with false cheeriness, guiding Lucy to sit down without looking. "Fernanda, right. Nice to meet you."

Heading back to her seat, Fernanda flashed Cornelia a triumphant smirk. Dottie had wedged her in between two female guests, instead of one of the eligible men, which made Fernanda feel slightly better about destroying one of her Scalamandré-upholstered dining room chairs.

Cornelia cast a cutting little smile in Lucy's direction as the guests reclaimed their coats. Then her eyes narrowed. "Oh, dear! I think you might have sat in something," she announced loudly enough for the other guests to turn and look.

Lucy whipped around to check out her backside. Sure enough, a huge smear of crème brûlée now covered the seat of her beautiful silk dress. "My dress!" she shrieked, eyes wide with panic. "It cost, like, a thousand bucks! I've never even worn it before! I'm going to throw up, I swear to God." She hopped around in a circle, a bit like a dog chasing his own tail.

Wyatt bolted to her side. "Calm down," he said. "Thanks for a lovely evening, Mother." He helped Lucy with her coat, hustling her along toward the elevator.

He hates me, she thought miserably. Lucy felt exhausted from nervousness. *I'll never fit into this world. I should just save us both the disappointment and back out now.*

Max caught her attention as they waited for the elevator doors to open. "Hey! I'm sorry about your dress."

"Thanks," Lucy said quietly. "I know I shouldn't mention how much things cost, but—"

"Lucy—" Wyatt warned her over his shoulder.

"No, it's nice to meet someone who actually appreciates the value of a dollar. My sister and Cornelia, they practically toss their clothes after one wear."

"Seriously? I make a lot of my own clothes, so they mean something to me." Wyatt suddenly had a grip on her elbow. She stopped herself short. She'd almost forgotten she was pretending to be someone else. "It was nice to meet you," she said, as she and Wyatt wedged themselves into the elevator next to Eloise and Trip. Her eyes met Max's briefly as the doors shut.

"Someone's got an admirer!" Eloise teased.

Despite her many failures, not to mention Wyatt's stony silence, Lucy couldn't help but feel a tinge of happiness as the elevator plunged down to the lobby. At least she'd managed to make a favorable impression on one person that evening. And a handsome one person at that.

16

Bright, cultured, beautiful, and the heiress of a major timber fortune . . . have you met her yet? If not, you will soon—and you're in for a delight. Lucia Haverford Ellis, graduate of Miss Dillard's and old chum of Wyatt Hayes (they're still just chums, if you believe them) has burst onto the New York social scene like a much-needed breath of fresh air.

—Rex Newhouse, www.rexnewhouse.com

I do *not* get it." Cornelia speared a fork through a bite of veal and shoved it between her glossy lips. Then she grabbed a roll and tore off a significant piece, plunging it in olive oil. "Did you see him put his hand on the small of her back and sort of glide her around the room? Totally trying to get to me. It's beyond obvious."

Uh-oh, Fernanda thought. *Cornelia downing carbs is never a good sign.* She looked around Fred's to see if anyone was watching. Cornelia had become a semi-celebrity, and Fernanda didn't want rumors of her friend's distress-eating spreading from Barneys to the rest of the civilized world.

"Why aren't you touching your food?" Cornelia stabbed at her veal so viciously her friend shuddered.

"I didn't notice any lower-back thing," Fernanda said, cramming her mouth with a bite of chop-chop salad. She hoped the next table was out of earshot.

"Whatever. He brought her to his mother's house. What is that about?"

"She told Max that they're practically family. Old friends. Nothing romantic between them."

"Like family?" Cornelia took another bite of her roll and lowered her voice to a hiss. "Please. I lost my V to my 'cousin' Selden. Don't be so naïve. This Lucy chick's got her gold-digging hooks into him."

"Well, she doesn't hold a Rigaud candle to you," Fernanda said. "I'm sure he'll come to his senses." *At least Cornelia didn't read Rex Newhouse's blog today,* thought Fernanda, *or she'd be flying off the handle.* Her personal assistant must have wisely decided not to print it out with the rest of her morning reads (ever since a Parisian dermatologist had warned Cornelia that sitting in front of a computer could prematurely age her skin, she'd hired a girl to surf the Web for her). Rex had devoted an entire post to Lucia Haverford Ellis. Clearly, he was just as enamored with the newcomer as Max and Wyatt Hayes were. In the short time since Dottie's dinner party, Lucy had shown up on Wyatt's arm at three different events. To make matters worse, she'd been flawlessly beautiful and heavily photographed at each one. She called to mind a young Katharine Hepburn, thought Fernanda—the slightly boyish, strong beauty that only good genes could account for.

"Uh, waiter?" Cornelia heaved an irritated sigh, holding up the bread basket for a refill. "I know he will, but when? It's been six weeks already."

Fernanda made neutral noises and took another bite of salad. She was running out of comforting words. As usual, Cornelia hadn't asked about her budding romance with Parker Lewis, and bringing it up would have been insensitive to her friend's current heartache. She pushed her thoughts elsewhere. "How was Tamsin's bachelorette?"

"Misery. Her friends from Trinity put together this horrible bar crawl—we had to drive around the city on a 'party bus' and wear sombreros and act like we weren't roasting in cheese-ball hell."

Fernanda tried again. "Is Tam getting excited for the wedding?"

"Getting emaciated is more like it. She looks like a blonde bobble-head. Really let the Adderall thing get away from her. It's super tragic."

Fernanda nodded. "Do you think it'd be wildly too soon to bring Parker to the wedding?" Oops. She had Parker on the brain, and the question she'd been weighing for days had just kind of popped out. "I don't know, it would be really fun to have him there—"

"Are you insane?" Cornelia asked. "Definitely, definitely too soon."

"You're probably right." Fernanda couldn't help feeling disappointed, but it was sage advice. "Plus I'd hate to call Tamsin two weeks before the wedding, pleading for a plus one."

"And there'll be a lot of cute guys there—all the New York boys plus the Palm Beach crowd, and Henry Baker's San Fran people. You don't want to put all your eggs in one basket, Fern. I mean, Parker did just get divorced. He's probably not looking for anything serious right now. I don't want to see you get hurt again."

Fernanda swallowed. She knew Cornelia was just looking out for her, but sometimes her best friend had a knack for saying exactly what Fernanda didn't want to hear. "You're probably right. It just feels different this time."

Cornelia rolled her eyes. "You say that every time, right before you go 'method' and start acting like a total stranger. Remember Brice, that lax-player from Dartmouth? You hid your Gucci and started doing keg stands every night. Then for Mark, you became, like, this silent geisha, until he dumped you for his intern. And then Armstrong, that club promoter—God, that was the worst. You had to spend a month at Promises, remember, to get him—and everything that came with him—out of your system."

"My track record is lousy, I know." Fernanda was not enjoying Cornelia's guided tour down memory lane. "But that's the thing about Parker. He's so laid-back, I feel like I can be myself around him. You're right, though, I know you're right. Why rush it?"

"Exactly," Cornelia agreed, sitting back in her chair. "You don't think Wyatt would bring Skankerella, do you?"

"He wouldn't!"

"He'd better not." Cornelia swallowed the rest of her roll. "It's bad enough that he's going to see me in that hideous bridesmaid gown. I'll never forgive Tamsin for choosing it. Not a drop of sex appeal. But at least it might keep her father from groping me in the receiving line." Cornelia's BlackBerry buzzed on the table. "Hi, Daph," she said, holding up a manicured finger to Fernanda. "What do you mean, his *wife doesn't want me there*. I've got to be there. Howard Galt's sixtieth birthday is all anyone's been talking about for weeks. I can't miss it." She cocked her head. Fernanda could hear Daphne's high-pitched voice yammering. "Fine, work on it. And I'll see you tomorrow at two. Have your assistant Berry me Dafinco's address."

"I still can't believe you're going to have your own perfume," Fernanda said when she'd hung up. "Like SJP or J-Lo—"

"Please. We're only selling *Socialite* at Bergdorf, Barneys, and Saks Fifth Avenue—each bottle costs at least $250, the glass is handblown in Italy."

"Handblown. Amazing. I can't wait."

Cornelia reached across the table to spear Fernanda's two remaining croutons. "So Howard Galt's birthday party is supposed to be major. But his lame-ass new wife doesn't want me there. Like I'm still interested in that dinosaur—I'm *so* over my old guy phase. Whatever. Can we shop? My stylist has been pulling up the pukiest stuff lately. Even the stuff I have to pay for is hid. You've got to help me."

"I'd love to!" Fernanda said. All of Barneys was underneath them and she'd called in sick at Christie's that morning. "I need something, too. Parker wants us to have dinner with some of his friends from—"

"You're the best!" cheered Cornelia. "Your turn to pick up lunch, sweetie?"

Fernanda tried not to mind. "You bet," she said, waving for the check.

Wyatt, wearing only a towel, padded across the white-tiled floor at the Racquet Club. After a full morning at his computer, composing the early chapters of his book, he was looking forward to his steam-sauna-pool routine. He was *really* working again; his deal with Harvard University Press had been made official last week. If *The Overnight Socialite* became the crossover academic-and-commercial knockout he and Kipling thought it could be, it would be worth all his efforts.

Max Fairchild, also clad in a towel, was an intrusion on these thoughts. "Wyatt! I was hoping to run into you, man."

Wyatt grimaced. Judging by Max's absurdly chiseled physique, the guy spent way too much time working out. "How are you?" he asked, hoping desperately that Max wouldn't try to keep the conversation going. He really needed to unwind.

No such luck. "Well, I'm good. I mean, I'm okay. But I was wondering about something. Er, *someone*. Are you dating Lucy? The girl you brought to your mother's house?"

"Lucy? No, she's just an old friend." Wyatt recited the party line, but he also felt territorial. The last thing Lucy needed was a distraction.

"Okay, that's what she told me, too. So you wouldn't have a problem with my taking her out?" Max looked elated.

"I wouldn't have a problem with your *asking* her out," Wyatt replied. "But don't be upset if she puts you off. She's very serious about her work. Doesn't have much time for a personal life."

Max nodded. "Well, I've got to try. She's one of the cooler girls I've met in a long time. You going to the steam room, too?"

"Sauna," Wyatt decided. He'd had enough of Max Fairchild. "See you around."

"She should call this *Spill in Aisle Three*," Lucy muttered, looking at one of the pieces with open bewilderment. Wyatt stifled a laugh. They'd crossed the threshold into the art exhibition of new works by Libet Vance. It was already filled with downtown galleristas posing thoughtfully in front of the installations.

Libet, daughter of a famous bad-boy artist, had expressed herself by configuring pieces of whole fruit—pineapples, mangos, Asian pears—into what could be roughly described as sculpture. Some of the bananas were beginning to spot with brown—a giveaway that the artist had thrown together her entire show that week. Libet

might view it as art, thought Lucy, but most people she knew would
consider it last Monday's breakfast.

Wyatt looked at her critically. "Are you chewing gum? Spit it out!
You look like a cow chewing her cud."

Lucy sighed. She and Wyatt had been out several times this
week, and each time he found something minuscule to freak out
over. She spit her fluorescent Bubbalicious into the palm of her
hand. "Are you in an especially bad mood tonight, or is it me?"

"Throw it out! What if someone wants to shake your hand?"

Lucy just laughed and tossed it into the trash can behind the bar.
"It's gum, Wyatt. Do you honestly think people are paying such close
attention?"

"Of course they are. You just entered a party on my arm." He gestured toward two photographers, currently photographing Libet and
her father in front of a wreath of mangos and kiwis. "They'll zero in
on us next, just watch." Lucy straightened her dress, a bronzed-
jacquard sheath that Eloise had pulled for her. It set off her olive
skin and dark hair perfectly. "Now follow me, I want you to meet
Rex Newhouse," Wyatt said. "You need to thank him for his profile."

"So how are things going with Wyatt and his new girl?" probed
Binkie Howe. She and Dottie were catching up over cocktails at the
Colony Club. "He seemed smitten at your dinner party. Oh, was
Cornelia fuming!"

"They're just friends," Dottie said. That was what Wyatt wanted
her to say, wasn't it? It was easier than the truth, that was for sure.

"Friends, my foot. He had that glow, Dot. That glow you and his
father used to have. I've seen it all before!"

The mention of her late husband made Dottie's heart ache, as it
always did. How she wished her son could find that kind of love.
Instead, he was taking advantage of a poor girl who didn't have family or friends around to protect her. The day after her party, she'd
cornered him at his apartment and begged him to reconsider his actions. What would happen to Lucy after Wyatt's little experiment
had run its course? How would Lucy feel when he revealed her as

a fraud, an impostor? Wyatt had spewed some nonsense about making sure Lucy found a nice job working for some designer, as if that were compensation for turning her life upside down. She'd raised a man who was incapable of thinking beyond himself.

"Mark my words," Binkie continued. "She's the one!"

Dottie smiled weakly. "She does seem lovely, doesn't she? I just hope she can survive my son."

"You're overreacting. Nobody even noticed!" Lucy chased after Wyatt, who had charged ahead to wave down their car on Little West 12th, but it was hard to navigate the cobblestones in heels. They'd barely arrived at Libet's party when he pulled the rip cord.

"Nobody noticed, *thanks to me*," he said, not looking at her. He rapped on the car window, waking Mark the driver, who unlocked the doors. "I yanked you out of the room—"

"He's Bono! He's used to being photographed."

"You sprang at him with your camera phone like a tourist hopping off a bus in Malibu. You can't seem so starstruck! What did I tell you about visible signs of excitement?"

Lucy groaned. "I know. But my friend Doreen is *such* a fan—"

"You're clearly not ready yet for civilization. We need more practice." Wyatt pulled out a cigarette and noticed his hand was shaking slightly as he lit it. If she kept screwing up like this, his book would flatline.

"I don't! Honestly, Wyatt, I get it—"

"Then explain why you asked me to hold your purse so you could hitch up your—I don't know what, your undergarments? Or why you insisted on touching your earrings ten times a minute to make sure they hadn't slipped from your earlobes?"

"It's nerve-racking, wearing a hundred thousand dollars' worth of jewelry clipped onto each ear!"

"You made that abundantly clear."

"Okay, I'm sorry!" She sank into the backseat of the car, exhausted. "But I thought Rex and I had a nice conversation. I said all the stuff we'd talked about—"

Wyatt took a deep breath. "You were fine with Rex. That's true. But we still have work to do. I don't think you realize how much is at stake for both of us."

Lucy glanced over at him, a sudden sympathy in her eyes. "The watch has been in your family for a few generations. It must have a lot of sentimental value, huh?" She rested her hand on his arm. "I don't want you to lose. I'll work harder."

He nodded, feeling a pinprick of guilt for not sharing his real incentive. "We've got a few more parties this week. Just enough time to get you fully prepped for the wedding next weekend. Your first *real* test."

17

Wyatt lit up a fresh cigarette and surveyed the vast back lawn of the Hayes estate, bursting in tropical lushness. He didn't know whether it was the Florida heat or the anticipation of the evening's events that had provoked the sheen of perspiration on his face and neck. Tonight would be the wedding of the year: the union of two old and powerful families from opposite coasts, two glamorous young socials, one ironclad prenup. Wyatt wiped his palms on his Turnbull & Asser tuxedo pants. He was nervous enough to be the groom. The balmy air seemed laced with excitement, even danger—how often could you say that about a Saturday night in Palm Beach?

Because Dottie was spending a week at Lyford Cay, a vacation from her life of leisure, her palatial Spanish-style spread belonged to Lucy and Wyatt for the weekend. Wyatt had momentarily worried that it might feel awkward, just the two of them inhabiting this house—but after spending 24/7 with each other for over a month, it would have felt more peculiar if Lucy were more than a shout away. So she was staying in the yellow room, he in the blue. (Dottie's home also boasted a violet room, an apricot room, a sand-and-turquoise room, and a periwinkle-and-sage room—with so many spare bedrooms, the primary colors had quickly run out and she'd had to turn to the Crayola spectrum, plus combos.)

Wyatt knew that people would see the two of them arrive together and assume that the Hayes hacienda had become a love nest. Their careful story that he and Lucy were old friends, like cousins, had met implicit resistance with everyone except Max Fairchild: it was a detail people quickly overlooked in sizing them up as a couple. Wyatt had decided to stop fighting the current. If the social world and its onlookers saw them as a dashing duo, why not? She'd cleaned up so well—so beautifully, in fact—that he no longer worried about his rep. Besides, it only strengthened the impression that Lucy had taken her rightful place of prominence in East Coast society.

Tonight would mark Lucy's biggest and riskiest test yet. She had more or less survived Dottie's dinner party, Libet's opening, a black-tie fundraiser for Mimi Rutherford-Shaw's baby-based nonprofit (the cause du jour), and a few cocktail parties where she'd floated through conversations by nodding and saying little. But the Winthrops constituted true society, as one of the oldest families in New York City. Their ancestors had helped drive the Dutch out of New Amsterdam in 1665. And the Bakers were old San Francisco. Both families had lavish homes in Palm Beach, the perfect location for the convergence of the twain. Tonight was one of those events that brought nearly all the relevant members of the Social Register together. If a meteor hit the Bath & Tennis tonight and immolated the entire Winthrop-Baker wedding reception, society would be reduced to Donald Trump and Paris Hilton.

If Lucy could fool the Winthrops, the Bakers, and their friends—all of whom had been born with entire silver place settings in their mouths—into believing she was one of them, and not an ordinary girl raised above a cocktail lounge in Minnesota, Wyatt would be well on his way to winning the bet with Trip and, more important, writing a successful book. He planned to devote an entire chapter to Lucy's behavior at tonight's wedding. And if she failed? If she revealed herself as stainless steel among the sterling silver? The ride would be over. The book would be over. His new feeling of purpose—and the fun he was starting to have with Lucy—would be snuffed out like a candle in a hurricane.

He put out the cigarette on the handpainted Spanish tiles, but stayed out on the terrace to let the smell of smoke dissipate. Lucy was on him constantly about his smoking, so much that he'd cut back to avoid hearing about it. But tonight, with his nerves a jangled mess, he couldn't resist.

Sufficiently aired, he straightened his bow tie and strode inside into the bedroom wing. "Ready?" he called, knocking on Lucy's door. He could hear her moving about the room, humming to herself.

"Almost!" She let him in as she slipped on a pearl-and-diamond earring. She was wrapped in a midnight blue silk gown that she'd borrowed from a designer he'd never heard of—someone Eloise had recommended. It was a good recommendation. Lucy's gleaming hair was pulled up Grace Kelly–style, exposing the unexpectedly delicate nape of her neck. Her dark eyes twinkled with excitement, and the blush of her face gave her a vital glow. Wyatt, who'd spent a lifetime knowing exactly what to say to women, was shocked to find himself speechless.

He stepped back to take her in. This wasn't the moment to lose his critical eye, his ability to pick out the tiniest flaw—

"I was worried that the dress would drape wrong on the hips. But it's fine, right?" Lucy said. She moved past him to the bureau, where she dabbed a single drop of rose oil behind each earlobe. She'd once told him that she'd worn the perfume for as long as she could remember. An enchanting, subtle fragrance, it was one of the things the old Lucy Jo had done right.

"You might take off one piece of jewelry." It wasn't really necessary, but it felt unnatural to look at her and offer no suggestions for improvement.

"Really? But it's all so—"

"The well-dressed woman always removes one accessory before leaving the house."

"I know, Coco Chanel, but can't we make an exception? It's all so beautiful." She glanced down at the art deco diamond bracelet circling her wrist. It was a stunning complement to her chandelier earrings.

"It's my mother's rule, too, and she's right. You don't want to look like Harry Winston chucked his entire front counter on you."

"I hardly think—"

"Take something off."

Lucy looked at him and removed one earring.

"Cute. Take off the bracelet. The earrings are enough. Anything more distracts from your . . . presence."

Lucy looked at him curiously and slipped off the bracelet.

"There, much better!" Wyatt stepped back again and took her in. She did look gorgeous. Perfect, actually, from the burnish of her hair to the petal-pink toes. He felt an odd stirring that he decided was pride. "Let's go. The car's in the drive."

"My first wedding!" Lucy exclaimed as she hurried down the stairs in front of him. "Eloise says they flew in thousands of orchids from Thailand for the reception. How insane is that?"

"None of your friends back home are married?" Wyatt had been on the wedding circuit for the past decade, at least ten a year.

"A few, but either I couldn't get home or there was a shotgun involved. Do you think Tamsin will have a long train like Princess Di's?"

"You never know. I'm sure she's pulled out all the stops." They emerged onto the front portico just as the evening light made the fish pond glow gold in front of them. Wyatt looked at her again and smiled, opening the door of his mother's Mercedes for her. "You look beautiful, by the way." There, he'd said it. Nothing to be nervous about. He'd been complimenting girls since he was, oh, seven years old.

Lucy looked at him sideways again, as if she weren't sure what to make of him.

"That was a compliment, Lucy. Say thanks."

"Thank you," Lucy said. She slipped gracefully into the passenger seat and looked up at him. Her eyes were luminous. "Sorry, it's—you just don't seem like yourself tonight, that's all."

He waited for her to pull her dress so it wouldn't get caught in the door.

"That was a compliment, Wyatt," she said. "Say thanks." He laughed, despite himself, and shut the door for her. As they drove past palm trees toward the setting sun, Wyatt felt a new sense of calm. The girl next to him was radiantly lovely, educated in arts and culture, and full of charm and confidence. It was easy, even for him, to forget that he'd made her that way.

"I'd say fifteen, twenty max," Wyatt said, checking his watch.

Trip eyed the watch lustily, too. "Fifteen at the most. Want to put a thousand on it?"

"Wait, you think the *ceremony* will only last fifteen minutes?" Lucy whispered. "What gives?" She was genuinely surprised, and not a little disappointed. "They're not going to, like, plight their troths and exchange their dowries and everything for an hour? I thought that rich people loved their pomp and circumstance."

"Not as much as they love their gin and tonic." Wyatt fanned himself with the hand-calligraphied program that each guest had been handed upon entry. The foursome was seated in a back pew of Bethesda-by-the-Sea, a beautiful neo-Gothic church festooned with orchids, white roses, and lilies.

"Waste of flowers for fifteen minutes, if you ask me. I hope they give them to the local hospitals or something." Lucy swept her eyes over the nave. There were a dozen men in black lurking in the shadows. "I can't get over all the Secret Service dudes."

Wyatt followed her gaze. "The ex-presidents, veeps, and heads of state in attendance tonight nearly outnumber the bridesmaids."

"Ooh! Ooh, they're starting!" She squeezed Wyatt's arm with excitement as the organ swelled into Mendelssohn's Wedding March and seven blonde bridesmaids in lavender silk taffeta began their slow sashay down the aisle. Lucy, who had a full line of bridesmaid dresses drafted on one of her many sketch pads, winced at the sight of these. The color was fine, but the dresses were drowning in bustles and bows that made even the bride's scrawny older sister look like she had junk in the trunk.

Cornelia, the prettiest in the bunch, was fourth in the lineup—the power hitter, Lucy thought. Like a heat-seeking missile, Cornelia immediately locked her eyes on Wyatt and Lucy, and as she passed by their pew, her posture noticeably stiffened. Lucy quickly removed her hand from Wyatt's arm.

"How long were you and Cornelia together?" she asked him as the last bridesmaid sauntered by.

"I don't know. Six months? Maybe seven?" Wyatt kept his eyes trained on the bridal party eddying around the altar.

"Why'd you break up?"

"What? Oh, I don't know—the usual reasons."

"No, really. I don't get it. She's mythologically beautiful. And you guys totally add up, like Ken and Barbie Rockefeller."

"Long story," he murmured, barely moving his lips. He seemed irked by her comment. "This isn't the time or place."

She tilted her head. "You know, that's what you always say when I ask you a personal question."

"Only when you ask it in the middle of a wedding ceremony, and we're surrounded by crowds of people."

As the San Francisco Philharmonic—flown in at the insistence of the Bakers, who were major patrons—began to play Pachelbel's Canon to signify the entrance of the bride, the enormous double doors of the church opened and the congregation rose. Tamsin began her walk toward the altar. Lucy noticed that she was wearing a simple strand of pearls and matching earrings, but the pearls were huge, as if the oysters had been taking steroids. Her poofy Oscar de la Renta gown, constructed out of what Lucy estimated to be at least fifty yards of heavy silk, swept both edges of the aisle, leaving little room for her father. He practically had to bend sideways at the waist to take her arm.

"Too much dress for her," Lucy whispered to Eloise after the bride was a safe distance past them. Then she caught herself. "I mean, don't get me wrong, she looks absolutely beautiful—"

"She does. She really does. But wouldn't that diaphanous Angel Sanchez gown that Libet wore to New Yorkers for Children—in white, I mean—have been perfect?"

"*Just* what I was thinking."

The bridegroom and his best man, both in morning suits, emerged into the chancel as Tamsin and her father approached. "Henry looks drunk," Trip observed. True enough, the groom did appear to be swaying back and forth. Max Fairchild, the nearest groomsman, discreetly reached out a hand to steady him.

As Tamsin and Henry whipped through their vows and exchanged platinum rings, Lucy tried to ignore Cornelia's death glare from the row of otherwise beaming bridesmaids. But she couldn't help noticing that Max Fairchild, whose hand propped up the inebriated groom during the entire ceremony, barely took his eyes off her either.

"You poor thing. Must be so hard seeing Wyatt here with another girl!" Leslie Reynolds, plumpest of the bridesmaids, elbowed for mirror space next to Cornelia in the chintz-rampant ladies' room of the B&T, where the reception was taking place. Leslie and Cornelia had been roommates during their sophomore year at Groton—the same year that everybody became aware of Leslie's crush on their algebra teacher, penchant for day-of-the-week granny panties, and smattering of back hair.

"Why would it be hard?" Cornelia answered smoothly. Leslie, along with some of the other bridesmaids, clearly relished her discomfort, and she refused to fuel their schadenfreude. "Wyatt and I are taking a break. He's seeing other people and so am I. We needed our freedom before making a lifelong commitment." One of the other girls gave her a pitying smile. *Haters,* she thought. *Don't think you'll be invited to the wedding, bitches.*

"So who's your date tonight?" Leslie reapplied her lipstick and then blotted it on a piece of tissue.

"Haven't decided yet," Cornelia said.

Leslie didn't seem impressed. "I would absolutely die if I saw Jackson with another girl. Especially one who looks like that Lucy." Jackson was her boyfriend, a towheaded dope.

"You think she's cute?" Cornelia gave a dismissive snort, running a hand through her golden curls. "Wyatt's being patient with me. We're secure in what we have. We don't need to cling desperately to each other." The other bridesmaids kept their faces blank to show they weren't buying it.

"Photo time!" Tamsin's sister poked her head into the ladies' room. The girls grabbed their lavender clutches, and after a final hopeless tug at their ill-fitting dresses, flurried out.

"Les, wait a minute," Cornelia said, still taking in her own reflection. She faced her frenemy with wide eyes. "I have to congratulate you. What are you, now—three months? Four?"

Leslie's mouth opened in protest. Then her hand flew to her belly. "What are you talking about? I'm not—"

"C'mon, sweetie. I spotted your pouch the second I saw you! Smart play. Now Jackson might agree to marry you, right?" She unleashed her most venomous smile. "Don't worry, I won't breathe a *word*. You know how good I am at keeping a secret."

"We just walked in, Max," said Wyatt slowly. Max had beelined for Lucy no more than thirty seconds after she'd entered the reception on Wyatt's arm. She was flattered, of course, but wished she could have a moment to catch her breath. "Maybe Lucy would like a drink? I know I could use one."

"Thanks, man!" said Max with an earnest grin. "I'll take a Ketel One and soda, if you're heading that way."

Judging by his expression, thought Lucy, that wasn't what Wyatt had in mind. They were interrupted by Binkie Howe, Dottie's friend, who gave Wyatt an affectionate kiss. "I must say, you make the most beautiful couple," she said, addressing Lucy and Wyatt. "It's good to see you happy, Wyatt."

"But they're not a couple!" Max interjected. He seemed oddly authoritative on the matter, thought Lucy. "They're just old friends. Grew up together. The kind of chemistry you'd have with your—how'd you put it, Wyatt?—your sister."

"That's right," said Wyatt.

"Will you all please excuse me for a moment?" Lucy withdrew, then wove her way through the rush of lavender bustles before swinging open the door of the ladies' room. She saw Cornelia chatting with one of the bridesmaids and immediately panicked. Pretending not to recognize her would make matters worse, so Lucy waved her glass of Veuve Clicquot. "Hey, Cornelia!" she said, heading quickly for a stall.

When Cornelia gave no immediate response, the other bridesmaid, a horsey girl with wheat-colored hair, stuck out her hand. "I'm Leslie." Lucy had to approach them more closely in order to shake it. "Leslie Reynolds. I don't think we've met."

"Lucia Ellis . . . Lucy."

Cornelia still hadn't peeled her eyes away from the mirror to acknowledge Lucy's presence, which—even by Dayville standards—showed a complete lack of manners. "Hello, Cornelia." Lucy took the lead. "We met at Dottie Hayes's dinner party."

"Did we? I'm terrible with names. And faces. And there were so many new ones that night." Cornelia said *new* as if she really meant *grossly disfigured.* "I adore Dottie, but she'll invite almost anyone she meets into her home."

Lucy actually had to gasp at the blunt-object force of the insult. She had the sinking feeling that Cornelia saw right through the ruse that seemed to be fooling everyone else. There was something in Cornelia's condescending tone that thrust her right back to carrying a tray at Nola Sinclair's show. But then Lucy happened to catch a glimpse of herself in the mirror. The mirror—an unexpected ally. It took her a moment to recognize the elegant, poised young lady staring back at her.

I'm really not the same girl I was just weeks ago, am I? And I don't need to take this crap from anyone. Fighting the urge to kick Cornelia right in her lavender bustle, Lucy smiled at her instead. "I understand," she said. "You must meet so many new people, going out as much as you do, night after night after night."

"*Me?* What makes you think I go out a lot?" Cornelia looked deeply annoyed.

Bull's-eye. Wyatt had taught her that if there was one thing a socialite couldn't abide, it was being called social. "Well, your photo

is in the paper just about every day. It's like you're running for office!" She laughed, making the jab passive-aggressive. Leslie
laughed, too, but nervously. She edged toward the door.

"You're too funny," Cornelia said. "Actually, I'm quite the home-
body. I love nothing more than a quiet dinner at home with friends."

"Well, then, the Waverly Inn must be your very own dining room!"

Leslie, looking like an accidental spectator at a dogfight, gave a
mini-wave before heading out the door. "Good to meet you, Lucy."

"You, too. See you out there."

Cornelia had finally turned to face her. "So how do you know
Tamsin?"

"Through Wyatt. Actually, I'd never met her before tonight, so it was
generous of her and Henry to include me. How do you know her?"

"We grew up together in Northeast Harbor."

Lucy smiled. "I love the Hamptons."

"Northeast Harbor's not in the Hamptons. Try Maine. I'm surprised you didn't know that, given that the Hayes family has been
going for generations. Didn't you and Wyatt grow up together?"

Lucy's stomach tightened, but she knew Cornelia was the type
of social predator who could smell fear. "Our families are close, but
we didn't exactly grow up together. I mean, he's much older. Closer
to your age than mine." *That was for the cab.*

"I should go," said Cornelia, lips pursed. "Tamsin expects us to
have our pictures taken in these gag-inducing dresses."

"They wouldn't be so bad without that bustle. When you get
home, just snip off—"

"You think I'm wearing this again? When I get home, I'm going
to have this dress incinerated." Cornelia grabbed her purse. "Have
fun tonight, Lily."

"Lucy," she said. But Cornelia had already sailed out of the bathroom.

Wyatt forced himself to stay at the table, watching Lucy work the
crowd from a distance. You could see at a glance that there was
something different about her, he thought, something that marked
her apart from the other women in the room. As she drifted effort-

lessly from one conversation to the next, he fought off the urge to guard her, to stand by her side and make sure nobody else latched on too tight.

"I'm going to lose this bet, aren't I?" Trip sat down next to Wyatt, drink in hand.

"Looks that way."

"Eloise thinks she's a great girl." He paused. "That what you think, too?"

Wyatt knew what his friend was asking. "I think you're going to lose this bet."

"Dance with me," Cornelia purred, pulling Wyatt toward the dance floor crowded with cheek-to-cheek couples. Lucy Ellis was nowhere to be found. The Starlight Orchestra was playing the first notes of "It Had to Be You." Cornelia had changed out of her bridesmaid dress into a slinky Halston; after her run-in with Lucy, she'd dispatched her driver to fetch it from home. This wasn't the time to play with one arm tied behind her back. Now she felt sexy again— and she didn't care whether Tamsin was pouting about her perfidy to the other girls. As far as she was concerned, Wyatt Hayes IV was the main attraction tonight. Tamsin might as well have eloped with her vodka-sponge of a husband.

"This is our song," she told Wyatt over her shoulder, finding an empty spot.

"We don't have a song, Cornelia."

"We don't? We should. What about 'I Want You Back'?" She laughed softly, pressing her body into his as they moved deeper into the crowd.

"Subtlety has never been your strong suit." Wyatt straightened his arms to create some distance.

"Subtlety is overrated. How about 'Endless Love'?" She pulled him right back.

"That'd be inaccurate," Wyatt said evenly, "considering that our relationship *did* end."

"*Voulez-vous coucher avec moi ce soir?*" She breathed the words into his ear in a perfect French accent. Wyatt let out a small sigh.

I'm getting to him, Cornelia thought with satisfaction. He had that unmistakable, thirsty look in his eyes, as much as he tried to fight it. Cornelia loved that look. From her cousin Selden to the college history professor to the string of men she'd dated in New York— some married, some not—that look always made her feel powerful. Seductive. Like her mother's daughter. Wyatt was the anthropologist, but it was Cornelia who understood how helpless the male of the species could become when attractive females signaled their desire. As Wyatt lowered his lips to her ear, Cornelia felt a delicious shiver pass through her. Victory was imminent.

"Cornelia, it's not going to happen," he whispered. She reared back, and saw that the look had vanished.

"You don't mean that." She kept moving her body in time to the music, but inside she felt slightly panicked. It was hard to feel seductive in the face of cold rejection. How would her mother take control of the situation?

"I do," he said, more firmly this time. "And it'd be a good idea for you to accept that. You have your choice of men—"

"Is this about that girl you brought? Your childhood buddy? There's something sketchy there, Wyatt, I can't put my finger on it—"

"Cornelia, lower your voice." Wyatt tried to edge her off the dance floor. She dug in her stilettos so the two of them spun right where they were.

"If you're even *thinking* about choosing that nobody with childbearing hips over me—"

"This has nothing to do with Lucy," Wyatt said between gritted teeth.

Cornelia, her glance roving over his shoulder, noticed a scene that made her very happy. "I hope not, because she's practically sucking face with Max Fairchild by the bar." She grabbed Wyatt's chin and turned him around—just in time to see Lucy and Max down shots and then burst into a spasm of hysterical laughter that practically drowned out the trumpet solo. Cornelia felt Wyatt's bicep tense.

"Excuse me," he said. He unlatched himself from Cornelia and strode off toward the bar.

She froze. Cornelia Rockman had never been abandoned on a dance floor. She had certainly never been abandoned for another girl. If the band was still playing, Cornelia couldn't hear the music—she was deafened by her inner scream. She watched with incredulous revulsion as Wyatt eased Lucy away from Max and started to hustle her outside. Then she felt every other couple on the dance floor notice that she was alone, the still point in their turning universe.

"Exactly where you want him?" asked Leslie Reynolds, who happened to be dancing with Jackson a few feet away.

Cornelia went stiff with rage. "Twins run in your family?" she countered. Then, fuming and humiliated, she charged off the dance floor.

"I think we should dance!" Lucy said, leaning into Wyatt as he swept her past the dining tables toward an outside door. She twisted away from Wyatt's grip and busted out her best disco strut in the middle of the crowded room.

"We're going to get some fresh air," Wyatt repeated.

"Are you upset about something?"

Without another word he herded her out into the hall and down the steps into the humidity, then past the valet area where some older guests were already lining up to go home.

"Uh-oh, Wyatt is *unhappy!*" she said, giggling—and then shut up when she saw the hard angle of Wyatt's jaw. "What's the matter? I'm just having fun." What a killjoy. He might be irritated, but she was having, bar none, the best night of her life! Five glasses of champagne had washed away the sting of Cornelia's rudeness and filled the party with instant best friends. How had she ever thought of these good folks as snobby? And then there was Max, who'd come right up to her after dinner while Wyatt was off having one of his cigarettes. They'd been doing tequila shots and cracking each other up ever since. Max was telling her about how the bride had pulled him into the coat closet just weeks before and tried to mack with him. Now it seemed kind of sad—but the way Max told it made her want to bust a gut.

Anyway, she was just thrilled to have made another friend. Eloise, Trip, and now Max. Her circle was rapidly expanding!

"Will you stop weaving like that? You're making a fool of yourself!"

"I'm tipsy. There was barely any food on the plates!" Lucy cupped her hands around her mouth and pressed against his ear. "I guess they had to cut corners somewhere—"

"Daniel Boulud catered. What did you expect, the all-you-can-eat buffet at Sizzler?"

That seemed a little harsh, but she wouldn't let it spoil her mood. "So I got a little carried away. Max kept—"

"Right. You got carried away by Max Fairchild."

"What? Max is a nice guy. Oops—" She would've tripped on the curb if Wyatt hadn't grabbed her arm in time.

"You're not right for each other." Wyatt pulled a cigarette from the breast pocket of his tux.

"You said you'd stop!" Then his statement pierced through her haze. "Why aren't Max and I right for each other? Because he was born into some fancy family and I wasn't? Not everyone sees the world that way." Without warning, hot tears sprang to her eyes. Why had Wyatt spent weeks building her up, making her believe she could fly in this crazy world of his—only to trash her when she did?

"Relax! Relax." Wyatt met her eyes for an instant, then looked away. "I meant, *you* could do better. Max is fine, but I see you with someone more dynamic."

Lucy's spirits lifted as quickly as they'd dropped. Wyatt cared about whom she dated? It was the first glimmer that he saw her as more than a vehicle for winning his bet with Trip. "I'm flattered," she said.

"Yeah, well—I see how hard you're willing to work. And I know that you help your mother financially. It's admirable. You've turned out to be a much finer person than I'd originally judged."

"Thank you," she said, touched by the rare praise. They endured a strangely uncomfortable moment of silence before Wyatt found more words. "We should go back inside so I can introduce you to people. Don't lose sight of tonight's mission: it's your chance to connect with the who's who of society. Maybe they'll even want to buy a dress from you someday. Are you feeling a little clearer?"

"Yes, thanks," Lucy said. She straightened her dress. "Do I look okay?"

Wyatt lifted a stray piece of hair from her face, grazing her cheek.

She inhaled sharply at the unexpected touch, and he retracted his hand as though he'd been burned. "Perfectly fine," he said crisply.

18

Wyatt's Book Notes:

There's a ritualized behavior that primatologists call "lip-smacking." Monkeys and apes are known to "lip-smack" potential rivals as a disarming gesture, putting them at ease before stabbing them in the back. Not unlike the socialite who air kisses her rival with feigned warmth, then blackballs her membership at the Colony Club.

Cornelia waited impatiently for her PowerBook to boot up. She'd locked the door of her Old Hollywood–inspired office, decorated in dusty rose and high-gloss white, so that her nosy staff wouldn't wander in and find her incongruously seated in front of the skin-ravaging computer. Getting some dirt on her rival would be worth the extra Botox. Cornelia carefully hunt-and-pecked "Google." Then "Lucia Haverford Ellis." The screen loaded so quickly that Cornelia gasped. Twelve thousand four hundred mentions. She clicked on Rexnewhouse.com and scanned the puff profile he'd written the month before. *Timber family. Miss Dillard's School. Fashion aspirations.* Nothing she didn't know already. There was Lucy at Save Venice, Lucy at the Explorers Club for a book launch, Lucy at a dinner party hosted by Leslie Reynolds just last night—they must have exchanged contact info at the wedding. All the mentions had occurred within the month of January, which only fueled Cornelia's gnawing question: Where had this girl been before she was suddenly *everywhere*?

Frustrated, she clicked through to Parkavenueroyalty.com, only to find more infuriatingly glamorous photos of Lucy at various parties. When the home page fully loaded, Cornelia let out another gasp. Lucy, wearing a white Prada dress that Cornelia's stylist said she couldn't get for another month, had deftly scaled the ranks to number one socialite! Cornelia had been demoted to number two. She ran through the reader comments, all of which gushed over the newcomer's grace and beauty. "She and Wyatt are the cutest!" weighed in some loser with the screen name 10021diva. "So glad he dumped Cornelia and found a class act!"

Cornelia slammed her laptop shut. It was bad enough Lucy appeared to have stolen her man. She wasn't going to steal her crown, too. She picked up the phone and dialed Anna Santiago's number.

"Hello, darling!" Anna said breathlessly. Cornelia could hear the whir of her stationary bike. She was always working out.

"Sweets, a favor. Are the invites for the Vanderbilt gala with the printer yet?"

"I just sent in the proofs. Why?"

Cornelia bit her lip. "Would it be impossible to pull them back and add just one more name to the host committee? It would mean so much to me, or I wouldn't ask."

"Lucy! Lucy!" Lucy whipped her head around to see who'd shouted her name. To her astonished delight, it was one of the many photographers flanking the red carpet at the screening of the new Gus Van Sant film. "Who are you wearing?" he shouted, already snapping her showstopping dress.

"Marchesa!" she called back, remembering Angelique's pose and throwing her chin back with saucy abandon. She wished she'd been able to pull together her own dress for the event, but she'd been out at parties nonstop, cutting drastically into her design time. It didn't matter, she reassured herself—the dress Eloise had pulled for her was fabulous, and the important thing, for now at least, was to boost her visibility. As the photog continued to click away, others followed suit.

Some of them didn't know who Lucy was, but it was clear that she was somebody.

After stopping to spell out her name, she made it through the press gauntlet to meet Wyatt inside Soho House's barely lit lobby.

"We're getting there," he said, holding her hand as they stepped into the elevator.

Friends hold hands, she told herself. Ever since they'd returned from Palm Beach, something seemed to have changed. Maybe it was her imagination, but Wyatt didn't seem as critical as he'd once been. He seemed to be actually enjoying their time together. As they settled into the darkened movie room, their arms grazing because of the tightly packed seats, Lucy felt a frisson of excitement bloom inside her. "Wyatt, thank you," she whispered.

He looked at her and smiled. "My pleasure."

"I'm so grateful for everything you've done for me. I—" she struggled to express herself. Maybe this wasn't the place to do it. "Do we have anything on the calendar tomorrow night?"

"Cocktails for the School of American Ballet, then dinner with Mimi and Jack."

"Can we get out of it?"

He looked at her with concern. "I'd rather not. You're on the committee now—it wouldn't look right. What's the matter?"

"I, um"—Lucy suddenly felt shy—"I'd like to have you over for dinner. You've treated me to so much. It's the least I can do."

"You cook?"

"Of course I cook." *A bit of a bluff*, she thought, *but how hard could it be?*

"I'd enjoy that." Wyatt looked touched. "How about next week, instead of tomorrow? Maybe Tuesday? We'll have Howard Galt's birthday party behind us."

"Perfect. Show up hungry."

"It's a date," he said. An unfortunate figure of speech. At the mere mention of the D-word, both Wyatt and Lucy riveted their eyes on the movie screen, and they didn't speak again until the lights came up.

* * *

"What do you mean, you haven't told her?" Trip carefully lined up his Calloway driver and squinted off the roof into the distance. It was an unseasonably warm day. He'd begun renting a penthouse apartment solely for its rooftop, allowing him to practice his swing midweek by driving balls into the East River. The lavish four-bedroom apartment was now the home of two of his maids. "What happens when your book gets published and Lucy's exposed as a fraud? You can't keep what you're doing a secret from her forever."

"I know that," Wyatt snapped. He pulled a club from his golf bag. The issue had been on his mind more and more lately, but he wasn't any closer to reaching a resolution. He'd gone through all the possible scenarios in which he could tell Lucy, but in each one, she'd be left hurt, angry, or worse. "But I can't tell her *now*. It would corrupt the scientific nature of the experiment—"

"Bullshit," Trip remarked. He halted his swing and looked directly at his friend. "Be a man and admit you're scared. You like this girl. You should have told her at the beginning, but you didn't, and now you don't know how to break the news that you're planning to blow her cover."

"I *like* this girl?" Wyatt repeated incredulously. He had to admit— he enjoyed her company. They'd developed a friendship, thanks to the countless hours spent working on their shared project. But if Trip was implying there was something romantic between him and Lucy—

"Fine, don't admit it. But don't pretend you don't care about her feelings." Trip executed his swing, sending the golf ball sailing off the roof and toward a buoy marking the ferry path. "I see the way you look at her. Maybe you're in denial, but nobody else is."

Suddenly Wyatt's interest in golf evaporated. What was supposed to be a relaxing diversion had become a reminder of the stress that had kept him awake the night before. He packed up his clubs and headed for the door. "See you tonight," he called over his shoulder, as Trip launched another golf ball over the FDR.

Cornelia grabbed the baby from a bassinet and cradled it in her arms. It was a scrawny thing, not particularly attractive, but then she'd always considered all babies—let alone these underfed Romanian orphan babies—to be highly overrated in their cuteness, much like kitten heels. "Don't you dare spit up on my Valentino," she whispered, a beatific smile on her face, but the red-faced little creature was making no promises.

"Cornelia, can we get a few shots?" asked one of the photographers who'd been sent to cover the Baby Love Sip 'n' See at the Tribeca Grand Hotel. As she hefted the surprisingly weighty child in her arms, Cornelia decided that this charity, the brainchild of Mimi Rutherford-Shaw (as though she weren't procreative enough with two little brats at home), was just about the most annoying one in town. Most charities didn't require you to rub shoulders with the beneficiaries of your efforts: Cornelia was on the advisory committee for Save Our Children with Rickets, but she didn't have to stand around all day propping up knock-kneed kids. Baby Love was different. Mimi's recently launched nonprofit provided for the needs of underprivileged and orphaned infants in the greater Manhattan area, and she was vehement that this Romanian mini-crop awaiting adoption wouldn't turn out normal if they didn't get lots of kisses and cuddling from strangers like Cornelia. Puh-leeze. Growing up, Cornelia's mother had reserved displays of maternal affection for when the cameras were rolling. Her nannies had all been stiff-upper-lip Brits whose idea of warmth was an approving tap on the head. If that was such a negative, where was the outreach for underhugged daughters of privilege?

Still, Mimi had arranged for a whole battalion of photographers to cover the cocktail hour, so Cornelia smiled as one snapped away.

"How long do we have to stay?" she asked Fernanda once he'd retreated.

"An hour? Maybe two?" Fernanda seemed to be in no rush. Her baby, a fat little dumpling of a girl, was actually pretty adorable, whereas Cornelia's had the sullen pout of an infant Simon Cowell.

"An *hour*? No, sorry. I'm meeting my image consultant for dinner at La Grenouille. What the hell are we expected to do with these babies for an *hour*?"

"I'm not sure . . . I think we're supposed to read to them."

"Read to them? Do they even speak English?"

"It's supposed to stimulate language development in babies,"

Fernanda said. She'd been paying attention when Mimi Rutherford-Shaw described the mission, whereas Cornelia had stayed glued to her BlackBerry. The crisis at hand: Daphne was still trying to sort out her invitation to Howard Galt's sixtieth tomorrow night, an unmissable event.

"This thing hates me," Cornelia said when her baby started to wail again. "He sounds like a fire engine."

"He's just frightened by all the noise in here. And he's probably not used to being held. Don't worry, he'll calm down."

"Before or after I shoot myself?" Cornelia slung him onto her left forearm, fished around in her Bottega Veneta bag, and pulled out a carefully folded *WWD*. She lifted the newspaper and began to read as though it were Mother Goose. "The Seventies are revived this spring as denim companies embrace lighter wash and retro fits." The baby stopped crying. Cornelia raised her eyebrows and continued. "Change is in the air at Halston—"

"He smiled at you! Hand me the Eye section?"

"We're not done with it." Cornelia clutched it tightly. Then she lowered her voice. "Have you talked to Lucy yet?"

She glanced across the room to where Lucy and Eloise were sitting. Seeing Lucy in her skinny jeans and Chloé blouse, with leather bracelets wrapped on one wrist, Cornelia felt like a fuddy-duddy in her tweedy suit. She hated to admit it, but Wyatt's new flame had a semidecent sense of style. She wondered who her stylist was and if she could steal her away. Maybe it was Eloise, who had great downtown flair. Holding two babies each, the duo were taking turns reading aloud from a big book of fairy tales. *Show-offs.*

Tamsin and Henry's wedding the weekend before had left the stench of humiliation in Cornelia's nostrils. She still couldn't get over how Wyatt left her cold on the dance floor, in front of all those wedding guests, to go wrench Lucy away from Max. Suddenly his little game of hard-to-get didn't seem like such a game. Cornelia had watched as he'd led Lucy outside. They were gone for too long—longer than it would take to chain-smoke three cigarettes, she'd calculated—and Cornelia had started to wonder if they'd made an early departure. But then they'd returned to the party, flush-faced, obvious—rubbing their togetherness in Cornelia's face, mortifying her in front of everyone.

"I haven't talked to her yet, but I promise I will." Fernanda pulled *Goodnight Moon* out of the basket on the table and cracked open the spine.

"What the hell are you waiting for? Anna's holding back the invitations! We need to lock Lucy in now!"

"It just feels awkward with Eloise around."

"What is *wrong* with you?" Cornelia snapped. Fernanda had gone so mushy and useless since she started dating her troll-man and his pet ferret. "Forget it. I'll ask her." She dumped her orphan back into his bassinet and strode across the room. Seeing her, Eloise and Lucy wrapped their arms more protectively around their babies, making Cornelia feel like the Wicked Witch of the East Side. *What do they think I'm going to do, eat them?*

"You girls are naturals," she said.

"Aren't they sweet?" said Eloise. "I don't know how I'm going to say goodbye!"

"I know, I know." Cornelia suppressed an eye roll. "Listen, Lucy, I could use your help. This year I've been asked to chair the Young Patrons of the Vanderbilt gala. I'm supposed to rally the support of friends and make sure we've got the best possible crowd there. Would you be interested in joining the benefit committee?"

Lucy looked confused. "Me? Really?"

"It's always the same old people, and I'm desperate for some fresh energy. Please? And don't worry, there's nothing to it. You invite a few friends, you wear a dress by the designer sponsoring the event—this year it's Roland Philippe, so it's guaranteed to be fabulous—and you show up for photos. Please say you'll do it?"

Lucy paused. Then she smiled, as though she'd decided to trust Cornelia. *Idiot.* "Okay, sure. Thanks."

"Fabulous! You're the best. Eloise, you'll be there, right?"

"Wouldn't miss it," Eloise said dryly.

"Maybe El could be on the committee, too?" Lucy asked.

"Oh, um—of course!" God, the girl was sticky sweet. As a kid, she probably let everyone on the playground cut ahead of her in the line for the slide. "Well, I'd better get back to the little precious. Thanks again."

Cornelia nearly skipped back across the room. It was almost too easy. Lucy had no clue whom she was dealing with . . . but she would, soon enough.

19

"All this for a *birthday*?" Lucy murmured as Wyatt escorted her down a hallway covered in gold leaf. Six concert violinists serenaded them on each side. She pulled her sable wrap more tightly around her shoulders, although it wasn't cold. "This tent is bigger than Dayville. Howard must be fucking loaded!"

"A lady never uses the word 'loaded,'" said Wyatt, the corners of his mouth lifting slightly. "Or that other word."

Lucy had to admit, there was something to be said for entering a party like this one on the arm of a man like Wyatt. She would've been a nervous wreck without him, even now, when she'd grown accustomed to going to three parties a night and hobnobbing with the snob mob. She'd seen him in his tuxedo dozens of times now—his tuxedos, actually, although they varied almost imperceptibly—but the impact never seemed to diminish. It turned out you could find

someone to be an arrogant jerk and still have your breath occasionally whisked from your body when he picked you up for the evening, or crossed the room with your drink in hand. She wasn't
interested in Wyatt romantically, but that didn't mean she couldn't
appreciate his unique presence.

"Five years old, tops." Wyatt nodded at the Galt family crest that
had been emblazoned on the tent. It was illuminated by a spotlight so intense that the ships in Oyster Bay Harbor could discern
not only the tiger midpounce, but the arrows and shield, too. The
tiger was about to ravage a wounded fox, which coincidentally happened to be the name of Howard's largest competitor, Fox Equity
Partners.

"You just can't help yourself, can you?" Lucy had to laugh.

The birthday fête was being thrown at Windsong, Howard's magnificent seventeen-bedroom estate facing the harbor, although the
house itself had been deemed unsuitable because the formal dining room could accommodate only two hundred of the eight hundred invited guests. Instead, an enormous gold-and-silver pentagon
had been erected on the sprawling property.

The tent—if such a vast and sturdy structure could be called a
tent—comprised five equally cavernous rooms, each a perfect
replica of one of Howard's "favorite places": the Metropolitan
Opera (complete with Renée Fleming belting out arias with the
accompaniment of a thirty-piece orchestra); his home in St.
Moritz; the spectacular rooftop terrace of the Hotel Russie in
Rome, with a frescoed depiction of the city's seven hills; the locker
room of an NFL team he owned; and the vast bow of his 120-foot
yacht, which spent most of the year anchored in the south of
France.

"Hot toddie?" asked a model-waitress when Wyatt and Lucy entered the St. Moritz room. Lucy's jaw hit the faux-snowy floor. Designed to replicate Howard's sprawling Swiss chalet, the party
planners had constructed an indoor ski slope, on which members
of the Olympic ski team were currently doing runs. The decor was
a PETA nightmare, with furs draped over couches and floors, and
a chairlift gleamed from one side of the mini-mountain, transport-

ing slightly bewildered guests up to the highest peak. A trough of Iranian beluga caviar beckoned from the summit.

"What do you think the purpose of this extravaganza—the underlying purpose—is?" Wyatt whispered in her ear. He could have said it loudly. Nobody was close enough to hear their conversation; the space was so vast that guests orbited stiffly around each other.

"I don't know, to celebrate? Ring in a new year, kabillionaire-style? Leave everyone else wondering where they went wrong?"

"Good answers. It's to show the world, in no uncertain terms, that he's made it. Which Howard clearly has, financially speaking—his fund went public for five billion in '04." Wyatt scooped some ground-level caviar onto a mother-of-pearl plate. "In my field we might call Howard an aggrandizer; having made his dough, he's now looking for social acceptance on the highest level. Hence the party. Throw an event like this one, and you obligate the entire guest list to reciprocate in some way—whether it's a useful introduction, a letter of recommendation to a club, inclusion at the most exclusive tables. A party can be an incredibly useful tool in building alliances and, ultimately, gaining social dominance."

Lucy took this in. She was starting to enjoy Wyatt's theories. "So why are you and I here, if Howard's party is just about racking up the IOUs?"

"If you're going to be the reigning socialite in this city, you need a foothold in all these different worlds. The Howard Galts of the world hold a certain kind of power. I'm not so naïve as to think that the old WASP establishment is the only one that still matters."

"Admit it, you came for the caviar," she teased, watching him spoon still more onto his plate.

"Wyatt! Lucy!" Meredith Galt, a petite, surgically beautiful brunette, darted toward them like a silverfish. She pressed each of them against her sequined gown, her protruding ribs making for a notably uncomfortable embrace. "I'm so glad you could be here. It means the world to Howard to be surrounded by his close friends tonight."

"We wouldn't have missed it, Meredith," Wyatt said.

"Yes, thanks so much for having us," Lucy said. "This party must've taken months to plan—"

"A year, darling, with a dozen so-called 'planners' on board to help. Of course, I ended up doing almost everything myself. When you have the *vision* of what you want, it's easier to do than to delegate." She spoke as though her inspiration were on par with that behind the Sistine Chapel. "I told one of the planners that we wanted doves to be released at midnight, and she brings me these mottled, gray birds—I swear they were pigeons! Can you imagine? But it's done. All for Howard, you know?" She smiled with feigned modesty.

"And it's amazing," Wyatt said. He took a deep breath, inhaling for two.

"Isn't the air especially amazing?" asked the hostess.

"The air?" Lucy and Wyatt looked at her blankly. The caviar, the monogrammed everything, the ski run—*amazing*. But the air? Come on, now.

"Imported from Switzerland. Cost a small fortune. But it adds a certain authenticity, don't you think?" Then, remembering the business at hand, Meredith fixed Wyatt with her dark eyes. "Make sure you find Howard, won't you? You know my husband. He'll get deep into conversation with some brilliant curator—we've got several here tonight, of course—and completely lose track of the hours. He has such an insatiable passion for art!"

"We'll make sure to find him," Wyatt said.

"Howard's into art?" asked Lucy as they made their way further into the vast tent. It surprised her—although she'd met him only once, at a dinner for the Central Park Conservancy, from the way he'd massacred his steak and limited his conversation to berating tax hikes on the nation's top-earning one percent, it was hard to imagine he had a softer side.

"Doubtful. Meredith's been buttering me up for weeks; she wants Howard's name on a wing of the Vanderbilt, and she knows I'm on the board. Nobody's going for it, no matter how big the check."

This was even more surprising. "But there are names plastered all over the museum. The bathroom stalls are in somebody or other's honor."

"Howard's richer than Croesus, but he's rubbed a lot of the board members the wrong way. Still, Meredith's his most ambitious wife yet, so maybe she can pull it off."

Lucy suddenly felt a blast of the chilled mountain air. "I never realized the social world was such a calculating place. Doesn't anyone operate without an agenda?"

"Not really. But you'll get used to it."

Lucy shivered. "I hope you're wrong about that."

Theo Galt remained quiet and watchful. Over the shoulder of one of his father's business associates, his eyes were trained on a gorgeous gazelle in a saffron silk dress. Lucia Haverford Ellis. She was a stunner, but not like the dime-a-dozen beauties he collected in L.A. You could tell this girl had class. And Theo was a sucker for class.

This wasn't a first sighting; he'd actually done some homework on Lucia (Lucy, as she modestly preferred to be called) after glimpsing her across the room at a crowded downtown exhibit several weeks before. Some socialite had tacked the contents of her fridge on the walls. He'd been immediately transfixed as Lucy floated around the gallery kissing friends and glancing at the artwork only as much as necessary. Her apparent boyfriend—some buttoned-up dude named Wyatt Hayes, whom his stepmother seemed to revere—hadn't left her side for a moment, but then he'd pulled her out of the party abruptly. Theo could understand why the guy was so possessive; he would be the same way, if given the chance.

"Your father was among the brilliant few to foresee the subprime disaster," gushed the associate, who seemed to be squeezing in as many compliments per minute as he could. "He deserves every penny of the billions he made."

Theo watched Lucy laugh at something her date whispered in her ear. From the way she tilted back her head, exposing her graceful throat, he could almost hear her tinkling laugh from across the room. According to Rex Newhouse (the authority on such matters, his stepmother informed him), Lucy hailed from an old-line Chicago family who'd made their fortune in the timber industry. She devoted her time to philanthropy and fashion, wrote Rex. And the dozens of photographs confirmed that her legs put Elle Macpherson's to shame.

When Wyatt strayed momentarily to pick up the seating cards, Theo gave a discreet nod to a lanky blonde bombshell in a dress the size of a Post-it note. She quickly descended from her box in the Metropolitan Opera tent and glided across the room to intercept him.

With Lucy unguarded, Theo made his move. He didn't bother to excuse himself mid-conversation from his father's drone. He knew the man would be forgiving. The gazelle looked up when he was less than ten feet away, as though sensing his approach. Up close, Lucy's neck was long and graceful. You could tell she'd studied ballet for years.

"Theo Galt. I'm Howard's son," he told her, stretching out his hand. There was no better opening line, as long as the girl knew who his father was—and more importantly, that his net worth equaled the GDP of Cyprus. And, of course, everyone in attendance tonight knew both.

But Lucy only blinked, as though stunned that anyone would dream of approaching her. It was appealing. *A challenge.* When she spoke, Theo was surprised by the strength of her voice. "Lucy Ellis. Good to meet you."

"I know who you are." He smiled confidently. "I saw you at that gallery opening, the one with all the fruit, but you left before I could get to you."

He made her laugh. "You must not have been trying hard enough."

So there was a flirt underneath her icy heiress façade! "You're right, and I take full responsibility. But I didn't give up after one at bat. I asked my stepmother to make sure we were seated next to each other this evening."

"How flattering. I assume she granted your request?"

I assume she granted your request, Theo repeated in his head. He would've gotten a giggle from a girl in L.A. He really had a thing for this Lucy. Perfectly proper, but there was something behind those extraordinary eyes that suggested she might be fun, too. "Actually, no. She didn't want to piss off your date, some hoity-toity dude I apparently should've heard of?"

Lucy laughed again. He was on a roll. "That would be Wyatt," she said.

"So I had to switch the cards without her knowing. Now Wyatt's seated next to my date. Look, they've found each other."

Lucy followed Theo's pointed finger. The blonde was draped over Wyatt's arm, laughing way too hard at some story he was telling. Lucy turned her attention back to Theo. "You're telling me that you gave up Irina Natrolova to sit next to me? In case you didn't realize, she's the face of Prada. I'm the face of *nada*." She laughed, and a tiny snort escaped. Blushing, she clapped her hand over her mouth.

"No-brainer," Theo said, worshipping her.

"No, seriously, that trade is just foolish. You could bounce a quarter off that girl's—" Lucy quickly stopped herself. "I mean, she's gorgeous."

Theo laughed. "And here I thought you society chicks were supposed to be all reserved."

Lucy looked upset, as though he'd criticized her by saying she had a personality. When she spoke again, it was in a more subdued voice. "So do you work in finance, like your father?"

"Nah, I'm kind of the black sheep. I dropped out of college—my old man was horrified, which was only one of the reasons I did it— and fled to Los Angeles when I was twenty. I've never looked back. I needed to make something of myself, without his help."

"I get that," Lucy said. "So, may I ask what you made of yourself?"

Theo took a sip of his drink. Lucy didn't waste much time with small talk, which he found winning. "Well, I drifted around for a few years, promoting parties, pretending to produce films. BS-y Hollywood stuff. Then one night I was in a club in Compton, and I heard this fierce young rapper by the name of Sweet T. Somehow I convinced him to let me represent him. Things just went from there; now I work with a few dozen performers and have my own label. It sounds corny, but I kinda fell ass-backward into my calling."

"You seriously discovered Sweet T?"

"You've heard of him?" Was it Theo's imagination, or did she look impressed? He was shocked. Sweet T hadn't permeated the "mainstream" market yet—let alone the rich New York heiress market.

"Uh, well"—Lucy seemed to falter—"my, um, staff used to play his stuff. I'm not a huge rap fan. Classical music and opera are *so* much more my thing. But I appreciate talent when I hear it."

There was definitely more to this Lucy Haverford Ellis than met the eye. Theo was intrigued. "I'm glad I switched the seats," he said, guiding Lucy toward their table. He noticed that she glanced over her shoulder, presumably to look for her lost date. But Wyatt was too preoccupied with Irina, who was listening to him with wide-eyed interest, to notice.

"Me, too," Lucy said, accepting Theo's arm.

Lucy tried not to panic.

She could totally handle dinner without Wyatt next to her, kicking her foot whenever she started talking too much. Theo's full-court press was nothing to worry about. Nor was the fact that Mallory Keeler, the editor-in-chief of *Townhouse*, was right across the table, watching her closely through her horn-rimmed glasses. Wyatt had warned her that Mallory made a business of knowing who everyone was, whom they were sleeping with, where they got lipo, how much they'd overpaid for their apartment, which nursery schools had wait-listed their tykes. It was no secret that Mallory had been digging for information about Lucia Haverford Ellis, the enigmatic newcomer who was suddenly turning heads.

I can handle this, she thought.

She got through the first five courses—there were nine total, each served by her own personal server. But when she was taking the first bite of the seared duck foie gras, Meredith Galt—surprisingly strong given her Chihuahua proportions—pulled her stepson away from the table to introduce him to a few guests. And Mallory, barely missing a beat, slid into his empty chair.

Lucy put down her fork. She felt her posture straighten. She'd met Mallory at Topsy Matthews's at-home trunk show for the baubles she'd collected in India, but she and the editor had barely spoken.

"Stunning dress, Lucia," Mallory said, eyeing Lucy from head to pin-thin heels. It didn't feel like a compliment, not the way she said it.

"Please, Mallory, call me Lucy." She fought down her nerves. "You look lovely, too." Mallory was dressed in black Armani, a little severe but it suited her.

"Fendi, right?"

Lucy was surprised by Mallory's accurate guess. "That's right. The invitation said the dress was 'bear market,' and I had no idea what to wear. I would've shown up in a fur coat and shopping bag, if my friend Eloise hadn't stopped me."

Mallory smiled. *She should smile more*, Lucy thought. *Softens her whole face.* "Mind if I run that in my coverage of tonight's party?" Mallory asked.

"You're covering the party for *Townhouse?*"

"Just a little something for the social diary section. We've only got a skeleton crew of reporters, so I write whatever needs to be written. Speaking of, I hear Cornelia Rockman was vetoed from the guest list by Galt's wife. Any truth to the rumors that the two of you are at each other's throats? She doesn't seem like your biggest fan."

"Is that right?" Lucy remained carefully wide-eyed. No way was she going to get dragged into mudslinging. She didn't need Wyatt to tell her *that* was a bad idea. "I think Cornelia's lovely, actually, and she does so much good for the city's public institutions."

Theo, having wrested himself free from his stepmother, returned to the table. He hovered, clearly wanting his seat back.

"I meant to tell you, Mallory, that article you wrote on the history of tuxedos was riveting," Lucy said. "I read that issue cover to cover."

"Really? It's nice to hear that someone actually reads our stories. We're like the *Playboy* of the Upper East Side—everyone picks up *Townhouse* for the pictures, much as I'd like to pretend otherwise."

Now it was Lucy's turn to smile. Maybe Mallory wasn't as scary as she seemed. Just a hardworking professional, like Lucy—or like

Lucy *would* be, once this socialite nonsense had served its purpose and she was working for a designer and climbing the ladder again, a few rungs higher. "At least they're picking it up. That's the first step."

"Mal, you should convince Lucy to be your next centerfold. I'd buy a few thousand copies myself," Theo said. "Now get out of my seat. I don't have much time to convince her to dump her uptight boyfriend for me."

Lucy bristled, but Mallory didn't seem to mind. "Actually, Lucy, we're shooting a huge fashion spread at the Central Park Zoo—profiling the most visible, stylish girls-about-town. Cornelia, Libet Vance, Anna Santiago, and a few others have all signed on, and we're devoting ten full pages of the next issue. We're raising awareness for the Wildlife Conservation Society. I'd love to include you in the lineup."

"Really?" Could it be this easy? Could she have arrived at the top of the pecking order so soon? Lucy glanced across the room to where Wyatt was seated—but with Irina next to him, cooing in his ear, he seemed to have forgotten that she was at the same party. It irked her that he could be so easily distracted. "I'll think about it, Mallory. Thanks."

As if she'd ever turn down such an amazing opportunity. Fortunately, Lucy had remembered just in time what Wyatt had taught her: *Seem to take the attention of others for granted, as though it were your birthright. Never appear to be courting the press.*

"I hope you'll do it. It'll be very elegant, I promise." Mallory stood up. "Theo, you're an ass." She said it with affection, and he laughed, jerking his thumb in the air. Then Theo plopped down next to Lucy, draping an arm over the back of her chair.

Wyatt stifled a yawn. It always surprised him how quickly the initial enthrallment of perfect beauty could wear off. Even at the height of his modelizing, he'd recognized the need for novelty to stave off his boredom. Irina had entered hour three of detailing the petty catfights among catwalkers; she'd introduced such a confusing mosh of names that Wyatt was reminded of a Tolstoy novel, except for her lack of plot.

At least he had all of Rome to gaze at. He had to give Meredith Galt credit—the artist she'd found had replicated the view with stunning accuracy, capturing the magic of Trinità dei Monti, St. Peter's, and Piazza Venezia. Renée Fleming sang in the next tent, her agile soprano voice ringing through the air, supported by the thirty-piece orchestra. If he could have been spending it with Lucy instead of the drone by his side, it would have been a great night.

"You seem distracted," Irina said, resting a hand on each side of her twenty-four-inch waist.

Women had been saying that to him his entire adult life, Wyatt realized. He looked over at Lucy, who was seated to the right of Theo Galt in the Metropolitan Opera tent. *Ridiculous, this whole spectacle—we shouldn't have come. Who throws a party like this in his own honor, besides perhaps Louis XIV?* "Not at all," he told Irina. He forced his eyes back toward his dinner companion, which shouldn't have required as much discipline as it did. There was a time in his life when he would have listened to Irina recite the phone book, if it meant she'd go home with him. "You were telling me about how Daniella stole Dasha's, um . . . her feathers?"

Wyatt watched with mounting discomfort as Theo and Lucy left their seats and headed toward the empty dance floor at the center of the pentagon.

"Her peacock feathers! *Exactly*," Irina said. "She had to take the runway during the Dior show without two of her plumes. It was devastating . . ." As Irina continued her sad tale, allowing Wyatt to turn his attention back toward the central dance floor, he saw that Theo now seemed to be grinding up against Lucy. Was that his idea of a waltz? Had the man no sense of propriety? He was like a dog in heat. Worse, Lucy hadn't slapped him yet.

"The waiters better start checking pulses!" Theo grabbed Lucy and pulled her closer. She glanced around and saw that he was right—at every table, some of the guests were swaying a little or bobbing their heads, but overall there were few to no signs of life. They were the only ones dancing. Frankly, she'd rather be in her seat, too, enjoying her banana caramel dessert.

"You're not what I expected," Theo said.

"What'd you expect?" Uh-oh. She thought she'd been playing the part well.

"You know—a typical Park Avenue princess, terrified of how others are judging your every move—" He grabbed her hand and pulled her even closer. "Come to Spain with me."

"What?" Lucy was sure she couldn't have heard him correctly.

"I leave tomorrow for Barcelona. Come with me!"

Lucy stopped allowing Theo to push her around in small triangles. Barcelona on a whim, with a man she'd just met? She didn't even have a passport. The trip to the Palm Beach wedding had been her first time on a plane, a fact she'd kept even from Wyatt. Was this really how the rich lived, Theo and Trip and all these other heedless men, picking up and going whenever and wherever they felt like it? Inviting virtual strangers along for the ride?

"Why don't you call me when you're next in New York?" she asked. Theo Galt was undeniably attractive, but she wasn't ready to be whisked away. Besides, what would Wyatt think? She glanced in his direction, and for the first time all night, found him staring directly back at her. He drew a finger quickly across his throat, the universal symbol for "cut it out." She looked away.

"Fair enough," Theo said. "I'll just have to invent a reason to be back in New York soon."

A few brave others had joined them on the dance floor, now, but Lucy wanted to sit more than ever. She turned her back on Wyatt and his presumptuous hand gestures. How dare he tell her what to do, when he'd abandoned her for the entire night? She wondered if she'd have to find her own ride home. Better than suffering the awkwardness of riding along next to him and Irina.

Suddenly, from ten feet away came a thunderous crash—one of the ceiling lights came spiraling down, sending up a splash of electric sparks. "Fire!" someone screeched.

Lucy whipped around. The young woman next to her pointed a panicked finger toward a nearby table. As flames began to lick up, smoke billowed, and the once reserved crowd immediately devolved into frantic animals, rising up, kicking back their chairs, hiking their ballgowns to their hips, and stampeding to the exits.

When Lucy looked back, Theo was gone, snapped up in the melee. She strained to find Wyatt, but couldn't. She moved as quickly as she could to one of the exits, jostled by the type triple-A crowd, the toxic odor of the fake-Italian piazza burning her nose. Her heel—those goddamned five-inch heels—twisted and she could feel herself start to go down, pulled into the current of moving moguls.

"Got you," Wyatt said, scooping her back up. He kept her in his arms, moving deftly toward the doors. Lucy looked back over his shoulder, not believing the devastation. One of the handpainted frescoed walls had collapsed onto the ground like an overdone soufflé. Rome was burning. And Wyatt was rescuing her from it all.

20

There will be occasions when the cook has the night off, and the couple has no plans to dine out. Thus the young lady should be schooled in the preparation of satisfying yet elegant meals that will remind her husband of his sound judgment in choosing a mate.

—*Sarah Birmingham Astor*, The Navigation of Society

*L*ucy! Hey, Lucy!"

She glanced across Lexington Avenue to see Max Fairchild waving frantically to catch her attention. *That's how I know him.* The memory slammed against her. Unfortunately for Max, he was wearing the same camel-colored trench coat he'd been wearing that rainy night back in December, immediately reminding Lucy of the gutless jerk who'd swiped her cab and left her standing in a puddle. When Max dashed across the street and kissed her hello, she couldn't erase the dismay from her face quickly enough.

"Are you okay?" he asked. "What's wrong?"

"I'm fine!" she said, recovering. She wasn't about to blow her cover. "Sorry I haven't returned your call yet. I've been so busy getting everything in order for my *Townhouse* shoot." *Too bad he's an ungallant cab thief,* Lucy thought, *because he's very cute.* He wore a moss green corduroy blazer and faded jeans, and his golden curls were unruly enough to suggest he wasn't too vain. "How are you?"

"Just lucky I bumped into you," Max said. "Any chance I could take you to dinner this evening?"

Dinner! Lucy glanced at her watch in a panic. Wyatt would be at her apartment in just twenty minutes and she had so much to do. "I'm cooking for Wyatt tonight. A little thank-you for all he's done for me, you know, introducing me to all his friends, showing me around New York." She held up the black and gold bag from Garnett Liquor, clinking bottles together. "Another time? May I call you tomorrow?"

"Of course. Have a nice dinner." Max looked so disappointed that Lucy instantly forgave him for the cab incident. He wasn't a bad person, she could tell—just a bit of a wimp. Then, remembering the duck à l'orange she'd left in the oven, she took off down the block in a full sprint.

"Will you please relax?" Trip said in an infuriatingly calm voice. "You're getting yourself worked up over nothing."

Eloise watched with shock as he crossed his modern, sparely decorated living room to pick up last week's half-finished *Times* crossword puzzle from the coffee table. He settled into an Eames chair. He uncapped his pen. All in all, thought Eloise, he was acting as though he hadn't just detonated an A-bomb.

"*Nothing?*" she repeated. Everything in Trip's black and gray living room seemed to have turned flaming red before her eyes. The old Eloise—the sweet girl who didn't want to pressure her boyfriend, who didn't want to force his hand—had officially left the building. That girl had gone dashing down the block as though there were a five-alarm fire in her boy shorts.

"I just don't think it really makes sense to redo my closets to accommodate your shoes, since you'll be moving back into your place pretty soon." Trip said the words slowly, as though dragging out his statement would make it any less incendiary. "I was just being practical—"

She shook her head so hard she could feel her brain quiver.

"When you ask your girlfriend of eight years to move in with you, Trip, it's not exactly *implied* that she'll be moving back to her place in a few months!"

Trip looked thunderstruck. "What? I just assumed—" He caught himself. "You're right, El, we never talked about it." He put down the crossword and scratched the stubble on his chin. "So you want to stay here? Sell your place? Is that what you're saying?"

"I want to know we have a future together." She covered her face with both hands, rubbed the deep crease that had formed between her eyes. She was losing her grip on anger—she could feel it melting, and a deep sadness was filling its place.

Trip pulled her hands down and gave her a light kiss. "Of course we do, El. You know we do. That's never been a question, at least not for me." There was genuine concern in his eyes, she was relieved to see.

"So you see us getting married and having kids someday?" There, she'd asked. The big, scary question that she'd been too chicken-shit to ask for the past several years was now hanging in the air between them. She could puke.

"Kids, sure. I mean, not right now, but maybe someday."

Maybe someday. Eloise forced herself to press on. "And marriage?"

"I thought we decided marriage wasn't us. That we'd do the Kurt Russell–Goldie Hawn thing instead."

Eloise struggled to contain herself. "When did *we* say that?"

"I don't know, I just thought we were on the same page." "We're as committed as any of the married couples we know. It's just a piece of paper."

"Then what's the big deal? We could just go down to City Hall and be done with it in an afternoon."

"You really think your mother's going to go for that?"

"Trust me, my mother would be thrilled to get a postcard from the drive-thru chapel in Vegas."

Trip held out his hand, and Eloise reluctantly took it. His cashmere sweater smelled of cigar smoke. "I didn't know this was such a big deal to you, babe."

"It is," she said, wiping her nose on the sleeve of her plaid pajama top. She realized just how badly she wanted a commitment—not to satisfy her mother or anyone else, but for her own sense of security. "It really is."

Trip's face had grown noticeably paler, but he wasn't running for the door. "Let me think, okay? It's a lot to take in all at once."

Eloise nodded, burying her head in the crook of his arm. It sure as hell wasn't unfolding like a fairy tale, but at least she'd broached the subject. Now she just had to be patient. She'd had practice.

When the doorbell rang, Lucy yanked the casserole dish out of the oven and dashed into her bedroom to change. Why did Wyatt always have to be so terribly punctual? *The escargots were my first mistake.* She ran a brush through her hair and swiped on some lip gloss. That beurre blanc sauce, so simple in Julia's *Mastering the Art of French Cooking*, had translated into a gluey mess, and the snails looked revoltingly gelatinous. She'd settled instead for a simple green salad, the ingredients of which she happened to have in the fridge. Then, by the time she got home from the liquor store, the smoke detector had begun to screech, and she'd opened the oven to find her duck à l'orange was charred. Net-net: at 7:45, just fifteen minutes before Wyatt was due to arrive, the "home-cooked gourmet meal" she'd promised was a blackened mess in the garbage pail. At least she hadn't set the place on fire.

Speaking of, they hadn't spoken much since Howard's sixtieth went up in flames last weekend. Nobody had been hurt, which was the important and rather miraculous thing, and Howard had been able to keep his wife from throwing herself in front of the fire engine. And now it was Tuesday, the agreed-upon night of their so-called date. Lucy wished Wyatt had never called it that. They'd had dinner together plenty of times before, though rarely just the two of them—and never for the sole purpose of enjoying each other's company.

"I'm coming!" she hollered, racing for the door while buttoning the front of her dress—which was one of Wyatt's favorites, the one he'd complimented her on when she wore it to the committee luncheon for the Vanderbilt gala. Lucy opened the door to see Wyatt standing there with a gift-wrapped box in his hand. He was wearing the soft cashmere V-neck she liked—a good color on him, navy blue—and she caught the subtle scent of cologne as he walked past her into the apartment.

Her heart was suddenly in her throat. *It's Wyatt, for God's sake,* Lucy thought. *I spend a hundred hours a week with the guy. And I want to slap him during at least sixty of them.*

"Thanks for having me." He wiped his hands on his trousers. So he was nervous, too. That was his tell.

"Thanks for coming!" she chirped. "Wine?"

He nodded with great enthusiasm. "Red, if you have it." He took a seat on Eloise's Brunschwig & Fils club chair as she went into the kitchen to pour. "Dinner smells delicious. Must admit, I'm famished. I spent the entire day working; it was five before I looked up at the clock. I skipped lunch and everything."

Lucy grabbed the wine and two glasses and glanced doubtfully at the sorry-looking dish she'd pulled from the oven. She had ended up throwing together a main course of . . . Hamburger Helper. Terrible. She loved the stuff herself, and she'd picked up a box along with some ground beef to have on hand for the rare nights she didn't have a dinner engagement and could cook at home. But in no way would it satisfy Wyatt's refined palette. At least she had the salad, plus some chocolate-dipped strawberries for dessert. Still, it wasn't much of a thank-you gesture.

"What are you working on?" she asked, leading him over to the small dining room table, where she'd already put out the salad. Wyatt always complained about waiting for a first course.

"Oh, you know—" Wyatt trailed off. He never wanted to talk about his work. Maybe he thought it'd be too far over her head, or maybe he just liked to leave it behind at the end of the day.

"I want to read your stuff someday." Lucy pulled out the cork and poured.

"Sure. Of course. Though it's pretty dull." He took a large sip of his wine. "This is good. You pick it out yourself?"

She nodded proudly. His twenty-hour wine tutorial hadn't been wasted. "Speaking of work, I called Mallory's office yesterday and told her I'd do the *Townhouse* spread. And even better, when I told her I was an aspiring designer, she told me I should bring some of my own dresses to wear! Can you believe it?"

Wyatt's face lit up. "That's great news! Of course I can believe it. I've seen your sketches—they're terrific." He took a bite of his salad. "Now you just need to find your own original vision, that's all."

She set down her wineglass. "What do you mean?" She had plenty of vision.

"Oh, just—think of the sidewalk artists we pass on our way into the Met. Some of them can replicate the masters with great accuracy. It would take a trained eye to tell a real Rembrandt from the one we saw on the curb. It takes talent to imitate so flawlessly. But it takes genius to create the original."

Lucy pushed her plate away. "My work *is* original, Wyatt. You don't know what you're talking about."

He seemed surprised by her reaction. "Don't be offended. I'm just saying—and you have to admit it's true—each page of that sketchbook you showed me was heavily influenced by another designer's vision."

"So what? You're saying it's wrong to find inspiration in other people's work?"

"I'm sorry I said anything. I didn't mean to upset you."

"Why would I be upset? You've just called me a rip-off artist." But even as she said the words, Lucy had the feeling he was absolutely right. She'd taught herself by studying the greats—Dior, Lagerfeld, Valentino—but had she ever designed something that was uniquely *her*? What would something uniquely *her* even look like?

"Just because you *haven't* done something doesn't mean you *can't* or you *won't*. I believe you have it in you. Don't forget, I'm an equity holder in Lucy Ellis Designs."

She breathed again. It was one thing to take Wyatt's criticism of her posture or her hair, another entirely when her work—her passion—was under his microscope. "I guess I'll have to figure it all out before the *Townhouse* shoot."

"You'll need some money to get everything made. Just tell me how much."

"I—no, I mean, I'll figure it out. I've taken enough from you already. And I mean, jeez, you saved my life on Saturday night!"

He brushed it off with a wave of his hand. "Got me away from Irina. God, she was a bore. Quite the sprinter, though."

Lucy cleared their plates and fetched the main course from the kitchen. This was the moment she'd been dreading. She watched him take his first bite of Helper. Wyatt immediately sank back in his chair, eyes closed, and Lucy could feel her stomach drop to street level. What had she been thinking? Who served a packaged meal to a gourmet like Wyatt?

"I can't believe it." He opened his eyes, but still looked dumbstruck. "You've matched her recipe perfectly! Did she teach you how to make this?"

"What are you talking about?"

"Boeuf à la Margaret! It was my all-time favorite dish as a child. I used to beg Margaret to make it every single night, and it's just as good as I remember. You weren't kidding when you said you could cook."

Was he serious? From the way he was gulping down forkfuls of Helper, it seemed that he was.

"Well, I made plenty," Lucy said, beaming. No need to give away Margaret's secrets. Watching Wyatt gobble down his dinner, she saw what he must have been like as a little boy.

"Theo Galt hasn't been in touch, has he?" he asked between forkfuls.

"Oh, he called yesterday. To make sure I'd survived, you know."

Wyatt shook his head. "Very nice. Where was he when it counted?"

"He says he got caught up in the swarm of people, and when he went back to look for me, I was gone."

Wyatt snorted. "I almost forgot. Open your gift." He picked up the box from the floor next to him and slid it across the table at her.

She opened the box and found a fine leather portfolio binder, absolutely gorgeous, a major upgrade from the plastic one she'd been using since high school. Just looking at it made her feel inspired. "Wyatt, it's beautiful," she said. "You shouldn't have."

"Something to capture your vision," he said.

21

Never wear anything that panics the cat.

—*P. J. O'Rourke*

*F*ull diaper. Those were the words that flew to mind when Lucy tried on the monstrosity of a dress that arrived by messenger to her door just three hours before the Vanderbilt gala. A mustardy yellow guaranteed to make any skin tone look malarial, with a saggy cowl of a bodice and a huge pouf at the hips that made its way around to an enormous bustle and tight mermaid train, the dress made her look like she was packing a loaded Pampers.

"You can't wear that monstrosity in public!" Eloise declared, diplomatically given the circumstances, as she circled the dress. "I don't get it. Roland's line is so glam—look, even the label looks like it was stitched on by a two-year-old." The dress Philippe had sent for Eloise to wear to the event, on the other hand, was a one-shoulder Grecian-inspired gown in black silk. It was gorgeous, and perfectly suited Eloise's willowy frame, ethereal beauty, and current golden-blonde extensions.

"Is it really that awful?" Lucy pulled the hanger off the doorframe and held the gown up to her body, hoping to see it in a new light. She and Eloise had decided to get ready together before the gala, which meant that hair and makeup artists would be arriving any moment—Wyatt insisted on the full works before such a big event. Lucy's dress had been late in arriving, so now her hands seemed tied. Eloise had called Roland's office, but of course there was no answer. He was off getting ready for the Vanderbilt gala himself, no doubt.

"It's the most hideous thing I've ever seen in my life."

Lucy groaned. "So what should I do? We're all supposed to wear his dresses, right? I don't want to be a poor sport."

"We'll trade," Eloise said heroically. "I've been going to these stupid things for so long, nobody's paying attention to what I wear. Trip barely notices La Perla these days. I'll just duck around the red carpet."

"There is no way I'm letting you trade with me." Lucy was touched, but resolute. "You're a stylist. This dress will ruin your credibility." She squinted her eyes at the dress, praying for a vision. "What if I just made a few alterations? Do you think Roland would mind?"

"Honey, you would only be doing him a favor. Show up wearing *that*"—she pointed to the dress and involuntarily shuddered—"and his reputation will be just as cooked as yours."

Lucy grabbed her sewing basket and pulled out her scissors. Where to begin? The heavy yellow fabric had been stitched together with fluorescent threads, topped by a mammoth magenta explosion about the size of her head on the derrière. *Bye-bye, bustle, if that's what you are.* She snipped with the precision of a surgeon removing a tumor. *And mermaid train, don't get too comfortable.*

"Will you have time to take in the hips?" Eloise suggested after Lucy had cut the train and rehemmed the bottom of the dress. "That'll help a lot, I think. Here, let me pin." She set to work.

Forty minutes later, the intercom buzzed—Henri and Elizabeth, the beauty team, had arrived. Eloise lifted her head from the dress. "I think I *like* this dress. Is that possible? You just performed triage!"

"It's wearable now, right?"

Lucy slipped into the streamlined gown. She'd gotten rid of most of the inflammation. The color was still not great, and if anyone got too close they might notice the stitchwork was rushed, but it would photograph just fine. She spun in front of the mirror, scrutinizing their work. Not bad at all. She just hoped Roland Philippe would agree.

Fernanda pinned back her glossy hair, then changed her mind and let it swing down. Her mother watched her in the mirror. She always watched her daughter prepare for events, and tonight was more momentous than usual. "Thank him again for that dinner, won't you? Wear it down. It looks lovely down."

"You sent him a note, *and* thanked him twice yourself. I think Parker understands that you enjoyed your meal." Fernanda smiled indulgently at her mother. She was glad her mother approved so wholeheartedly. She and Parker had grown very close in just a few short weeks, and she'd specifically asked Roland's assistant to send her a dress in ivory—a subliminal suggestion, she hoped.

"Fernanda?" said her mother, untwisting one of the dress's delicate straps. "This is what I've always wanted for you, dear."

When Fernanda was fifteen years old, her mother sat her down during spring break and told her—in the stark terms that can only be uttered between mother and daughter, and even then only after a few cocktails—that she'd need to marry someone wealthy. Specifically: very wealthy. That goal had been reinforced, though never again so directly, for the past fifteen years. Fernanda had never questioned it, not really. She wanted the comfortable life that her mother wanted for her. Despite her high marks at St. Paul's and her Dartmouth diploma, neither woman considered that Fernanda could go out and earn that life for herself.

And now it looked as though she'd finally found success. Not only that—she really liked Parker. She could be herself with him. *In fact*, Fernanda thought as she gazed in the mirror, *it's possible that I'm even falling in love.*

"Lucy! Eloise! Over here!" a photographer called out.

Shoulders back, belly in. Arms held ever so slightly away from the body to avoid any unfortunate fat-squish. Chin slightly lifted. Lucy ran down the checklist of directions Wyatt had given her on posing, feeling more like a Balanchine ballerina than a girl getting her photo snapped. Lips parted. Forget saying cheese—it spread out the cheeks too much, very unflattering.

Just when she'd gotten into position, Lucy felt a tap on her shoulder. She turned around to find a pretty blonde in a dither. "I'm Laurel, Roland's assistant?" She had a lilting voice that turned almost everything into a question. "Is there a reason you're not wearing Roland's dress?"

Lucy cringed. So much for her delusion that nobody would notice. "I can explain—" she began, although she had no idea what that explanation might be. "I just made a few changes to it."

"What are you talking about? This isn't the silver dress we sent you yesterday."

"Yesterday?" Lucy's sense of suspicion began to tingle. "I got this dress a few hours ago. It didn't fit properly, so I made a few alterations—"

"Alterations? The dress we sent you had absolutely nothing in common with what you're wearing now." Laurel pinched the fabric between her fingers. "This is polyester? Roland is allergic to polyester—he practically breaks out in hives if it's in the same room."

"I knew it!" Eloise exclaimed. "I knew Roland had nothing to do with this dress! It was hideous, Laurel. Lucy worked some major magic to get it looking this good."

"So what happened to the dress we sent?" Laurel looked totally panicked.

There was a sudden commotion from the photographers. The girls craned their necks to see who was commanding the carpet and camera bulbs—and it was none other than Cornelia Rockman, wearing a silver gown and emerald earrings.

"*That's* your dress!" Laurel was fuming. "I sent it myself to be sure there'd be no mistake? The messenger said your doorman signed for it? How did she end up with it?"

Lucy didn't answer. She'd heard stories about husband hunting and nanny poaching on the Upper East Side, but dress-napping? That was a new one. Cornelia was a pioneer.

"Listen, Lucy, I'm sorry this happened? Hopefully we can find another occasion in the near future? So much from his new line would look beautiful on you."

"Of course," Lucy said. "I'm sorry it didn't work out this time."

After Laurel had marched off to find Roland, Eloise turned to Lucy with unease in her eyes. "I know it's just a dress, but it's still creepy. What are you going to do?"

"What I have to do," said Lucy. One thing she'd learned from Rita: you don't start a fight, but if someone else does, you finish it.

She strode over and took her place next to Cornelia, who gave Lucy's dress a confused once-over. Sticking her right foot out ever so slightly, angling her hips for the most flattering angle, Lucy could feel the photographers shift their attention toward her.

"Who are you wearing, Lucy?" called out one reporter.

"Just something I whipped up at home."

"Roland didn't give you a dress to wear?" Cornelia had the audacity to feign concern.

"Cut the bullshit, Cornelia." Lucy dropped her voice so only her red carpet nemesis could hear her, and she kept her expression pleasant. "I know what happened. And if it's a turf war you want, that's what you'll get."

Several hours later, Fernanda nuzzled up to Parker in the backseat of the Town Car. "My place?" he asked, giving the driver directions after she nodded her sleepy consent. They'd been among the very last to leave the gala, dancing and knocking back glass after glass of champagne. It was nearly three, and she could barely keep her eyes open. In fact, she might have drifted off to the land of Nod on their drive downtown had Parker not whispered three electric words in her ear.

22

Lucy Ellis, squired as usual by Wyatt Hayes IV, stole the red carpet at last night's Vanderbilt gala in a little something she "whipped up at home." The girl never ceases to amaze.

—Rex Newhouse, *www.rexnewhouse.com*

Theo kicked his feet off the desk and peered more closely at his computer screen, which he'd just refreshed to find newly posted photos of Lucy at the Vanderbilt gala. She looked even more stunning than he remembered, dressed in a golden gown that flattered her complexion and dark hair. But there was Wyatt, lurking in the background of several candid shots, looking smug. Theo had been kicking himself ever since the conflagration at his father's party. How he wished he hadn't panicked at the first taste of smoke in his mouth and sprinted for the nearest exit; if only he'd done the more gentlemanly thing, he might've gotten a leg up on his East Coast competition.

His eyes fell on a photo of Cornelia, who, he conceded, had also looked gorgeous in a silvery dress. Maybe he should help her. A quick recording session, just to see if she had any talent, might not be a bad idea. His father would hate that he was doing it—that one bathroom grope had cost him more than the collapse of Wall Street—which sweetened the idea in Theo's mind.

But then his thoughts turned back to Lucy. How could he make it up to her?

The next morning, as Lucy lay in her sudsy lavender-and-honey bath, chilled cucumber slices resting lightly on her eyelids, she felt . . . well, as tightly wound as the spring in a pogo stick. Lately, even in the rare moments when she had time to unwind, her mind raced. She took a deep breath as the hot water melted her muscles, sore from yesterday's rigorous double workout with Derrick. She rested her head against a rolled-up Egyptian cotton towel, and then lifted her pedicured left foot onto the bathtub's porcelain ledge, watching the steam lift off her exposed leg. Just minutes before, from the window seat, she'd watched snow come petaling down to the ground. *Relax,* she told herself. But she couldn't. It was impossible to stay in the moment.

In the past two months, she'd been transformed from Wyatt's plus one to a bona fide It girl. First came the invitations to store, restaurant, and club openings. Book launches. More benefits than one human being could attend. Ladies' luncheons. Screenings, the occasional premiere. Birthday parties for people she'd met once or twice. Then there'd been a flood of dinner invitations buzzing through her BlackBerry, at least two on any given night: the Hendersons at Elio's, the Martins at their home on Central Park West, the van Severs at Swifty's. The alligator Smythson appointment book that Wyatt had given her was overflowing. And so was her closet— since apparently one of the golden rules of the socialite biz was that you couldn't wear the same outfit twice.

And the barrage of press was just plain mind-boggling. This morning, she'd flipped open the *New York Times* to discover her first party photo on Bill Cunningham's Sunday Styles page, a rite of passage if ever there was one. She'd clipped it out, neatly storing it in the cream-colored box her first pair of Manolos had come in, along with a photo of her from Tamsin and Henry's wedding that *Quest* had included in their coverage of the event. There was even a little photo of Lucy, taken at Libet's exhibition, in this month's *Vogue*! Lucy Jo Ellis—well, Lucia Haverford Ellis, but close enough—had appeared in *Vogue*!

And then there was the *Townhouse* spread, now just two weeks away. And of course, the legendary Forum Ball—the exciting, if terrifying, culmination of their experiment. She still couldn't believe she'd be there.

The doorbell rang, breaking her thoughts. *Probably the messenger with my dress for tonight's dinner.* She pulled herself out of the bubbles and threw on a fluffy white robe. Max had called earlier that week and asked her out again—she'd had to decline. He was starting to take the hint, she hoped. Even if she had been romantically interested in him, which she just didn't think she was, her calendar was fully booked. Tonight she and Wyatt were heading to an intimate dinner for eight at the Waverly Inn. The group, comprised mainly of cooler-than-thou downtown scenesters who called themselves artists but didn't seem to produce very much art—had as little to say as their more buttoned-up Upper East Side counterparts, but Wyatt insisted she make inroads into every "scene." Lucy always angled to sit next to Wyatt, who never suffered a shortage of unexpected opinions.

"Coming!" she called, tying the sash tight and leaving little puddles across the living room floor with each step. She unlocked the door and gasped.

"Lucy Jo!"

"Rita! What are you doing here?" Lucy asked, unable to keep the panic out of her voice.

Rita—a short, stout woman with brassy highlights self-streaked through her copper hair—pushed a copy of *Vogue*, open to the spread with Lucy's photograph, into her daughter's face. "Some way to greet your mother! You don't return my calls, so I had to come in person." She barreled past Lucy, knocking her with an alarmingly large suitcase and taking in the apartment. "This is your friend's place? Cute." Then she flashed an ear-to-ear grin and dumped the suitcase on Lucy's left foot.

"What are you doing here?" Lucy repeated, feeling ill.

"I guess you were waiting to tell me?"

"What are you talking about?" Lucy asked.

"Your new life, kid!" She waved *Vogue* in Lucy's face again. "My friend Brenda brought it in to the salon. At first I wasn't sure it was you. You look different, so *classy*. The city's been good for you. Anyway, they got your name wrong—where'd that *Haverford* come from?—but there's no mistaking my little girl."

My little girl? Those words had never left her mother's mouth before. Lucy, feeling weak, sat on the arm of the couch.

"You didn't mention that you were famous!"

"I'm not. It's just one photo, Rita."

"But you should see how many photos there are of you on the World Wide Web!"

Rita had learned to use the Internet? The sky should be falling at any moment.

"Bren's boyfriend looked up the name on his computer. Pulled up a website that shows photos of you out on the town every night, dressed to the nines, rolling with a bunch of Richie Riches." Rita whistled through her front teeth.

Lucy, suddenly hot, shoved open a window in the living room. "Why didn't you call first? I could've planned better—"

"Thought I'd surprise you!" Rita fingered Eloise's curtains. "Brenda was tickled to take care of the kitties, so I packed a bag and hopped on the bus!"

"How long can you stay?" Lucy asked feebly.

"I'm in no rush!" Rita looked pleased. "And here I thought you were strapped, working for that designer. I guess you just got a big raise, huh?"

"Actually, I lost my job before Christmas. I should've told you sooner."

"So where's the money coming from?" asked Rita. "Are you dancing? I always said you'd be able to make good money, and now you look better than ever—"

Lucy shuddered. Only her mother would view exotic dancing as a promising career choice. "Nothing like that. It's, um, a social experiment. My friend Wyatt's a biological anthropologist—a scientist who studies the relationship between humans and primates—and he's been teaching me how to be, um, a socialite." The experiment had stopped seeming weird to Lucy, until she said it out loud. "When it's over, he's going to help me get a job working for an amazing designer, a job I couldn't seem to land on my own."

Rita nodded approvingly. "I saw that Wyatt guy. Quite the looker. Is he also your beau?"

"No! No beau! No." Lucy could see Rita's mind working. "It's just a business proposition. That's all."

Now it was Rita who looked shocked. "Hold on, now! It's one thing to dance—hell, I'd do that myself if I still had the body for it. But I didn't raise my daughter to—"

"*Rita!* Wyatt and I are strictly platonic. We're just working together, like, professionally."

"What's in it for him? You'll get a leg up in the fashion business, but what's the gravy on his potatoes?"

Lucy let out a frustrated sigh. "It's a bet with one of his friends. These guys, Rita, they're not like the guys we know back home. Wyatt's got spare time on his hands."

"And spare money, seems like. So he's using you as a guinea pig—and bankrolling this new swanky lifestyle."

Lucy hated feeling like a kept woman, and she could hear the ka-ching sounds going off in Rita's head. "Well, more or less. I borrow a lot, too. That dress I wore in the *Vogue* photo was borrowed from an up-and-coming designer."

"You know I have nothing against borrowing," Rita declared magnanimously. "Share the wealth, I always say. Speaking of which, I spent my last dime coming out here. I had to get a New York wardrobe, once I saw how swanky you're looking these days." She unzipped her suitcase and pulled out several tiny little dresses, each in a different animal print. "I brought my nails, though, so once we find a few investors, I'll be back in the black."

The relative peace of Lucy's warm bath seemed lifetimes ago. "I don't have any money, Rita. I'm just as broke as I've always been."

Rita didn't look concerned. "Your friend Wyatt does, though, right?"

"I can't ask him for money. He's done too much for me already. But listen, in a few months, when I've got my career going full-steam, I can help you—"

"You're selling yourself short." Rita Ellis lowered her voice. "I'm sure you could find some way to convince this guy to part with some cash. Use your feminine wiles, darling—"

Lucy felt the anger rising in her chest. "In a few months, Rita, when it's my money to give. You know I'll be there for you. That's the best I can do."

Rita frowned hugely. She shook her head. "I come all the way out here, leave my whole life behind—"

"If you'd called, I would've told you to stay home!" Lucy snapped. As soon as the words left her mouth, she could feel them hit Rita hard. She'd never spoken so disrespectfully to her mother. Rita's penciled eyebrows arched in hurt surprise, before forming an angry downward arrow.

"I didn't realize!" Rita declared. She grabbed her suitcase and moved toward the door. "I won't stay where I'm not wanted!" She waited a beat, giving Lucy the chance to stop her before charging out of the apartment.

Lucy let her go. She watched the door slam behind her mother.

Her hands trembled as she headed back into the bathroom and pulled the plug in the tub. She watched the iridescent bubbles swirl down the drain as though pulled by some invisible hand. *She's never exactly been Mother of the Year.* Lucy pressed both hands over her face. *She could ruin everything for me.*

She walked to the apartment door, then changed her mind. *No. Too much at stake.* Lucy glanced in the entryway's gilded mirror. She'd developed a habit of tucking invitations into its ornate edges. They were too beautiful—the hand-engraved calligraphy, the Mrs. John L. Strong card stock—to hide, or keep stacked on a tray. Now the mirror was starting to look overgrown, almost wild. Lucy could barely see her own reflection.

She threw on her snow boots and raced out the door after her mother.

* * *

Trip had cooked dinner, set a small table in front of the fireplace, and uncorked a bottle of wine they'd bought on their last trip to Tuscany. Eloise didn't need her mother whispering in her ear to wonder if he was up to something. Ever since their blowup about the closet last week, he'd been quieter than usual. At the end of the meal, Trip dipped fresh biscotti into the vin santo and brought it to her lips.

"You make me so happy, El." His voice was lower than usual. Eloise, watching him over the flickering candles, felt her heart start to pound. *It's happening.* She realized just how badly she wanted it. "We were made for each other." Trip reached across the table for her hand.

A moment of silence passed. Then another.

Reach into your pocket. Drop to one knee. Please!

As though she were controlling his thoughts, Trip moved one hand slowly toward the pocket of his sport coat, and extracted a small midnight blue box. She shut her eyes. Her joy was overwhelming. When she opened her eyes and then the small box, she saw before her not an engagement ring but a plain brass key.

"Happy Valentine's Day. Since we're officially living together," he said, "I thought you might like your own key." He smiled as though he were the sweetest, most thoughtful man on the planet. Eloise wanted to dive across the table and bite his face.

"But Trip, darling, I've had keys for the past four years," she said carefully.

"Really? Well, right, but this is sort of a *symbolic* key. To show we've taken the next step in our relationship."

She wished she could feel excited about that. "Unlocks the same door, right?"

"Well, yeah, but—c'mon, El, it's a sign of our new commitment."

She could feel her heart harden against him. She was thirty-five years old. How could Trip really expect that sending his household manager to Ace Hardware constituted an adequate "sign of commitment"? She pushed her chair away from the table.

"Where are you going?"

"I think I need to spend the night at home. I mean, my home. By myself." Her voice was croaky. She didn't have much time before this became a bigger, more unpleasant moment than it already was. Eloise escaped as quickly as she could, grabbing her coat and pretending she didn't hear Trip calling her name.

Ground rules. Lucy would simply explain to Rita that she wouldn't be able to run roughshod over her entire life. There would be no borrowed earrings, credit cards, prom dates like old times. There would be boundaries. Lucy rested her full basket on the counter in front of the Duane Reade cashier. Rita had reluctantly agreed to set up camp in Lucy's old Murray Hill studio (Wyatt had been paying her rent, presumably so she could move back in after the Forum—one of those thoughts she preferred to avoid). The place was just as Lucy had left it—inhospitably bare-bones—so she was stocking up. But that would be it. She would not be pulled into the cycle of providing for Rita's every need.

By the time she'd hauled the heavy bags back to Eloise's apartment, Lucy felt okay. Better than okay, really. Maybe it was time to give Rita another chance. She opened the door just as Rita unleashed a peal of laughter. And then—

"I should've told him where to shove that key!" *Eloise. Fark.* She must've come home and met Rita.

"I know I just met you, honey, but can I tell you what I think?" Rita asked. Lucy rounded the corner of the foyer to find her mother dispensing Kleenex and advice to a tear-streaked Eloise as they lounged on the sofa like sisters in a very peculiar sorority. She felt a rush of concern for her friend; Trip must have really stepped in it this time. "Get yourself knocked up. Call me old-fashioned, but he sounds like the kind of guy who'll do the right thing."

"*Rita!*"

"Not like this one's old man," Rita thumbed toward her daughter. "Saw the pregnancy test next to the sink and ran out so fast he left a jackass-shaped hole in the door."

"Heartwarming," Lucy remarked. She put down her bags. "El, what happened? Yesterday you seemed so happy—"

"Yesterday I thought I'd be engaged today!" She choked back sobs. "Rita's been great, Luce. I told her she's welcome to stay here"—she heaved for breath—"as long as she needs to."

Rita, still patting Eloise's platinum blonde spikes, looked up and smiled. "Lucy thinks I'll embarrass her," she said, playing the martyr to the fullest. "I know she's trying to convince everyone she comes from a highfalutin' family, but I won't blow her cover. I know how to act classy. I've watched *The Real Housewives*. I know how to act like a rich bitch."

"I'm sure you do," Lucy said. She straightened her posture, summoning up the inner alpha that Wyatt had been helping her to find. "But you can't blow this opportunity for me. I won't let you. Either lay low in Murray Hill until the Fashion Forum Ball, or take the next bus back to Dayville." She ignored the horror-stricken look on Eloise's face. Her friend didn't understand.

"Fine." Rita pouted, but then turned to look at Eloise brightly. "Have I showed you my nails, doll?"

23

Wyatt's Book Notes:

L. enters new situations with trepidation, and appears overly impressed with existing alphas. Missteps still abound. For example, upon spilling some red wine on the light-colored couch of a hostess, L. made a squawking display of cleaning it up, revealing her subordinate status. I told her afterward she should have apologized quickly and called for the maid—something I had witnessed C. do just months before.

*O*n the Harvard Club's wood-paneled grill room, Dr. Kipling crooked one bushy white eyebrow as he lavished butter on his popover. "Define 'not so sure.'"

Wyatt folded his hands over his plate. "About the ending, I guess."

"The ending? The subject goes to the ball, passes herself off as a socialite to the most discerning critics. It's the final moment in her transformation to alpha female. You're nervous, I understand. But I've read your research, Wyatt, and the first several chapters. Maybe you're not so sure about this book, but I am."

Wyatt frowned. He wished Kipling would stop referring to Lucy as "the subject." How could he explain that the problem wasn't his confidence, but his conscience? If he published the book with all the details of the past two months spelled out, fingers would instantly point to Lucy, even if he shortened or changed her name.

She'd be exposed as a phony, and Wyatt knew that many of the people she'd come to think of as friends—the ones inviting her to dinner every night, asking her to join their committees—would drop her faster than they could say "not our kind, dear." At the beginning he hadn't given it much thought, but as the end of their experiment drew closer, the exposure was starting to feel a bit—

"Cold," muttered Kipling. "Damn bisque is room temperature at best. This place is going downhill."

Maybe he'd let Lucy read the manuscript herself. Let her decide if she could handle it. But then he cringed, thinking about how she'd react to certain observations in *The Overnight Socialite*. It wasn't too great a mystery: she'd think he was a heartless snob. And could he blame her?

"This book is going to reinvigorate your career," Kipling said, reaching for the second popover when it became clear that Wyatt didn't have much of an appetite. "I knew I wasn't wrong about your potential."

"Trust me," said Cornelia, pushing back the unsightly plastic goggles the perfume nerds had forced her to wear. "This is *Socialite*. It's perfect. Can't you smell the unmistakable aroma of old money?"

One of the nerds cleared his throat. "But our focus group—"

Cornelia was resolute. She threw off her goggles, stripped off the lab coat, and headed toward the door. "Screw your focus group," she told them over her shoulder. "This is my perfume."

"You heard the girl," said Daphne, scuttling along behind her.

"I can't believe how cool you're being about this." Lucy sat on the couch, flipping through one of the photo albums Wyatt had brought over for her to peruse, so she would better learn some of the names and faces that she'd supposedly known since birth.

"She's your mother, Lucy." He took a bite of his Boeuf à la Margaret. For the past two weeks, since their first homecooked meal together, they had fallen into the habit of having dinner at her place on Sunday nights, some downtime in which they could review how the campaign was going. "It sounds like you made it very clear what we're doing, and that she'll need to keep a low profile until the ball. But actually, I'm glad she's in New York. You'll want family around when this is all over."

Lucy flipped a page of the album. She wasn't looking forward to the end of the experiment as much as she would have predicted at the beginning, with the exception of her double sessions with Derrick, which she couldn't wait to be done with. Even though she'd hopefully be in a better place all around—working for a great designer, living independently, not exhausting herself on the social circuit quite as much—she wondered if she'd miss hanging out with Wyatt every day. She suspected she would. "What was it like having such glamorous parents?" she asked, pausing over a black-and-white photograph of his parents in the drawing room of their Fifth Avenue apartment. It had to have been taken New Year's Eve decades ago, judging by their sparkly party hats and noisemakers and the champagne on ice in front of them. Wyatt's father's arm rested on his mother's shoulder; her head was tipped back, mid-laugh. They looked—besides elegant and dressed to the nines— genuinely happy, the kind of happy you can't fake.

"I never thought of them that way," Wyatt said, leaning in to see what she was looking at, and inadvertently replicating his father's pose. "How'd your work go this week? Any inspiration?"

Lucy shook her head. She'd spent the afternoon flipping through her portfolio before concluding that none of her designs—not the metallic jumpsuit with a chain-link belt, or the mod minidress, or the bustier-based gown with a plunging back—were good enough for her debut as a designer in the pages of *Townhouse*. The shoot now loomed just a week away. "I wish. I'm dry." Being out and about had honed Lucy's sense for what the best-dressed desired in their clothing. It was as though her sketches had been transformed along with her, growing dowdier as she became more chic. Wyatt was right: they were all over the map, lacking a cohesive style that was unmistakably hers. She was proud of her ability to imitate Narciso Rodriguez's structured, sensuous designs, but what could she bring to the table that was fresh and innovative?

"You'll get there," he told her.

Lucy wished she shared his confidence.

Wyatt was happily ladling more Boeuf à la Margaret onto his plate when the phone rang. The caller ID bleated out *Theo Galt* in robotic tones that echoed throughout the apartment. Wyatt looked surprised. "That guy's still calling you? You'd think he'd take a hint by now."

She glanced up from a photo of Wyatt's mother smartly turned out for a luncheon. Lucy recognized the Colony Club in the background. "What do you mean?"

"Well, after he left you to die at his father's party, I just assumed you'd negged him."

She laughed. "I think you're being a little melodramatic, don't you? Anyway, we met for a quick drink last week before the Museum of the City of New York party." She set aside the book and picked up her bowl of Helper from the coffee table. Frankly, after all the amazing meals she'd had recently, it tasted pretty revolting. But Wyatt couldn't get enough of it.

"You never told me that." He seemed hurt.

"Sorry, I should have," she said quickly. "It was just a drink—to be honest, it slipped my mind. I've been so focused on the shoot, and the fact that I may be about to blow the biggest opportunity I've ever been given."

The phone stopped ringing and the answering machine blared on: *Lucy, babe, this is Theo. Loved seeing you last week. I'm back in town at the end of the month, and this time I'm insisting we spend as much time together as possible. Call me, babe.*

"He's *insisting*?" Wyatt exaggerated a shudder. "That guy makes my skin crawl."

"He's harmless." Lucy liked Theo and found his interest flattering, but she hadn't thought about him much since their last encounter. "Anyway, I don't think someone who dated Cornelia can really pass judgment. The more I know about her, the less I get it. I mean, obviously she's beautiful—but you spent a lot of time with her."

Wyatt swished his wine before taking a pensive sip. "Well, I like women with strong personalities, who aren't afraid to express their opinions."

"But come on. Cornelia's strong like toxic fumes."

Wyatt laughed. "She and your Theo would be a decent match for each other."

"He's not *my* Theo. Okay, so you like strong women. What else?" This was progress, thought Lucy. She was finally getting Wyatt to open up about something personal; usually he changed the subject. After spending so much time together, she'd developed a natural interest in what made him tick.

"I don't know . . . intelligence is obviously important. Physical appeal, a sense of grace. Brunettes more than blondes, I don't know why. Someone who's not just a social butterfly but has a desire to do something with her life."

Lucy sat up, paying closer attention. Maybe she was giving herself too much credit, but it kind of sounded like he was describing—

"Someone who doesn't take herself too seriously," he continued. "But has serious goals."

Is he talking about me? At a party the week before, she'd caught him watching her across the room, and for a fleeting moment she'd thought she'd seen something rise in his eyes. Was Wyatt falling for her?

"Not too wrapped up in her looks. Vanity is the kiss of death," he continued.

Lucy glanced down at her outfit: Levi's and a Vikings T-shirt. Vintage Lucy Jo. She could feel her heart pick up its pace. Would he try to kiss her? Did she want him to? Without thinking, she pulled the pencil out of her bun, letting her hair fall in waves to her shoulders. "What else?" she prompted, feeling an unexpected exhilaration. When Wyatt took a long sip of his wine and looked deep into her eyes, she actually shivered.

"Well, it helps to come from the same kind of background," he said after giving it some more thought. "Cornelia's grandparents lived next door to mine in Maine. There was that sense of shared history."

Lucy bit her cheek. Hmm. "But that's not, like, *the* most important thing."

"Maybe not, but relationships are easier when you've been raised with similar expectations and standards." He said it casually, oblivious to her flushed cheeks. "But anyway, enough about me. You're the one who's got quite a collection going. Max Fairchild. Theo Galt. Top socialite and femme fatale rolled into one. I just hope you won't let it distract you from the purpose of what we're doing."

"Do I seem at all distracted?" Lucy couldn't keep the snap out of her voice. For a moment, she'd felt an involuntary excitement at the thought that their charade of a relationship might become something real. Now she wanted to slap the smug off his face. Her instincts had been right the first time they met: Wyatt Hayes was nothing but an arrogant snob. How dare he give her butterflies?

"Well, I'd keep your distance with those guys. Remember, they think you're some socialite with a huge trust fund and blue-blood lineage." Wyatt chuckled, which fanned Lucy's irritation.

"So they're just gold diggers? Social climbers?" Lucy could feel her heart begin to pound again, this time with real anger. She stood up, hands around elbows. "No way would they be interested in the real me."

Wyatt put down his glass and looked up at her with amusement. "It's just well known that Max's family has fallen on hard times and that the Fairchilds need to marry well, and that Theo's hungry to make inroads into certain circles. So it might not be a total coincidence that they both zeroed in on you right away."

"And it's impossible that they might have liked me?" she retorted. "Found *me* attractive? That's inconceivable to you, I guess."

"What?" He looked taken aback by her reaction. "No, that's not what I meant—"

"I know exactly what you meant," she said, eyes blazing. She stood up. "You know what, Wyatt? You should leave."

He made a face. "I'm just trying to look out for you."

"Well, don't. Max and Theo might not be up to your so-called standards, but at least they treat me like an equal!"

Now Wyatt stood. "And you're implying that I don't? I've been very fair—"

"When you look at me, you see someone you want to *pass off* as an equal to your hoity-toity crowd. You see the difference?"

"You're right. I should go." Wyatt grabbed his coat and scarf from

Bridie Clark

the closet. "Thanks for dinner. Oh, and the character assassination. We should do this again."

After he slammed the door, Lucy grabbed the nearly empty wine bottle and plopped down on the thick shag carpet. She felt shaky from yelling, from allowing her emotions to go haywire. She had to nip this Mr. Darcy love-hate thing in the bud. For many reasons— the top one being that it was pathetically one-sided. And it would never work between them, she reminded herself, pouring the dregs of the wine. She wanted a guy who'd love her in couture or comfy sweatpants. A guy who drank beer, regular old beer, and didn't in-sist on some ridiculously overpriced imported lager every time. A guy who cared more about the Rangers game than the Asian-art auc-tion at Sotheby's. Wyatt was completely right, now that she was thinking about it with a clearer head—coming from a similar back-ground did make things easier.

Besides, better that life remain uncomplicated by romance right now. She had work to do. She couldn't fail. She'd been planning to give herself the night off, but now that Wyatt was gone—she had to get back to the work that remained her passport to freedom and success. It was why she had spent the past two months pretending to be someone she wasn't.

Stooping to pick up the albums he'd left behind, Lucy paused mid-bend to look again at the photo of his parents. She stared and stared.

You never know when inspiration will hit you smack between the eyes. She rushed over to her sketch pad with the album in hand. Grabbing her pencil, all thoughts of Wyatt flew out of her mind as Lucy began to put her vision on the page.

24

Contrary to general belief, humans imitate apes more of-
ten than the reverse.

—*Primatologist Frans de Waal*

*I*nside the luxe trailer parked on Fifth Avenue in preparation for the *Townhouse* photo shoot, Mallory Keeler snatched Lucy's green velvet cocktail dress off the rack and examined it with a furrowed brow. "You seriously made this?" she asked, flipping the hanger to examine the back.

"Yes, but I—I brought other options—" Panicked, Lucy pawed blindly through the other outfits she'd made. *Damn.* She must have forgotten the red dress, her favorite, with hand-sewn rosettes framing the dramatic back, in her bleary-eyed rush to get to the shoot on time. Doreen had spent days following her pattern. She still had the fuchsia slubbed-silk dress with teardrop-shaped cutouts at the neckline—a loose adaptation of a dress Mrs. Hayes had worn in one of the album photos—and the high-waisted twill trousers with a bateau blouse. She'd pulled two consecutive all-nighters and enlisted Rita's help in order to finish on time. They'd even had a rare mother-daughter outing, the two of them scouring the Garment District in search of materials: luminous silk, rich herringbone tweed, creamy chiffon so diaphanous it danced even when the elevator door closed. She'd thought her mother would be freaked out by the frenzy of the Garment District, as she herself had once been, but Rita seemed to roll with all of it.

"Forget the other options," Mallory declared. "I want you in this one." Mallory turned to her assistant, Emiku, who sported a Britney-style headset and a no-nonsense expression. "Give her the diamond earrings on loan from H. Stern." She turned back to Lucy, her eyes unblinking behind her horn-rims. "What were you thinking for shoes? Emiku, show Lucy what we've pulled."

Lucy felt the relief deep in her bones. Mallory's approval meant she'd cleared another hurdle. She had found her vision: thoroughly modern classics, inspired by the vintage photographs in Wyatt's album but streamlined and sexy *and* practical enough for the girl in Dayville. Her pencil had pirouetted over the page. She'd closed her eyes and seen an impossibly chic woman strolling down Fifth Avenue in a pea-green belted suit with a velvet collar. She had smelled the gardenia tucked into a socialite's twist of hair as she floated around the dance floor wearing a white-and-gold silk organza gown.

"What do you think about these peep-toes?" Emiku asked, holding out a pair of fabulous Louboutins.

"I think I'm in love," Lucy said.

She'd barely slept the night before, thanks to a combination of nerves and last-minute finishing touches. In truth, even if she hadn't been overwhelmed with work, she knew she wouldn't have slept much that week. Wyatt had kept his distance since their fight, which had thrown her off. For professional reasons, Lucy longed to have a man around the house. More times than she could count, she itched for his opinion, but her fingers refused to dial his number.

"Why don't you get dressed?" said Emiku, as efficient as her boss.

"Might as well get started without the other girls, since who knows when they'll show up."

Of the four socialites being photographed for *Townhouse*, Lucy was the only one who'd shown up on time to prep for the shoot, in which they'd mingle with the polar bears and lemurs at the Central Park Zoo. Lucy bet it never crossed the other girls' minds that *Townhouse* had a budget to keep; every hour the hairstylists, makeup artists, photographer, and photographer's assistants waited was on the books. No wonder poor Mallory was inhaling coffee like a trucker with eight hundred miles to go.

Ducking behind the makeshift privacy curtain, Lucy slid the green dress over her head, careful not to smudge the siren-red lips the makeup artist had so artfully drawn. She looked closely at the woman in the full-length mirror that had been propped up against the wall. If she passed this woman on the street, Lucy might look twice—in appreciation of her beauty, and because there was something vaguely familiar in her face—but she would never presume to say hello. Her hair was thick, glossy, and perfectly styled in loose curls. Her pore-less complexion seemed bathed in candlelight. She'd slimmed down, although her body still had some healthy curves. Perhaps it was vain, but for the first time in her life, Lucy fully appreciated her own beauty.

She heard the door slam, and a moment later, Libet Vance's nasal voice echoed through the trailer. "She *made* these? Shut up!"

Lucy poked her head out from behind the curtain to discover the leggy blonde "artist" thumbing through the clothes she'd brought. Bond-girl contender Anna Santiago, Libet's plump-lipped best friend ever since they'd debuted together at Le Bal Crillon, was perched at her shoulder checking out Lucy's clothes with equal enthusiasm. Anna's daddy, a Venezuelan oilman, loved to spoil her in any way she could dream up. Jewelry, cars, the $250,000 Hamptons rental—so far, Anna had proved herself very imaginative. Lucy encountered them both regularly out on the circuit, but they'd exchanged only the most cursory small talk.

"You like?" Lucy tried to sound confident, but it was intimidating to watch firsthand the reaction of two of the most stylish girls she'd ever met.

"Of course! I had no idea you had talent!" Anna slid into the chair to have her makeup done, folding her slender legs underneath her. She lit up a cigarette while the makeup artist tested foundations to see which one best matched her golden skin tone. "You have to make me something! That fuchsia silk dress would be perfect for my friend's wedding in Bogotá next month."

"I'm loving these pants," Libet added, holding up a charcoal gray, high-waisted, wide-legged pair with gold stitching along the seams. She was wearing what appeared to be a shoelace tied around her forehead. "They remind me of a killer pair my mom wore in the Seventies. Would you ever make me some?"

"Absolutely!" Lucy tingled with joy. These girls were gorgeous, famously chic, and photographed wherever they went. If they wore her clothes—and dropped her name as the designer whenever reporters asked—it would be exactly the kind of exposure she needed to start her own label. The day couldn't be going any better. She couldn't wait to tell Wyatt.

"Lucy, what do you say we get a shot of you surrounded by penguins?" suggested the photographer, Giles, whose French accent seemed to fade in and out like the signal on a cheap radio. "A take on that famous Marilyn Monroe moment in *Gentlemen Prefer Blondes*."

She was just about to follow him outside when the door slammed open and Cornelia, breathless, blocked the entrance.

She wore a plush pelt—a questionable choice for a day at the zoo—and sunglasses that overwhelmed her petite face. With her lackey Fernanda two steps behind her, Cornelia coolly scanned the room, as though she had arrived at her family's estate to discover squatters in the foyer. When her eyes landed on Lucy, her icy expression suddenly broke into fury. "What the hell is she doing in that dress?" she demanded, her sharp voice carrying over the suddenly still trailer. "Everyone knows that green is *my* color!"

Is this chick for real? Lucy stifled a nervous giggle. The place was otherwise silent.

"We can shoot you both in green," Mallory said. "Lucy made this gorgeous dress, and I'm going to insist that she wear it."

"Wait, you *made* a *green* dress for yourself?" Cornelia, her upper lip curled in a sneer, crossed the space in two steps until she was right under Lucy's nose. Lucy's nervous giggle grew too big to contain; it broke forth from her pursed lips and seemed to smack Cornelia in the face. "It's so not funny," Cornelia said, shaking her head without breaking her glare.

"You don't own the color, Cornelia." Lucy refused to be bullied. "Grass is green, so is money—"

"I see," Cornelia said. The temperature lowered another ten degrees. Libet and Anna exchanged wide-eyed looks in the makeup mirror. "I'm sorry, Mallory, but I refuse to be part of this shoot if *she's* in it, too."

"You're not serious," Mallory said. She white-knuckled the back of a makeup stool. "I understand there's some tension, but you can't back out now—"

"I can and I will," Cornelia declared, turning her killing stare on Mallory. "So you either choose me, or this random newcomer whom nobody ever heard of two months ago."

Lucy sucked in a breath. All her hard work, all the late nights spent hunched over the sewing machine—and now Cornelia was robbing her of her big opportunity to show her stuff.

"Sorry, Cornelia. But if you force me to choose, I choose Lucy." If Mallory had struggled to reach her conclusion, she didn't show it.

And just like that, Manhattan's reigning socialite was dethroned. Cornelia didn't move right away. She stood in the doorway, almost panting from the shock of Mallory's decision. "Fine, I'll stay in the shoot. But I'm not standing next to her." She huffed over to the makeup station. Instead of feeling victorious, Lucy couldn't help feeling a little frightened.

"Cue the penguins!" Giles shouted.

Lucy took her position while a keeper from the zoo ushered in the funny birds, their tiny wings flapping, to waddle around her. She tried her best to look natural despite the oddity of the situation—the professionals staring at her from every angle, the silver reflectors washing away the shadows from her face, the hyper-daylight glare of the lights towering around her, and of course, the strange tuxedoed penguins at her feet. One of Giles's assistants scrambled to adjust her hair, while another buzzed around her head with a light meter. "Relax your face, Lucy," Giles commanded.

"Like this?" She tipped her chin up slightly and angled her hips toward the camera, just the way Angelique had taught her.

"Perfect. You're a natural. Just like that." Giles clicked away madly while Lucy held her pose. "Now let's try—"

"Excuse me!" Cornelia, on deck for her shoot after Lucy, stomped her foot. "Why does Lucy get to be photographed with those adorable penguins, while I have to cozy up to a disgusting two-toed sloth? Is it even safe? I mean, that thing has three-inch claws!"

"Maybe she'd prefer the poison frogs," the zookeeper behind her muttered.

"You'll be fine," Mallory said wearily. "Now, will you keep it down?"

"*Lu-u-uce!*"

Lucy froze at the unmistakable sound of her mother's voice. Running through the gates of the zoo enclosure, Rita waved the red dress like a matador. "Your beautiful dress! You left it—"

Before she even knew what she was doing, Lucy pushed through the crowd of penguins to intercept her mother. "Thank you, Rita, but you didn't have to bring it all the way here—"

"Nonsense, doll, it's your favorite." Rita looked brightly at the group, clearly hoping to be introduced. Lucy didn't say anything. "Well, I should be going. Don't want to hold up the works! Good luck, Luce, I'll see you later."

But Cornelia stepped forward before she could go. "Are you her PA?" She scrutinized Rita's face. Lucy felt herself squirming.

"Am I her *what*?" Rita repeated. Then she chuckled. "No, I'm her MA—"

"She's my, um, manicurist." Lucy couldn't look at her mother as she said it. She'd never felt so low in her life. When Giles barked at her that they needed to get started again, she gave her stricken mother an apologetic shrug and slunk away, disgusted with herself. She'd make it up to Rita later. Once she was a success, she'd set her mother up for life. But the thought didn't ease the knot in her stomach.

"Wait up!" Cornelia finally caught up with the mysterious russet-haired woman walking furiously fast down a path in Central Park, her arms wrapped around herself in the cold, her chin against her chest. Something about Lucy's reaction had piqued Cornelia's curiosity. "Rita, wait!"

The woman froze as though she'd been caught. She turned around. "What can I do for you?" she asked. Her face was worn, and her makeup was distressingly evident.

"I'm absolutely desperate for a good manicurist. May I get your card? I'd love to make an appointment."

"Oh, I—Lucy's very possessive. She doesn't like for me to take on other clients."

Lucy has her own private manicurist? And Wyatt called me *high maintenance.* "I certainly won't tell her. Name your price."

Open Sesame. Rita unfurled a smile. "Here's my number, doll," she said, pulling a Bic out of her oversize tote bag, taking Cornelia's hand, and scribbling the digits across her palm.

25

"I am ready," said Emma, "whenever I am wanted."
"Whom are you going to dance with?" asked Mr.
Knightley.
She hesitated a moment, and then replied, "With you,
if you will ask me."

—*Jane Austen, Emma*

$\mathcal{L}$et's not discuss Eloise and Trip anymore," Wyatt said. "We only argue. She's a big girl, Lucy. If she wants to wait around for him, that's her call." Wyatt clinched his navy blue blazer together with one hand and raised his shoulders toward his ears against the chilly February air. "Where's Mark with our car? Dinner starts in fifteen minutes and it's all the way in SoHo."

"I just don't get it," Lucy said, unable to keep the irritation out of her voice. Ever since Wyatt had unknowingly jilted her, her annoyance with him had stayed on a low simmer. She was exhausted from the *Townhouse* shoot that morning—less because of the shoot than her troubled conscience over how she had treated her mother—and yearned to chase down Rita and make things right. But Wyatt had refused to let her cancel their plans. "Trip says he's in love with Eloise. So how can he live with making her so unhappy?" she asked. The wind slapped at her bare legs, goose-bumping her skin.

"'Men marry because they're tired,'" Wyatt quoted. "Maybe Trip's not tired yet. I put *Dorian Gray* on your reading list, right?"

"I read it in high school. Come on, I know you're not that cynical. You were raised by lovebirds. *I'm* not even that cynical, and my mother was always fuzzy about the identity of my dad. The best she could offer was a short list of candidates, two of whose last names she'd never known."

"I guess life in Dayville was more fun than you make it out to be," he said teasingly. "Anyway, you can't seriously think it's wise for Trip to propose if his heart isn't in it."

Lucy exhaled in frustration, her breath creating a brief cloud. "Let's just take the subway. The President's in town—traffic will be horrible."

"The subway?" Wyatt looked pained.

"The subway. Or can't you stand such proximity to the great un-washed?" She began walking toward Lexington. "Maybe you'd rather wait for Mark, who's probably stuck in traffic, and then inch your way down to Prince Street. I'm sure Mimi won't mind if you're an hour late to Jack's surprise dinner."

"You're in some mood tonight." Wyatt followed her, shaking his head. "Is your mom all set up at your old place?"

"Yeah. She went kicking and screaming, but she went." She hadn't told Wyatt about Rita's nearly disastrous appearance at the shoot. No doubt he'd panic about the risk she posed to their experiment. Lucy didn't want to think about that.

"Would she be more comfortable somewhere else? I could put her up at the St. Regis or something."

Lucy, softening, slowed down so that they were walking in sync again. "That's very generous of you, Wyatt, but my old apartment is perfectly fine. Rita's already made it look like home. Besides, I don't want to add the St. Reg to my tab."

"Don't worry about the cost. You said she was a big help with the dresses for *Townhouse*, right?"

Wyatt had Rita's back? She looked at him. Lately, he'd been saying the opposite of what she expected more and more. "Come on," she said, taking his arm. "There's a Number Six train with your name on it."

"Thanks for seeing me on such short notice," said Cornelia, stretching her fingers flat on the makeshift manicure table like a cat fanning its paws. "I raced here straight from the shoot." Rita's "salon," a grubby Murray Hill studio draped in cheetah-print fabric, heightened her suspicions that Rita was more than a mere manicurist to Lucy Ellis. Then again, Cornelia had given that creepy hair guy on the Lower East Side steady business until she found mouse skeletons under his bathroom sink. "My nails are a mess. I haven't had a decent paint job in days."

Rita inspected Cornelia's fingers, holding them so close to her face that Cornelia could feel her breath. *Ew.* This had better be worth it.

"Have you considered acrylics?" Rita asked.

"Acrylic *nails*? Um, no. Can't say that I have."

"You should." Rita whipped out a black plastic box from underneath her table. In glittery letters across the top were the words RITA'S ARTISTIC ACRYLICS. "I've got a whole line of 'em. You might like the set with the Hollywood sign?" She held up the long green nails. "No? How about the many loves of Jack Nicholson? I just silk-screened that skinny Lara Flynn Boyle girl on the pinky."

"How about a regular manicure? Do you have Sheer Bliss?"

"Sheer Boredom, you mean?" Rita pantomimed a yawn. "C'mon. At least let me give you the Anjelica Huston thumbnail."

"Gimme all ten. I wouldn't dream of breaking up a collection." If she wanted to get the dish on Lucy, Cornelia knew she'd have to commit. Besides, Lucy's nails always looked fine. If she trusted this lady—

"Good choice!" Rita clapped her hands like a cheerleader. "Excellent choice."

Cornelia settled back in her chair. Time to get down to business. "So how'd you and Lucy meet in the first place?"

Rita looked perplexed. "Lucy and me? Why, I guess I've just known her forever."

Cornelia frowned. Answering the question seemed to make Rita a bit emotional. *Interesting.* Worth probing. "So you must know Wyatt really well, too."

"Oh, of course. Sweetheart of a fella, that Wyatt."

Now I know she's lying. "Yeah? Think there's something between them? I adore Lucy, but you know how tight-lipped she can be."

Rita peered at Cornelia's thumb. "I don't know. She wouldn't tell me that sort of thing, either." Was it Cornelia's imagination, or did Rita seem a little sniffly over her lack of insider info? "Lucy Jo is very private."

"Lucy Jo?" *That was a new one.*

"I mean *Lucy*." Rita looked flustered. "I have another client named Lucy Jo. I swap their names up all the time. Sweet girl, Lucy Jo."

Cornelia didn't know exactly what she was after from this woman, but she knew she wasn't getting it. "How long have you been in New York, Rita?"

"Not long, but I love it. Finally a city that can keep up with me!" She grabbed Cornelia's hand and pulled it closer again, filing the top of her nail to prep it for the acrylic. "How about you?"

"Oh, born and bred. But back to—"

"I guess your parents gave you everything your heart desired, didn't they?" Rita paused, almost wistful, before applying the first coat of toxic-waste glue to Cornelia's nail. Then she pressed it with the nail, which featured a garish portrait of Michelle Phillips. "You all real close?"

"Me and my parents? I see them twice a year. The whole family congregates for an annual meeting each spring. And every November, my mother throws herself a lavish birthday party and expects me to show up, even though she practically ignores me."

Rita nodded, lost in her own thoughts. "Maybe she doesn't know how to make things right. Maybe she wishes she could start over."

Cornelia hated when barely literate beauticians went Dr. Phil on her. "Yeah, well, too late. She was a miserable mother. Three years in a row, she made the orthodontist rip out my braces in time for her birthday party, and then screw them back on the following week. God forbid I wasn't perfect."

Rita looked appalled. "I never did anything that bad! And so expensive."

"So you have kids?"

"Oh—just the one. A daughter."

Cornelia stared at the hideous acrylics Rita was gluing onto her fingernails, praying they'd be less painful to remove than her braces. She had to move the conversation back to Lucy. "Lucy's gotten very chummy with Jack, you know. Nicholson." Who cared if it was true or not? "They chat all the time. She was his date for his last premiere."

Rita looked up, stared at her, and shoved her chair back from the table. "Are you serious? Jack Nicholson? Her *date*? But she knows he's my all-time favorite leading man! She knows that! How could she keep something like that from me, her own moth—" she stopped herself mid-screech—"her own *manicurist*!?" And just as quickly as she'd lost her composure, Rita's face seemed to melt. She slumped back in her chair. Rita was *crying*. Sobbing, really.

"Rita," said Cornelia, patting the older woman's curly head. Delight flooded every cell of her size-two body. She'd hoped to get a little dirt on her nemesis, but now she sensed there was a landfill overflowing with it. "I can see you're in pain. You need someone to talk to. Why don't we go out for a drink?"

At first, Wyatt thought that the twenty-something girls across the fluorescent-lit subway car were staring at him. Then he realized that Lucy was the object of their infatuation. Of course she was. She was enviably chic, in a well-cut Libertine blazer and skinny jeans. They probably recognized her from the pages of last month's *Vogue*.

"Forgot to tell you," she said offhandedly. She hadn't noticed the girls. "Margaux Irving's office called. They'd like me to auction off the gown I'm going to wear to the Forum Ball. You know, the gown I've been working on with Doreen and Eloise. All proceeds go to the museum. Of course, I told them I'd be honored."

Wyatt felt his spirits lift. The one salve for his conscience was witnessing her growing success as a designer. "That's terrific. Just think, you'll be up there, onstage, in front of the fashion world, in the gown *you made*—"

"Alongside gowns by Ralph Rucci, Vera Wang, Ralph Lauren—" Lucy gulped, looking into his eyes with sudden panic. "Wyatt, it'll be like a battle of the peacocks up there! What the hell was I thinking?"

26

```
To:        mallorykeeler@townhouse.net
From:      cornelia@rockman.net
Status:    URGENT
Subject:   will be 20 minutes late xoooxxxoo
```

*C*ornelia had spent an hour pulling together the sexy secret agent look. Stepping out of her Town Car into the dank morning rush-hour air of Midtown Manhattan, she turned up the collar on her trench coat and tucked the incriminating manila envelope into her Louis Vuitton tote. Inside it was more ammo on Lucy Ellis than she'd ever dreamed of having in her arsenal.

Just two days earlier, after convincing a woebegone Rita to join her for drinks at a dive bar around the corner from her "salon," she'd gotten Lucy's mother—*Lucy's mother! It still seemed too delicious to be true*—to spill everything. Dayville, Nola Sinclair, Wyatt's insane attempt to create the perfect socialite—it finally all made sense, Lucy's sudden emergence on the scene and Wyatt's unwillingness to take Cornelia back. *I was too much woman for him*, she realized now. Wyatt apparently preferred a girl who'd take his orders, say his lines, play her part, and in Lucy he'd found a flesh-and-blood blow-up doll. Cornelia had assured Rita endlessly that Lucy's secrets would be kept in the vault. But the morning after the drunken girl talk, a Sunday, Cornelia's PA had done some online digging to find an incriminating photo of an unnamed cater-waiter crashing through Nola's runway—now the contents of her manila envelope. Cornelia had always had a sneaking feeling that Lucy looked familiar, and now she knew why. You had to look at the photo under a magnifying glass to identify the girl, but Cornelia had a feeling the readers of *Townhouse* would do just that.

She slid into the ripped pleather booth of Midway Diner, wrinkling her $50,000 nose at the thick smell of ketchup and fried eggs.

"I'm on a deadline," said Mallory Keeler as soon as Cornelia sat down.

"Didn't you get my text, sweetie?" Cornelia asked. "Terrible traffic from uptown."

"I came from uptown, sweetie."

"Did you? Well, I'm sorry," Cornelia said. She smiled, hoping to move the conversation back onto friendlier terrain. She still hated Mallory for humiliating her by choosing the Interloper over her at Saturday's *Townhouse* shoot. It had taken a great deal of pride-swallowing just to pick up the phone and dial Mallory's office. But this was worth it. "You look pretty, Mal. Loving that choker." The choker actually looked like something you'd buy on Canal Street for five bucks, Cornelia thought, but then, what did this dowdy editor know about style? It was still bizarre to her that Mallory was tight with Theo Galt.

"You excited about the perfume launch, Cornelia? I hear your face will be spread across a billboard in Times Square, impossible to miss."

"I know. Can you believe it? And we're giving away a bottle in all the Fashion Forum's swag bags."

"I heard, I heard. And you're thinking about doing a reality show?"

Cornelia nodded her head. "It's so crazy. I don't know how all this happened, you know? One minute Patrick's snapping my photo at some parties, the next thing I know I'm, like, a *brand*."

"Ask Daphne, your publicist," Mallory deadpanned. "She probably has some idea how it happened."

The 'tude! It was such a drag when wallflower types couldn't get over their jealousy issues, but that was the story of Cornelia's life.

A waitress with a distressing number of facial piercings materialized next to their table, pad in hand. "More coffee?" she asked, and Mallory nodded. "And what'll you have?"

"Do you have espresso?"

"This look like a Starbucks?" asked the waitress, lisping around the enormous stake she'd paid to have driven through her tongue.

"I'll have half a grapefruit." It peeved Cornelia that the waitress gave no sign that she recognized her, but that would change soon. For a split second, as she pulled her own silver out of her Vuitton tote and handed the bewildered waitress her porcelain bowl (she'd never eaten in such a dive before, and wouldn't dream of trusting the dishwashers' standards of cleanliness), Cornelia wondered why being famous mattered to her as much as it did. But the thought evaporated quickly, as it had before, leaving her to the task at hand. She gave Mallory a cunning little smile and rested her elbows on the flecked linoleum table.

"So what's up?" Mallory crossed both arms. "Why did you invite me here? This doesn't seem like your type of breakfast boîte."

"I didn't want to be seen," Cornelia whispered. "I really, really shouldn't be getting involved." She whipped off her oversize sunglasses. "But I want to bury the hatchet. You didn't know what you were doing at the shoot this weekend. Lucy Ellis conned you along with everyone else. So . . . I forgive you."

"Very big of you," Mallory muttered.

Cornelia chose to ignore the sarcasm. "When I heard that you were writing an exposé about the fraud Lucy has perpetrated, I thought I owed you a sit-down."

"The fraud? What fraud?"

"Sorry, were you hoping to keep your exposé top secret? I'm afraid the word is out."

Mallory sighed. "I have absolutely no idea what you're talking about."

"But it's the talk of the town!" Cornelia lowered her voice, as if the diner's seedy patrons were undercover for *Town & Country*. "Mallory Keeler's riveting tell-all—it's all anybody could talk about last night."

"Come on, Cornelia, enough. I'm not planning any tell-all, and I'm not enjoying your little game. Some of us have jobs that require actual working, you know."

The audacity. Cornelia could barely speak. But then she envisioned the cover of *Townhouse* bearing Lucy's humiliating runway photo, and found her voice. "If you're not already planning to write the article, you should."

Mallory just shook her head. "You've made it clear that you don't like Lucy." Cornelia bristled, but said nothing. "But that doesn't mean you can make up vengeful stories—"

"Make up stories?" Cornelia was unable to keep her fury under lock and key any longer. "You know what, Mallory? Your dinky magazine doesn't deserve an article this big. Keep writing your little fluff pieces. I'll bring this to the *Times*." She stood up quickly and grabbed her bag. Why had she expected this pasty little nobody to grasp the injustice Lucy had committed? "I thought you were a serious journalist. Clearly I was wrong."

Mallory studied her face. Then she gestured for Cornelia to sit down again. "Okay, I'm listening. What've you got?"

That's more like it. Cornelia settled back onto the bench, relieved. With a Cheshire cat smile, she slid the manila envelope across the table.

Thirty blocks downtown, in Parker Lewis's tranquil cream and charcoal gray master bedroom, Fernanda cracked open one eye and nearly purred with contentment. She took a moment to drink in the gentle light seeping around the edges of his window shades, the deliciousness of their entangled limbs and Parker's warm breath on the back of her neck. Her hair was in sex knots and her face was frighteningly devoid of makeup, but for once, Fernanda didn't care.

She was engaged. Well, no, but as good as engaged. Parker, last night over dinner in front of the roaring fire, had told her that he wanted to spend the rest of his life with her. Her relief had bordered on ecstasy. She didn't even shout out her ring preferences (a cushion-cut bordered by two sapphires, no skimping on the carats) right away.

"I'm holding you hostage," he murmured, stirring behind her. "I'm thinking homemade blueberry pancakes, maybe a snowy walk with Mr. Fursnickety, and then we light a big fire and spend the rest of the day curled up right here."

"I have no say in the matter?" she teased, but it was music to her ears. She dreaded calling in sick again, especially since her boss at Christie's had just come through with that raise, but there was no real debate inside Fernanda's head.

"If you want," said Parker, "you can have banana pancakes. But otherwise, no, you have no say."

Fernanda rolled over to kiss his neck. "What about work for you? You don't need to go in?"

"Work can wait for a day," he said, sitting up. "Work's not what's really important, is it?" He kissed her forehead, and then swung his legs over the side of the bed. "Now, stay right there. Breakfast is coming to you this morning."

Just one more thing to love about Parker, thought Fernanda, cozying back down under the covers. He was so senior—not to mention successful—at the bank that he no longer had to put in face time or deal with a boss breathing down his neck. He could afford to be laissez-faire. Not like the junior investment banker she'd dated who was one step away from wearing diapers on the job to avoid time-wasting bathroom breaks. Parker seemed to have a grip on the whole life-work balance thing.

That he was twenty years older seemed only a selling point to Fernanda, as was the fact that he wasn't what you'd call "conventionally handsome." Although she found him adorable, to the rest of the world Parker was undeniably squatty, hairy, and bow-legged. His face had character, as her mother put it, but the character was comic: slightly bulbous nose, toothy grin, eyes set a bit too close together. Fernanda was the looker of the pair, which worked just fine for her. It meant she wasn't as painfully aware of the lines and creases that her dermatologist couldn't erase. Parker managed to make her feel hot and young.

"You're spoiling me, Park," she called after him, propping herself up on her elbows. "What did I do to deserve the royal treatment?"

"Like you really have to ask?" he yelled back from the kitchen.

She felt such a rush of joy that her chest almost ached. Sternly, Fernanda reminded herself not to get carried away. She wasn't married yet. There could be complications. After all, traces of the ex-wife were everywhere. She'd found an old tube of mascara in the bathroom cabinet, and even a few stray tampons in one of the drawers. The ex's name was still on half the mail Parker received.

It was hard not to get a teensy bit excited, though. She'd met his friends, and they seemed to like her. He'd charmed her mother, which hadn't been difficult, and made an effort to get to know Max. She'd helped him make his cozy new Tribeca pad feel like a home (while secretly plotting their triumphant return to uptown life, where they really belonged).

Even before last night's conversation, the temptation to call St. James's—anonymously, of course—to check if they had any Saturdays available for weddings next fall had proved too strong. She'd held herself back from trying on bridal dresses at Vera Wang, but only just. If he proposed, she could have all the details of their wedding planned in under a week, right down to the *Fernanda & Parker* typeface on the matchboxes. She pulled herself out of bed, traipsing naked across the room to retrieve her BlackBerry from her bag. The only thing separating her from a perfect day was this phone call to her boss, so it was better to get it done with early—preferably while she could still leave her feeble excuse on a voice mail.

Five missed calls. Four from Cornelia—her friend had a habit of calling incessantly until Fernanda answered—and one from her mother. But first, her boss. Thankfully, she got his voice mail. "Martin, this is Fernanda. I'm afraid I'm not feeling well again, and I don't think I can make it to work." Her voice was still gravelly with sleep, which conveniently made her sound ravaged by bad sinuses. "I'll be checking e-mail, you know, between naps and a doctor's appointment. See you tomorrow."

"Breakfast is served," Parker said, appearing in the doorway with a rattan tray loaded with food. Pancakes, a small pitcher of OJ, and steaming hot coffee—Fernanda's mouth watered. No wonder she'd gained five pounds since they'd met. Normally she'd throw herself on the Jill Pettijohn cleanse immediately, but Parker said he liked her better with some meat on her bones—and Fernanda actually believed him.

"Smells delicious," she said, jumping back in bed and pulling the sheets loosely around her. She looked up at Parker and smiled seductively.

"Let's let it cool," he said, nearly throwing down the tray on the nightstand and diving on top of her.

Over her squeals, Fernanda could hear her BlackBerry buzzing. She tried to block it out, but involuntarily tensed—what if it was her boss? "Hold that thought," she said, wiggling out from under Parker and reaching for the phone.

But it was Cornelia's number flashing on her screen. "Her fifth call this morning. I wonder if something's wrong."

"With Cornelia? Trust me, plenty's wrong." Parker sighed. "But go ahead, pick up. We have all day together."

Fernanda smiled gratefully, then said, "Hey! How are you, C?"

"You sound happy," accused Cornelia. "Do you know how many times I've called you?"

"I'm sorry. What's up?"

When Cornelia spoke, her voice was so cold that Fernanda shivered. "I finally nailed her, Fern. She's been passing herself off as an heiress, when she's really to the trailer born."

"You mean Lucy? What did you do?" Fernanda felt the cold current pass over her again. Cornelia's vindictive streak could cross the line into downright frightening territory. She'd once ratted out a "disloyal" college friend, a girl working for *Glamour* and struggling to make ends meet, for selling a few leftover beauty products on eBay. The girl had been banned from Condé Nast for life. And Cornelia had started those nasty rumors about Mimi Rutherford-Shaw getting lipo every month, and about Anna Santiago and her stepbrother. She kept Page Six on speed dial. Cornelia had done something really bad this time, Fernanda could feel it.

"It'll be such thorough public humiliation that she'll be flipping burgers in her sleepy little hometown before she can blink." Cornelia cackled—or maybe it was just a bad connection. "With straw between her teeth and her tail between her legs."

"Is that really necessary?" Fernanda looked at Parker and suddenly felt ashamed of how evil her best friend sounded. "I mean, so she's self-made. So she took a few liberties with the truth—"

"*Self-made*? She's a work of fiction! Wait till you see the photos from the Nola show." There was that bad connection again. "I mean, it's just too good. The little gold digger is about to get all the attention she craves. It just won't be the *kind* of attention she craves."

Fernanda was starting to feel ill. Parker watched her intently. "Don't do it, Cornelia," she said quietly, aware that she was lighting a short fuse.

"What did you say?"

"Don't do it. It's—I don't know, it's just really mean."

"Mean? Tell me you're joking. The girl stole everything that mattered to me—"

Fernanda took a deep breath and tried to be brave. "She didn't really steal Wyatt. And anyway, it's time to move on. There's amazing stuff happening in your life right now, but you're consumed by the negative."

"Have you lost your mind?" There were shards of ice in Cornelia's voice. "Believe me, she deserves everything that's coming her way. It's all coming out in *Townhouse*."

"So you got Mallory Keeler to write a nasty piece about her—"

"You can call it nasty. I call it *true*," Cornelia said with chilling intensity. "And speaking of the truth? You might want to run some due diligence on that guy you're dating. A friend on his old co-op board told me that he's practically broke. The ex took most of his money; his investments and restricted stock are tanking; he's probably getting fired, and he's leveraged up the wazoo. Has Prince Charming mentioned any of that?"

"You don't know what you're talking about," Fernanda retorted, wanting to reach through the phone and slap Cornelia. *Hard.* Her chest felt constricted. The room was wobbling. Maybe she was having a heart attack.

"Just ask him," Cornelia snorted. "It figures. Didn't Freud have some theory about girls being drawn to men who remind them of their fathers? So it'd make sense you'd fall for a failure."

Fernanda felt her insides deflate. She ended the call without another word.

"Are you okay? What the hell was that all about?" asked Parker.

"You don't want to know." Fernanda plopped on the edge of the bed. She couldn't look at him.

"What do you mean, you haven't told her?" Dottie, who'd been examining one of the fabric swatches her decorator had left for the new draperies in her living room, looked up at her son. He was visiting her at home again—since when did Wyatt do that?—and he looked slightly unkempt, like he'd barely bothered to shower before wandering over. "Isn't the Ball the Saturday after next?"

"But the book won't be out for months after that. It still needs editing, and of course, an ending. I have plenty of time before . . . she needs to find out."

Dottie drew her petite spine up to its greatest height. This had gone on long enough. Her son may have been brilliant in his way, but apparently he needed the basics spelled out for him. "You need to do the right thing. For her sake, and your own. I see how you look at her when she's in the room with you. She's a special girl, Wyatt. Who cares if she's not"—she lowered her voice—"pedigreed. I don't, and you shouldn't. I want you to be happy. Frankly, Lucy seems to share our values more than any of the fly-by-night party girls you've dated."

Wyatt looked at her like she'd announced a move to Vegas to join Cirque du Soleil. "I've grown very fond of Lucy, of course, but that doesn't mean—"

Dottie sighed. "You're only fooling yourself, darling."

27

Wyatt's Book Notes:

Because male bowerbirds of New Guinea aren't much to look at, they compensate by constructing elaborate houselike bowers to lure potential mates. They feather their nests with colorful objets d'art—ornate crests, fans, plumes, and tail streamers dropped by their neighbor, the bird of paradise. Impressive real estate can be more effective than a great matchmaker. Men in New York society don't need to be told.

$\mathcal{L}$ucy gingerly carried her masterpiece into Eloise's living room, where Wyatt sat on the couch waiting for the unveiling. "I can't believe I'm asking you this—but please, be critical." The dress had turned out just as she'd imagined it, thanks to Doreen's careful execution, and struck her as exactly right for the Ball's "Fauna in Fashion" theme. It was regal without being princessy, and she felt a surge of pride knowing it was her very own creation. *Tout le monde* who mattered—she'd even begun thinking in French Snob, thanks to Wyatt—would see it on display at the Ball next Saturday.

Wyatt looked at the dress, then raised his eyes to Lucy. "It's perfect," he said. "I can't believe you did this. You're—"

She interrupted him by letting out a squeal, feeling the knots in her stomach release for the first time all week. The dress was ready. So was she.

"Listen," he said. He squirmed in his chair. "I've been meaning to talk to you about something."

"Wait, just hang on a sec." She ran into her bedroom, grabbed the envelope off the bureau, ran back, and waved it at him. "Before I forget, here's the money from my first commissions. Libet and Anna both placed orders after the *Townhouse* shoot. Doreen says she'll have them finished in a week or two." She handed it to him. "I've kept a pretty careful tally of how much I owe you, Wyatt. This is just a start."

Wyatt looked down at the envelope in his hands. "I can't take this—"

She'd expected resistance. "Of course you can. You're my first investor, and you made all this possible. I know you hate mushiness— but you've given me so much more than money. You've completely changed my life."

He turned the envelope over, uneasily. "I can't take credit for what you've done."

"We've both done it. Team effort." She smiled. "What did you want to talk about?"

"Huh? Oh, never mind. Nothing important."

Eloise took one last look in Trip's bathroom mirror before grabbing her clutch and racing down the stairs to the waiting car and her soon-to-be fiancé.

This had to be it. She was terrified to hope, but really, Trip had given her no choice but to have the utter expectation of a proposal. For starters, he'd announced that he'd made reservations at an "undisclosed location," and Eloise would be brought there blindfolded. Last week she'd overheard him talking on the phone in his study about making a "huge commitment," and being finally ready "to pull the trigger." She'd stood at his study door a second longer than she should have, unable to tear herself away, and had distinctly heard her boyfriend—her soon-to-be fiancé!—say that he'd "been thinking about it for a long time, but now the timing feels right." Besides, after their last fight, Trip would have to be a complete turd to lead her down the wrong path again.

Eloise smoothed down her Brian Reyes dress, an understated white and tan strapless with a sleek silhouette. Paired with a cashmere cardi and simple clutch, it was just the demurely sexy look she needed for the night.

Her BlackBerry buzzed. "Sweetie?" she asked, picking up. "I'm on my way right now."

When she emerged from her building, Trip was standing outside the Mercedes, holding a dozen red roses and a blue and gold Hermès scarf. "No peeking," he instructed, giving her a surprisingly languorous kiss before tying on the high-end blindfold.

Heart galloping, Eloise groped her way into the backseat. "Hi, Raoul," she giggled, waving her hand blindly.

"Hello, Miss Carlton," the driver answered. "You're a good sport."

The drive took longer than Eloise had expected. Maybe it was the blindfold, maybe it was her nerves, maybe it was Trip's uncharacteristic silence from the seat next to her—but what was probably a ten-minute trip felt more like an hour. Finally, Raoul pulled to a stop and she could hear him shift into park.

"We're here?" she asked.

"We're here, baby doll," Trip said, holding both her hands. "Can you handle the suspense for one more minute?" She nodded, smiling, while Trip got out of the car. A moment later, the door on her side opened, and his hand took hers again, helping her out.

"Where are we?" she twittered, loving every second as Trip led her forward. She could hear their feet crunching on gravel, and then the silk blindfold was untied—

"Surprise!" Trip shouted, as she struggled to orient herself.

They were standing on the dock of the Boat Basin on the Upper West Side. Eloise recognized the site from her early days in New York, when she'd lived in the neighborhood. "Are we taking a boat ride?" she asked. It was the perfect night for a proposal on the Hudson River, with Manhattan on one side and a deep orange sunset on the other.

"We're taking *many* boat rides," Trip said. He pointed to a flagblue Hinckley docked close to where they stood. A huge American flag was mounted off the rear on a mahogany pole, and printed in navy-and-gold block letters on one side was the name *Eloise.*

"There she is," Trip said. "The Hinckley T38R Convertible. Hand-built, open all the way up to the cockpit. You and I can take her to Nantucket this summer—it'll be amazing."

Eloise just stared at the boat that bore her name. "This is my surprise?" she asked, feeling seasick.

Trip, who'd been looking at her with hopeful anticipation, suddenly realized what he'd done. His face dropped. "Babe, I haven't forgotten about our conversation. I promise. I just need some more time. I thought you'd be excited—El, you look kind of green."

"You're not planning to propose tonight?" she asked.

"El, lovebug, we've talked about this," he said. He shut the car door so Raoul, staring straight ahead in the driver's seat, wouldn't hear.

"So you're *not.*"

"I thought you'd be excited! C'mon, sweetie, I'll give you the tour, you'll love it—"

"There is no chance I'm stepping on that boat." Eloise felt seconds away from a Krakatoa-style eruption. "You need to tell me right now, Trip, right now—are we getting married or not?"

Trip stared at her. "You're not serious. You can't expect me to respond to an ultimatum like that, to agree to change my entire life— you know how I feel about marriage."

"Does it matter how *I* feel?" Eloise demanded. The crux of their problem, she suddenly realized, was Trip's unwillingness to put her needs ahead of his own. "What kind of sicko plans this whole blindfold thing"—she threw the Hermès scarf on the ground. He tried to put his hands on her shoulders, but she shrugged them off violently—"and doesn't propose?" She was going to puke.

"Don't do this, El. We just moved in together—"

Her anger left her winded; she struggled to catch her breath. "Don't you dare act like I'm rushing you!" Eloise opened the car door and threw herself in. "Raoul, please take me home." But she could see the driver pause, not wanting to piss off his boss. *It's always about Trip. Trip's program, Trip's feelings, Trip's decisions.* She got out of the car. It was hard to control her body, but she did, running as fast as she could in four-inch stilettos.

"Eloise, please wait!" Trip dashed after her, grabbed her arm, and forced her to teeter.

"Don't speak to me unless you're ready to propose!" she shouted at him.

She was that girl. He'd turned her into that girl.

She kept on running, running, running. Past the crowds perusing the fruit stands outside Fairway, past the sidewalk where John Lennon was shot, past the evening joggers in Central Park to Fifth Avenue. One of her feet was bleeding, the other felt raw with blisters, but she didn't care. The sun was gone by the time she reached her own block. Eloise was too devastated to cry.

"Hello, Justine. This is Alison Pearce, Parker Lewis's new secretary. Mr. Lewis asked me to call you for a copy of his most recent summary of assets. We didn't receive one last month. Maybe because of Mr. Lewis's recent move? I know everything's been a little chaotic. Uh-huh. Uh-huh, perfect. Could you fax it to two-one-two, five-five-five, nine-eight-two-zero? Thanks, Justine. I'll let you know when it's come through."

No sooner had Fernanda hung up the phone than she heard the squeak of the front door hinge and the sound of Parker dropping his keys on the console table.

"Parker, is that you?" she called, running a hand through her freshly blown-out hair and trying to calm herself. He could have easily caught her mid-snoop; she was getting sloppy. "In the bedroom, sweetheart!"

"Hey, hon. This is a nice surprise." Parker, wearing a pin-striped bespoke suit and a robin's egg blue tie she had picked out for him at Bergdorf, looked a bit weary as he crossed the room to kiss her hello. "Dinner's at eight, right?"

"Yes, but I told Nelson and Ava that we'd swing by their place at seven for a quick drink. Is that okay, darling? Didn't your assistant mention it?"

Parker glanced at the clock. It was already six thirty-seven. "Maybe she did. It's been such a crazy day, Fern. Have you seen the news? The financial markets are taking a historic beating—"

Fernanda uncrossed her legs and stood up from the bed. "Poor puppy," she said, smooching his neck. She hated when he got all doomy-and-gloomy about the economy. "A nice night out with friends will cheer you up."

Parker looked unconvinced. "Where are we going?"

"Bouley. Ava made the reservation."

"Fine, but if Nelson Miller orders the eighty-eight Château Haut-Brion like he did last time, he's paying for it. After a day like the one I just had, it will *not* cheer me up to drop a thousand bucks on dinner."

Fernanda, horrified, stopped inspecting herself in the mirror and whipped around to face her boyfriend. "Parker! Say you're joking. You would *never*—"

Parker looked at her blankly. "I'll get changed fast, and then we can go."

"Okay!" she called after his retreating back. She pushed out of her mind the specter of an embarrassing moment with the dinner check. Parker would never be that gauche. "I laid out some clothes for you. Figured you'd want to change out of the suit you've been wearing all day."

Parker popped his head out of the walk-in closet. "I'm a fifty-two-year-old man, darling. I've been capable of dressing myself for a few years now." He said it lightly, but she could tell she'd over-stepped.

"Just trying to help!" she called, hiding the hurt in her voice. Parker really was in a black mood today. You'd think he'd show some gratitude for the effort she'd put into eradicating his ex-wife's tack-ola influence on his wardrobe—he had more Gucci loafers than you'd find in Cipriani on a Saturday night.

"I know you are, sweetie." Parker, now in his boxers, sat down on the chaise in the corner and patted the spot next to him. Fernanda perched beside him, careful not to wrinkle her sapphire-toned Michael Kors frock. "You know what it is? I just need more downtime. It seems like we're always running somewhere. I need a night or two each week where it's just you and me, some takeout, in our PJs by eight." He smiled, and Fernanda smiled back—although she felt more like crying. PJs by eight? The mere mention of downtime was such a *downer*.

Ever since Cornelia had planted the nasty little bug in her head, Fernanda had been obsessed with sleuthing out the truth about Parker's financial solvency. She'd started with his BlackBerry and e-mail account, logging in whenever she had the chance (his password had been easy enough to guess: Fursnickety, that nasty little vermin his wife had understandably left behind). Other than the pang of guilt she'd felt after reading an e-mail to his college buddy in which Parker had gushed about how happy Fernanda made him, she hadn't gotten much out of her efforts. Then last Friday she'd overheard him wrapping up a call with someone named Justine. When she teasingly asked about the other woman, he'd revealed that she was his private banker at JP Morgan—and so, of course, Fernanda had seized the first opportunity to scroll down in his BlackBerry call log and take down Justine's information for herself. She'd phoned from his apartment so that her number wouldn't pop up on Justine's caller ID. It was risky, but Justine didn't seem to suspect anything.

Was it wrong? A gross violation of his privacy? Clearly, yes and yes. But she was her mother's daughter, after all, bred to care about money first and foremost.

"Are you okay, babe?" he asked, touching her cheek. He turned on the lamp next to the chair, warming the room in a soft yellow light. "I'm not saying I don't want us to have a social life. Just more balance. Like maybe this weekend, you and I could go away to my cabin in the Adirondacks and just—"

"This weekend?" Fernanda nearly hyperventilated at the thought. "That's impossible, this Saturday is the Fashion Forum Ball! I've had my dress for four months! Cornelia's one of the Ball chairs and she'll kill me if I'm not—"

"Okay, okay," he said, taken aback by her impassioned response. Fernanda thought she heard him sigh. "Another weekend, then. No big deal."

As he stepped into the closet to dress, she dashed off to the fax machine, where Justine's report was waiting.

28

The countdown is on, fellow fash-addicts! Tonight is the glitziest, most exciting party of the year, the nexus of East Coast aristocracy and old Hollywood glamour, of dazzling haute couture and American heritage, of five-star fame and fifth-generation power. It's the Fashion Forum Ball, and we'll be on the red carpet to give you your fix.

—*www.fash-addict.com*

*N*ow do you remember why eating is kind of important?" Lucy clucked, circling Eloise with her pincushion.

With a sigh, Eloise hitched up her flax-colored strapless dress—ingeniously decorated with pheasant feathers and antique beading and right on the money for the Ball's celebration of fauna in fashion. The dress had been designed by Lucy, Eloise's designer of choice these days, and stitched with the expert help of Lucy's former Nola Sinclair colleague Doreen—but it was now dangerously loose on Eloise's diminished frame. Since the breakup with Trip, her appetite had collapsed and she'd been subsisting on the three C's: coffee, champers, cigarettes. "Just don't let me dance. This dress will be down around my waist by the first chorus. No offense to your pinning job, of course." Eloise lifted her arm so that Lucy could get in a bit closer.

The two friends, at Wyatt's insistence, were getting ready in a lavishly appointed suite at the Carlyle. It was an extravagance, but it was the only surefire way to avoid wrinklage; the museum was just three blocks away from the hotel. Since two that afternoon, Eloise and Lucy had been ensconced with an entourage of hair and makeup gurus. Eloise had to admit that the suite—with its framed architectural renderings by Piranesi and its sweeping view of Central Park—was a refreshing change of venue, considering she hadn't been out of the apartment or her sweatpants since Trip broke her heart.

Feeling a familiar lump in her throat, Eloise reached for her pack of cigarettes. "What if he shows up with a date? I mean, it's possible—"

"He's not showing up with a date, El. I called Margaux's office myself. Trip RSVP'd solo. Double- and triple-confirmed."

"Fine, what if he goes home with someone?"

"I will personally kick his ass down all fifty front steps of the museum. But he won't. This is Trip we're talking about. He might be an idiot, but he's not a bad guy."

Eloise let out a deep exhale, but wasn't reassured. She wondered if she'd ever stop feeling queasy. "I'm sorry, you must be so sick of listening to me."

"I'm not. You're being incredibly strong." Lucy smiled kindly at Eloise, dodging the small cloud of smoke she'd just exhaled and putting the final pin in her bodice. "There. You look beautiful."

"Thanks," she answered. She just hoped Trip would think so. "So do you, Luce, really." She just knew that Lucy's diaphanous cream-colored gown, hand-pinked at the edges, would steal the show. The soft layers of chiffon made it look like she was walking through clouds, while the bodice was molded perfectly to Lucy's svelte silhouette. The dress reflected a vision and attention to detail one might expect from a Paris couturier, not a girl from the Midwest. Lucy looked like the modern embodiment of the Roman wilderness goddess Fauna, from the warm olive undertones of her skin to the delicate gold Manolos that laced up her legs.

"Can I admit something?" Lucy walked to the window and looked out at the sun melting over the trees of Central Park. "I know I should be nervous about the auction, the press reaction to my gown, meeting Margaux Irving for the first time—and trust me, I am." She shivered at the thought. "I really am. But my mind keeps racing with . . . I don't know, *other* thoughts. I'm just not sure what will happen after tonight with me and Wyatt."

As distracted as Eloise had been with her own crisis, she wasn't blind to the growing chemistry between her friend and Wyatt. "Listen, four months ago, Wyatt was pretty much a nightmare, in terms of women. Selfish, shallow, elusive—"

"Obsessed with his place in the world. Yeah, I know—"

"But he's changed a lot. Frankly, more than I thought Wyatt would ever be capable of changing." So unlike Trip. Eloise poured herself another glass of Veuve Clicquot, hoping it might inspire a more festive mood, or at least steady her nerves.

"He's still Wyatt, though." Lucy waved her hand, reaching her limit with a topic that clearly made her uncomfortable. "Anyway, I shouldn't be thinking about this stuff. I should focus on getting through tonight."

"Me, too." Eloise smiled wanly and gulped down her champagne, feeling it burn her throat just a little. If only the bubbles could eat away the ache that seemed to permeate her entire body. Then maybe she could smile and giggle and pretend to have a merry old time at the Ball. "I just can't believe he hasn't called. Eight years of talking all day long and then radio silence."

"I still wish you'd come with us," Lucy said, watching her with concern.

She knew Lucy meant well, but the last thing Eloise needed was to show up as their third wheel. "Max will be a great escort. We've got the whole unlucky in love thing in common, you know?"

"Max and I are just friends, Eloise. We don't have that kind of chemistry. He hasn't called me in weeks."

Eloise took this in. "I admit I don't hate the idea of Trip seeing me walk in on the arm of one of the best-looking guys in New York. And Max is a total sweetheart."

"That's the spirit." Lucy lifted her glass. "To Trip Peters eating his heart out."

"I mean, *everyone* complains about divorce settlements and the tanking economy. I just assumed Parker's complaints were, you know, the universal kind." Fernanda looked at her reflection in the mirror, weighing whether to wear her grandmother's pearl necklace with the diamond and ruby clasp, or something younger, more modern. She decided on the pearls. "But it turns out he really is as broke as Cornelia said, or nearly."

"I can't believe Binkie didn't tell me this before you got so involved!" Her mother was outraged, just as Fernanda knew she'd be. "Binkie's known him through the opera for years. She *must* have known his wife took everything." Absentmindedly, Martha smoothed Fernanda's beautiful mane of hair with her hand. "I'm sorry, sweetheart, I'm terribly sorry."

Sorry for what, exactly, Martha didn't specify—but her expectation that Fernanda would end things with Parker and try her luck elsewhere was tacit. Fernanda frowned. *Funny how just last week she was raving on and on about how she's never seen me happier, more relaxed, more in love.*

"Don't think about it now. Just have a wonderful time tonight and we'll figure out what to do in the morning." Martha paused, tapping a finger to her lips with a fresh thought. "Incidentally, I hear Morgan Ware's marriage is a little wobbly these days. Maybe he'll be at the Ball?"

"You're not bailing." Wyatt was holding firm on this one. The final night of their experiment, the big test—Trip had to be there, no matter how stinking a mess he'd made of his life. Wyatt needed a wingman. As it was, he was so nervous his skin actually itched. He'd been dressed for the Ball for over an hour, and though he looked highly presentable in his Turnbull & Asser tails, his dark hair slicked back in the same debonair fashion his grandfather had worn in the '20s and his father had worn in the '60s, Wyatt had never felt less sure of his footing.

"But it's Eloise's terrain, not mine. All her froufrou fashion friends will be there, whispering in her ear that she's better off without me." Trip stared at his reflection in the mirror, disheartened. He pulled dolefully at the undone white bow tie around his neck. He'd been struggling with the thing for twenty minutes. "Thirty-six years old and I still need help getting dressed."

"They'll whisper *that* whether you're there or not." Wyatt was sick of hearing Trip whine about his self-created predicament. Although in the past he'd felt vaguely impressed by Trip's marriage aversion, now—thanks in part to Lucy's insights on the subject—he was starting to view it as selfish and immature. "Eloise is a one in a million girl and you've been stringing her along for years. I say this as someone who cares about your happiness: get over yourself and make a commitment."

"Dude, you think you're in a position to lecture about doing the right thing?"

Trip was right, much as Wyatt hated to admit it. Wyatt directed his pacing toward the antique demilune on which several crystal decanters were displayed, and poured himself a fresh scotch. He hadn't slept all week. He'd thought seriously about backing out of his book contract with Kipling—he thought about it day and night, in fact. But the publisher was practically giddy with enthusiasm, calling every day to check on his progress. If he bailed now, that door would be closed to him forever. Still, how could he root for Lucy's success tonight, knowing that the higher she climbed the farther she'd have to fall?

"My God, will you stop that?" Trip snapped. "You're driving me insane."

"Stop what?"

"The pacing! You haven't stopped moving since I got here! I know you're nervous, but it's annoying as hell!"

"It's my goddamn study, and I'll—" Wyatt's eighth-grade response was interrupted by the ringing phone. He picked up.

"I'm ready if you are," Lucy said, excitement in her voice.

What if she never spoke to him again?

"I'll call you when I'm a block away," he said, and clicked off.

"Where's Margaret?" said Trip. "I need her to tie this goddamn thing for me."

29

*L*ucy stared out the window of the limousine, clutching her minaudière. She'd spoken very little during the short ride to the museum, distracted by how handsome Wyatt looked and how close he sat next to her in the backseat. Her hand fluttered up to touch her hair, in which she'd pinned the gorgeous art deco diamond butterfly brooch that Wyatt had sent to the hotel that afternoon. "I've never seen anything like it," she said. Its wings were spread, as though it'd been captured midflight, and it gleamed against her dark walnut hair.

"It belonged to my great-great-grandmother," he said, watching her. "I thought you might like to have it."

Lucy spun to face him in the backseat. "*Have* it? I just assumed it was on loan for the evening. No way, Wyatt, I can't possibly accept such a valuable heirloom—"

"It would mean a lot to me if you did. You deserve it. You've worked hard, Lucy, and this is your night. Besides, it suits you."

Wyatt sounded curiously earnest. Moved by his generosity, she leaned over and kissed his cheek. "I don't know how to thank you, Wyatt," she whispered, keeping her cheek close to his for a moment longer than necessary. "You've changed my entire life, just like you said you would."

But her gesture had the opposite of its intended effect. Wyatt kept his eyes rigidly trained forward, like a little boy wanting to keep distance between his lips and Aunt Edna's. Lucy pulled back, mortified.

"I can't take credit. You're the star," he said quickly. "We're here." She forced herself to smile. "Look at all the press. They're as perceptive as bird-watchers in Central Park, knowing exactly which arrivals merit the swing of their lenses. But in this case they're more interested in the female of the species—rightly so, given the more distinctive, rich coloration of their attire."

Her knees had started to quake underneath her gown. "Could you hold off on the zoology for a minute? I'm petrified."

"Sorry." Wyatt reached out and grasped her hand. "Don't be nervous. This is your moment to shine. I'll be waiting upstairs with champagne. You can do this, Lucy."

Before she knew it, the door of the limo was opened for her. As soon as her second Manolo hit the red carpet, Lucy could hear the paparazzi—there seemed to be hundreds—yelling her name, louder than the crowd at a Vikings home game. *Overwhelming* couldn't begin to describe the feeling of taking her first steps in front of this battalion. The mad staccato of their flashing cameras created a blinding wall, making it impossible to tell who was screaming at her to *Turn! Twirl! Smile!* And how did they all learn her name? It took Lucy's breath away—she'd walked several red carpets before, but this one marked a new level of pandemonium. One photographer reached out to grab her arm, only to be immediately bodychecked by a brawny security officer in black.

"Thanks," she said, feeling a bit like prey, and the officer nodded. *Wow*. Wyatt had prepped her, but she had to see the ferocity of the camera crews, scratching and elbowing to get their money shot, to believe it. All their lenses were pointed at her. Even better, at her gown.

This is it, thought Lucy, *the make-or-break moment. If my gown gets good reviews, I'm one huge hurdle closer to becoming a designer. If it doesn't, I'll be forever branded a fashion victim.* She took a deep breath, tried to seem confident, and smiled coquettishly. A few steps closer, the riffraff pushed against black velvet ropes manned by PR girls and more security. Lucy stepped gingerly past this crowd, her eyes locked on the stately museum, which spanned five city blocks. It, too, was dressed magnificently for the occasion. Crimson carpet had been laid down the fifty front steps with military precision, and enormous white spotlights illuminated the iconic stone façade.

"Lucy! Lucy!" called out a fresh-faced kid Lucy recognized from the pre–Academy Awards coverage on E! He leaned so far over the velvet rope that his upper body was nearly horizontal to the ground. "Who are you wearing tonight?" he yelled. His cameraman, whose assistant shoved a fuzzy mike near her head, zoomed in for the close-up.

"My own design," she answered, savoring each word. She'd rehearsed this moment for weeks, on top of dreaming about it for years.

"Wait, did you say you *made* the dress you're wearing tonight?" The boy reporter looked incredulous. He pointed at her. "*That* dress?"

For once, her red-carpet smile was genuinely felt. "That's right. I designed it, and then a wonderful friend and I produced it." Props to Doreen. "Do you like it?" she asked, flirting a little.

"You look hot! You definitely get my vote for Best Dressed!"

The short exchange seemed to set off a frenzy among the reporters, as they began shouting their questions rapid-fire at Lucy. Over the roar, she couldn't make out what anyone was saying, so she waved politely and started to move on down the carpet. Leave them wanting more, Wyatt had always coached her. She hoped he was right, but then he'd never steered her wrong. She took a few more steps, basking in the glow of the spotlight. *This is my moment,* she thought, *the moment when I fully step into the life I was meant to have*—

"Luuuuuce! *Lucy Jo!* Over here, doll, over here!"

Oh no, no, no, no, no.

Rita's voice—the same abrasive accent that Wyatt had spent days training out of Lucy—cut through the deafening noise to assault her daughter's ear. At the sound, the air seemed to *whoosh* out of Lucy's lungs. Before she could stop herself, her eyes found her mother on the other side of the rope. Rita, sausaged into a god-awful sequined dress, had elbowed her way through the phalanx of photographers and seemed to be having a heated debate with the towering PR girl standing guard.

"She won't let me in, even though I've got a ticket right here!" Reaching one hand into her front-and-center cleavage, Rita fished out the ball's distinctive green and gold invitation. It looked terrifyingly similar to the one that had been delivered to Lucy herself, inside an extraordinary hand-stitched envelope made of thick leaves and gold thread. And there was the envelope in Rita's other hand. Lucy heard herself groan.

"I don't know who you mugged to get this ticket," sneered PR Girl, "but you're not coming in." She turned to Lucy, a mean little smile on her pretty little face. "I mean, I would get so Margauxed!" The famed editor had inspired her own verb, meaning to flay silently but thoroughly.

Get this under control. Lucy desperately wished Wyatt was with her. He'd handle the situation and she could go back to smiling for the cameras. She prayed her mother wouldn't blurt out that they were related, or something equally damning. Her mind raced for a solution that wouldn't destroy her mother's feelings.

"Go ahead—tell her you know me, doll! Tell her you're my—"

"Rita!" Lucy shouted, catching both women by surprise. "Um,

could I talk to you for a moment? Somewhere a bit more private?"
She shot PR Girl a look she hoped would be interpreted as "my
manicurist is clearly off her meds, but I'm such a good person that
I'll take time out of my very important night to make sure she's okay."
PR Girl, puzzled, just shrugged and opened the velvet rope for her.

Lucy pulled her mother out of earshot on the museum steps. She
couldn't risk the chance of the two of them being photographed together. Luckily Gisele and Tom Brady had just arrived and were
temporarily diverting everyone's attention.

"*Taa-daa*! Betcha didn't expect to see me tonight, did ya?" Rita's
hair had been teased into an elaborate nest of tendrils, and she wore
a corsage—a corsage!—of carnations and baby's breath on one wrist.
Rita looked like a prom queen on Social Security. Completing the
look was the clunky camera around her neck and a stack of glossy
photographs under her arm. "Did you know George Clooney's coming tonight?" Rita waved a photo of him. "I'm gonna have him sign
it: 'To Rita, one sexy *mamasita*!' Cute, right? This event is the mother
lode of celebrities!"

"Rita, why are you here?" The air was colder once you stepped outside the fray, and Lucy shivered. Leave it to Rita to spoil her golden
moment. To put her obsession with celebrity above her daughter's
hopes and dreams. This was the worst, most selfish thing her mother
had ever done, which was saying a lot.

"I wanted to be here for you." *Did Rita actually look proud of herself?* Lucy bit back her scream. "I haven't always been the best
mother in the world, but I'm here for you now. To support you, doll."

"How did you get a ticket?" Her mother had managed to snag a
ticket to an event that had closed its doors to several Fortune 100
CEOs?

"I cannot reveal that information." Rita, in a mock-serious voice,
mimed zipping her lip and tossing away the key.

"I'm sorry, Rita, but you can't be here," Lucy said bluntly.

Rita looked hurt, but quickly recovered. "I thought you'd appreciate that I was, you know, *here* for you—here to support you—"

I will not feel guilty about this. Lucy was too close now to have

Rita blow her cover. "It's going to be a madhouse. Why don't you relax over at the Carlyle?" She struggled to keep her voice low, but the
situation was getting increasingly desperate. "I already have a room
there, and it's only a few blocks away. You could order room service,
take a nice hot bubble bath—"

Rita shook her head and laughed. "And miss all the action? Not
on your life!" But then her face fell for an instant as she seemed to
catch Lucy's drift. "Unless you really don't want me here."

Lucy glanced over her shoulder. Libet and Anna had just arrived
and were reveling in the press attention. Meanwhile, she was running
out of patience. So she didn't want her terminally tacky mother to
spoil Wyatt's bet, torpedo her soon-to-launch career, and ruin the
biggest night of her life—did that make her an awful person? Why
did Rita always have to be the child in their relationship? No wonder
it had felt so good to be taken care of during the past three months.
It was a first.

"Well?" asked Rita petulantly.

Lucy looked back at the red carpet, then at Rita. "Can't you let
me enjoy the spotlight for once?" she blurted out. "Does everything
always have to be about you and what you want?"

Her mother looked stunned. She began to blink her eyes quickly.
She took a raspy breath. "Have your spotlight, then." Her lower lip
began to tremble. "You've changed, Lucy Jo. You used to be a good girl.
You used to understand what it meant to be family. Now I don't even
know you. Maybe you look all fancy, but the old Lucy Jo was a hel-
luva lot classier." She gave her daughter a last accusatory glare, then
pushed her way through the crowd toward the street.

Lucy stood shocked into silence. For a moment, she thought
about running after her mother. But instead she turned, slowly,
back toward the red carpet, swallowing the lump in her throat. As she
climbed the remaining stairs to the museum's front entrance, she
heard a photographer call her name and glanced over her shoulder with a carefully executed smile, striking the pose she'd practiced so often. Soon she was rewarded with a tidal wave of
flashing cameras, the supernovas of fame. She turned slightly so

the photographers could capture the floating layers of her gown in movement. She posed as though her future depended on it. Because it did.

I'll make it up to Rita later, Lucy reassured herself, slipping through the doors into the party of a lifetime. She tried to ignore how much her heart ached.

30

Great apes . . . make great fakers. Frans B. M. de Waal, a professor at the Yerkes National Primate Research Center and Emory University, said chimpanzees or orangutans in captivity sometimes tried to lure human strangers over to their enclosure by holding out a piece of straw while putting on their friendliest face. "People think, Oh, he likes me, and they approach," Dr. de Waal said. "And before you know it, the ape has grabbed their ankle and is closing in for the bite. It's a very dangerous situation."
—The New York Times, *December 12, 2008*

*I*s that a chipmunk?" Lucy pointed at the birch branch, but before Parker Lewis could turn his head, the tiny little creature had scurried away. Of all the things Lucy had imagined she might see inside the social event of the year—the rustling of one-of-a-kind couture; jewelry worth more than most people's houses; immaculately preserved society doyennes—she hadn't figured on live fauna.

"I should've brought my ferret, but he's not trained. Apparently all the animals in attendance tonight had to finish more school than your average ophthalmologist."

Lucy giggled harder than Parker's joke merited, thanks to her runaway nerves. His was the first familiar face she'd seen when she entered the vaunted marble hall of the Heritage Museum, and she'd latched on to him immediately. Wyatt hadn't been kidding when he called the Fashion Forum Ball the Super Bowl of fashion, as well

as being Lucy's chance to rub shoulders with the crème de la crème
of international society. He'd prepped her that this wasn't a "pack a
table with your friends for twenty grand" benefit, and that guests
were chosen with greater care than vice presidential candidates.
Margaux's team of A-list arbiters made snubbing an art form. It
made Rita's ticket an even greater mystery.

"Where's Fernanda?" she asked, to be polite.

"Oh, Cornelia dragged her off to the powder room." He waved his
hand. "I'm sure she'll be back in a few hours."

The Natural History wing of the museum had been transformed
into an enchanted forest, with hundreds of rare butterflies flutter-
ing above the crowd and touching down on the branches of the live
birch trees. Apparently they were surrounded by an entire ecosystem,
from the chipmunks to the songbirds Lucy could hear lightly chirp-
ing in the background. *How Rita would've loved it in here,* Lucy
couldn't help thinking. Her mother had been born to exclaim over
spectacles like this, and all the twinkling lights made it look like the
room had been BeDazzled.

"George Clooney, two o'clock," whispered Parker.

Another reminder of the disappointment in Rita's eyes. The
thought made Lucy's conscience feel like lead. She distracted
herself by once again scanning the crowd for Wyatt. When she finally found him, despite his brush-off in the limo, Lucy couldn't
unlock her eyes. As usual Wyatt cut an incredibly soigné figure;
in his well-cut tails, he was a standout even among the highest
ranks. Clooney didn't hold a candle. Wyatt's handsome face was
animated by the story he was telling. She was so transfixed that it
took Lucy a moment to notice that Wyatt was speaking to Margaux Irving.

Lucy's stomach lurched. Margaux was dressed to intimidate in a
voluminous taupe gown with enormous mink shoulders and a
matching train. It felt too soon in the night to face such a major
challenge, but Lucy knew she had to go over—Margaux was in sky-
high demand; it was unlikely Lucy would have two chances to meet
her. Snagging a glass of champagne from a waiter with a tray, she

told Parker she'd be right back. "Oh—and thank you," she said to the waiter, almost forgetting.

Wyatt beamed at her as she approached. "Lucy! I was hoping you'd find us. Margaux, this is Lucy Ellis. Her gown will be auctioned tonight."

"Of course," Margaux said, extending her long, thin hand toward Lucy. Her voice was surprisingly—well, human. Even feminine. And up close, her skin looked bizarrely flawless and untouched by age—so much so, Lucy wondered if she might have a gnarled portrait aging in an attic somewhere. "Lucy's photo has run in my magazine, Wyatt—I know very well who she is."

Don't blush. Don't curtsy. Just look her square in the eye. Meeting Margaux required nearly as much protocol as an audience with Queen Elizabeth, and Wyatt had coached Lucy well. The key was to seem deferential but not obsequious. "I'm delighted to meet you," Lucy said, shaking the proffered hand. She suppressed the urge to kiss the enormous pink diamond bauble on the older woman's finger.

Margaux gave Lucy a cool once-over—taking in her modern Grace Kelly updo, lingering for a moment, maybe two, to assess her dress, and ending with her delicate stilettos. Her face gave away nothing. "Who designed your dress? I don't recognize it."

Lucy cleared her throat. Moment of truth. "I designed it myself," she said, mustering all her confidence. Wyatt discreetly took her hand in his, which she so appreciated. Having him next to her always gave her extra oomph. Maybe because she sensed that he cared as much about Margaux's approval and Lucy's success as she did.

"Yourself?" Margaux arched a perfectly sculpted eyebrow. "Where did you study?"

Lucy glanced quickly at Wyatt. "I'm self-trained. I've loved fashion since I was a little girl." She tried to keep her voice steady and relaxed, as if chatting about her designs to Margaux Irving were an everyday occurrence. "When I was a teenager, I took apart a vintage Chanel dress to understand exactly how it had been constructed, the way an aspiring engineer might take apart a radio." She didn't mention that she'd found the dress serendipitously at the local Salvation

Army, or that she'd had to pay the eighty-dollar price tag on layaway. "It's always been my dream to be a designer."

Another loaded pause as Margaux stepped forward slightly to examine the dress from another angle. "And where did you have it made?"

"In my own living room." Lucy lifted up her train. It had taken weeks of labor to make the floaty confection. "I worked with another seamstress in order to finish in time. And my friend Eloise Carlton—I believe she's worked for your magazine—helped with the fitting."

Margaux swept around her. "I must say—"

Lucy drew her breath in anticipation, but before Margaux could deliver her verdict on the gown, a young assistant flew at her. The girl's face was flushed with panic. "Margaux! I'm so sorry to bother you, terribly sorry, but we're having a little issue with some protesters!"

Uh-oh. This would not be pretty. Lucy felt so sorry for the assistant, who would doubtlessly get Margauxed for the breathless interruption, that she was temporarily distracted from her own suspense.

The editor in chief cast a withering look. "Such as?"

"They just doused three of our guests with red paint on their way in, and they say they'll only stop if they can have a word with you."

"I don't negotiate with terrorists."

"I know, but . . . we've received word that Mary Kate, Kanye, and Demi and Ashton are all circling the block, afraid to get out of their cars. These protesters don't care about the police, about spending the night in jail—they just want to talk to you."

That's kind of bad-ass, Lucy thought, although she selfishly wished it didn't have to interrupt her tête à tête with Margaux. She'd never understood carcass chic, or how designers and their clients could look the other way while little bunnies in China went to their slaughter. She favored Stella McCartney's animal-friendly approach.

"Enough." The stony-faced editrix turned back to Wyatt and Lucy. "Please excuse me." She swept away before they could answer—before she could give any indication of feeling toward Lucy's gown.

Now what? Frustrated, Lucy let out something between a groan and a sigh, and Wyatt slipped his arm around her. "I'm sure she loved it," he said. "How could she not?"

Despite knowing better, she couldn't help feeling a little thrill from his unexpected closeness. "She must rock in poker. But thanks."

"Trust me, I'm sure she was a fan. And everyone else will be too. You're beautiful—" Those last two words seemed to slip out, and once they had, Wyatt quickly dropped his arm. The same cloud she'd felt in the limo passed over them, reminding Lucy that she had to get her feelings in check. Wyatt was nothing more than her friend—a surprisingly loyal and supportive friend, but just a friend. "There's Parker and Trip," he said, changing the subject. "Let's see if they're at our table."

"That's Walker Gregory, director of the museum." Wyatt discreetly pointed as they made their way through the crowded room to find their seats. The Grand Room (not only an apt description, but the name of the family who'd endowed it) was a sight to behold, even for Wyatt's jaded eyes. Amazonian vines and foliage hid the ceiling and walls, while the tables were covered in crisp linens, heavy silver, and Meissen porcelain, creating a sense of civility in the exotic wilderness. Walker, Wyatt observed, was seated to the left of Meredith Galt, who'd recently made an enormous gift to the Fashion Forum. He and Lucy had been seated prominently, too, he was pleased to note.

Speaking of Galts, there was an unwelcome one waiting when they reached the table. "Theo, what a fun surprise!" Lucy exclaimed, rushing over to kiss him hello.

"Swell tux," Wyatt said, shaking Theo's hand. It was black-on-black, cheesy as hell. "Very Steven Seagal." He took his seat. Wyatt wasn't sure why the discovery of Theo grinning from the seat next to Lucy's irritated him so much—ditto Lucy's effusive reaction to seeing him—but it did. He'd have preferred a table in Siberia to an evening spent witnessing Theo's slimy moves. Besides, for all Theo knew, Wyatt and Lucy really *were* a romantic item—so where did he get off with the full-court press? No doubt the guy had asked to be seated next to Lucy—since the museum was now in such debt to his family, nobody had the stones to say no. See how they felt when the Hayes Foundation reevaluated its portfolio of philanthropic contributions next year.

"Are you okay?" Lucy whispered when Theo was distracted by a passing friend. "You seem upset. Is it Theo?"

"Never mind," said Wyatt. If he tried to explain his feelings, he knew he would sound jealous, or possessive of a woman he had no right to be possessive of. Wyatt glanced down at the event card to the side of his plate. "So it looks like the auction will take place before dinner."

"I'm glad," she said. "I won't be able to enjoy myself until it's over."

As soon as the words left her lips, Walker Gregory took the stage. As the waitstaff silently set the first course, the audience craned to see the small, patrician gentleman who for decades had maintained the museum's preeminence. Walker welcomed everyone to the Ball, thanking various patrons and boasting of high-profile recent acquisitions, but Wyatt wasn't listening. He heard his own name mentioned, but even that failed to steal his attention away from the young woman sitting next to him. The magnitude of what Lucy was about to do—presenting not only her gown, but herself, to the most discerning style cognoscenti on the planet and asking for their approval in such a public and vulnerable way—was only now fully hitting him. She nervously clutched his hand under the table. At that moment, Wyatt wasn't thinking about his book, the experiment, his stake in the night. He just prayed Lucy wouldn't be crushed in front of everyone who mattered to her career. She'd come too far and cared too much.

"Will all the participants in our fashion auction please join me?" Walker asked, prompting Wyatt to squeeze Lucy's hand extra hard.

"Ouch!" She laughed a little as she stood. "You're even more nervous than I am, aren't you?"

"These ladies have generously agreed to auction the dresses they're modeling this evening," Walker continued, "and all proceeds will go toward continuing the Heritage Museum's tradition of excellence."

Wyatt watched with tense pride as Lucy threaded her way to join the museum director onstage. All the other women who were lining up next to her, besides hailing from the most prestigious families in American history, had chosen gowns made by established American designers such as Ralph Lauren, Michael Kors, and Nola Sinclair. He thought Lucy was the most self-assured and elegant of the bunch, and that her dress matched her as the most beautiful—but what if nobody else admired it enough to make a bid?

Compare her with Cornelia, he thought, watching his ex glower next to Lucy in a celadon Ralph Rucci gown and a painted-on smile. Cornelia could don ten tons of diamonds and still lack Lucy's sparkle. He'd taught Lucy the manners, the savoir faire—but she'd always had an inherently noble character. It showed through in everything she did, from her ready devotion to Mimi Rutherford-Shaw's nonprofit to her tireless work ethic, from her immediate curiosity about art and culture to her unwavering modesty and sense of self. He knew she dreamed of making it big not only for herself, but also so that she could provide for her mother. Seeing her on that stage, he saw her clearly for the first time.

"Can you believe she made that dress?" Theo, leaning across Lucy's now empty seat, had the audacity to smile at Wyatt as though they were old chums. "Girl's got serious talent."

"She's got a very bright future ahead of her," said Wyatt. He tried not to think about how his book might stall her career before it started.

The Sotheby's auctioneer called the room to silence. "First we have a Rodarte gown, worn tonight by Miss Libet Vance. Can I start the bidding at ten thousand? Ten thousand from the woman in red. Twelve? I have twelve thousand dollars from the gentleman at the back of the room." The auctioneer continued to rattle off bids. "Fifteen thousand for this one-of-a-kind gown. Going once, going twice— sold to the woman at table twelve for fifteen thousand dollars." Anna Santiago's Nola Sinclair dress—a vampiric mountain of heavy black lace that made Wyatt shudder—went on to sell for a respectable seven thousand, and then Cornelia's gown for an impressive twelve.

"Last but not least, we have a beautiful gown by"—the auction-eer paused to make sure he was reading the program correctly—"Lucy Ellis. Is that right?" Lucy nodded, an easy smile on her face. If she was nervous about her dress's being on the block, it didn't show. Wyatt felt he'd absorbed all her anxiety, compounding his own. He reached quickly for his water glass, nearly knocking over his wine. He didn't think he could stand to watch. "She's wearing her own creation, ladies and gentlemen. I'll start the bidding at five thousand dollars. Can I have five thousand for this stunning gown from Lucy Ellis?"

Echoing Wyatt's worst fears, the Grand Room remained silent. Guests actually stopped chewing, holding their silverware frozen over their plates. Eloise, seated with Max at the next table, shot a glance toward Wyatt, eyes wide with panic. Wyatt himself had stopped breathing. The silence was unbearable. He got ready to raise his pad-dle. Lucy would be devastated that he'd had to come to her rescue, but it was better than watching her endure this silence for another minute.

Theo's hand shot out to grab his own paddle. "Don't you fucking dare!" Wyatt said, glaring. The thought of Theo Galt owning Lucy's dress appalled him.

"I think you're missing the point of an *auction*," Theo whispered back. "Besides, I've decided I want to back her. Help her start her own label."

"She's already got a swarm of people who want to back her, includ-ing me." He spoke without thinking. "She doesn't need your—"

"A one-of-a-kind original by Lucy Ellis," repeated the auctioneer. "Doesn't she look lovely in it? Can I get five thousand for this ex-ceptional gown?"

Before either man could get his paddle in the air, a timid voice called out from the back of the room. "Five thousand!"

Wyatt, exhaling for the first time since Lucy had left her seat, lifted out of his chair to behold the angel who'd bought her gown. Fernanda Fairchild sat with her paddle trembling in the air.

Shocked, Wyatt's first instinct was suspicion—why would Cornelia's BFF stick her neck out to save Lucy? But when he turned to the stage to catch Cornelia's reaction—face purpling with rage, jaw dropped—he realized there had just been a major social defection. Fernanda, it seemed, had found her backbone.

With the ice broken, Wyatt watched with glee as paddles began flying faster than the auctioneer could call. Every female in the room seemed to grasp how special Lucy's gown was, and as Wyatt knew, it was a room full of women accustomed to getting what they wanted. Wyatt caught Lucy's eye; because he knew her so well, her cool expression betrayed her elation. If she'd won over this room, the core of chic, there'd be no stopping her.

"Twenty thousand," declared a distinctive voice from the front of the room. Heads whipped around to see who'd more than quadrupled the original ask.

"Margaux Irving! We have twenty thousand from the incomparable Margaux Irving!" the auctioneer chirped. Wyatt, unable to control himself, jumped up from his seat applauding—luckily, others followed quickly. Margaux had made history by raising her paddle—in the decade he'd been attending the Ball, Wyatt had never seen her bid on a gown. "A high bid from the one and only Ms. Irving! Ladies, gentlemen, do we have anyone who'd like to top that?"

Paddles stayed down, as the guests weighed their desire for the gown against the danger of alienating the powerful editor, but the buzz in the room was deafening. His eyes locked with Lucy's in triumph, and she flashed him a huge grin. Cornelia, meanwhile, seemed to be slightly convulsing next to her.

Since nobody seemed to be finding courage, the auctioneer brought down his gavel. "Sold to Margaux Irving for a very generous twenty thousand dollars."

She did it! Pure jubilation coursed through Wyatt's veins. He felt high. Eloise and Theo and Max were toasting all around him, but once again Wyatt was only truly aware of Lucy, slipping quickly through the crowd, beaming, pausing here and there to graciously accept congratulations from new admirers. When she finally made it back to their table, Wyatt couldn't stop himself—he pulled her close and kissed her, hard, with all the pent-up passion he'd been denying for weeks. When she pressed back against him, her lips petal-soft but her kisses firm, it was all he could do not to carry her out of the party and straight to his bed.

The book. It flickered momentarily across his frontal lobe, forcing Wyatt to pull back.

"Wyatt?" she asked, touching his arm.

The world had returned to spinning on its axis, but everything seemed changed. Theo, Wyatt noticed with satisfaction, had slunk off toward the bar, trumped by the kiss he'd been forced to witness. Max and Eloise had quickly absented themselves, too. Lucy was looking at him in a new way, her face lit with hope and curiosity. He could see in her eyes that she'd wanted that kiss as much as he did.

The book, the book, the book. "I—there's something I need to do," he said.

"What, gloat?" She smiled, teasing him. "Give Trip a pass tonight. It can't be easy for him, watching Eloise with Max. You can rub victory in his face tomorrow."

She has no idea, thought Wyatt, unable to bear his duplicity a moment longer. He cared way too much about Lucy to hurt her. "Just give me a few minutes. I'll be right back." Before she could utter a word of protest, he stood and headed quickly for the door, resolved in what he had to do.

"What the *hell* were you thinking, bidding on that dress?" Cornelia kept her voice low so that only Fernanda and Parker could hear. She'd charged straight to their table as soon as the auction was over, head spinning with anger. "Lucy was twisting in the wind until you opened your fat mouth!"

"Calm down," Parker said slowly. "You're overreacting." Fernanda, her face even paler and more drawn than usual, didn't say a word. She sat with her arms crossed, not meeting Cornelia's eyes, like a prisoner of war anticipating torture.

"Does the troll *speak* for you now, too?" Cornelia could feel a familiar hot darkness welling up inside her. She'd felt it for the first time when she was sixteen and her mother had forgotten that it was

Parents' Weekend at Groton and flown to Verbier with her Swiss "friend" Jacques instead. It was a dangerous feeling, Cornelia knew that. Her mother had returned from the slopes to find her friends all gossiping that she had chlamydia. "You're just lucky your grand gesture triggered a bidding war, Fernanda. Where would you have gotten your hands on a spare five thou? You would've had to harvest a kidney—what's the going rate for the internal organs of an aging, insolvent social has-been?"

"There's something seriously wrong with you," said Parker, his cheeks flushing. "Anyone ever tell you that?"

"Oh, please. You're pathetic," she spat back at him. "Broke, bald, boring—no wonder your wife dumped you. I guess Fernanda here is the best you can do." She let out a laugh. "Do you have any idea how many men ol' Fern here threw the cat to during her twenties, hoping one would make an honest woman out of her?"

"Get away from us, you viperous beast!" Parker flew to his feet, while Fernanda remained slumped, face buried in both hands. Though he was considerably shorter than Cornelia, the sheer force of his outrage pushed her back on her heels.

She became aware that people were starting to pay attention. "No need to make a scene," she sneered, pulling herself together. Cornelia Rockman would not be reduced to hysterics in the middle of the social event of the year. She would not raise her voice. She was, after all, a lady, and these two losers were *so not worth it*. Without a backward glance at Fernanda, she turned on her heel and walked away, ending eighteen years of friendship.

In a quiet corner of the now forsaken room where they'd had drinks, Wyatt punched in the phone number and prayed for voice mail. After all they'd been through together, he had no choice. Lucy was a human being, not a chimpanzee under observation. His mother was right: it was time to think of someone besides himself, for once.

"Wyatt!" Damn it, Kipling had picked up. Wyatt could hear the din of a restaurant in the background. "Good to hear from you, son, even at this late hour. Have you—"

"I'm sorry, sir, but I can't publish the book," Wyatt blurted out. With the utterance of each word he felt more weight rise off his heart.

"El, think you ought to slow down just a bit?" Lucy eyed her friend with concern. After Wyatt had abruptly vanished, leaving her stunned and breathless and bewildered by their kiss, she'd found Eloise with Max at the bar. Eloise, normally poised and soft-spoken, was in her cups—no state to help Lucy decode Wyatt's hot-and-cold behavior—and had just overridden Max to order yet another martini.

"I'm *celebrating*! My girl just *dominated* the auction!" Eloise leaned across the bar to snag one of the jumbo martini olives. Then she fell on Lucy, holding on for dear life. Max put an arm protectively over Eloise's fragile shoulders and tried to help her stand.

"Why don't we celebrate with some bread and coffee?" Lucy flagged down a passing waiter and made the request.

"Good idea," said Max over Eloise's head. "She hasn't touched a bite."

"I can hear you!" Eloise laughed, leaning on Max. "How can I eat when my boyfriend is doing the bump-and-grind with some *Gossip Girl* castoff?" She waved her pointed finger toward the dance floor, but Lucy couldn't see Trip anywhere. Eloise accepted her fresh martini from the bartender, who shrugged at the look Lucy gave him. As she brought the glass to her lips, it tipped a little and sent a splash down the front of her beautiful strapless gown. Eloise stared at the graying stain for a moment, before swinging her head back up with a grin. "Wet couture contest!" she hooted, swallowing more gin.

Max lunged for a napkin and held it in front of her as her gown went translucent. "We need to get you home," he said.

"Just one dance," Eloise slurred. She took Max's hand and dragged him toward the dance floor. Short of carrying her out of the ball caveman-style, there didn't seem to be much he could do.

Lucy was distracted by Wyatt's hand touching down on her elbow, a light contact that nonetheless sent a shiver throughout her whole body. "Sorry to rush off like that. Now the night's all ours." He smiled, his blue-gray eyes twinkling, and grabbed two champagne flutes from a nearby table. He handed her one, grazing her hand. "So."

She smiled softly. "So."

"Three months went by fast, didn't they?" He studied her face.

"If you weren't the one living on kale and exercising five hours a day," she laughed. But it had. She took a sip of champagne, the bubbles tickling the roof of her mouth. Wyatt slipped an arm around her waist, his hand pressing against her back. It felt overwhelming and strangely natural at the same time.

"It went by fast for me, then. Too fast." He leaned toward her, kissing her again—it felt more deliberate, this time, but even more delicious. *Could this really be happening?* Lucy had never believed in fairy-tale romance—Rita and her short list had stripped away the veil from her young eyes—but she was now faced with mounting evidence that Happily Ever After could actually . . . happen. Once she made things right with Rita, her life would be perfect. "I don't want this night to end," she murmured, kissing him between words.

"Sorry to break up the gropefest." Cornelia, looking rosy-cheeked, materialized next to them. The pin-thin blonde flashed them a sticky sweet smile, laying her hand on Lucy's arm and reminding Lucy of Wyatt's observation that *a smile is sometimes the social animal's way of baring her teeth.* "You've had quite a night for yourself, haven't you? It's just too bad your mama wasn't here to see it, Lucy Jo. I pulled every string I could think of to get her that ticket."

So Cornelia knew. Thinking of the way she'd treated Rita, Lucy wanted to sink through the floorboards. "The two of you met?"

"Oh, yeah. Rita and I had quite the catch-up." Cornelia cocked her head. "You can't miss the family resemblance. The nose, the hips . . . She told me about how you worked all through high school as a waitress at the local truck stop. What a refreshing choice for the heiress of a major timber fortune. And then your job in Nola Sinclair's factory—"

Wyatt exploded first. "Enough! I don't know what your point is—"

Cornelia smiled. "Wyatt, darling, I think you do. Lucy here is a complete fraud. She's your doll, all done up in the right clothes and jewelry, with the right fork in her hand. At first I couldn't understand how you could leave me for"—she waved a hand in Lucy's direction—"this. But I get it now. You weren't equipped to handle a real woman. You needed to find a little toy, a chess piece you could manipulate however you wanted."

The Grand Room was spinning, Lucy struggled to breathe—

"Now the rest of the world is going to find out your weird little secrets. Next week, *Townhouse* is running a cover story exposing all Lucy Jo's lies. Mallory's writing the final paragraphs tonight." Lucy gasped. She *had* thought the editor gave her a strange look when she'd waved at her across the room during cocktails. "I thought you'd want to know before it landed on your doorstep."

"You've gone too far, Cornelia," she heard Wyatt say, but his voice sounded far away from her now. "There's no reason to attack Lucy just because things didn't work out with us—"

Cornelia snickered. "Don't flatter yourself. You were always waxing on about how I should contribute more to the public good. Well, exposing this liar is my contribution." And with that, Cornelia strutted away, leaving a whiff of acerbic perfume in her wake.

Lucy's humiliation cut so deep that she couldn't breathe, as though she'd been swinging from the chandeliers, fallen, and landed flat on her back. She couldn't find her voice to speak. The ball, the museum, shrank away from her. Wyatt's hands were on her shoulders, trying to comfort her, but Lucy couldn't raise her eyes to meet his. Everything was lost: Wyatt's bet, the approval of all the people she'd come to know, the career she'd worked so hard to attain. He'd be humiliated right along with her. She'd even wounded Rita. Now she'd never be able to make it up to her by offering help, a boost, a better life.

"It'll be okay, I promise," Wyatt said, but she knew he was lying.

"I need to get out of here." Lucy still couldn't bear to look at him. Tears stinging her eyes, she gathered the skirts of her gorgeous, hopeless gown around her, turned, and dashed out of the ball.

31

I don't care what is written about me so long as it isn't true.
—*Dorothy Parker*

*M*ax?"

"Yes, Eloise?"

She laughed at his formality, resting her spinning head against his chest. She resisted the urge to lick one of the studs on his tuxedo shirt. "I like your pecs."

"Thank you."

"I'm so glad you came to the ball with me. I don't know what I'd do if you weren't here."

"Drink yourself even sillier?" He smiled tenderly at her. "I'm glad, too. Now why don't you let me take you home? We'll pick up a pizza on the way. Sober you up a little."

"Just a few more dances," Eloise insisted, finding her energy again. All she hoped was that they were making Trip—last seen gyrating with his girl to "Fly Me to the Moon"—good and jealous. She wrapped her arms around Max's neck. "Dip me!" she whispered, and Max nervously obliged. Eloise dipped, dipped, and kept dipping— forcing Max to haul her up like a fishing net full of cod.

"Eloise, I'm taking you home *now*," he said after returning her to her upright and locked position, and this time she could tell he wasn't taking no for an answer. He pressed her body tightly against his, lifting her off the ground and carrying her off the dance floor. It felt nice, and then it felt rather embarrassing.

"Hey!" she cried, pounding his chest. Was anyone watching this? He didn't even bother stopping at their table and she had to snare her purse off the chair as they passed. How humiliating! Her date was acting like a Neanderthal! God, she hoped Trip didn't notice. "Put me down right now, Max!" she yelled as he carried her right over to the coat check, catching the attention of the couple in front of them in line. She slapped his back for emphasis.

Max reluctantly lowered her feet to the ground, but stepped in front of her so she was out of view. Only then did Eloise notice that the top of her dress, still damp and vaguely transparent from the martini she'd spilled on herself earlier, was now resting comfortably around her hips.

"You're sure you want to leave so early?" Parker said after Fernanda had whispered as much in his ear. He excused himself from Jack Rutherford-Shaw and followed her a few steps. "I haven't even gotten you onto the dance floor yet."

"I've had my fill," said Fernanda. Cornelia's attack had exhausted her, but she'd expected as much when she raised her paddle. She hadn't thought her friend would go on to lacerate Parker. He'd brushed off her hurtful comments, but she could tell they stung. And then Cornelia had filleted and broiled Lucy—she must have, anyway, by the look of the poor girl's tear-streaked face when she ran out of the Grand Room.

Parker kissed her cheek. "Let me just say a few goodbyes. Two minutes."

"I'll meet you outside."

Moments later, standing on Fifth Avenue, eyes cast up at the softly lit museum, Fernanda shivered. She held her mother's mink coat together, one gloved hand at her throat, the other holding the swag bag from the ball, from which peeked out a bottle of Socialite, Cornelia's perfume. She knew she'd never wear the stuff. Their friendship, so central to the past two decades of her life, was over.

She noticed her brother easing a very intoxicated Eloise Carlton down the museum steps. "Max!" she called out. He looked up. "Here, take our car. Parker and I can hop in a cab."

Max raised both eyebrows. "You sure? That's really nice of you."

"I can occasionally be nice." She let out a little laugh. But it occurred to her how infrequent those occasions were, and she felt ashamed. "Really, take it. Parker won't mind." She waved her brother toward the waiting town car and hurried over to help him. Max opened the door for Eloise, who had gone boneless, and the two of them struggled to help her inside.

"Thank you," he said, walking around to the other side to get in. She nodded, watching the car pull away from the curb.

But it would take more than a few little gestures for Fernanda to feel virtuous.

"Sorry to leave you waiting!" Parker jogged down the steps, a big grin plastered on that funny face of his. He pulled her into a squeeze. "Proud of my girl. You did the right thing tonight, you know that?"

"I hope you don't mind, I gave our car away to Max. He was playing Knight in Shining Armani to Eloise Carlton."

"Of course not." Parker stuck up his hand for a yellow cab. With his other arm, he kept Fernanda close.

If I marry this man, she thought, watching the glittering crowd waltz the night away behind the museum's enormous windows, *there'll be no Park Avenue.* Parker, no longer the scrappy young man he'd once been, seemed to accept his changed circumstances with calm resignation. *There'll be no Christmases in St. Barts. No six-carat anything. No house accounts on Madison Avenue; no salesgirls falling over themselves the moment I enter a boutique because they know I've got more money than most investment banks.*

"You lit up that room," he whispered, kissing her cheek. She could see he meant it. Fernanda liked the woman he thought she was. She decided, then and there, that she wanted to become that woman.

"Parker," she said softly, filled with a certainty unlike any she'd ever known. She grabbed both his hands and pushed thoughts of her mother's reaction out of her head. "Parker, will you marry me?"

Around three in the morning, Lucy hitched up her gown and stepped on the escalator heading down into the bowels of Port Authority. She'd been all over the city in desperate search of Rita, who wasn't picking up her phone—traipsing from dive bars her mother had mentioned to the studio apartment in Murray Hill, a depressing tour of the old life that Lucy herself would be heading back to. She'd murdered her feet in her stupid stilettos and gotten nowhere. Then, remembering the hurt on Rita's face, she headed back across town, through the neon blare of Times Square, to the bus terminal.

Sure enough, there was Rita, sitting on a bench in front of the Greyhound Departures screen, flanked by a homeless man and a grumpy-looking older woman in a velour sweatsuit. Rita's mascara had bled down her face, making her look like a cross between Alice Cooper and Marion Cunningham, and she was still wearing her sequined mini. She was drinking something out of a paper bag—Zima, if Lucy knew her mother. Despite her aging hooker appearance, there was something innocent about her, like a kid waiting for the school bus, and Lucy felt a rush of affection. And shame. How could she have allowed her ambitions to so cloud what truly mattered?

"What are you doing here?" Rita asked, looking up when Lucy ran over to her.

"About time, if you ask me!" breathed the woman in a heavy Bulgarian accent, and the man nodded. Rita had clearly briefed her new friends about her daughter's recent behavior.

"Rita, I'm sorry. I shouldn't have treated you that way."

"Why aren't you at your party? Did something happen? You look upset!"

Does Rita care more about what I'm *going through than what* she's *going through?* It sure sounded that way. "It was a disaster," she admitted. She told her mother about Cornelia's revenge.

"Maybe nobody will care?" Rita suggested. But Lucy wasn't so naïve. The *Townhouse* piece would give her a notoriety that would be impossible to outrun. The invitations would stop coming. Nobody would hire her; nobody would want the Page Six mentions, the negative association with a known liar. Including Wyatt, Lucy thought miserably. She knew he was too much of a gentleman to ditch her in her hour of need, but once the reality set in—and he saw his own name smeared all over the press, too—he'd come to view her as an obligation, a headache, and nothing more. She nutshelled all this for her mother.

"It's *all* my fault!" Rita buried her face in her hands, choking back a sob. The homeless man patted her back like they'd known each other for years. "I can't believe I trusted that girl. I don't know what I was thinking." She looked up at Lucy, tears of regret rolling down her cheeks. "I've ruined everything for you, just like you were afraid I would. You have every right to hate me. I am so sorry, Lucy Jo, I— I'm going back to Dayville. I won't bother you anymore."

"I might be heading to Dayville with you. But not tonight." Rita's sincerity broke Lucy's heart. The homeless man offered up his seat, which she gratefully accepted, and then she wrapped her arms around her mother. "It's not your fault. I shouldn't have been ashamed of who I am or where I come from."

Rita, sniffling, wiped her nose on the sleeve of her bolero jacket. "No, you shouldn't." Her voice was gentler than Lucy ever remembered it being. "I meant what I said. Lucy Jo Ellis is the classiest person *I've* ever met. I mean, you've spent your entire life taking care of me, even when I"—she took a jagged, tearful breath—"didn't deserve it. You've worked hard to make something of yourself. You've got real talent, not like those other girls who just flit around looking pretty and doing nothing all day. And you're a good person, Lucy Jo."

"Maybe I used to be." The ball seemed decades away from her now. The red carpet, the auction, the kisses—had any of it really happened? Her stomach growled, bringing her back to the present. She hadn't eaten all night—or for the past three months, it seemed. "Who wants a pretzel?" she asked the little group, and three hands shot into the air. Lucy headed over to the twenty-four-hour cart, paid the exhausted vendor, and handed off the pretzels.

"Let's go," she told her mother. She picked up the suitcase at her mother's feet.

"You mean to the Carlyle? You said you have a room there?"

"Nah, let's go home. Murray Hill." Maybe it was shabby, maybe the floorboards tilted too much, maybe there were occasional water bugs (a sweet nickname for cockroaches) in the bathroom—but at the moment, Lucy didn't care. She wanted to be in a place that reminded her of who she really was. Tomorrow she'd figure out what to do with the smoldering remains of her life.

"Even better." Rita grabbed her duffle bag and slung it over her shoulder, waving goodbye to her pals. "I think you'll love what I've done with the place."

At 6 AM the following day, Trip lifted the skinny arm that had been flung over his bare chest. The redhead it belonged to didn't stir. What the hell was her name? Trip could barely remember his own. He took in his surroundings—more boudoir than bedroom, with the gothic black curtains and burgundy walls, and littered with a shocking number of Red Bull cans. Her heavy black dress lay in a heap on the floor, like the remains of a melted witch.

Trip sidled two inches toward the edge of the bed. *Good.* Now he just had to make it to the front door without waking the girl, and he'd be free. His head ached like a calving glacier; his mouth was the Sahara. Trip's left foot touched the ground first, careful not to pull the black satin sheets. He didn't know girls slept in black satin sheets. He didn't want to know. Then his left hand. Just as he was sliding his body toward the ground, he heard her snort.

Trip froze mid-slide. The girl was quiet again. He lowered himself a few more inches, still balancing on one hand and foot. His tux lay in the corner, next to the witch puddle. Just the sight of their discarded clothes made him feel sick. He remembered how she'd shoved him backward on the bed last night, playing the tiger. Then he remembered seeing Eloise lace her arms around Max Fairchild's neck.

"Omigod! Are you *okay*?" the girl asked, sitting up and pushing her red fro out of her face. The sound of Trip throwing up in one of the gift bags they'd received leaving the ball, the first thing he could grab, had woken his bedmate.

"Sorry," he said lamely, not wasting a moment in wiggling into his pants and buttoning his dress shirt. He needed to be elsewhere immediately. To his dismay, the girl pulled herself out of bed and walked across the room toward him, draped in her satin sheet. "You can, uh, keep my bag," Trip said.

"I don't care about that." She pressed a finger against his chest.

"Really, I insist," Trip said, jamming his foot into his shoe while holding his puke-filled bag. A puke-filled bag of expensive, useless stuff: the perfect metaphor for his life. He grabbed the other shoe and headed for the door. "Anyway, thanks for everything"—he fumbled with the doorknob.

"*Clarissa,*" she said. "Aren't you even going to put on your other shoe?"

"Right," he said, already savoring the sweeter air in the hallway. "In the elevator!" He was being a complete jerk, Trip knew, but all he could think about was getting home and putting last night behind him.

"Jaaaaack!" Mimi Rutherford-Shaw shrieked from her dressing room in Bedford, where she'd been kitting up to go riding. The ball had interrupted their usual weekend routine; they'd had the driver take them straight from the Heritage Museum to their country house in the wee hours of the night. "Jack, come here! Look at this!"

"What is it, Mims?" her husband called back from the bedroom, where he was still lounging in his pajamas with the *Wall Street Journal*. She ran to the doorway and ripped open her shirt, revealing her epic set of double Ds. That got Jack's attention, and he put down the newspaper. He squinted at her chest, first with interest and then in horror. Then he rushed over. "What the hell happened, Mims? You burn yourself?" They both gasped over the purplish welts that had popped up like foothills across her mountain range.

Mimi, hand over mouth, picked up the swag bag she'd brought

home from the Forum Ball. "It's Socialite! Cornelia's perfume! I just spritzed the stuff and this happened!" She pulled out the glass perfume bottle and held it out to her husband. "Call Dr. Stone, Jack, and tell him I need to see him immediately!"

"Eau de Cornelia Rockman?" Jack muttered under his breath as he headed to the telephone. "You might've guessed that stuff would be toxic."

Eloise's eyes cracked open. She saw that her dress had been neatly hung on the back of the doorframe; her shoes were tucked under the bureau. A large bottle of Evian had been left on her nightstand, and she reached for it, moaning a little.

Eloise Carlton was not one of those people who experienced alcohol-induced amnesia, unfortunately, and as she slugged away at the Evian, her mind moved in painful, unrelenting circles through the night before. Trip, dancing. Eloise, drinking. Eloise, dancing, a demented Isadora Duncan, carried topless off the dance floor for all of New York society to behold, and deposited in a car by Max Fairchild.

I'll move away. Paris. Marrakech. Start over fresh, travel the world, be a woman who finds herself. My own version of Eat, Pray, Love. *Minus the* Love. *I'm in no shape for that. And the* Eat *will have to wait, too, until I regain the capacity to chew. Maybe my own* Drink, Hurt, Sob.

Just as she'd found the strength to sit upright, propped against pillows, the apartment doorbell rang. She jolted out from between the covers, hangover temporarily forgotten, and poked her head out into the hallway. Lucy's bedroom was empty. She hoped that her friend had enjoyed the triumph she deserved, riding on the wings of Margaux Irving's endorsement. The last she'd seen, Lucy and Wyatt were in a steamy-looking lip-lock, apparently coming clean about their feelings about each other.

The doorbell rang again.

Eloise knew it was Trip without cracking the door. He'd never let go of their relationship so easily. Whatever last night's waify redhead had offered him was nothing like the lifetime of devotion and companionship she could provide. A man like Trip knew quality, he knew girls like Eloise weren't disposable. She hurried into the bathroom and smeared toothpaste on her toothbrush, jamming it into her mouth as she flew back to the bedroom and scrambled for something to wear.

"Hold on!" she yelled, pulling a sweater over her head. Whipping off her enormous pajama pants (his, of course), she threw on a pair of cuter boy shorts while yanking hairpins out of the collapsed bun she'd worn to the ball. Then she dashed into the hallway, realized the toothbrush was still in her mouth, flung it over her shoulder into the kitchen, and opened the door. Her Tripless nightmare was finally over.

Expecting to see her beau down on one knee, Eloise instead found an empty hallway.

"Trip?" she called, wondering if he'd already retreated around the corner to the elevator bank. "*Trip!*" She yelled, even though she might rouse the whole floor on a Sunday morning.

When Max Fairchild sheepishly poked his head around the corner instead, Eloise felt her last hopes crumble inside her. She held on to the doorframe for support.

"Sorry, Eloise, I—I don't know what I was thinking, barging in on you so early. I brought some food—" Max trailed off, staring at the carpet. He was holding a grocery bag from Grace's. "I just wanted to make sure you were okay. Your phone was off. I tried Lucy's line, too, but she didn't pick up—"

"Trip and I are over," Eloise blurted out. There it was. Just saying the words out loud, her knees grew shaky, and the hallway suddenly seemed pixelated. "Trip and I are over," she repeated. The spots of light grew bigger. She felt her fingers slide down the cold wall.

Luckily, Max was there to catch her.

32

The highlight of last night's ball, as most will tell you, was Lucy Ellis's stunning self-made gown, which fetched a record twenty thousand dollars from Margaux Irving herself during the predinner auction. The lowlight? Well, put it this way: Nobody should be itching to try Socialite, the perfume just launched by Cornelia Rockman and our readers' vote for least-favorite swag-bag item *ever*.

—*Rex Newhouse, www.rexnewhouse.com*

*C*ornelia couldn't focus. Restless, she'd been awake since dawn, bustling around her apartment—writing half a thank-you note to the editor in Margaux's office whom she'd conned into giving her the extra ball ticket, then drifting to the bathroom to smear Crème de la Mer over her face, opening three invitations before flipping on the television and watching a few minutes of TiVo'ed *Access Hollywood*. There was an "is she or isn't she pregnant?" bit about one of Theo's clients, but it wasn't enough to keep her still.

It was more than the *post coitum triste* she often felt after coming down from the high of a magnificent social triumph. Last night's coup was her greatest ever. Last night, she'd successfully brought her nemesis down. She'd never forget the look on Lucy's face. Last night, Cornelia's perfume had gone home in a swag bag with the world's most influential tastemakers. So why did she feel more miserable than she ever had in her life?

Well, Fernanda, for starters. She'd been sold out by her best friend, who hadn't been the same since Parker came into her life. And then there was Wyatt. Watching her ex kiss Lucy, Cornelia had finally been knocked flat by the truth she'd spent three months furiously avoiding: there would be no reunion. She should have known when Rita had told her about the experiment that he was a lost cause—the old Wyatt, the one she'd known, cared where everyone came from and where they belonged. Watching him fawn over the girl from Missouri or Montana or wherever was the final evidence that the Old Wyatt had disappeared, and all the plotting in the world couldn't make New Wyatt look at Cornelia the way he looked at Lucy.

Was anyone still looking at her? She flipped through *Town & Country*: nary a photo. And she couldn't deny that Lucy had rocked that auction with the dress she supposedly made—another lie, no doubt—and that Margaux Irving and the rest of the crowd had kept their eyes trained on her. Cornelia had spent fifteen thousand on her Ralph Rucci couture, but only auctioned it off for twelve—did that mean she devalued the dress by three thousand dollars just by wearing it?

Fortunately, her phone rang, rescuing her from this troubling line of thought. "Bad news," Daphne said.

Cornelia put down the magazine. A chill prickled her spine. Daphne was the queen of spin—for her to consider something bad news, it had to be downright apocalyptic. "Don't tell me my show got canceled," Cornelia said, ready to whine hard.

"This is worse. You know those sample perfumes we put in all of last night's swag bags? The ones that went home with every single one of the ball's eight hundred and fourteen attendees? The perfume bottles that were supposed to give you exposure to the *ne plus ultra* of the fashion world?"

"Of course! Spit it out—what happened?"

She could hear Daphne take a deep breath. "I just got off the phone with Dafinco's CEO. Apparently they're already getting calls ranging from disgruntled to litigious from folks who spritzed on the perfume and broke out in *a horrible purple rash*. This thing is going to be all over Page Six, Cornelia, and it's going to be ugly."

"But that's ridiculous!" Cornelia jumped up from the breakfast table. "I've worn the perfume myself. That can't be true. These people are just looking to cash in—"

"I tried it, and it looks like someone spilled acid on my wrists. Trust me, it's true."

Cornelia stared at the innocent-looking pink bottle on her dresser. "Fine, even if it is true, it's not my fault. Their laboratory's to blame! They were the ones who got all self-righteous about no animal testing—"

"Listen, girl, you're not getting it." Daphne had never spoken to her so bluntly. Her publicist's lack of ass kissing, more than anything, made Cornelia realize the gravity of the situation. "Nobody gives a shit that Dafinco's to blame. You're the one they'll remember. Your face is all over the ad campaign."

"So what are you saying?"

"It's not good. We'll issue a statement. But you should keep a low profile until all this blows over. And by low profile, I mean: talk to nobody. Do you understand?"

Cornelia groaned. She'd envisioned Hollywood knocking on her door, but instead she'd be living like a shut-in? It wasn't fair. Nothing in her life was adding up the way it was supposed to. "What did I do to deserve this?" she wailed. Daphne didn't say anything, so Cornelia hung up. She hadn't cried since she was seven years old (she'd decided then that she would no longer give her mother the satisfaction), but she wished she remembered how. Wyatt's rejection, coupled with the blow up of her career, made her want to fling herself out her twelfth-story window. The only bright spot in her life, she realized, was the impending humiliation of Lucy Ellis, a girl Cornelia had come to hate with a fervor that scared even her.

"Wyatt?" Lucy called softly, cracking the door to his study.

He wasn't there, which surprised her. He'd spent every Sunday morning since she'd known him holed up in his study with the *Times* and his coffee. It had been one of the few times of the week she'd had to herself, back when she was Wyatt's 24/7 guinea pig socialite. But then, this wasn't a Sunday in ordinary times.

She didn't leave right away. His study, untouched by the shmancy decorator, reminded her of all the late nights she'd spent there under critical direction, working to please him, to transform herself into the socialite he had bet she could be. All the hours of training— the elocution, etiquette, art history, jet-set geography lessons; all the evenings spent playing backgammon and eating Chinese takeout. Lucy loved the wraparound bookshelves, brimming with his vast collection of books; the smell of worn leather; the overstuffed couch; the ancient oriental rug, threadbare in the circles that revealed Wyatt's near-constant pacing.

I came so close, she thought. *Margaux wanted my dress. Wyatt wanted me.* Feeling a lump in her throat, she scanned the photos Wyatt had displayed on one of the walls. There was little Wyatt on his horse . . . on his sailboat . . . on the shoulders of his aristocratically handsome late father. Wyatt with his crew team before his first Head of the Charles, arms flung around the necks of two teammates. The display was absurdly egocentric, of course, but it also revealed Wyatt's preoccupation with his place in the world. It was almost as though he didn't know who he was without the fancy hobbies, the famous friends, the fabulous settings. She looked at the grainy baby photo of Wyatt being bounced on Nixon's knee, the shot of him playing polo in Argentina. *I could help him define himself in a deeper way.* For the first time since Cornelia broke the news about the *Townhouse* report, Lucy paused in worrying about the negative effect it might have on him. Maybe, for Wyatt, a little social embarrassment could be just the push he needed to start living a more authentic life.

Without really meaning to, she had made her way around his entire study. On his desk, next to his Tiffany lamp, there was a small gold frame. Lucy leaned closer. To her surprise, it contained a photograph of *her*, taken during their weekend in Palm Beach at his mother's house. Relaxed by the pool, she faced the camera dead-on and was laughing, and she looked like herself—not posed, not perfect, not some socialite in a pretty dress, just herself. She'd forgot-

ten that he'd taken it. The sheer existence of the photo, let alone
its intimate placement in a spot where only Wyatt would see it, for
a moment took her breath away.

Her eyes fell upon a thick stack of paper on top of Wyatt's antique desk. THE OVERNIGHT SOCIALITE was printed on the top page,
along with Wyatt's name. The title pierced her with curiosity and
dread. Had he written a book? Since she'd known him, he'd been
hard at work on some mystery project that he never wanted
to discuss. Unable to control herself, Lucy flipped to page one
and read:

> *There was nothing extraordinary about the girl under the
> awning—not her beauty, birth, education, or profession. In fact,
> I chose L. as the subject of my experiment precisely because she
> was so unremarkable—one of the faceless, nameless many who
> immigrate to New York City from the hinterland, full of unreal-
> istic dreams.*

Lucy felt her heart drop. She skimmed down the page—which was
now shaking, along with her hand. It couldn't be real.

> *Just when I think progress is finally being made, L. blindsides me
> with an uncouth comment or action, or surprises me with her
> lack of basic cultural literacy. Last night, she asked if Edith Piaf
> was a kind of rice.*

Lucy flipped frantically through the rest of his manuscript, but tears
blurred her vision. There could be no explanation other than the obvious: Wyatt was planning to publish a book about their experiment.
Long before Cornelia even heard of Rita Ellis, Wyatt himself was
planning to expose her as a fraud to the entire world. She had never
felt more betrayed. She was nothing more than a trained dog to him,
a girl he'd plucked from obscurity and passed off as a woman with
class. No, worse—a trained dog wasn't humiliated in public. Wyatt
didn't love her—it was right there in black and white, impossible to
deny—he found nothing about her "remarkable" or "extraordinary."

The whole thing was just academic for him. *Just a topic for a book.* He had set her on a path to a humiliation that would deny her humanity and annihilate her ambitions. He obviously cared nothing about her feelings. He was worse than Cornelia—at least Cornelia had never pretended to be Lucy's friend.

"Lucy!" She hadn't heard the advance of his footsteps, and looked up to find Wyatt—unshaven, in an old sweater—standing in the doorway. He smiled. "You're here! I've been everywhere—Eloise's, the Carlyle—" He stopped short when he saw his manuscript, and her face. Lucy wiped away tears with the back of her hand, grabbed the pile of papers, and charged toward the door. Wyatt stepped back in alarm. "What were you doing in here?"

She flung the manuscript at his head. Pages cascaded over his shoulders.

"I can explain—" he began in the timeworn words of men who've screwed up big time.

"How dare you?" She ran to him, raising herself on her toes to come just inches from his face. Her entire body shook with anger. He looked petrified, scared speechless. "You should make sense of your *own* warped life, and leave mine alone!" Lucy hurled her way to the elevator bank, stabbing the down button. She heard Wyatt behind her, calling her name. The door opened and she rushed into it as he appeared in the landing. "Maybe I didn't grow up gagging on silver spoons, but I know right from wrong. I would never, *ever* stoop this low." Then the elevator doors shut on his stammering, bewildered face.

As it dropped nine floors to the lobby, Lucy fought the urge to crumple on the floor in tears. She'd endured Wyatt's constant criticism for months, and for what? So he could use her like this—destroying not only her dreams but her trust?

"Are you okay, Miss Lucy?" asked Howard the doorman, looking concerned as she made her way shakily through the lobby.

"Not really," she answered, but she shook her head when he asked if he could help.

Once outside, she took a sharp breath. The first notes of spring were in the air already, although the crocuses in the median of Park

Avenue had yet to emerge and she still needed a coat. She struggled to clear her head. The sky did her a favor with its shocking blueness; one of the neighbors had planted scarlet geraniums in her window boxes. *Wyatt doesn't own this*, she thought suddenly. *Wyatt doesn't own the taxicabs, swimming upstream like vibrant yellow fish, or the smell of roasting chestnuts. He doesn't own the bustling streets, the outdoor cafés, the symphony of car horns and dogs barking and distant sirens and people laughing in foreign accents.* When she'd first gotten off the bus from Dayville, Lucy had claimed all this as her own. And it was still hers, if she wanted it.

A young girl walked by with her mother and a beagle, pulling gently on the dog's leash, and Lucy envisioned an older, more sophisticated spin on her bright poppy-colored coat. She was surrounded by inspiration: the light slanting down through the buildings, the uneven sidewalk, the boy on a scooter whizzing past her. New York hadn't spit her out. She'd prove to Wyatt that she didn't need him to reach her dreams. She wouldn't sit idly by while *Townhouse* and Wyatt spun their own versions of the truth. As Lucy walked briskly back to Eloise's apartment, she could taste hopefulness in the air, and her mind started to weave a plan.

33

Twinkies have a shelf life of twenty-five days, not seven years, and certainly not fifty years. Even so, twenty-five days is an unusually long time for a baked product to stay fresh. The secret to Twinkies' longevity is their lack of dairy ingredients: because dairy products are not part of the formula, Twinkies spoil much more slowly than other bakery items. . . . According to Hostess, it takes forty-five seconds to explode a Twinkie in a microwave.

—*Snopes.com*

Dottie Hayes, over her cobb salad at the Colony Club, clucked in sympathy for the young lady sitting across the table. Lucy Ellis might not have sprung from the pages of the Social Register, but Dottie had long since decided that this girl, who could endure her son so graciously, was one of nature's aristocrats. Dottie was furious with Wyatt for not telling Lucy about his book—for not canceling it—months ago. Instead, the girl had been ambushed by it. Dottie was deeply relieved when Lucy called and asked for her help, and she'd invited her to lunch straightaway. "I'd be honored to lend my support, Lucy. Your work deserves a stage. Besides, after that knucklehead son of mine did—"

Lucy smiled, holding up her hand to stop Dottie. She looked crisp in a navy blue sheath, fresh-eyed and lovely. "Thank you. That's incredibly generous of you. We can't imagine a more beautiful setting than your library."

Dottie fiddled with her napkin, troubled. Lucy, to her credit, had yet to say a negative word against her son. Did that mean she might be persuaded to give him a second chance? Not that he deserved one, but her maternal loyalty required her to ask. "I've never seen Wyatt so tormented," she said softly, testing the waters. "He regrets hurting you very much. You know that he's canceled that awful book?"

Lucy sighed, but didn't say anything. She took a quick sip of her Pellegrino. "Maybe it'd be better that we not discuss Wyatt."

"I understand that, of course." But then Dottie, against her natural temperament and Lucy's wishes, forced herself to say more. "It's just that—you've had such a wonderful effect on him. In these last few weeks, when he had you in his life, he would call to see how I was doing. He seemed calmer, even *nicer*. Ironic, isn't it? That he's the changed person from all this."

"I'm grateful to Wyatt for all he's done, but I don't want to see him, Dottie. If that puts you in an awkward position, please just tell me."

"No, no." Lucy had spoken with such finality that Dottie didn't dare push the subject further. "He's the one who's created any awkwardness, not you, my dear." As much as she wished otherwise, perhaps Wyatt didn't deserve the girl seated across the table from her. She was hardworking, modest, loyal, curious—just what he had been searching for, and what Dottie had prayed for her son to find—but he'd betrayed her.

Dottie glanced around the members-only haven that felt like her second kitchen. Most of the women in the dining room knew Lucy Ellis, either personally or via the social columns in which Wyatt had made her an unlikely fixture. In days they would know her true provenance. They would read the slander spread by that shabby, overexposed vixen Cornelia Rockman. Dottie knew she had to do her part to make sure that the right people understood Lucy's innate elegance.

Besides, her plan sounded like fun. "Why don't you and Eloise stop by tomorrow, and we'll discuss the details," Dottie said. She had always wanted a daughter. She wasn't about to make the same mistake her son had.

* * *

"Oh, I'll just wait here," Wyatt said nonchalantly, moving toward the small couch in Eloise's lobby. Lucy was still living with Eloise, as far as he knew, and he was prepared to wait all day for her to come downstairs and hear his heartfelt apology.

"I'm sorry, sir, but you won't." The doorman, a gray-haired gentleman in his fifties, looked stern. "The young lady does not wish to see you. She made that abundantly clear."

Damn it.

Maybe he could appeal to the man's sense of romance. "I just need to make things right. I made a huge mistake, but I care about Lucy a great deal."

"Well, Lucy is an exceptional young woman. Always goes out of her way to brighten my day."

"You see why I miss her so much!" Maybe it was working. He couldn't tell. "I can't sleep, or eat—I just keep thinking about how she must feel." It was a strange relief to admit this to another person. The doorman nodded; it seemed he felt Wyatt's pain.

"You still can't sit here," he said.

"C'mon, man!" Wyatt, scowling with frustration, headed for the door. The tightness in his stomach was worse than ever. He'd have to find some other way to reach Lucy, to show her how sorry he was.

"And you might want to slow down on the flowers," added the doorman. "The ladies have very important business to attend to, and they don't need to be interrupted by deliveries every ten minutes. And pass that on to your friend Mr. Peters. I don't know what he's trying to prove with all those roses. He should've proposed to Miss Carlton years ago."

Wyatt, dropping his head, left the building.

"So Wyatt's been calling me nonstop," Mallory said, resting both elbows on the zinc-top desk of her midtown office. She directed this to Lucy, who had just lowered herself into a visitor chair next to Eloise.

"Has he?" Lucy held Mallory's gaze, not allowing the mention of his name or efforts to affect her. "Well, then, you know why we're here. Cornelia told us about your article."

Mallory frowned; bit her lip. "I like you. I even like the idea that
you put one over on the toffs that buy my magazine. But I'll tell you
what I keep telling Wyatt. *This is business.* I've got to think about
my newsstand numbers. Our advertisers are mostly luxury-goods re-
tailers, and they're getting massacred, which means we're getting
massacred. A story like this, like it or not, will drive sales."

It was the response that Lucy had anticipated. "We're not asking
you to kill the article. We're just asking that you hold it for the next
issue."

"You want time to flee the country? Sorry, but I don't want to get
scooped on this. I can't afford it."

"You won't get scooped," Eloise said. "You'll get a bigger story." She
slid the invitation across the desk, a reprint of a page from Lucy's
sketchbook with the event details handwritten in the margins.
Cheap, easy—they didn't have money or time to spare—and yet perfectly chic. They'd picked them up from the printer on the way to
Mallory's office.

"Interesting," said Mallory, frowning a little. "You've been planning
this for a while?"

They chose to ignore the question. "Lucy is poised to become a
darling of the fashion industry," said Eloise. "As you know, Margaux
Irving showed tremendous support by bidding on her gown—"

"Correction." Mallory cleared her throat. "She bid on *Lucia
Haverford Ellis's* gown. Who knows if she'll be equally impressed by
some small-town nobody. No offense."

"Just give us one week," Lucy said, trying to push past Mallory's
brutal candor. "Then you can go ahead and write about how I
conned everyone into thinking I was to the manor born. But that will
just be backstory. The *real* story here isn't about society scandal. It's
about reaching the summit—achieving a dream—the good, old-
fashioned New York way: by any means necessary."

Mallory considered this for a millisecond. "The society scandal
angle will sell more copies than your prairie-girl-makes-good angle."

"Ours will elevate *Townhouse* in a way that brings in more readers over time. Remember, you'll be the first to cover the story—the
whole story. It's an ASME award, Mallory. You'll be duly credited by

all the other press publications that will jump on this once it breaks. You'll be the authority, the talking head, for all the news outlets, boosting *Townhouse*'s visibility and your own."

"I'd agree to style the next three issues, free of charge," added Eloise, for good measure.

"You'd do that?"

"Sure. A little mutual back-scratching." Eloise smiled sweetly.

Mallory sat back in her chair, fingering the invitation, weighing the risks. "Screw me over on this, ladies, and I will make Cornelia Rockman look like a Sister of Perpetual Mercy. One week."

Wyatt squinted up at the sky, which was just growing light, and nervously took a seat on a green wooden bench. He hoped Lucy would be showing up soon, out for her typical early morning run. He felt more than a little creepy, staking her out like this, but she still refused to talk to him.

There she was! His breath tightened in his throat as he saw her running toward him, up the steps to the Central Park reservoir. She moved easily, like a veteran athlete, hair pulled off her face into a clean ponytail. Derrick would be proud. Just seeing her brought a wave of emotion—it was crazy how much Wyatt had missed her in just a few short days. He glanced at the sky. *Perfect*, he thought. *Couldn't have timed it any better.*

"Lucy!" he called out. She was in her own world, and didn't look up right away. "Lucy!"

Seeing him, her eyes widened and she stopped in her tracks. He pointed vigorously up to the sky, where a plane had traced out I'M SORRY in enormous fluffy white letters. "Please, please forgive me!"

She looked up. She read the message. Then she turned, without so much as a word of response, and sprinted back toward the Met.

Hearing the familiar buzz, Lucy stopped walking down Bleecker Street and glanced down at her BlackBerry. "I just got a text from Max. He's doing a Home Depot run and wants to know how many stages we'll need," she said to Eloise.

"Six. Small ones, just big enough for each model. Assuming they all agree."

Lucy wrote back quickly with both thumbs. "Thank God he's so good with his hands." She looked up to see Eloise blush. "I mean, handy. Dottie says we can build the pieces right at her house, by the way."

"Lucy"—Eloise reached out and touched her arm—"thanks for letting me do this with you. I—it's just a godsend, to have this right now."

"Are you kidding? There's no way I could pull it off without you. You're the best thing Wyatt Hayes ever added to my life." Lucy felt just as grateful to be busy—to be the mistress of her own fate, once and for all. She didn't have time to make sense of her conflicted emotions about Wyatt, which was good, because she had no idea where to begin. "We make a fabulous team." Arms linked, they headed inside to August, a quiet West Village boîte where they'd asked the other girls to meet them for lunch.

"So?" Libet asked as soon as they came into view. "What's up? Your e-mail said it was top-secret and urgent."

Lucy looked out at the clutch of young women, arrayed in their luncheon finery, some in clothing they'd commissioned from Lucy since the *Townhouse* shoot (*no wonder*, she thought, *that Doreen was able to quit her Nola job to focus solely on producing my dresses*). All the girls around the table knew her as Lucia Haverford Ellis, the Chicago heiress to a timber fortune who'd gone to the same sorts of schools they'd attended, who'd jumped onto the same committees and showed up at the same openings. The woman they knew wasn't Lucy; the woman they knew was Wyatt's creation. Rooted as they were in their Upper East Side–Hamptons–Palm Beach world, could they even *imagine* being the daughter of a manicurist from Dayville, Minnesota? Or for that matter, being the friend of that girl?

"Ladies," Lucy said, taking off her spring jacket and sitting at the head of the table. She took a deep breath and looked at Eloise, who nodded in encouragement. "There's something I need to tell you."

Wyatt hit the speakerphone button and dialed Lucy's home number. He'd lost hope that she might answer his call herself. Instead

he braced himself for her inevitable voice mail greeting, holding his
manuscript over the shredder with both hands.

"I've erased all the book files from my computer," he called out
after the beep. "And this is the sound of the last hard copy getting
shredded!" He began feeding page after page into the machine's
waiting teeth, hoping the gesture might summon her to the phone,
but nobody picked up.

Libet twirled around Eloise's living room. "This is too gorgeous. You
said I get to keep it, right?"

Lucy nodded, her pursed lips holding a row of pins. "C'mere," she
managed to get out, and Libet stood still to be fitted. Lucy expertly
pulled in the fabric around the socialite's bony bottom. *Shoot.* Libet was so greyhound-thin that getting the hips to fit caused a puck-
ering at the waist. If she had more time, Lucy could redo the whole
dress. But she had a mere four days left and two more looks to fine-
tune. Doreen had been working at a turbocharged pace, too, and
Lucy couldn't ask any more of her.

"It's cool you're doing this, Luce," Libet said. "I mean, you're
an artist. Just like me, you know?" Lucy thought of Libet's rotting
fruit and smiled politely. "I've got your back two hundred percent.
I had a friend in high school who was poor, and she was, like, *so*
great."

"Remember, you can't tell anyone about any of this," Lucy said,
still struggling with the pins. She took a step back and looked at her
model. "Libet, I'm going to ask you a favor. Please don't take it the
wrong way."

"Anything, sweetie."

"Could you possibly . . . eat a few cheeseburgers this week? Some
Häagen-Dazs? The thing is, the dress will fit perfectly if you gain
five pounds. Otherwise, it'll cost me hours of work, and I don't have
an extra minute between now and Saturday."

At first Libet looked horrified. Then, accepting the sacrifice she'd
been asked to make, she nodded gravely. "*I'll do it*," she declared
with great feeling. "For you, Lucy, I will gain five pounds."

"Wow, that's great. Thanks so much."

"You said I get to keep the dress, right?" Libet tilted her head, straining to hear. "Do you hear music outside?"

"Oh, that. There's a boys' choir singing outside the window."

"What?" Libet rushed over to look. "There's two dozen kids on your sidewalk!"

"Wyatt and I heard them perform last month at a benefit for a settlement house, and I told him how much I loved it—"

"So he sent them over to serenade you? *Omigod!* That is so sweet!"

Lucy just shook her head. "Over-the-top gestures don't make what he did any better. Besides, I don't have time for a concert, personal or otherwise, right now. I'm not even sleeping this week."

"You're tough, lady," Libet said with admiration. "I'd totally melt. I hear Wyatt's a wreck. Mimi said Jack said he's been moping around the Racquet Club."

"Poor guy," Lucy said, shoving in her final pin. But as much as she hated to admit it, it was getting harder each day to bar Wyatt from her thoughts. She deleted his messages without listening, afraid of the effect his voice might have on her. She had to stay strong—she couldn't let him distract her from what really mattered, and she didn't know if she'd ever be able to trust him again.

As Libet slipped back into her street clothes, Lucy rummaged through the kitchen cabinets to find her a gift: a huge tub of Nutella. Four days, two looks to go.

"Please," Wyatt begged, following Rita as she hurried down 33rd Street toward the subway stop. "I just need to talk to her for one minute. Could you convince her to give me a minute?"

Rita stopped at the top of the stairs, clearly contemptuous. "Maybe I could, but I won't. And let me tell you something else. I got your note about wanting to 'fund' Rita's Artistic Acrylics. *Insulting*, Mister. As if I would sell out my own daughter for a bribe like that!"

Wyatt groaned. He'd known that offer was a bad idea, but was running out of good ones. "I'm sorry, Rita, I'm just—*desperate*." Wyatt couldn't believe he was saying that about himself, but it was true.

"Why are you so worked up? I figure a guy like you could get any girl he wants."

"Lucy's irreplaceable."

Rita seemed to soften a little, perhaps sensing his agony. "Well, give her time. Lucy just might come around, you never know." Wyatt, clinging to the sliver of hope she'd just offered, watched as Rita headed down the stairs and out of sight.

"Where the hell is everybody?" Cornelia scowled into the phone when Anna Santiago's voice mail picked up again. Bad enough that she was persona non grata at Dafinco, which had immediately yanked her perfume off the shelves and suppressed news about the rash of rashes as if it were another Chernobyl. Bad enough that Daphne couldn't get the MTV producers to return calls about her reality show.

But what made it all worse was that even Fernanda wouldn't talk to her.

Despite Fernanda's blatant disloyalty at the ball, Cornelia had decided to be the bigger person when she heard about her friend's surprise engagement. (She'd gotten the news from one of her maids, who knew one of the Fairchilds' maids, and she never received so much as an e-mail from Fernanda herself. She was willing to overlook that, too.) If Fernanda could get over Parker's distressingly six-figure annual income, then Cornelia would, too. But how could she be supportive if the girl refused to speak to her? Fernanda picked up the phone each time she called, only to immediately hang up in her ear.

Cornelia headed into her white marble kitchen, carefully avoiding eye contact with mirrors. She hadn't left her apartment since the ball—the perfume debacle and subsequent whispered bad-mouthing had essentially put her under house arrest, and it was shocking how quickly her carefully maintained looks had run wild with nobody there to see them.

Her hair was now kinked and curly, her nails were a ragged mess, and she hadn't showered for at least two days. It felt strangely good to let herself go. *I've had to be perfect for twenty-seven years*, she realized, pouring some more vodka into her coffee mug, which she used before noon for propriety's sake. *Townhouse* would be out in just a few more days, ending the Lucy dynasty and restoring Cornelia to the top of Manhattan's social order. Then her little vacation would be over.

Returning from their pilgrimage to Costco in Queens, Rita and Margaret appeared in the doorway of Dottie Hayes's library, each holding a megabox. "Got the Twinkies, got the Bagel Bites!" Rita announced.

"You are the best!" Lucy jumped up from her sewing machine to help them with their loads. "And the wine spritzers?"

"But of course!" Margaret smiled. "We'll load up Mrs. Hayes's refrigerator. Keep working."

"You sent more flowers?" Wyatt was seated across from Trip at their usual table at Bar & Books, a half-empty pack of Dunhills on the table between them. They'd been camped out for an hour, swilling scotch and trying to make sense of the situation. Lucy still wasn't returning his calls. It had been five days. He had tried everything: repeatedly leaving voice mails with apologies so profuse they startled him; continuing with avowals that his manuscript had been shredded, then burned, then buried; begging a tightlipped Eloise and even more tightlipped Dottie Hayes to intervene. His own mother had stiffly told him to "leave my Lucy alone." All had failed. He felt like an exile from his own life. During the past three months, Lucy Ellis had become the first person he spoke to in the morning and the last person he spoke to at night, but even still, Wyatt was surprised at how bereft he felt. Without her, and with the burden of his own guilt and hubris, he was a man deprived of oxygen.

"Of course," said Trip, who had his own problems. "Eight dozen red roses. A dozen for each of the years I've been blessed to have Eloise in my life. I've been sending 'em every day, I don't care what that doorman told you."

Wyatt groaned. "Jesus, you really wanted to remind her of how *long* it's been?"

Trip scratched his head. "Maybe that's why she hasn't responded."

"Or maybe she's buried in roses and can't see the telephone."

"Let's talk about something else." Trip stamped out his cigarette into the ashtray, now overflowing with their dead butts. "Is your publisher going to let you try another topic?"

"Doesn't look that way." Kipling hadn't been angry at Wyatt for leading him on; he'd been badly, perhaps permanently, disappointed. Thinking about the book reminded Wyatt of Lucy's hurt expression when he walked in Sunday morning. "She must have flipped through the first half, to get so riled up." Wyatt rubbed his forehead with his palm. "She doesn't even care that I backed out of my publishing deal."

Trip tilted his head. "Well, you should have been up front with her from the beginning."

"Aware of that," Wyatt said curtly. "God, I'm starving. Of all the weeks for Margaret to call in sick."

"Listen, at least Lucy hasn't already started dating Max Fairchild. Can you believe that guy? What a vulture."

"What, moving in on a girl whom you left hanging for eight years?" Wyatt finished his drink and gestured for a refill. "Eloise gave you many chances, Trip."

"Yeah? Well, you spent every day with Lucy. Plenty of opportunity to be honest."

Irritated with each other and themselves, they both stared glumly into their brown water. Then Wyatt remembered something. "Hey, I owe you this." He took off his wristwatch and slid it across the table. Thanks to Cornelia's meddling, he'd lost a bet he knew now he was a fool to have made in the first place.

His friend pushed it back. "Nah. It's yours, keep it."

"I insist. Deal's a deal."

"I don't want it!"

"You really are off your feed." Wyatt watched him with sympathy. "Why don't you just propose?"

But Trip just hung his head. "Maybe I should. I—I don't know. I still can't get there."

They sat in silence for another moment or two, until Wyatt slammed the table with his palm. "This is absurd. We need to clear our heads, stop our moping. Have some fun." Maybe he could get

Lucy out of his head. Find the guy he used to be before she came
into his life.

"What'd you have in mind?" Trip asked.

Eloise watched Max hammering away on the other side of Dottie's
library. His faded Springsteen T-shirt clung to his back a little; he'd
been hard at work for hours. She tried not to notice how strong his
arms were. *Max deserves more than a rebound fling, and I'm in no
shape for anything real*, she reminded herself. He reached into the
back pocket of his Levi's—a far cry from the custom jeans Trip ordered from Japan and had his assistant break in for six months—
and pulled out a Paul Smith hankie to wipe his brow.

When he caught her gazing at him, those light blue eyes meeting hers, Eloise blushed, running a hand through her currently jet-
black, short-cropped hair. "This is what you had in mind, right?" he
asked, thumbing toward the phenomenal ministage he'd been
building all morning. To her amazement, he'd found an old roller-
coaster car at a junkyard near Coney Island, spruced it up and
painted a whole line of cars into the background, and then constructed a frame around the whole thing. It was *incredible*. When
someone sat inside, it reminded Eloise of a photo taken during the
steep downhill drop of a huge coaster.

"Better, actually. You're really good at this." Not only had Max offered to take personal days to help them out, but he was an expert
carpenter. There was something sexy about a man who actually
knew how to *do* stuff. Trip's greatest skill—other than choosing
investments, of course—was outsourcing. Once, she'd noticed the
house manager scrambling into rooms before Trip entered them
to flick on the lights. It got that embarrassing, but he didn't seem
to care.

Max grinned. "I've always loved building stuff. In another life, I
would've loved to make my living at it. It comes a lot more naturally
to me than finance."

Eloise had a flash of Max living in an old stone cottage in Con-
necticut; a workshop in the garage; kids and dogs under foot. She
saw herself whipping up dinner in the kitchen, a good glass of Bur-

gundy next to the stove. Then she gave herself an inner slap. "So why don't you?"

"Have you *met* my mother?" He chuckled, returning the handkerchief to his pocket. "Maybe she'll lighten up now that Fernanda's engaged."

"You're thirty-four years old. Too old to be under your mother's thumb." She knew it was absolutely none of her business, and she should hold her tongue—but post-breakup, Eloise had found she couldn't hold back an honest opinion.

If Max was put off by her forthrightness, he didn't show it. "You're absolutely right," he said, passing the hammer from one hand to the other in contemplation. "Maybe I'll go for it."

"Well, that's the mantra of the week!" she said, smiling. Her BlackBerry buzzed—the buyer from Barneys, calling, she hoped, to confirm her attendance—and she bent to pick it up.

"Just for the record, I think Trip Peters is a fucking idiot for letting you go," said Max, eyes still on her. He said it with such quiet and unexpected intensity that Eloise froze.

Dottie Hayes surveyed her library, now utterly transformed. Lucy was still sewing feverishly, and Max and Eloise were hammering away on the finishing touches, but everything looked as good as ready. She couldn't believe the energy of these young people, Lucy in particular.

"Whaddya think?" Rita Ellis, who'd been bustling around the room, stopped for a moment next to her. "Not bad for a week's time."

"Not bad at all," said Dottie, walking over to inspect the stage where she herself would be showcased the next afternoon. "Rita, may I ask you something?" She gestured for the other woman to join her in a quiet corner of the room, where they could talk with more privacy. "It's about Lucy. I know she's been adamant about not allowing Wyatt to disrupt her this week, with so much to accomplish. But—"

"How would she feel if he happened to show up on Saturday?"

"Well, exactly." Dottie was relieved at not having to spell it out. Maybe this Rita woman, garish as she was, had some sense to her.

Rita studied her daughter from across the room. "I've been wondering the same thing. Truth is, I don't know. But they seem to have something special, don't you think? She wouldn't have been so upset about the book if she didn't care about him."

"I do hate to meddle."

Rita nodded. "But what if our kids' happiness is at stake?"

Wyatt tapped his old-school black book against the back of the driver's seat, trying to muster the proper enthusiasm for its contents, as the two of them sped downtown. "I'll call my old friend Marietta. Bikini model. She'll hook us up for a fun night."

"Great," said Trip, forcing a fist pump. "Great!"

"The sea is full of fish!" Wyatt proclaimed, watching the city blocks whiz past the car. A night out would ease their loss, offering up countless beauties whose hips didn't lie. Then maybe the one who wasn't speaking to him would fade from his thoughts.

Trip pulled out two Cubans from the inside of his jacket. He handed one to Wyatt. "Maybe we've been looking at this all wrong."

"To our freedom!" Wyatt seconded. He didn't much feel like smoking a cigar at the moment, but figured it was in the spirit of things. He thought about how Lucy had been on him to quit cigarettes; a fishwife, really. He pulled out his lighter. "Some new spots opened since I was last out. I really hibernated this winter, didn't I?"

But Trip, who was checking his voice mail, had stopped paying attention. He seized Wyatt's arm as if he were having a fever dream. "Somebody called from an unknown number, but the message is just static! I can't tell who it is!"

Such a response was *not* in the spirit of things. "Does Eloise have an unlisted number?"

"Maybe she was calling from a pay phone!" Trip played the message again, pressing it hard into his ear.

Wyatt frowned. "Why would she do that?"

Trip opened his mouth to offer a possible explanation, then shut it. Opened it again. Nope, still nothing. "Still, I should probably call her back, just to check."

"We're not supposed to talk about them tonight, remember?" said Wyatt, peeved. But Trip was already leaving Eloise a message. *Do*

I sound that pathetic with Lucy? he wondered, listening to his friend pant into the phone.

"I'm calling Marietta," Wyatt said to nobody. He cracked open the tiny book of phone numbers, carefully annotated over the years, and put on his glasses to read the small print. Next to Marietta's name, he'd written the word "body." Had he really written a note like that? It made Wyatt feel kind of slimy, but he dialed her number anyway.

"Hello?" A sultry voice picked up immediately. Wyatt could hear screams of laughter in the background. "Dylan, put that down!"

Here's hoping Dylan is a lanky model from Fort Worth.

"Mommy said it's time for bed, Dylan, right this minute"—then Marietta seemed to remember she'd picked up the phone—"who's this? Dylan, *no!* Mommy said *no!*"

Wyatt very quietly ended the call. He turned to face Trip, who was listening to his static-y voice mail for a fourth time. *Not helping.* Wyatt opened his black book again, read through the names of girls he'd known in a former life. *What's wrong with me?* In his hand was a catalogue of some of the world's hottest women, but he didn't feel like placing an order.

"Wyatt?" He turned to see Trip watching him. "Sorry, dude, but I don't know if I'm up for this. I miss Eloise too much."

Wyatt nodded. Their hearts weren't in it. He leaned forward and got the driver's attention. "Mark? You can just take us home."

"What? You forget something?" The driver was confused.

"Unfortunately, no," Wyatt said, sighing a little. They didn't speak for the rest of the ride.

"Oh! You're here," said Dottie, startled. "I thought you said you had a tennis match this afternoon."

"Canceled." Wyatt looked up from his desk, where he'd been staring at his photo of Lucy and waiting for the phone to ring. He'd had an interview that morning for an adjunct teaching post at Columbia, and they'd told him they'd be in touch soon. The position was the ocean floor on the academic food chain, but it was a job—and he'd realized that he couldn't rightfully beg Lucy to come back into his life unless he had one. Columbia seemed eager to fill the spot, which had been vacated unexpectedly, and said they'd call him that afternoon. It was now nearly four o'clock.

"Well, that's fine. I was just going to leave something on your desk. An invitation." His mother seemed unsure of herself. She approached his desk and held out the piece of paper.

He took it, reading through the details hungrily. "Good for her," he said quietly, as if to himself.

"Yes, well. Perhaps you should come."

Wyatt looked up. "She won't even return my calls. She doesn't want me there."

"She *says* she doesn't, but—"

"You think she might?"

"Have you learned your lesson? You'll appreciate Lucy from now on?" Dottie spoke as if he were still a little boy who'd finger painted on the walls. "She's a special girl. No more of your nonsense."

Wyatt jumped up from his desk and pulled his mother into a bear hug, catching her completely off guard. "I've learned," he promised, his words choking a bit in his throat. "You really think I should go?"

"Of course," said Dottie, touched by his unexpected display. "You love this girl, don't you? You can't let her slip away."

Lucy pulled Dottie's dress away from the sewing machine, snipping the orange thread from the bobbin. She glanced at the clock above the library mantel—only 9 PM. She'd expected to need another all-nighter in order to be ready for tomorrow, but to her astonishment, everything was in place and ready to go.

"Hey!" Eloise draped an arm over Lucy's shoulders. "Come grab a beer with me and Max. We're just going to Phoenix Park."

"I feel like I'm forgetting something."

"I know, but we haven't. I've been through the list five times. We're actually *ready*." She grinned at Max, who'd come up behind them. "This show is going to rock. We all deserve a drink."

"You guys go," said Lucy. She didn't want to get in the way of whatever was happening between the two of them. "I'm just going to head home. Maybe I'll sleep."

"Yeah? Okay. So, I'll see you in the morning."

Lucy gave them both a kiss on the cheek and they scampered off, leaving her alone with the oil paintings besetting the walls. Not for the first time, she wondered if she'd asked Dottie to let them use her home because it reminded her of Wyatt. Reaching for her Black-Berry, she scrolled down through her missed-call log to find only five from him that day—a significant drop-off from the day before. *Maybe he's giving up*, she thought, packing up her tote bag. The thought made her feel tired—or perhaps it was a week of little sleep that was the culprit. Lucy took one last glance around the room to make sure everything looked perfect, and headed for the door.

34

Please come celebrate the debut of
Carlton-Ellis
Saturday, March 21st
Presentation begins at 4 PM
800 Park Avenue, PH A

3:45 PM

Lucy crouched behind a rack of clothes in Dottie's spacious guest bedroom, which had been transformed into a backstage area. The girls were all ready, just getting the finishing touches from the top-flight entourage of hair and makeup artists Eloise had recruited. From this vantage point, all Lucy could see was shoes—sexy snake-skin stilettos, red velvet platforms, lace-up ballerina flats—stepping briskly in every direction, like rush hour in fashion heaven. She'd dipped beneath the fray, out of sight, under the auspices of searching for a vintage clutch that one of her models had misplaced. Really she'd just needed a moment to catch her breath.

"Room down there for me?" asked a voice belonging to a pair of Brian Atwoods that could get a girl in trouble. Eloise ducked into view, bending legs as skinny as a heron's. "You're hiding. The most thrilling day of your entire career—*our* entire careers—and you're hiding behind a clothing rack!"

"I'm just . . . you know, breathing. Or trying to."

"You have nothing to worry about, Luce. The sets are amazing and the place will be packed. Are you kidding? After the Ball auction, this is the place to be. Your dresses are *gorgeous*. Come on, stand up."

Lucy forced in some air, standing. She'd been so busy for the past week, she hadn't allowed herself to get nervous. Now, with the presentation about to start, she was making up for lost time. Maybe there would be goodwill in the room—at least for a while. But once the fashionistas and the society editors and *Margaux Irving* saw that her influences weren't just Paris and Milan and the ladies who lunch on the Upper East Side, maybe they would start to suspect the truth about her. And then at the end of the show, when she would have to stand before them all and . . . she shuddered. For a painful moment, as she stood there with Eloise, Lucy wished that instead of getting on that New York–bound Greyhound from Dayville she'd thrown herself under the front tires.

"Think it's time?" Eloise asked gently.

Lucy nodded, pushing some of her dark curls behind her ear. "Here we go," she said, catching her mother's eye across the room and flashing a thumbs-up.

"Girls, places!" Rita barked, understanding the unspoken order. When it came to corralling models, her brassy nature was an asset, and she'd done a beautiful job with all the models' manicures, giving each the dark red talons of a 1940s starlet.

As they emptied into the library, which rivaled a New York public branch in size and grandeur, Lucy surveyed the whirling blur of energy and vibrant hues around her. There was Fernanda, radiant in a daffodil-yellow frock with a flirty full skirt and a skinny belt, taking her place on the roller coaster set that Max had designed, her beautiful hair teased to look as though the wind were whipping through it. Dottie, regal in a cantaloupe-colored silk taffeta wrap dress that had a crisp yet feminine ruffle at the collar, took her place—as a shopper in a megastore aisle, inspecting the back of an open Cheetos bag with the gravitas of a philosopher. Her fingertips had been dusted orange, matching her frock.

Mimi, now hives-free, wore a dark gold linen-silk gown with hand-beading at the neck. Since her tableau had her shoveling fake snow (an homage to the Minnesota winter), Lucy had made her a fetching flax-and-gold puffer vest to layer on top. Anna, a sizzling vision in crimson, popped against the red-and-white checkered tablecloth of the Dayville pizza parlor Max had replicated based on Lucy's description. Lucy had also used the classic tablecloth fabric to make Anna's sash. And lastly Libet, who now filled out the bodice of her little white dress perfectly, sat in a truncated version of bleachers, watching a ball game wearing a foam finger and a backward cap. The red stitching of a baseball—iconically American— had been used, sparingly but evocatively, in a straight line down her back. Eloise made one last sweep, adjusting straps and pinning hair.

So far, so good, Lucy had to admit. Everything had shaped up beyond their expectations. Over the next hour, Eloise would squire buyers from Barneys, Bergdorf, and Saks, gathering their feedback and, Lucy hoped, orders. Lucy knew it was a long shot: all the other designers' fall collections had been presented weeks before. All they could do was pray that the buyers decided to do the unimaginable: exceed their open-to-buy dollar allocation toward a fall delivery because they strongly believed in the viability of the Carlton-Ellis brand.

While Eloise was trying to pull off this miracle, Lucy would be attempting one of her own: winning over Margaux Irving and the cabal of powerful fashion editors who'd agreed to spend their Saturday afternoon viewing the presentation. And, more frightening still, she'd reveal her story, which could leave these buyers and editors feeling tricked and hoodwinked, ready to rip apart the clothes—and their designer—thread by thread. If the Carlton-Ellis launch didn't succeed, and instead caused a stampede of cold feet, Mallory would have to run the original story she'd planned. It would be too late for a comeback.

"This is it," said Lucy, giving Rita a squeeze. She felt an involuntary twitch of missing Wyatt. Wyatt would look her over, tell her to stand up straight, hold her hand, the way he had done every single time she'd appeared in public as Lucia Haverford Ellis—his was a level of scrutiny that would drive most women crazy, but she found an odd reassurance in knowing that nothing escaped his critical eye. Besides, she'd always felt more confident, more sure of herself, when he was at her side, and when he said he believed in her, she believed him. But Wyatt had built her up only to knock her down. Now she had to stand on her own two feet.

"Open the doors!" she called out to Margaret.

Cornelia's bloodshot eyes opened a crack. Squinting half-blindly at the antique brass clock next to her bed, she was dismayed to see that it was four in the afternoon. She'd slept through the day again, following another sleepless night. Then she remembered: *Townhouse!* She sprang from the covers. The magazine with the exposé of Lucy was due to land on newsstands today, which meant that for the first time in a week, Cornelia had something worth getting out of bed for. She pushed the frizz out of her eyes and into the Scrungi she'd left on the nightstand. The photo of Lucy crashing through Nola's runway—would Mallory run that as the cover? Cornelia ached with suspense. Throwing on the hooded sweatshirt and yoga pants she'd been wearing for four days—slightly crusted with Domino's pizza sauce, but she was just running to the Korean deli on the corner and back—she flew out the door.

"Pack of Marlboro lights and this," she said, grabbing the magazine off the stand and waving it at the cashier. Giddy with anticipation, she stared at the cover. Fatso Mimi, surrounded by Romanian orphans? *What?*

"Fifteen dollars and fifty-six cents," said the cashier.

Cornelia patted the front pouch on her sweatshirt. No wallet, just her BlackBerry. "Sorry, I don't have any money on me."

"Okay," he said, reshelving the cigarettes. "I'll hold magazine for you. No pay, no read."

"You see me every day!" She couldn't catch her breath. "You know I'm good for it!"

"Never seen you before, Miss. Can't give things away for free."

She scowled at his obvious brain damage. Turning her back on him, she flipped through the magazine as fast as she could. Where the hell was the article? She reached the back cover—still no mention of her sworn enemy's fraud. A dark feeling began to spread inside of Cornelia. She flipped back to the table of contents. *No mention of Lucy Jo Ellis.* Her rage washed everything in white light and her head felt like it was going to blow up. She would strangle Mallory Keeler.

"Miss, you okay?" yelled the cashier. "You need nine-one-one?"

Cornelia closed her mouth. She hadn't realized she'd been screaming.

"Your phone! Your phone is ringing!" the cashier said, looking at her as if she'd escaped from Bellevue. "Maybe somebody who can come get you?"

Cornelia pulled her BlackBerry out of her sweatshirt. *Theo Galt.* She picked up.

"Hey, there," he said. "So I've been thinking about your musical aspirations. We should talk. Are you heading over to Lucy's thing? Maybe we could grab a bite afterward."

The only words Cornelia heard were: "Lucy's thing." She forced herself to focus. "Mmm. What's the address again? Can't find it anywhere."

"Eight hundred Park. So . . . dinner afterward?"

But Cornelia didn't answer. Unable to control herself, she was already running as fast as she could toward Dottie Hayes's apartment.

"This could be a terrible idea." Wyatt, straightening his tie in the reflection of the elevator doors, felt like he and Trip were seventh grade boys heading to a high school dance. His heart was knocking against his Adam's apple. "Eloise and Lucy don't want us there. I mean, they won't even talk to us. Maybe crashing—"

"Nut up!" Trip commanded. His face was pasty pale, but his gaze was steady. "This could be our only chance. We know where they are, and we know they won't run away. All I need is less than a minute." He wiped the edges of his mouth with his thumb and index finger, then reached into his blazer and pulled out a velvet box.

"Is that a *ring*?" asked Wyatt, floored.

"If this is what it takes to make Eloise happy, I'll do it. I just want her back." Trip stuffed the box back into his pocket.

The elevator doors parted, but Wyatt seized Trip's arm and held him back with more force than necessary. "Don't you *dare!*" He spoke quietly but forcefully—no way would he allow Trip to steal the limelight on Lucy's big day. "You will keep your mouth shut, and support the girls. You will not propose to Eloise. This event is *not about you.*"

Trip glared at him, but then begrudgingly agreed. "I'll ask her afterward, fine. Now let go of me?"

They stepped off the elevator and into Wyatt's childhood home, heading toward the library. Once inside, Wyatt couldn't help but swivel his head around like a wide-eyed tourist in Times Square, taking in the electric crowd that filled the transformed room. Everyone was buzzing over the socialites modeling Lucy's dresses on elaborate mini-stages—Wyatt's own mother was up there, he noticed, despite her general reticence to be in the spotlight. When he caught Dottie's eye, she winked at him—equally out of character, he thought, smiling nervously back at her.

As he walked closer to Libet Vance's stage, Wyatt began to clue in to what Lucy had done—the genius of the presentation she and Eloise had put together in just one week. She'd managed to marry her true down-home roots with high fashion, drawing inspiration both from the real-life American women she'd known all her life and the glamorous socialites she'd partied with all winter. Showing media savvy, she and Eloise had recruited the most press-magnetic socialites as their models—but set them in *tableaux vivants* showing life in the so-called "flyover states."

"She did it," Wyatt said, feeling overcome with admiration. His eyes quickly searched the room and found Lucy—luminous, powerful, poised, and holding her own with Margaux Irving.

Margaux, sleek as a panther in a slim-cut Prada shift, swept up next to Fernanda's roller-coaster scene. She gazed at the tableau as though it were a blank wall. "We've contrasted real American experiences with the gilded socialite," Lucy explained, forcing herself to stay calm despite the editrix's unsettling lack of a reaction.

"The dress is pretty," Margaux remarked.

Pretty. Was it a compliment? To Nola Sinclair and her cutting-edge supporters, *pretty* had been the dirtiest of words. But then again, *pretty* had been Lucy's intention. She'd designed dresses she herself craved: feminine, light, artfully and impeccably made, brimming with optimism. Clothes that made you feel just a bit more alive. The type of thing that hard-core fashionista Margaux could easily dismiss as too mainstream. She led the inscrutable editor over to Mimi's stage. "She's shoveling," said the editor coolly, casting her eye over the setting.

What did that mean? What could Lucy deduce from Margaux's statement of the obvious? Her palms had started to sweat. She looked across the room—past Mallory Keeler, scribbling notes furiously, past the well-heeled flock of editors (who'd deigned to come because Margaux had deigned to come), past the socialites who added beauty and gloss to a scene already exploding with both—to see Eloise showing the buyer from Saks Anna's dress. The buyer, nodding and looking closely at the sash, seemed impressed. But how would she—*they*—feel after hearing the truth about who Lucy was? Lucy now knew how things worked. Nobody would have offered Cornelia that ill-fated perfume deal if her last name wasn't Rockman. The fashion world seemed willing to consider the design career of Lucia Haverford Ellis—at least, they'd shown up to give her a chance—but how would they feel about Lucy Jo?

"Food's fabulous," gushed Rex Newhouse, snaring another sliced-up Twinkie off a passing tray. "You must share the name of your caterer." But then he noticed Margaux and retreated nervously into the crowd. The woman had a way of bringing confident men and women to their knees without saying or doing a thing.

"Would you excuse me just a moment?" Lucy asked Margaux, who was shocked enough to form a facial expression. Nobody, Lucy imagined, had ever put the editor on hold before. But if she waited a moment longer, she'd lose her nerve. It was now or never. "There's something I need to say." Catching Eloise's attention, she headed for the front of the room. Eloise did the same, white-lipped. Lucy felt grateful for having chosen to wear her high-waisted trousers; at least nobody could see her knocking knees.

Looking out over the room from in front of Dottie's double-height fireplace, they spotted Trip and Wyatt standing near the door. "What the hell are they doing here?" whispered Eloise.

Lucy's eyes locked with Wyatt's, and for a moment, she thought her shaky legs might actually give out underneath her. Then she pulled herself together, looking away. She couldn't indulge the feelings Wyatt provoked in her—not now, when her dreams hung in the balance. She had a job to do—and an unpleasant one.

"May I have everyone's attention, just for a moment?" she asked.

Mallory Keeler, who'd been interviewing Rita in a quiet corner of the room, looked up with rapt interest, as did the rest of the crowd. "We'd like to thank everyone for coming," Lucy said into a microphone that she picked up from the mantel. "Eloise Carlton and I are so proud to welcome you to the debut of Carlton-Ellis." The room broke into hearty applause. "Wait, please"—she held up her hands to quell the noise—"I have a confession to make."

Wyatt's stomach clenched, knowing what Lucy was about to divulge. Too many of the guests, he feared, had the loyalty of rattlesnakes.

"It's always been my dream to be a designer," she began calmly, in counterpoint to his own racing heart.

He was the first to glimpse Cornelia Rockman—barely recognizable, she was such a mess—barrel off the elevator, and Wyatt quickly intercepted her in the hallway. He hadn't seen such a dramatic makeunder since Cameron Diaz's in *Being John Malkovich*—her face was puffy, her hair puffier, and a rank, boozy smell emanated from her pores.

"She can't get away with this!" Cornelia hissed. "And neither can you!"

Wyatt shut the door to the library behind them. "Look at yourself," he said gently, pointing toward the nineteenth-century antique mirror his mother kept above a console table. The glass had warbled slightly, but the reality check still worked—and Cornelia blinked hard, taking in her reflection. "You really want everyone in that room to see you like this? Besides, Lucy's in there telling them the truth as we speak."

Cornelia looked beseechingly into Wyatt's eyes. He could almost feel her anger dissolving, leaving her limp. "I just want things to be the way they were," she said in a small voice.

To his shock, he actually felt sorry for her. He'd once had a similar wish, for a return to the old established way of life—thank God it hadn't come true. "We wouldn't have been happy. You want something else, Cornelia."

There was a loud flush from the nearest bathroom, and then Theo Galt rounded the corner, zipping his fly. Cornelia immediately covered her face with her hands, distraught. "Don't look!" she said, rushing to the elevator and jamming the door button.

Theo, rising to the occasion, hustled to her side instead of running away. "I'll get you home," he said, a hint of proprietary concern in his voice. They made an attractive couple, thought Wyatt as he watched them step into the elevator—or they would, once Cornelia washed her hair.

Crisis averted, Wyatt dove back into the library, where Lucy appeared to be mid-disclosure.

"Until a few months ago, I was making eight dollars an hour stitching zippers for Nola Sinclair," she said. "I have no pedigree whatsoever—"

"Pedigrees are for dogs!" Rita shouted.

"Dear Lord," breathed Rex Newhouse, transfixed. Wyatt noticed that Mallory Keeler was taking notes fast and furiously. Margaux Irving, on the other hand, was still as a statue, a hand planted against her lips. Wyatt didn't know if he could bear to watch Lucy so exposed, so vulnerable. Dottie, holding the Cheetos, looked almost as pained as he felt. Neither of them had ever witnessed such social courage.

"I'm a completely ordinary girl," she continued. "I grew up in Middle America, only we just called it America. Dayville, Minnesota. I chowed on pizza. I cheered at ball games. I watched too much bad television, waited in amusement-park lines, shoveled endless snow, shopped at Mall of America, bussed tables, clipped coupons, went to church along the side of a highway. That's who I am, and I shouldn't have pretended to be someone else. I like who I am."

Wyatt waited for her to mention his name, to say that Wyatt Hayes IV had put her up to the deception—but no, she was taking full responsibility herself. This was her story. It always had been, he realized. "Moving about this world of power and privilege has been the best apprenticeship a designer could ask for. It is filled with beauty and style"—her eyes met Wyatt's as she said this—"and I feel lucky to call all of today's models my friends. But I believe that it's my background, unglamorous though it may be in the eyes of some, that allows me to design what real women want. Our collection is meant to be as practical as it is inspirational; as flattering as it is fashionable. I hope you'll agree."

Lucy handed the microphone off to Eloise and Wyatt caught her eye again. She looked away quickly, before he could read how she felt about seeing him—before he could even summon up the smile, the nod of congratulations, the gratitude he wanted to express to her. Eloise put her arm around Lucy's shoulders and gave her a squeeze.

But the rest of the room appeared to be frozen. You could hear crickets.

"Did she say *Mall of America*?" Wyatt heard one member of the glossy posse whisper to another, clearly appalled.

Most people in the room—despite their lofty fashion credentials—had never heard the notoriously tight-lipped Margaux Irving speak. When she did, her words were as crisp as a sterling silver spoon tapping the side of a crystal glass. "There is nothing ordinary about the ability to construct magnificent clothes that elevate the woman who wears them," she told Lucy, loudly enough that Mallory Keeler, on the other side of the room, immediately scribbled down the rare quote. "Carlton-Ellis won't need my support, but you'll have it all the same." Then, nodding her head in benediction, Margaux swept out of the room. Taking their cue from on high, the crowd burst into fresh applause.

As the others in the room—Mallory Keeler, Rex, other journalists and fashionistas too well dressed for a Saturday afternoon—swarmed around Lucy, Wyatt held back. He caught his mother watching him from her stage. She raised her eyebrows in some kind of warning, then smiled.

"Saks might be interested in twenty doors across the U.S.," whispered Eloise as she passed. She gave Lucy a low five and a huge grin.

"That's incredible!" Lucy kept her voice down, too. "*Elle* wants to feature the line for an upcoming 'Fresh Faces' piece!"

"I can't believe it. Do you know what this means?"

Lucy giggled. "It means . . . howdy, partner, we're in business." It was exhilarating. And it felt damn good to be herself again, liberated from all the lies.

"You talk to Wyatt yet? I've been avoiding Trip."

Lucy shook her head. She didn't know what to say to him, or whether she was ready to forgive him. She let herself look down the long room to where Wyatt was standing, talking to Mallory. "Who do you think leaked? I didn't want him here. Or I *think* I didn't."

Eloise shrugged. "No idea. But I wouldn't be too hard on him. I heard he cut Cornelia off at the pass, before she could cause a major scene. And he seems really sorry—"

"Well, he should be," Lucy interrupted. But she had to admit, her anger seemed to have cooled considerably. She allowed herself another glance in his direction. He had never looked so forlorn. She thought of the note he'd sent her: *You've changed me. Let me prove it to you.* He *had* canceled the book, after all, which required sacrifice—something he'd never had to make before.

"I should get back to the buyers," said Eloise, giving Lucy a quick hug.

"Right! I should get back to the editors." She had a career to launch—or so she hoped. The fashion business was brutal, even if you had Margaux Irving's best wishes. She tossed her head, shaking off thoughts of Wyatt. They had time to figure things out.

"*Eloise!*" Both girls froze at the sound of Trip's voice. He charged through the room, parting the crowd. Eloise stared at him with mounting horror, but Trip didn't seem to notice. He was a man on a mission. Eloise clutched Lucy's arm.

"Trip, this isn't the time or place," Eloise whispered through a pained smile.

"I can't wait another minute to tell you that you're the best thing that's ever happened to me." He took both her hands and dropped to one knee on Dottie Hayes's Aubusson carpet. This seemed to get the crowd's attention, and several guests backed up to give him room.

"This is the most exciting presentation I've ever been to in my life!" Lucy heard the buyer from Bergdorf whisper. "Did they stage this?"

"I think I'm going to faint!" exclaimed Eloise's mother, who'd flown in from Boston to show her support.

"I've been a complete fool," Trip said. "If getting married is important to you, Eloise, then let's do it." He pulled out the black velvet box, fumbling it open to reveal a flawless seven-carat emerald-cut diamond, flanked by two smaller diamonds, on a classic platinum band. Eloise's mother gasped. "Will you marry me, Eloise?"

"We should talk, Trip," she said quietly, trying to pull him to his feet.

But Trip wouldn't budge. "Marry me, El."

Lucy covered her face with her hands, peeking out between her fingers. It was beyond painful to watch. He'd left Eloise with no choice. "It's too late," she whispered, distraught. Time seemed to stop for a moment as she ran out of the room.

Trip just stared after her, eyes wide. He stayed on one knee, like a linebacker suddenly bereft of an opposing team.

"Buddy, why don't you give her some time to think it all over?" Wyatt had made his way toward them. Lucy could hear real tenderness in his voice as he helped his friend get back on his feet. Trip hung his head, dazed, as though slowly waking from a tranquilizer dart.

"Did she just say no?" he asked Wyatt, dumbstruck.

"Let's get you out of here," Wyatt said. He looked at Lucy. It was the closest the two of them had been since she'd thrown his manuscript at him, and the electricity between them was so intense she felt every nerve in her body come alive. "I'm sorry about—well, everything," he said. Lucy just nodded, too stunned by the intensity of her feelings to gather words. A lock of hair fell in Wyatt's eyes, and he pushed it back. "Could we talk later? Maybe I could take you to dinner?"

She hesitated. "That sounds good."

"Really?" His face showed his surprise and delight. "You won't regret it, I promise." He started toward the door, his friend using him as a human crutch, but then paused again. "Congratulations. I'm so proud of you, Lucy."

"Wyatt?" she asked, a smile teasing her lips. "Please call me Lucy Jo."

Acknowledgments

My heartfelt thanks to David Groff, a phenomenal editor, poet, and person, and the dream team at Weinstein Books, especially Harvey Weinstein, Judy Hottensen, Kristin Powers, Katie Finch, and Rich Florest. I'm lucky to have Rob Weisbach as an inspiration and friend, and my agent, Daniel Greenberg, always in my corner with good advice. Larry Salz and Marissa Devins, thanks for your guidance and patience. Thanks to Aneta Golawska-Nowak. My gratitude to my best friends and family, who offered notes, encouragement and babysitting. Most of all, thanks to my husband John and our beautiful little love, Jane Louisa.